Ju

Jukeboxes

An American
Social History

by KERRY SEGRAVE

McFarland & Company, Inc., Publishers
Jefferson, North Carolina, and London

Library of Congress Cataloguing-in-Publication Data

Segrave, Kerry, 1944–
    Jukeboxes : an American social history / by Kerry Segrave.
       p.   cm.
    Includes bibliographical references and index.
    ISBN 0-7864-1181-3 (softcover : 50# alkaline paper) ∞
    1. Jukebox industry — United States — History — 20th century.
  2. Jukeboxes.   I. Title.
  ML3790.S384   2002
  306.4'84 — dc21   2001007161

British Library cataloguing data are available

Front cover image ©2002 PhotoDisc

Manufactured in the United States of America

McFarland & Company, Inc., Publishers
  Box 611, Jefferson, North Carolina 28640
   www.mcfarlandpub.com

Contents

Preface

This book looks at jukeboxes from their beginnings in the 1880s up to 2000. Their history is unusual in that after the birth of the jukebox, the music machine struggled along for almost 20 years, achieving no more than minor attention for brief periods within that two-decade span. Although Thomas Edison can be fairly called the father of the device, he quickly came to disown his child. Edison wanted a neat and well-turned-out business device — a Dictaphone. Instead, he got a juke. After a two-decade unsuccessful struggle to permanently establish itself as a part of the entertainment scene, the box disappeared for another 25 years. It was not technologically ready. The jukebox was also beaten out by other devices, musical and non-musical, and largely forgotten by the few people who had remembered it in the first place.

Suddenly, at the ripe old age of 45 or so, it sprang forth to enjoy a period of spectacular growth and popularity. To use an old cliché, the box was in the right place at the right time. Technological changes then favored the music machine and the end of Prohibition meant that a huge number of legal taverns opened up all over America, and taverns would always be the favored home of the box. In 1933 there were perhaps 20,000 to 25,000 jukes in America. The spectacular rise began the next year with approximately 300,000 jukeboxes on site by the end of the 1930s. That growth was all the more spectacular considering that America was in the grip of the Depression in that period. Most industries were happy if their sales did not decrease too drastically in those hard times. So financially healthy was the jukebox industry that it was able to usher in the luxury light-up era, in 1938, with the originally plain machines adopting more plastic and neon as they got gaudier and gaudier. During that time, and lasting through the 1940s, the box became a ubiquitous part of the American scene.

Throughout the 1950s the juke held its own but growth had ground almost to a halt. It was becoming a replacement industry, with assistance from a foreign market that would remain strong through most of the 1960s. Technology again turned against the jukebox; the recording industry began to undergo the first of many changes, none of which would benefit the jukebox. From the 1960s onward it was all downhill for the music machine. There was no steep decline, no single, dramatic, precipitating cause — just a slow and steady erosion of the popularity of the jukebox. Today it is largely irrelevant, forgotten once more.

Research for this book was conducted at the University of Victoria library, the University of British Columbia, and Vancouver Public Library. Among the materials consulted were newspaper indexes and periodical indexes and databases. Additionally, the back files of *Billboard* magazine provided extensive information.

1

The Jukebox Arrives:
A Dictaphone Gone Bad,
1870–1907

I don't want the phonograph sold for amusement purposes.... I want it sold for business purposes only. Thomas Edison, 1877

    The coin-in-the-slot device is calculated to injure the phonograph in the opinion of those seeing it in that form, as it has the appearance of being nothing more than a mere toy.... Thomas Edison, 1891

The jukebox, which became so prevalent in America during the latter part of the 1900s, had its origins a century earlier in the invention of the phonograph by Thomas Alva Edison. Although the date generally accepted today for the birth of the jukebox is 1889, the machine languished in obscurity for the following 45 years as it competed unsuccessfully with various other coin-operated music devices. The nickel-in-the-slot player piano captured more of the public's coins in that period.

Back in 1877 in a converted barn in Menlo Park, New Jersey, Edison was tinkering with some pieces of scientific equipment when he arrived at the solution to the problem of registering human speech. Upon making this discovery, Edison put aside his work on telegraphy to concentrate on his new brainstorm. On January 24, 1878, he sold his invention for $10,000 plus a royalty of 20 percent. From that transaction came the Edison Speaking Phonograph Company. Everyone associated with the phonograph at that time was convinced that the talking machine would be used in the same way as the telephone and the telegraph. That is, it would essentially be a business communications device, a forerunner of the Dictaphone. Reflecting on his invention in 1878, Edison suggested 10 possible uses for the machine, one of which was "reproduction of music." Still, no one saw the invention as viable in any way except as a business device.[1]

Some 500 of these phonographs were made and distributed to American showmen across the country. Apparently this talking machine was successful as a novelty, at least for a time. For about six months those machines worked almost nonstop as they kept people amused. But then the novelty wore off and the public suddenly drifted away. During 1878–1879 the machine was neither technically sophisticated enough to reproduce music nor technically ready to do office work. Edison was unhappy as he watched developments. What had been meant to be a national demonstration of the device to spark interest, especially that of business, had, as far as the inventor was concerned, backfired, with the whole thing becoming little more that a fairground sideshow. Writing to his assistant, Edison remarked: "I don't want the phonograph sold for amusement purposes. It is not a toy. I want it sold for business purposes only." The sudden loss of public interest in his device confirmed for the inventor that the talking machine's future lay not in entertainment, but in commerce.[2]

Meanwhile, two scientists, Chichester A. Bell and Charles Sumner Tainter, had begun, in 1883, their own experiments on the talking machine. On June 27, 1885, they applied for patents on their improved apparatus, the Graphophone. They had replaced the tin foil with a cardboard cylinder coated in wax and allowed the stylus to float over the grooves, held to the cylinder only by gravity. After raising enough money, the two men formed the American Graphophone Company in 1887 to manufacture and distribute dictation machines to industry and commerce. Upset by this turn of events, Edison turned back to his phonograph, determined to improve his machine. Within a year, patent wars were looming. In 1888 Pittsburgh millionaire Jesse B. Lippincott was successful in temporarily unifying the two groups when he formed the North American Phonograph Company to market talking machines to business firms, to substitute for a stenographer. Following commercial practices of the time, these machines would not be sold outright but leased. The telephone, then coming into its own, was also marketed that way. North American carved the United States into 33 territories and allocated those distributorships to respectable businessmen. Those 33 local firms would rent the devices to business enterprises within their areas for $40 per year. Local companies were responsible for maintenance on the units while the parent company was responsible for cylinders. Rentals were to be split between them on a 50/50 basis. However, the machine required much servicing, it generated opposition from stenographers, it required considerable skill to operate, the sound quality was not always good, and the executive dictating into the machine had to speak with particular clarity and was almost forced to shout into the tube he held over his mouth. Business was not good. Companies that did lease a unit seldom renewed those leases. Experience was showing that the widest and only immediate market for the unit was the amusement field.[3]

By May 1891, the number of companies distributing for North American had decreased from 33 to 19. At the second annual convention of the National Phonographic Association held that month, a poll revealed that at least one-third of all operating phonographs and Graphophones were actually being used for entertainment. During the 1880s the entertainment phonograph had not disappeared entirely. Public interest may have dropped sharply from 1878 to 1879, but it was not zero. In the hands of independent showmen the devices had continued to dispense material ranging from speeches to farmyard noises to music-hall jokes, but no music. But now, after 1888, with improvements in the technical quality and performance of the devices, a whole new world of sound entertainment opened up before them. Those later units were capable of playing music, although not of great quality. Showmen had managed to obtain some of those later units (even though they were supposedly not sold but only leased to business firms), and by 1890, nickel-in-the-slot phonographs were appearing in different parts of the United States. In fact, by that 1891 convention, many of those remaining 19 firms distributing for North American had themselves defected to the entertainment field.[4]

The first coin model appears to have been developed by Louis Glass, general manager of the Pacific Phonograph Company. That firm, which controlled California, Arizona, and Nevada under the North American plan, faced with declining revenue from business-machine rental, developed a nickel-in-the-slot cabinet for the phonograph. On November 23, 1889, it placed the first coin-operated phonograph in the Palais Royal Saloon in San Francisco. This date is now generally accepted as the "birth" date of the jukebox. That machine had four individual listening tubes, stethoscope-like devices that the customer placed in his ears. To hear the recording it was necessary to place a coin in one of the four slots, each of which controlled a tube. It also meant that a single tune could generate up to 20 cents per play. During its first six months at the Palais, this machine reportedly earned over $1,000 in nickels and by May 1891, Glass had placed similar coin phonographs at locations throughout San Francisco.[5]

On a trip East, Glass met Felix Gottschalk, secretary of the Metropolitan Company. That firm held the rights to New York City under the North American plan. Enthusiastic about Glass's financial success and over the success of the coin-operated weigh scale, he decided he wanted to market the coin phonograph nationwide. He headed the Automatic Exhibition Company of New York, incorporated in New York in February 1890, with a capital stock of $1 million to market the nickel-operated device. Gotts-chalk purchased the right to Glass's multiple-tube cabinet and combined it with the patents he controlled. Produced by Automatic was a 4½-foot-high, glass-topped wooden cabinet model that housed a single cylinder Edison machine and a storage battery. When the coin broke an electric circuit, the cylinder record was set in motion by a slide push bar. Patrons listened to the machine's single tune with a pair of rubber ear tubes connected to the front of the cabinet. At this time, there was apparently just one set of tubes per machine.[6]

Some 750 of these machines were placed in operation from Maine to Montana and were said to take an average of $2 a day each. Subject to mechanical failure and easily deceived by slugs, the units also collected a vast array of paper wads, plugs, buttons, and other items small enough to fit in the coin chute. By 1891, Automatic was forced to develop an improved model that was less susceptible to slugs and easier to service. The principles of successful jukebox operation in the modern era were evident even then. One of the Automatic Exhibition firm's merchandising comments noted, "Receipts increase or decrease in various machines as the records, which are changed daily, are good or mediocre, and different localities require different attractions." At the first convention of the phonograph companies, held in May 1890 in Chicago, the firm displayed its machine and described the income potential that lay in coin phonographs. Many of those struggling phonograph firms grabbed at the idea of getting steady revenue from coin machines— in order to finance the main goal of marketing a business device. Under a leasing system, Automatic furnished cabinets and coin mechanisms while the local phonograph firms supplied Edison phonographs and serviced the machines. Net profits were divided evenly between the two parties.[7]

Although the North American Company owned 15,000 shares in Auto-matic's venture, Edison opposed the use of the coin machine, as he felt it nullified efforts to make the phonograph a serious business instrument. Local phonograph firms were advised not to promote the coin-operated unit at the expense of the business machine. The inventor didn't like the enter-tainment units in 1877, and he felt the same in 1891 when he wrote: "Those companies who fail to take advantage of every opportunity of pushing the legitimate side of their business, relying only on the profits derived from the coin-in-the-slot, will find too late that they have made a fatal mistake. The coin-in-the-slot device is calculated to injure the phonograph in the opinion of those seeing it only in that form, as it has the appearance of being nothing more than a mere toy and no one would comprehend its value or appreciate its utility as an aid to business men and others for dic-tation purposes when seeing it only in that form."[8]

During its initial year, Automatic received a steady stream of requests, mainly from showmen at fairs and resorts, demanding records of songs and instrumental music. Thus the Columbia Phonograph Company became a recording specialist in 1890 and quickly came to dominate as a recording producer. All of their material was produced on wax-coated cylinders. Columbia also operated coin phonographs in Maryland, Delaware, and Washington, D.C. As early as June 15, 1890, it advertised that it would place coin phonographs on the premises of locations wanting them, "providing there is a fair chance of profit to the company." Within five months Columbia had 100 coin machines on location in drugstores, hotels, and depots in Baltimore and Washington. By the second phonograph convention in 1891, 16 of the 19 companies attending were in the coin-phonograph field, operating a total of 1,249 machines. The largest operators were the New York Company (175 units), the Old Dominion Company in Virginia (155), and Columbia (142). Many of the local firms had balked at the high percentage demanded by Automatic and had developed their own coin mechanisms. At that convention no less than six new nickel-in-the-slot devices were displayed, with prices averaging about $50 each.[9]

Typical of the minor boom enjoyed by operators of the time was the experience of the Missouri Phonograph Company. This firm had about 50 units in operation in St. Louis by June 1891 and was amazed when one of their first machines grossed $100 in one week. The company employed two "inspectors" who serviced each unit twice every 24 hours. The Louisiana Phonograph Company reported one of its New Orleans machines had taken in $1,000 in April and May 1891, the first months of operation. No commissions or share of the machine's take were paid to location owners in those early days, as the phonograph was considered to be a business booster, particularly for drugstores and saloons.[10]

As the North American Company had not encouraged the use of phonographs for entertainment, it remained for the territorial firms to produce their own records, which they sold at prices ranging from $1 to $2. Each record was an individual master, as there was no means at this time of reproducing the cylinders, of dubious acoustic and entertainment quality. Columbia featured John Philip Sousa's Marine Band, the Third Artillery Band, Shakespearean recitations, and Joy Y. Atlee, the famous "artistic whistler." In their 1891 catalog, 27 of Sousa's marches were listed; 36 selections by Atlee were also available. Another popular genre was comedy. Dan Kelly recorded a "Pat Brady" character for Columbia. One enthusiast in 1893 wrote that it was not uncommon to see men and women standing in line before those machines in many of the larger American cities to hear him sing and talk. Columbia was said to be shipping 300 to 500 cylinders daily from their catalog, mostly by mail order. Firms in New York, New Jersey, and Ohio also produced recordings that they claimed could be used for

5,500 plays. As records were fragile and easily broken, there was little opportunity to test such a wildly exaggerated claim. In St. Louis the Missouri
Phonograph Company was surprised to find that its tavern locations favored
church hymns and that the number-one hit of the barroom circuit was
"Nearer My God to Thee." In Cleveland the top nickel-grabber was "Night
Alarm," a band recording describing a fire, complete with calls of firemen,
ringing bells, and horses' hooves.[11]

Events moved swiftly during 1890–1894. The national network of established phonograph firms dispersed several thousand machines and trans-
formed the coin-operated phonograph from a fairground curiosity into a
minor industry. However, the North American Company was finding its
rental system to be unsuccessful. By July 1891, it was allowing territorial
companies to sell the phonographs outright. The high price of $190 for a
unit complete with batteries, ear tubes, blank cylinders, and sundries stym-
ied any large spurt in growth in the industry. Seeking sales, local firms
began to invade each other's territories, eventually forcing North American to take over the right to sell phonographs nationally, paying the local
concerns 10 percent of the sales price on machines marketed in their areas.
None of this would save North American, and the company declared bankruptcy in 1894. Edison then organized the National Phonograph Company
to market the phonograph as a music machine only.[12]

With coin-operated machines in a somewhat chaotic state, both Edison's new firm and its rival, the American Graphophone Company, felt the
solution lay in a phonograph so cheap and reliable the public would buy it
for home use. Although neither firm would ignore the coin-operated segment, both turned toward the home unit. In addition to a line of home models, Edison's National Phonograph Company made coin-operated machines,
most of which were operated by a storage battery and housed in a substantial four-foot high oak cabinet with the single cylinder mechanical works
displayed under a glass cover. It was equipped with ear tubes or a polished
brass horn. Variations of the Edison coin models appeared under the name
Ajax, Imperial, Regal, Climax, Vulcan, and Majestic, while Bijou and Excel-
sior offered a spring-motor version. Around 1906 the machines were standardized in the Windsor (battery), Eclipse (DC current), and Acme (AC
current) models, selling for around $65. Similar coin machines were pro-
duced after 1895 by American Graphophone, which used a Bell and Tainter Graphophone in lieu of the Edison unit. In 1898 Graphophone produced
what was the all-time low-priced coin phonograph, the spring-operated
Eagle, a nickel-in-the-slot counter model that sold for $20. But without the
drawing power of Edison's name on the machine display cards, the appeal
of the Graphophone was limited.[13]

From the beginning it was apparent that little money could be made from placing a single unit in a bar, then another in a restaurant a few blocks away, and so on. Machines were prone to slugs and breakdowns; patrons could only play a single tune. These units had to be visited far too often. One of the earliest, perhaps the first, phonograph parlors was opened in Cleveland in September 1890, by James L. Andem, president of the Ohio Phonograph Company. Andem realized that the single-cylinder machine could only coax one nickel from a customer and decided to group a dozen machines in one location where patrons were apt to listen to several units in succession. This was the first attempt to provide the patrons with "selectivity." An attendant who looked after the machine and made change serviced a parlor. The attractive surroundings and the variety of recordings drew the family trade, and by 1893 this was the usual method of operation for the several thousand coin phonographs in use.[14] Vitascope Hall, a parlor in Buffalo, New York, contained 28 of the latest Edison machines.

These parlors reached their popularity peak around 1897 and most cities in America and Europe had at least one. One in Paris, France, employed about 40 people and gave the customer a choice of some 1,500 cylinders. A patron entered the hall and sat at a station on the second floor where he called down his selection through a tube to an employee on the floor below. The employee retrieved the selection and loaded it on to a machine connected to the customer's station. Milan, Italy, had one called the Bar Automatico.

Andem had some advice at this time for his fellow parlor operators: "Cleanliness about the machines and their accessories cannot be enforced too rigidly ... the cabinets are kept highly polished, the glass clean, the machines bright, the announcement cards fresh and interesting; the phonograph slot business depends on the patronage of a scrupulous public whom it is well not to offend." With the addition of other automatic devices such as kinetoscopes, weigh scales, strength testers, electric shockers, games, gum-ball venders, and so forth, those phonograph parlors became even more popular and came to be known as penny arcades. Soon the phonograph was overwhelmed by other devices in the arcades it had created. It found itself unable to migrate to what would become its favorite locations decades into the future — taverns and restaurants — because it did not offer customers any choice and its unchangeable volume level was too low to be heard in such locations.[15]

One early attempt at producing a machine with selectivity was made in 1896 by the Multiplex Phonograph Company of New York that developed an attachment for the Edison phonograph that enabled patrons to rotate five cylinders. But the patron had to play each of the five tunes in succession; he couldn't skip from number one to number three without putting in a nickel for number two. Offering only partial selectivity and requiring ear tubes, the Multiplex attachment sold for $150 and was not commercially successful.[16]

Another flurry of technological development took place from 1905 to 1907. The Multiphone Company of New York developed a selective nickel-in-the-slot cylinder phonograph with a large magazine wheel containing 24 records. Known as the Multiphone, the unit had records mounted on shafts extending at right angles from the perimeter of a circular conveyor that looked like a tiny ferris wheel. The spokes of the wheel were numbered to

A phonograph parlor in 1896 in San Francisco. Those small towels hanging from each machine were used by customers to wipe off the ear tubes.

indicate 24 selections and customers used a projecting lever to turn the wheel until the desired tune was manipulated under the playing mechanism. Housed in a massive — eight-feet high, three-feet wide, and one-and-a-half-feet deep — bronze or mahogany cabinet, the front and sides of the cabinet were of beveled glass. One winding of a crank at the bottom would play 18 records. Early models had a speaker horn that was later incorporated into the top of the cabinet.[17]

The Multiphone Company attempted a large-scale chain operation. In 1905 they placed seven test models on location for a one-year period and discovered that each unit netted $363.50 per year after paying locations a 20 percent commission, record costs of $12.50 per year, and an annual maintenance expense of $25. Companies were then organized to operate the machines manufactured by the parent Multiphone Company, and in 1906 those concerns placed the devices on a percentage basis in their territories. Stock was sold to the public and dividends were paid from the machine's net earnings, 50 percent to the stockholders and 50 percent to the operating firm, which used its share of the profits to buy more Multiphones, priced at $250 each. However, the promoters failed to foresee the development and competition from rival coin phonographs and coin pianos, which were being sold outright to location owners. Thus, in 1908, the Multiphone Company went bankrupt.[18]

The last of the cylinder coin units was the Concertophone, a selective machine with a revolving magazine containing 25 records. First marketed in 1906 by the Skelly Manufacturing Company of Chicago and retailing for $325, the unit was powered by a spring mechanism. Housed in a six-foot cabinet with a speaker horn protruding from the top, it was operated by setting a metal dial on the side of the cabinet at the number desired. Then the patron manipulated the slide bar to maneuver the selected cylinder into playing position. In order to attract the curious, the cabinet had a glass front and a reflecting mirror that showed the machine's movements. At its initial location the Concertophone earned as high as $10 a day. Despite something called a friction amplifier, it apparently was still not loud enough, as the company went bankrupt in 1907. Both of these devices required a fair amount of work by the patron; they had to turn a selection handle and wind the motor. Both units played wax cylinder recordings. Because of advances in disk recordings, the cylinders were starting to disappear around this time.[19]

Gabel's Automatic Entertainer, a disk-record coin machine, debuted in 1906. Back in 1887, Emile Berliner had started experiments with a machine that played a horizontal disk. Its development took years. In 1901 the Victor Talking Machine Company of Camden, New Jersey, was incorporated. Berliner's Gramophone was simpler, more rugged, and disks could be stamped out in batches. So superior was the disk, compared to the cylinder, that in

1902 Graphophone converted its factory to manufacture a disk-playing unit. By 1902 Victor and Columbia began to offer the cylinder record serious competition with their disk recordings.[20]

One of the first attempts to market a coin-operated disk phonograph was made at this time by the Universal Talking Manufacturing Company of New York. It proved to be impractical. Around 1905, Julius Wilner of Philadelphia developed a nickel-in-the-slot machine that played 12 ten-inch disk records in rotation. When a coin was placed in the machine, the lowest record in a magazine was lifted on to the turntable for playing, while a sound box came forward with a new needle to play the record. Lacking the feature of selectivity, the Wilner device achieved no success.[21]

The first successful disk machine was John Gabel's Automatic Entertainer, a spring-operated coin phonograph using 24 ten-inch records, produced in 1906 by the Automatic Machine & Tool Company of Chicago. Twelve records were located in racks on each side of the turntable, and any record could be selected by turning a knob. Completely automatic, this unit had a 40-inch long transmitting horn at the top of its five-foot oak cabinet and large glass panels on three sides to keep its movements in full view. A new feature that simplified operation for the patron was a handle on the front of the cabinet that changed both the record and the needle and wound the motor with one turn. Above the turntable, a magazine held 150 needles, one of which was fed out for each record. Another new development was the sound box, which was controlled and moved over the record by a screw attachment. Equipped with a magnetic coin-detector to reject slugs, the Automatic Entertainer is today generally considered to be the direct forerunner of the modern-day jukebox. As with the other developments of this period, the Automatic Entertainer was not successful. Gabel stopped producing it in 1908.[22]

Competing against the phonographs of Edison and Graphophone in this period were coin machines that did not owe their existence to the phonograph or its patents. The forerunner of the phonograph in pioneering automatic music was the coin-operated music box that enjoyed some success at the turn of the century. An interest in mechanical things surfaced during the Renaissance, resulting in a variety of automata being produced from about 1500 to 1700. Examples included mechanical birds that chirped single tunes and dancing musical dolls. Although automatic music works first appeared in watches around 1750, it wasn't until 1815 that the manufacture of music boxes became an established industry in Switzerland. Then it became fashionable to incorporate tune players in items ranging from snuff boxes and jewel cases to small bottles and cane handles. From these novelties it was a short step to a music box that was a complete instrument in its own cabinet.[23]

Early models of those devices were operated by a pinned cylinder powered by a clocklike spring motor. Soon the boxes occupied a place in middle-class European homes similar to that enjoyed by the radio in America in the 1940s. The fixed cylinders in those units limited their repertoire to endless repetition. Finally, in 1878, an interchangeable cylinder was developed that permitted easy insertion and removal. Still, the units required four hand operations by the user, and acquiring additional music for the machines remained an expensive luxury. In 1886 Paul Lochmann revolutionized the industry when he developed the tune-sheet music box in Germany. Those sheets were steel disks in which notes were represented by perforations similar to the sound track in a player piano roll. Varying with the size of the music box, the disks ranged from 8½ inches to 27 inches in diameter and pivoted on an axis. These disks were machine-made, a development that meant production no longer required skilled craftsmen, and therefore they were cheap to produce. As a result, a short-lived American music box industry sprang up in northern New Jersey.[24]

Around 1886 Percival Everett patented a penny-in-the-slot strength-testing device in England. When he arrived in America to seek financial backing, he was persuaded to incorporate the coin-operation feature in personal weighting scales. Music boxes were incorporated in scales to give the user his weight for a penny and to attract additional patronage from onlookers whose attention was caught by the music. It wasn't long after that before coin-operated music boxes made their appearance. Gustav A. Brachausen was an employee of Polyphon Musik Werke, which manufactured the Polyphone, a tune sheet music box, in Leipzig, Germany. He was sent to America in 1893 to help establish the Regina Music Box Company, which was to produce the machines at Jersey City and Rahway, both in New Jersey. Brachausen developed a device that made coin operation supposedly foolproof by using an automatic slot-closing mechanism to prevent jamming while the box was playing. By 1895 he was marketing both penny and nickel coin-operated Regina disk boxes. Tunes could be changed by the owner periodically replacing the single tune sheet. A similar machine was the Criterion, made by the M & J Paillard Company of New York. Those firms and several others devoted most of their output to the production of disk boxes for home use and the music box soon became a standard piece of furniture in many American households.[25]

Between 1898 and 1900, Brachausen secured another patent for a device that enabled the machine to automatically change, select, and repeat tune disks. Equipped with a piano sounding board to give it volume, housed in an oak, rosewood, or mahogany cabinet that averaged six feet in height, and using a 27-inch disk, the Regina was sold to individual locations, mostly restaurants, cafes, and ice-cream parlors. Varying in price, depending on cabinet type, the units sold for over $500. Regina came to stock over 1,000 different tune disks.[26]

Around 1905 Regina produced the Automatic Reginaphone. This machine held six cylinder recordings mounted on spindles that revolved around a common center. When a coin was inserted in the machine, the spindles successively rotated individual cylinders into playing position. Intended for arcades and other locations, the Reginaphone was equipped with either ear tubes or a speaker horn. Improvements in this unit resulted in the introduction in 1908 of the Regina Hexaphone that featured a tune-selecting device by which the customer chose one of the six cylinders to play. While the arcade models had ear tubes, Hexaphones manufactured as crowd entertainers for cafés and saloons concealed the speaker horn within the cabinet. Although the Hexaphone, and other music boxes, quickly faded from popularity, the idea of concealing the speaker horn was eventually adopted by all coin phonographs.[27]

Despite the flurry of technical advances made by coin-operated music machines in the first six years or so of the 1900s, both the music boxes and the phonograph faded into oblivion from around 1907 to 1908. New forms of coin-operated devices squeezed space away from these devices in arcades. Cylinders and steel disks lost favor to records. Still, the quality of records at this time left much to be desired. Insufficient volume was one of the two main factors that condemned these devices. Squeezed out of arcades, the jukebox of this time had trouble moving to locations such as saloons and restaurants. The sound from a phonograph was tinny, muffled, and accompanied by a pronounced hissing as the stylus was dragged over the surface of the record. If one managed somehow to increase the volume, the hissing would also increase. In short, in locations with a fair amount of ambient noise, such as cafés and bars, these units were difficult or impossible to hear.

If the phonograph had been the only source of automatic music available it might have been more successful. However, it was not. The coin-operated player piano came to be the dominant form by which automatic music was received by the public. Also important in driving the early jukebox into limbo was the arrival of a new form of entertainment — motion pictures. By around 1907 the five-cent movie house (it came to be called the nickelodeon) was beginning to sweep America. It quickly captured the public's fancy and threatened the arcades. From centers offering state-of-the-art devices to a family trade, the arcade soon slipped into a more tawdry state as more and more of the public's coins went to the movies. Author J. Krivine observed: "By 1908, the public had virtually stopped dropping nickels into automatic phonographs.... During this period, the automatic band in its many wonderful manifestations was queen of the taverns." Walter Hurd, writing in 1940 as *Billboard's* editor, wrote, "The coin-operated piano had its big day during that period [between 1900 and 1925]." While it lent nothing to the mechanical development of phonographs, the coin piano "once and for all clearly demonstrated that high-priced coin-controlled instruments were an economically sound investment and would greatly increase the popularity and revenue of the refreshment places in which they were installed." Reporter Lewis Nichols, writing in 1941, remarked that a jukebox lobby group, the Automatic Phonograph Manufacturers Association, said that "public interest at that time [1906] was centered more in the coin-operated player piano (than in juke boxes)." In Chicago in 1907 there were 116 nickelodeons and only 19 arcades.[28]

Just after the end of this period, the Copyright Act of 1909 was enacted. This law exempted jukebox operators from paying any royalties on the copyrighted music they placed on their machines, which gave them and location owners a profit. Other elements of the entertainment industry that used the same music for commercial gain, such as motion pictures, radio, and television, were quickly compelled to pay royalties. However, a specific exemption for coin-operated machines protected them. Battles would be fought, and lost, for decades in an attempt to bring phonographs under the copyright provisions. It would be almost 70 years before the fight succeeded.

Before 1909, the copyright law did not protect authors against the unauthorized manufacture of their works. The law had been written in 1873, when phonograph records and piano rolls were unknown. Sheet music was the medium through which the public enjoyed new songs. Prior to 1909, the competitive situation among manufacturers of music rolls was intense and the question of authorship often wholly ignored. When Congress enacted that 1909 law it recognized that authors were entitled to be paid when their musical works were adapted to instruments serving to reproduce them mechanically; but in doing so it attempted to protect the smaller piano roll companies against a possible monopoly on the part of the Aeolian Company, a giant at the time. Instead of directly outlawing monopolistic practices by music-roll manufacturers, Congress adopted a scheme that had no precedent in American legislation. That scheme, part of the 1909 copyright legislation, became known as "compulsory license." Once an author permitted the recording of his musical composition, the law permitted any other company to record it on payment of two cents per record. There was no obligation to enter into agreement with the author or publisher or any requirement to insure actual payment of even the two cents. Before 1909, the author's right to control all public performances of his works was absolute. That conformed to the almost universal doctrine then, and now, prevailing throughout the developed world. The 1909 revision introduced the concept that only those public performances of musical compositions that

Good Music makes the Drinks Taste better

Drop a Nickel

THERE'S A **WURLITZER** Instrument Here

An early Wurlitzer ad to entice customers into a location.

were for profit were within the scope of copyright protection. The language in the act that exempted phonographs stated, "The reproduction or rendition of a musical composition by or upon coin-operated machines shall not be deemed a public performance for profit unless a fee is charged for admission to the place where such reproduction or rendition occurs."[29]

Half a century later, during 1959 hearings on a bill to end the exemption, a Library of Congress statement was submitted that claimed hearing records of the 1909 Copyright Act exemption showed the juke escape to have been a "last-minute affair," not even mentioned until three weeks before the committee report was issued. Librarian of Congress Quincy L. Mumford quoted from music trade publications from the 1909 period and deduced that the exemption was "incorporated in the bill at the suggestion of the Wurlitzer and DeKleist interests." However, the librarian also noted that hearings of the 1909 report said the coin-operated machine exemption from performance royalty "is understood to be satisfactory to the composers and proprietors of musical copyrights" and the so-called penny parlor was said by one publisher to be of "first assistance as an advertising medium."[30]

During this period, and into the end of the 1930s, the jukebox was not called by that name. Phonograph, automatic phonograph, or music machine were terms commonly used, among others. Tallahassee, Florida, operator Lon Bagnall declared at the end of 1939 that the name originated in Tallahassee, in a dime and dance place with an automatic phonograph in the corner. "Somebody called the automatic machine a jook organ (don't ask me why) and the name stuck. Before long the dime and dance places became jook joints." Going jooking meant to go dancing and also meant making the rounds of two or more jook joints. *Billboard* commented that the terminology writers used to describe automatic phonographs "has descended in many cases to the use of the words 'juk boxes' or 'jook organs.'"[31]

Around the same time, a Florida operator identified only by the initials F.T.G. hoped *Billboard* would spearhead a campaign to replace the term "juke-organ." He claimed Miami newspapers used the term often, particularly in describing cases in which locations stayed open after hours and disturbed neighbors with loud music. "Consequently coin phonographs are associated in the mind of the general public with juke joints of the cheaper variety.... Juke-organ is not an accurate description, it is not flattering, and it lessens public acceptance of coin phonographs as a major form of musical entertainment." F.T.G. suggested perhaps holding a nationwide contest to find a new name. *Billboard's* editor observed that the subject had been raised before. He felt "music boxes" was the most acceptable term then in use since it did not have any "evil associations" with jukeboxes. "A few publications opposed to the automatic phono business for one reason or another are playing up the use of the term 'juke box' in order to injure the music trade," he added. "Newspapers also use the term carelessly." The expression "juke box" was said to be most annoying to operators in southern states, especially Florida. One unidentified official of the phonograph manufacturers association took a different position and suggested it might be more feasible for the industry to accept the term "juke boxes" and make the best of it.[32]

According to Geoffrey Parsons Jr. and Robert Yoder, writing in 1941, the work "jook" had African origins and meant "dance." It was put into the vocabulary by Blacks in the South where any somewhat rowdy roadhouse had long been called a jook joint. Automatic phonographs installed in Southern jook joints became known as "juke boxes."[33]

Author Vincent Lynch reported that writers Oliver Read and Walter Welch claimed the term had its immediate origin in "jook," an old Southern word of African origins used among Blacks, which meant "to dance." Eddie Adlum, publisher of *Replay*, suggested it could be a corruption of "jute," and that people who worked the southern jute fields frequented the low-down roadhouses where the automatic phonographs first arrived back in the 1920s. Thus, jute joint became juke joint, and the music machine became the jute, or juke box. Adlum also believed, with others, that the term had more overt sexual connotations, like "boogie," and that a juke joint was a whorehouse, a jukebox kept the patrons dancing.[34]

In 1946 jukebox manufacturer AMI vice president De Witt Eaton sent out instructions to distributors, salesmen, and operators to drop the term "juke box" and use "music vendor" instead. He argued that youngsters who initially put the term "juke box" into the American vocabulary eight years earlier were now "sedate married folks and today's young people are tired of it." He added, "Music vendor has the crisp, compact expressiveness of today's vocabulary and applies perfectly to all forms of coin-operated music, phonographs, wall boxes, telephone and personal music."[35]

Twenty-five years later, in 1971, Fred Granger, an executive with the trade group Music Operators of America, said he was conscious of opinion against use of the term "jukebox" and there was nothing wrong with the term "coin-operated phonograph." However, he admitted that attempts to use another term always proved futile. Granger commented that when he talked to somebody outside the trade "and go into any kind of explanation about the business using a term other than jukebox, you almost always end up with the person saying, 'Oh, you're talking about jukeboxes.'" He thought the term did conjure up the image problem the industry had always had, but stated that they weren't "going to cure the problem with another name for jukebox." Additionally, Washington Congressmen, whom his trade group lobbied every year, were also "accustomed" to the term.[36]

The *Oxford English Dictionary* defined "juke" as of West African origin meaning disorderly or wicked. It defined the term (and its spelling variants) as a roadhouse, or brothel, especially a cheap roadside establishment providing food and drinks and music for dancing. The earliest reported uses were 1935 and 1936. A second meaning was to dance, especially at a juke joint, or to the music of a jukebox, with a first reported usage in 1933. The first reported usages of jukebox (jook organ) were in 1937 and 1939.[37]

A typical jook joint in the Southern United States, circa 1941.

Although the juke industry disliked the term, the media quickly adopted it. Just as quickly, it was adopted by the public. Several general news magazines used the term in 1939 and 1940 and after that there was no turning back. *Billboard* never used the term in its own text until a couple of years after 1939. Occasionally it used the term when it printed a direct quote from another source, but it remained uncomfortable with the term, as it backed the industry. The jukebox industry disliked the term because it felt it conjured up images of Blacks, poverty, disorderly people, and so forth. Once the mainstream media and the public adopted the word, though, the battle for a different term was lost.

2

The Piano Outplays the Box, 1907–1933

"[My Wurlitzer coin piano] has increased my bar trade at least from $6 to $10 per day." J. H. Doherty, Denver bar owner, 1910.

"The Peerless [coin piano] stimulates the appetite, increases the thirst, lightens the feet and spirits, and loosens the strings of the pocketbook." Peerless brochure, ca. 1910.

"Prohibition had been repealed and bars were opening up all over. People needed cheap entertainment, and I got to thinking about music." David Rockola, 1934.

Automatic pianos and other single-instrument music machines also came from European beginnings wherein, by the early 1800s, larger machines were developed before the smaller machines. These were basically mechanical pipe organs. The next evolutionary step was the addition of drums and various other percussion instruments to imitate a small band or orchestra. These early orchestrions (as they came to be called later) were the playthings of kings and queens at the start of the 1800s. By the early decades of that century, those mechanical organs and orchestrions had become fairly popular. Manufacture of these units was then centered in Germany. Beginning around 1857, the pinned wooden cylinders used in the machines started to give way to perforated paper rolls. Costing $50 to $100 or more each, cylinders were expensive, large, and unwieldy. In comparison, perforated paper rolls playing the same tune cost only a few dollars each and could easily be stored in a small space. Cabinets grew more ornate and sometimes contained moving effects such as revolving windmills, dancing waves, and cascading waterfalls. From the German house of Ludwig

Hupfield of Leipzig came a mammoth orchestrion, the Helios V, which was 14'9" tall, 19'9" wide, and 8'2" deep. It was claimed to represent all the instruments of a military and concert band of about 100 to 200 performers.[1]

Musical quality of the orchestrions was said to be very authentic. One early admirer was composer V. Lachner. In 1849 he wrote: "It is not merely mechanical performance, without life or soul, that reaches the ear of the hearer; no, he fancies that he is listening to the work of living human forces, conscious of their artistic aim." Around 1915, in a press release about one of its large units, the Rudolph Wurlitzer company said: "The Wurlitzer PianOrchestra is so nearly a 'human' as to defy detection. There is nothing of the mechanical in its playing. Seated in another room, and not knowing of the existence of this instrument, you would never question but that this is a real flesh and blood organization of trained musicians." In America during the 1880s and 1890s orchestrions were mostly imported from Germany and were sold to financiers, industrialists, and other wealthy individuals for home use. Only a very few were sold to business establishments. As United States manufacturers entered the field, Germany's influence faded, ceasing altogether with the onset of World War I.[2]

Scottish immigrant and machinist John McTammany developed the player organ in America. By 1874 he had made his first three Automatic Air Organs, while working for the firm of Boyer & Swain. Shortly thereafter, he took over the Munroe Reed Organ Company of Worcester, Massachusetts, and developed the player piano. In 1877, M. Debani of Paris, France, invented a piano with a second set of hammers operated from above by the movement of a tune sheet — a board with pegs sticking out from it, which was moved across the hammers. Similar to McTammany's machine, both were patterned after the old barrel-organ principle. The Pianola was invented in 1897 by E. S. Votey. This was a separate unit designed to make any piano into a player piano. Based in Massachusetts, the Aeolian Company soon developed a device that could be installed in their new pianos, turning them into players. By around 1900, nearly all the piano manufacturers were equipping their pianos with player mechanisms, constructed so as to be unobtrusive with the controls hidden behind sliding doors.[3]

American manufacturing activity in the coin-operated piano field was pioneered by the firm of Roth & Engelhardt (later to operate as F. Engelhardt & Sons, Peerless Piano Player Company and National Electric Piano Company) of Johnsville, New York. Beginning with their small "D" model in 1898, this company marketed several dozen different models under the names of Peerless and Engelhardt. Those units ranged in size from a small cabinet-style piano playing a range of only 44 notes to large orchestrions consisting of upright pianos with case extensions containing many instruments added on top. An entire keyboard model had 88 notes and was equipped with a rewind music drawer mechanism holding perforated rolls containing 15 selections. Some units already had two separate rolls for continuous music. As one rewound, the other played. Orchestrions sometimes exceeded $10,000 in price.[4]

As the 20th century began, conditions were favorable for music machines, at least for some of them. A new style of music, ragtime, grew to become America's favorite. At the same time, the new marches of John Philip Sousa, along with the works of George M. Cohen, were being hummed and whistled everywhere. Automatic music meant people no longer had to attend a concert or gather around a regular piano with sheet music to hear these numbers. They only had to drop a coin in a slot. Historian of these devices Q. David Bowers said about the first few years of the 1900s, "Saloons, candy stores, billiard parlors and, yes, even brothels—none were quite complete without a coin piano near the door to lure in the customers."[5]

If the arrival of motion pictures helped drive the music box and phonograph into oblivion, it widened the market for coin pianos and orchestrions. To attract paying customers to theater box offices there was no substitute for having one of these units playing nearby. Inside the theaters a new breed of automatic musical instrument, the photoplayer, evolved. Almost every maker of coin-operated pianos in business between 1905 and 1925 also had a line of photoplayers. Those devices, marketed under such names as "Pipe-Organ Orchestra" (Seeburg) and "One Man Orchestra" (Wurlitzer) usually consisted of a piano and several ranks of pipers plus assorted traps and percussion instruments housed in side chests. What set them apart from orchestrions were their sound effects gadgets. One photoplayer contained the following effects: fire gong, auto horn, automobile exhaust, Chinese cymbal, bird whistle, cowbell, wind, waves, telegraph key, crackling flames, horses' hooves, and so forth. Music could be made to conform to the film by going forward or backward on the roll.[6]

One of those attracted to the coin-operated piano field was Rudolph Wurlitzer. At the beginning of the 20th century his firm was well established and well diversified in the music field. Rudolph was born in Schoeneck, Germany, on January 30, 1831. He founded the Wurlitzer business in 1856 and began importing musical instruments from Europe. The Wurlitzer family traced itself back to Saxony where, in 1659, Nicholas Wurlitzer, son of a swordsman, turned his talents to making lutes. It remained a musical family ever since. Rudolph left Europe and landed at Hoboken, New Jersey, in 1853, with little money and only a negligible knowledge of English. Working at various jobs in different cities, Rudolph found himself in Cincinnati

Opposite, top: An ad for Peerless coin machines. *Opposite, bottom:* An ad for the Wisteria, a Peerless orchestrion.

DID you ever hear of the London tailor who noticed that when a street piano came under his window and played "God Save the Queen" the machines of his operators slowed down to keep time with the music?

It took him just about a minute to size up the situation.

He hired a man by the day to play good, rollicking, *swift* tunes, with the result that the work of his shoproom trebled itself. This was a natural, though unconscious, result, an instinctive compliance with the demand of the musical tempo.

Does your enterprise need a stimulant?

Give it some *Peerless* tonic and watch it brace up. The *Peerless* is a business booster of the Big Bull Moose variety. It will change the entire atmosphere of your establishment and put backbone into the most spineless employee. It will give *you* an optimistic viewpoint that by natural attraction will induce patronage.

The *Peerless* will advertise you. It never gets tired, doesn't belong to the union, works overtime without extra pay, never gets sulky or dopey, has no bad habits, and is always "fit" and ready for business.

The *Peerless* stimulates the appetite, increases the thirst, lightens the feet and the spirits, and loosens the strings of the pocketbook.

It's a coin-coaxer, a money-wheedler, a nickel-winner.

It's the *big thing* for which you have been looking.

Do your requirements call for a single piano or an orchestra?

The *Peerless* supplies either—in fact, two, three, four or five instruments in one.

Try it! Put one in your establishment, bait it with a nickel and watch the people bite. The next nickel and the next and all the rest will come out of your customers' pockets.

Make it easy for them—have the slot connections where they can't help but see them. The suggestion is all that's needed.

Tell us what you need, and we will recommend the right instrument.

Mail communications will have our immediate attention.

THE PEERLESS PIANO PLAYER CO.
F. ENGELHARDT & SONS, Proprietors
ST. JOHNSVILLE, N. Y.
NEW YORK   CHICAGO

MODEL "WISTERIA"

PEERLESS AUTOMATIC PIANOS HAVE PLAYED THEIR WAY THROUGH ALL PUBLIC PREJUDICES

THERE was a time when a favorite argument against the Automatic Piano was that the individuality of the performer was lost. Some daring and original souls discovered, and with much simplicity and the courage of their convictions, asserted that the individuality of the average performer was a good thing to lose. The truth of this statement came home to many an employer, and a tide set in in favor of the Automatic Piano.

There is nothing more trying nor tiring than to endeavor to dance to uncertain and fluctuating measure, and the faultless time of the Peerless is an inspiration to rhythmic movement, whether it be in the gymnasium or ball room. The demand is for real music correctly rendered and in the creation of the new type depicted above, the purchaser has what he has been looking for all these years.

As an economical and satisfactory substitute for an individual performance for all public amusements, the arguments in its favor are too obvious to require mention. The PEERLESS pays for itself in a short time, and immediately becomes an appreciable profit-compelling asset.

A NICKEL DOES THE TRICK

MADE BY THE

PEERLESS PIANO PLAYER COMPANY
General Offices: 316 South Wabash Avenue, Chicago
Factories: St. Johnsville, N. Y.

a few years later. Near where he worked was a retail music store which, thought Rudolph, had an inadequate and overpriced stock. Determined to capitalize on this, the young man sent his savings of $700 back to family connections in Europe. They returned crafted instruments, which Rudolph sold directly to retailers. By 1861, he had established a factory at Cincinnati to make instruments for martial music. His biggest customer was the military. Soldiers marched to the beat of drums and the blare of bugles made by Wurlitzer. By 1865, Wurlitzer was the largest outlet for band instruments in the United States.[7]

In 1890, the Rudolph Wurlitzer Company was incorporated. Although in those early years most of the company's efforts were concentrated on regular musical instruments, the firm became increasingly aware of the demand for automatic music devices. Around 1893, the company secured a sales distributorship from Regina, which lasted about 10 years, becoming in time the largest single sales outlet for the various Regina musical products. In 1896, Wurlitzer persuaded Regina to equip some of its music boxes, particularly the large 27-inch disk machines, with coin slots. Having good success with those large, glass-fronted "Orchestral Corona" models provided Wurlitzer with more evidence of the potential for coin-operated music.[8]

Wurlitzer's large-scale entry into the field of mechanical music began in 1897. In that year, Eugene DeKleist, a maker of barrel organs, was trying to expand his business. He went to see Rudolph, who encouraged DeKleist to develop and build a coin-operated piano. After two years of work, the new piano was marketed in 1899, under the name of the Wurlitzer Tonophone. For the music source, DeKleist used pinned cylinders similar to the ones in his merry-go-round organs. The electrically operated device had a capacity of 10 tunes and played upon receipt of a nickel. Wurlitzer's first order with DeKleist was for 200 Tonophones, at a cost of $200 each. Reportedly it was a big success from the moment it appeared. The success of the device led to the development of many other types of coin-operated machines. Several varieties of coin pianos were produced at the DeKleist factory and marketed under the Wurlitzer name. As he grew rich, DeKleist paid less attention to his business, resulting in a decline in product quality and an increasing number of customer complaints. In 1909, the DeKleist firm was taken over by Wurlitzer when the latter formed a new corporation, the Rudolph Wurlitzer Manufacturing Company.[9]

The 1899 Tonophone was among the first coin-operated pianos to appear in America. A major factor contributing to its success was the firm's flair for advertising. In their brochures, ads, and other sales and promotional material, Wurlitzer sold not just the machine but also the concept of coin-operated music. An early ad stressed that music was a source of revenue, claiming

THE TONOPHONE
Automatic Piano with Nickel-in-Slot Attachment.

STYLE 1 Oak or Mahogany, including one cylinder, with direct current motor, **$600.00**

STYLE 2 The same equipped with alternating current motor, **$650.00**

SOLD FOR CASH OR ON MONTHLY PAYMENTS.

Extra cylinders, 10 tunes, $40.00   Cylinders exchanged for $5.00

The Wurlitzer Tonophone.

that testimonials showed their music machines returned as high as 300 percent, and never less than 50 percent, on investment. Music stimulated business by causing people to enter an establishment, who might not have, and spend money. Again Wurlitzer cited reportedly unsolicited testimonials that said that some of their automatic music instruments increased bar trade by 25 percent. The ad also stressed the "charming" influence of music, that is, it soothed, refined, and elevated: "The classically inclined can be accommodated as well as the admirer of ragtime." Additionally, the ad stressed that one had to have music if one wanted his location to be trendy and with it.

Promotional material argued, "the modern saloon has become the magnet for the better element of the male community." That had happened because of the "charming" influence of music, the prevalence of art in those places, and "the congregation of men occupied in different callings who meet for quiet interchange of thought." Wurlitzer's brochure concluded, "Let us once more impress upon the proprietors of modern cafés and other public places, that you must have MUSIC to attract the better element, and as long as it is profitable and increases your trade, why not have it?" A testimonial from James Cunningham, owner of the Metropole bar, said he had purchased a Tonophone four months earlier for $650. Since that time it had taken in $668.20 and increased his bar trade.[10]

The public liked the honky-tonk sound of coin pianos and liked the Tonophone. One disadvantage of the machine was that new cylinders cost $40 each. To ease this burden, cylinders could be rented for $5 each. Any one of the 10 tunes on a cylinder could be selected simply by turning the arrow on a circular dial on the outside of the cabinet. On other coin pianos there was no selectivity, and the patron often had to listen to many unwanted tunes before his number moved to the front of the rotation. Tunes on the Tonophone played through twice, for one nickel. However, that was more out of necessity as the limited amount of space available on the cylinder dictated that each number had to be short; often with a refrain or two omitted. Accepting only five-cent pieces, the Tonophone's coin slot was also equipped with a slug detector.[11]

Coin-operated pianos of all kinds were curiosities in the very early 1900s. Regardless of the type and quality of music they played, they usually drew a steady flow of business. At that time the New York *Sun* wrote: "The restaurant dearest to the men of Washington Market acquired a Tonophone (electric piano) for its main dining room the other day. The patrons patronized it liberally and there was continuous music from noon till evening, which the waiters seemed to enjoy as much as anybody." Testimonials by the dozens were said to have poured into the offices of Wurlitzer and of its distributors.[12]

Tonophones were produced from 1899 to about 1908. Production of the model was stopped in favor of the Wurlitzer 65-Note Player Piano, which replaced it as the basic full-sized coin piano in the company's line. Using perforated paper rolls, each roll contained five tunes and cost $4.50. Considering the technical advances that had been made in Europe by the late 1890s, the Tonophone, with its outdated pinned cylinder, was obsolete when it was first placed on the market. Wurlitzer admitted this when it included the following in a catalog for band organs, around 1912: "We know the old-fashioned pinned cylinder ... could never be adapted to the purpose, because of the harshness of the music; the lack of means of regulating the

Remember! The TONOPHONE is the only Automatic Musical Instrument where any one of the ten tunes can be played at any time. This is impossible on instruments where Paper Rolls are used. The Tonophone has an indestructible cylinder—no Paper Rolls.

Some People will always make money no matter what they do   (They are the fortunate kind)

Some People will never make money for they never have an opportunity   (They are the unfortunate kind)

Some People make money because they are wide-awake and grasp every opportunity   (They are the sensible kind)

Some People never make money, for they fail to grasp the opportunity offered them   (They are the foolish kind)

WHICH CLASS DO YOU BELONG TO?

The sensible kind we hope, for here is an opportunity to make from

100% to 300% on a Safe Investment

The following figures taken from TESTIMONIALS in our possession show that **THE TONOPHONE** is beyond a doubt

THE GREATEST MONEY-MAKER ON EARTH!

And at the same time a wonderful **Business Stimulator**

As it will increase your trade 25 to 50%

NAME	ADDRESS	Earned per Month	Yearly Average	Interest on Investment
Jas. Cunningham	St. Louis, Mo.	$167.05	$2004.60	308%
Am. Liquor Co.	Denver, Col.	142.50	1710.00	263%
Evans & Cammack.	Marion, Ind.	140.15	1681.80	258%
Wm. J. Bley	St. Louis, Mo	127.45	1529.40	235%
Fred. Suhr	St. Louis, Mo	124.00	1488.00	229%
Frank P. Madden	Stockton, Cal.	96.00	1152.00	177%
Trede Bros.	Red Bluff, Cal.	80.00	960.00	148%
Jake Weber	Columbus, O	68.80	823.60	126%

We can furnish hundreds of Testimonials to show that the Tonophone will not pay less than 100% on the Investment.

Now is the Time to Buy! Cash or Monthly Payments!

Testimonials to the money-making ability of the Tonophone.

tempo; the trouble and time necessary to change the music; the impossibility of putting a complete waltz or two-step on a cylinder (the music can not be any longer than the circumference of the cylinder); and the expense of new music...." However, the Tonophone did serve to introduce America to coin-operated Wurlitzer music. The firm had just one model on the market in 1899, the Tonophone, but by 1908 it had dozens.[13]

The Wurlitzer 65-Note Player Piano

Height, 4 ft. 10 in.   Width, 5 ft. 2 in.   Depth, 2 ft. 3 in.

PRICE—Complete, with Electric Motor and 1 Roll of Music, containing 5 selections.....$700.00

Extra Music Rolls, 5 selections each...................................... 4.00

Shipping Weight, 1,025 pounds.
Net Weight, 755 pounds.

Wurlitzer's 65-note player piano had clear glass panels which revealed the machine's interior.

Introduced around 1902, the 44-note Pianino was the first Wurlitzer coin piano to be operated with a perforated paper roll. Compared to the Tonophone, the Pianino was intended for those who wanted a smaller or less expensive machine. Other firms had such models. The Mills Novelty Company's Automatic Pianova automatically rewound the roll at the end in 30 seconds and cost $500. Each roll had six numbers and played for 12 to 15 minutes total. A roll cost $4.50. Pianinos remained good sellers for almost 30 years. An innovation on this model was its coin-detector slot. With this device the Pianino could take several nickels at a time, resulting in larger receipts for the location. A customer could drop five nickels, one at a time, into the slot. Additional profits could be made by deploying cast-iron wall boxes at various booths in restaurants, and so forth. The $10 to $15 cost per wall box normally paid for itself quickly by the added business that it generated. To provide a variation in the sound of the Pianino, each machine was equipped with a mandolin attachment.[14]

Another variation came a few years later in the form of the Wurlitzer Violin Pianino. In addition to the piano/mandolin sound of the Pianino, these units featured 21 violin pipes and 21 flute pipes that produced an accompaniment. Usually the Violin Pianino sold for around $200 more than a regular Pianino. Thus, in March 1920, a Pianino sold for $575 while a Violin Pianino was listed at $750. When Wurlitzer introduced its 65-Note Player Piano in 1908, this paper roll–operated model replaced the Tono-phone as the firm's standard, large coin-operated piano. Featuring a roll rewinder, magazine coin-detector slot, mandolin attachment, and electric lights for illuminating the interior while it played, the unit cost $700. Extra five-tune music rolls were priced at $4 each.[15]

During this pre–1910 period, Wurlitzer opened a retail store on West 32nd Street, New York, which displayed and sold orchestrions and coin-operated pianos. The firm also sited those machines in various places with a commission to the location owner of 25 percent of the gross take. A different roll of music was put on the machine each week. Reportedly, some locations took in $18 or more per week. If receipts in a particular spot were less than $2 a week, the machine was removed. Sometimes people would cheat the piano by tying a string on a nickel so that it would not drop all the way through the mechanism. Iron washers with holes would not work, but they could prevent real nickels from going in by jamming up the works.[16]

Chicago-based Wurlitzer sales agent Sam Winter had spent some time trying to get a bar proprietor to take a machine. Finally the barman asked Winter how much commission he would get if he allowed a coin-operated piano in his establishment. Winter explained it would be better to buy a unit. The price was $700 with terms of $70 down and $7 a week for 90 weeks. If the machine took in $10 a week the barman kept $3 and gave the Wurlitzer collector $7. Unconvinced, the barman said he might be better off with 25 percent of the take and nothing else to worry about. Said Winter: "If you can find operators to give you 25 per cent, even 50 per cent, buy their own instruments, take care of them on the commission basis, it surely ought to be a better proposition to buy your own instrument and get all the receipts." Winter also explained that Wurlitzer did not change music

A box full of nickels on the bar and two more on the floor. Evidence of the Tonophone's drawing power. Hoeffler was a Wurlitzer distributor.

rolls (on a purchased machine) and "you don't want us to change rolls … in the first place you have no choice…. Changing rolls for you, you will be unable to please your customers … and the result would be a loss of trade, not a gain." What was interesting about these arguments was that a few decades later the juke industry would adamantly declare that locations could not buy machines (they had to take them on a commission basis from operators) precisely because it was impossible for a location owner to buy a machine outright and make a profit, for various reasons. One of them was that the location owner knew nothing about music selection, compared to the operator. Yet back around 1910, when makers tried to sell units directly to locations, opposite arguments were trotted out.[17]

Cabinets, grill work, and glass work on the Wurlitzer models all got more elaborate as time passed. The Wurlitzer PianOrchestra (orchestrion) sold for $4,050 in 1920. The most expensive machine in the firm's stock was the Paganini Violin Orchestra. Standing 11'4" in height, 8'10" in width, and 6' in depth, it had a shipping weight of 4,200 pounds and cost $10,000. Most of these Paganini units were not coin operated. They were intended to provide background or mood music for exclusive country clubs and similar places. They were, of course, designed for establishments wanting an alternative to live musicians and their associated costs. However, the PianOrchestra was advertised and promoted to places that wanted coin-operated music.[18]

Chicago's Marquette Piano Company marketed its Cremona line of coin pianos around 1905. Some incorporated a tune selector, a rare feature that permitted the choosing of a favorite tune on a particular roll, instead of the usual practice of having to hear whatever came next in the rotation. After the selection was made, the roll would race ahead or rewind to the start of the desired number. However, Marquette, which sold its Cremona line for $500 to $650, did not actively promote its tune selector, nor did it usually mention the feature in its ads. Apparently it was subject to breakdown and was difficult to service.[19]

Another leading manufacturer of the day was the North Tonawanda Musical Instrument Works, formed around 1906 or 1907. The Pianolin, a small arcade-type piano that used an endless roll, was the best known of its products. Two letters in praise of the Pianolin were sent to the company in 1910. One was from Grand Rapids, Michigan, bar owner Bert Wosinski, who said that in the first four days he had the unit in his bar it took in $31.65 and "helped the bar trade wonderfully." Tonawanda, New York, bar owner William Kolpack claimed his Pianolin was averaging over $100 a month and it had increased his "bar trade from $5 to $8 per day." Denver, Colorado, bar proprietor J. H. Doherty stated that his Wurlitzer coin piano had grossed $92 in six weeks and "it has increased my bar trade at least from $6 to $10 per day." In this period, various other single-instrument music machines were developed and marketed, such as an automatic harp, automatic banjo, automatic violin, and so on. None of these achieved any type of success. Only the automatic piano, and more versatile orchestrions, enjoyed continued public favor and success.[20]

The Wurlitzer PianOrchestra provides high-class entertainment that makes business hum

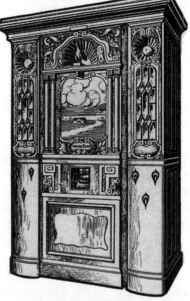

**One thing is certain—
you want more business!**

**A Wurlitzer PianOrchestra
will get you more
business**

Wurlitzer PianOrchestras are right now getting more business for 762 other men in your same line almost everywhere the sun shines. (Testimonials by the basketful.) What a PianOrchestra has done for others it will do for you.

The Wurlitzer PianOrchestra will give you entertainment of cabaret variety—at practically no cost.

The public drops the coins that play the music, thereby putting the instrument upon a basis that is self-paying.

You have heard the beautiful music of a 10-piece orchestra and have seen couples dance the fox trot, one step and hesitation, and you wished perhaps, that you could afford to employ a 10-piece orchestra and make your place just as attractive.

We can place a *PianOrchestra* in your establishment—give you practically the same volume and quality of music as a 10-piece orchestra, and you can add these entertainment features or dances and draw just as big crowds.

**The Wurlitzer PianOrchestra
provides just the entertainment that everyone likes**

There is as much difference in the quality of its music and the "music" of a majority of automatic musical instruments as between a human orchestra and a hurdy-gurdy. The Wurlitzer PianOrchestra is so nearly a "Human" Orchestra as to defy detection.

There is nothing of the mechanical in its playing. Seated in another room, and not knowing of the existence of this instrument, you would never question but that it is a real flesh and blood organization of ten trained musicians.

The music rolls which it plays are cut by a new process. The selections are all up to date.

The Wurlitzer PianOrchestra is equipped with the wonderful AUTOMATIC ROLL CHANGER

that makes it possible for it to play as many as thirty different selections without change or attention — classical, operatic, dances, songs, and all the national airs. A musical program of from one and a half hours' to three hours' duration, can be arranged without attention.

Every feature of this Automatic Roll Changer is patented by the Rudolph Wurlitzer Company, and cannot be found in any other instrument.

Now Read the Special Offer Below

SPECIAL OFFER FOR IMMEDIATE ACCEPTANCE

You know that everybody likes music and if you can provide the music that they like best, you are bound to make your place more attractive.

ENCLOSED YOU WILL FIND A RETURN POST CARD. If you will fill in and mail back this card AT ONCE we will write you a personal letter and make a special offer for immediate delivery of a Wurlitzer Style 47 PianOrchestra, upon terms that will make it practically self-paying.

All you do is install it. We will not only show you a way to get your money back, but a way to make the instrument an extra source of income.

Our Style 47 PianOrchestra, here illustrated, is only one of many attractive styles.

It will cost you only a one-cent stamp to get our beautiful art catalogue in fine colors, and a great variety of other high-class literature, which you will find very interesting reading.

Our proposition to you is an exceptional one. Do not toss this circular aside. Mail back the card now and hear the proposition anyhow!

THE RUDOLPH WURLITZER CO.

121 E. FOURTH ST.
ALBANY, N.Y., 17-19 Green St.
BUFFALO, N.Y., 701 Main St.
BOSTON, MASS., 630 Washington Ave.
COLUMBUS, OHIO, 57 Main St.

329-331 S. WABASH AVE.
CLEVELAND, OHIO, 800 Huron Rd.
DETROIT, MICH., 26 Adams Ave. W.
DAYTON, OHIO, 133 Ludlow St.
KANSAS CITY, MO., 1016 Walnut St.

LOUISVILLE, KY., 652 S. Fourth St.
MILWAUKEE, WIS., 133 Second St.
PHILADELPHIA, PA., 912 Chestnut St.
ROCHESTER, N.Y., 570 Main St. E.

113-119 W. 40th; 114-118 W. 41st.
SYRACUSE, N.Y., 437 S. Clinton St.
ST. LOUIS, MO., 1109 Olive St.
SAN FRANCISCO, CAL., 985 Market St.

Wurlitzer's PianOrchestra, one of its most expensive machines.

Charlie Weber's San Francisco saloon was described as one of the city's brightest night spots in 1904. Near the door was a Tonophone. After realizing his $600 machine had paid for itself several times over, Weber paid $3,500 for the company's PianOrchestra. Both played a tune for a nickel. The latter was described as follows: "Near the top, over 10 feet from the floor, a large jeweled bulb begins to rotate, throwing sparkling and brilliantly colored rays of light from the many facets of the circular mirror behind it." A few miles away at the seaside Cliff House, General Manager J. M. Wilkins noted with amazement that his two coin pianos, costing him $650 each, had paid for themselves in just a few months. The story was said to be much the same in other places such as St. Louis, Chicago, New Orleans, New York, and so on, in 1904.[21]

A second name that would become synonymous with jukeboxes, besides Wurlitzer, was Seeburg. Justus P. Seeburg was born in Gothenberg, Sweden. After graduating from a technical institute there in 1887, he came to the United States, where he worked for various piano companies. Around 1902–1904, the J. P. Seeburg Company was formed. In its early years the firm was involved in making piano action mechanisms. Seeburg introduced

Charlie Weber's bar. Tonophone on the left, PianOrchestra at the back.

its own coin piano in 1907. Three years later it debuted its orchestrion model, a restyled piano with the addition of a violin sound, cymbals, and other percussive effects. Both units were powered pneumatically with electrically driven bellows. By 1911, the firm had a variety of products on the market, including a photoplayer, several large orchestrions, and several varieties of smaller coin pianos. As well, Seeburg manufactured organs for the theater and for the home. Initially, Seeburg also functioned as an operator when it placed some 500 of its own coin pianos on location. It was a short-lived experiment with the firm selling its operating business to concentrate exclusively on manufacturing. Seeburg became recognized as one of the larger manufacturers of coin pianos in the world. A 1918 Seeburg price list showed 18 different models varying in price (retail) from $350 and $650 at the low end up to $2,850 and $4,000 at the upper end. Wholesale prices were given as 40 to 50 percent of retail.[22]

Coin pianos and orchestrions owed part of their success to the aggressive merchandising and promotion methods used by some of the estimated 100 manufacturers and marketers in the field. Most of these machines were sold directly to proprietors of taverns, hotels, restaurants, and so on. Very few operators, who bought machines from the distributors and placed them in locations for a percentage of the take, existed in this period. A sales invoice for an early pneumatic orchestrion, dated July 22, 1905, listed the sales price, including installation, as $11,559.85. The cost of 12 paper music rolls was included. The customer bought 36 additional rolls at $10 each. A used orchestrion, along with 12 rolls taken in trade in the transaction, was valued at $2,900. Obviously, only the most prosperous could afford the high-end models. Perhaps as many as tens of thousands of the coin pianos and orchestrions were placed in locations throughout America in this period, indicating wide public acceptance.[23]

Testimonial letters from customers attested to the money-making abilities of these machines. Pioneer operators— mostly location owners— lost no opportunity to merchandise their automatic music, using a great variety of progressive promotional gimmicks. One of the earliest methods was a simple placard for mounting in the establishment's window or directly on the machine. One of the first of these was made available by the coin piano manufacturer, the Link Company. It read, "Drop a Nickel in to Hear the Latest Dance and Song Hits as Played By a Link Coin-Operated Piano." The name of the establishment was printed in a lower corner of the card. Another early leader in the provision of in-location music promotion materials was Wurlitzer. The firm made available a variety of advertising cards bearing such slogans as "Drop 5¢ in the Slot For A Real Concert," "Good Music Makes The Drinks Taste Better — Drop A Nickel," and "Drop A Nickel and Fill The Air With Beautiful Music."[24]

Distinctive and–
Complete

STYLE L AUTOMATIC ORCHESTRA

SEEBURG Automatic Instruments

THE LEADING LINE

Distinctive because of pronounced artistic superiority in design. Every SEEBURG instrument incorporates individuality of style and instrumentation.

Complete mechanically—complete musically—complete throughout the entire line

Seeburg Automatic Instruments
— SOLD TO —

THEATRES	RESTAURANTS	RINKS
LODGES	CABARETS	CAFES
CONFECTIONERS	DANCE HALLS	

WRITE THE

J. P. SEEBURG PIANO CO.

209 Republic Building   CHICAGO, ILL.

One of Seeburg's elaborate and ornate orchestrions.

Drop a Nickel and fill the air with beautiful Music

"DROP A NICKLE IN"

TO HEAR THE LATEST DANCE AND SONG HITS
AS PLAYED BY A

"THE BEST NICKLE PIANO IN THE WORLD"

Wyoming Valley Music Co.
Wilkes-Barre, Pa.

Drop 5¢ in the slot for a Real Concert

One of Wurlitzer's promotional brochures read, in part, "With the great strides forward in the production of automatic instruments, has come a popular demand for music in all public places where people congregate for social intercourse, or to while away an idle moment, so that today it can be safely said that no public place is complete without its music of some kind." It added, "Nothing is more attractive in a public place or recreation or amusement than music, and the general public is not slow in showing their approval by opening their pocketbooks to pay for it..." Another Wurlitzer flyer read, in part: "...nothing adds more to the patrons' pleasure than the sweet strains of music, or brings larger returns on the investment.... We can show many instances where our automatic instruments have been the means of increasing the bar trade from 10 to 25 per cent. Aside from this increase of the bar trade, there is positively no legitimate investment that can be made in connection with the café business that will pay such heavy dividends." Music was not an afterthought in such establishments. Rather, it was an integral part of the location's ambience, as much a part of the atmosphere and decor as the color scheme.[25]

The Niagara Musical Instrument Manufacturing Company provided a dinner menu listing musical options alongside the food choices as part of a promotional package for restaurants that contained its EnSymphonie automatic pipe organ. The Peerless Piano company had a flyer that stated, in part: "The Peerless will advertise you. It never gets tired, doesn't belong to the union, works overtime without extra pay, never gets sulky or dopey, has no bad habits and is always 'fit' and ready for business. The Peerless stimulates the appetite, increases the thirst, lightens the feet and spirits and loosens the strings of the pocketbook. It's a coin-coaxer, a money-wheedler, a nickel-winner. Try it! Put one in your establishment, bait it with a nickel and watch the people bite." With all this hype, coin pianos and orchestrions became quite popular. By 1914, Wurlitzer alone boasted that 10,000 of its automatic music machines were in use in the United States.[26]

If some of the people involved in the coin-music industry understood the importance of song selection in generating income for their machines, some ignored it. Bill Shayne recalled that he started working for the Miami-based Dixie Music Company in 1913, when he was 17. At that time, he remembered, "we serviced our locations with pianos instead of phonos ... we gave the matter [of song selection] little or no consideration."[27]

Very reliable, some of these coin pianos were still in service decades later. Harry Graham, executive with Marquette Music Company in Detroit, said, in 1938, that the old coin pianos "...cost us $500 ten years ago—we

Opposite: **Examples of more ads designed to attract customers. Note that the Link ad had trouble with the word "nickel."**

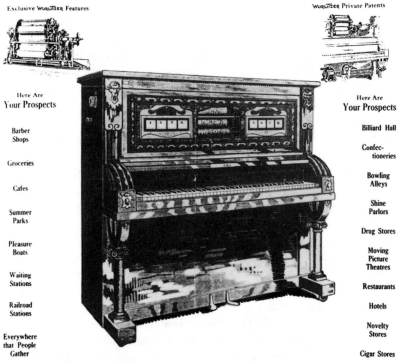

Exclusive WURLITZER Features

WURLITZER Private Patents

**Here Are
Your Prospects**

Barber
Shops

Groceries

Cafes

Summer
Parks

Pleasure
Boats

Waiting
Stations

Railroad
Stations

Everywhere
that People
Gather

**Here Are
Your Prospects**

Billiard Hall

Confec-
tioneries

Bowling
Alleys

Shine
Parlors

Drug Stores

Moving
Picture
Theatres

Restaurants

Hotels

Novelty
Stores

Cigar Stores

Here is the Big Money-Maker

The bright, cheery Gay Music of this style IX Musical Instrument will attract crowds. The crowds will increase the cash receipts of your customers. This is the modern up-to-date wonder. These are its exclusive advantages. Only the Wurlitzer Musical Instrument has the "Roll Changer" that has SIX SEPARATE ROLLS of music with FIVE TUNES TO EACH ROLL. Thirty distinct popular medlies. The patrons are enabled by a device to select their own style of music, just what they want; Ragtime, Classic, Jazz, or Hawaiian Tunes. The "Roll Changer" is at the top of the Piano, very easy to attend, no unpleasant stooping on the knees required. Our DIRECT SHAFT DRIVE does NOT stretch nor break like the animal belting on other makes of Electric Pianos. A big Saving in Time and Expense itself. Gives absolutely perfect tempo for dancing. You do not need to sell these Wurlitzer Wonders. THEY SELL THEMSELVES. All you need to do is deliver the instrument and collect the money.

Send for Special Dealer's Offer

Make More Profits at Less Worry and Expense

Mail in the enclosed card for our SPECIAL DEALER'S OFFER now. There is a limit to the time to establish new dealers and the number we want. Don't Wait. Mail the card now. No obligation. We have a proposition on which you CAN make more money. This is indeed a rare opportunity. Your bank book can be full of money and your heart full of appreciation of your wise decision. Will you miss the chance to Make Real Money. You can wait too long. Decide now.

Send Card Now—Don't Wait!

The Rudolph Wurlitzer Company

121 E. Fourth Street, Cincinnati, Ohio

Note the long list of potential locations cited by Wurlitzer. Two of the most popular location types were omitted — brothels and speakeasies.

couldn't sell them today at any price." His company had one restaurant location that had continued to use a coin piano (owned by the restaurant) up to early in 1938. According to Graham it took in only $2 a week. After Marquette put in a modern jukebox (on a commission basis), "it is grossing much more."[28]

Chicago's Green Lantern Tavern had both a modern jukebox and a coin piano of undetermined age on its premises in 1947. The piano averaged 480 plays a week, compared to the modern juke at about 440. Only two original piano rolls were left; each contained 10 songs, lasting about three minutes each. Song selection was not possible; the next tune on the roll was the one that played.[29]

Through 1920, coin pianos and orchestrions were the dominant music machines. Still, the average restaurant or saloon probably had no automatic music device located on their premises. If they did, it was probably one of the lower-priced coin pianos. Then a series of disasters struck the industry. Prohibition spread throughout America on a local option basis during World War I. In January 1920, Prohibition was adopted nationwide, marking the end of the best customer of the coin-operated business. Saloons and bars all across the land closed their doors, at least officially. The bootleg operations and speakeasies that replaced them compensated for the loss only to a minor degree. For all practical purposes, the era of large orchestrions came to an end with Prohibition in 1920. After that date, the number of larger machines sold was but a small fraction of the amount sold during the height of the market from around 1905 to World War I. Most machines sold in the 1920–1930 era were smaller units. Radio arrived on the scene in the 1920s and came to dominate entertainment in that decade, soon to be found in every living room. Music was a regular feature of early radio. It was free and it offered something else the pianos could not — vocals. Sound movies, which completely revolutionized the motion-picture business in 1926 and 1927, took another good customer out of the market. Seeburg had been a major supplier of music machines to the silent theaters, as was Wurlitzer. The pipe organ, supplied by the latter to cinemas, came to be affectionately called "The Mighty Wurlitzer." By this time, around 1927, the coin-piano industry was finished. In fact, the coin-machine industry overall was in trouble. Arcades, also hit by the movies, then by radio, had fallen drastically in public favor. Customers were tired of the limited array of games available.[30]

Yet even as the industry languished, the background for revival was being established. Just before the Depression arrived in 1929–1930, the vending machine took center stage among coin machines. Journalist H. F. Reves commented: "To some it seemed that everything in the way of standard, tangible merchandise, might more economically be sold by machines than by ordinary retail stores and clerks." Detroit's Cunningham Drug Store undertook an experiment in 1929 at its main Griswold Street store when it installed about 50 machines in all. Those venders, each dispensing a different, single item, ran some 60 feet along the wall in one part of the large store. A change machine was also installed. The machines took 5-, 10-, and 25-cent coins. After only a few months, the experiment was abandoned for

Four Vital Factors

that interest YOU most as a Live Wire Dealer

The Musical Instruments Themselves	The Manufacturer's Reputation	Your Own— Profits	Sales Help that Bring Business
Regardless of the Public Place you desire to install one, we have just the style, size and price that will close the sale for you. Every combination of Musical Instruments have been built to satisfy the most subtle fancy of the prospect. Piano with single Piano, with violin and flute, up to an assembly of 23 different parts—a complete orchestra or band if desired. All played by paper rolls. The very latest hits are always ready as soon as they come out. The Artistic case and finish make the Wurlitzer Automatic a big attraction.	How long has he been in business? How has his merchandise stood the test? What is his rating? All these questions are proper for you to know. All we need to do is write, ask or phone any owner of a Wurlitzer Musical Instrument you know. Then will be your proof. Then look in Dunn and Bradstreet. The name of Wurlitzer has always stood for the highest perfection in musical merchandise of all characters. A ten million dollar corporation.	Here are your biggest interests most naturally. Is it not logical that you can make more money? In less time by selling one Wurlitzer Musical Instrument for 1500 dollars or more than if you had to sell three Pianos? Of course you can increase your profits? In the first, your competition is null while in the Piano it is your big factor. Study it out yourself. Larger Sales, Larger Territory, Larger Profits in Less Time. Can you afford to miss this opportunity?	Here is just the angle that counts the most. If you can multiply your efforts by "well written," "logical," convincing sale literature and have your prospects come to you instead of finding them yourself, could you not close more sales and make more money? Let us show you the sale helps we create. Thousands and thousands of dollars are invested in them each year. Certainly you know the value of such Sale assistance. This is our service to you.

It is Easier for You to Sell Wurlitzer *Musical Instruments—They're Known All Over the World*

Wurlitzer constantly encouraged piano dealers to handle the Wurlitzer line.

LOOK, WHO'S HERE!

Our big Kansas City Branch is Open and Ready for Business with a full line of Wonderful

Wurlitzer Automatic Musical Instruments

The finest display of Self-Playing Musical Instruments ever shown under one roof in this state. We manufacture 50 different styles, suitable for every purpose for which music is desired. Wurlitzer instruments are known as perfection the world over. There are none "just as good". We have been 56 years in the business and make and sell more self-playing, coin-operated musical instruments than all other firms combined.

Come in and hear the new Flute and Violin Pianos (the latest Wurlitzer inventions) and the PianOrchestra (automatic orchestra.)

THE RUDOLPH WURLITZER COMPANY

World's Largest Manufacturers of Automatic Musical Instruments

1027 MAIN ST.	DERNBERG BLDG.	KANSAS CITY, MO.

BOTH PHONES: MAIN 4584

A 1912 postcard announcing Wurlitzer's opening of a branch office in Kansas City.

unclear reasons. One was that the change machine was too liberal in accepting slugs—giving out five good nickels. As well, the machines took up a lot of floor space and were awkward to restock. For a brief time in this period, organized labor was worried about the potential threat posed to retail workers. However, the Depression took the wind out of the sails of these machines. They settled down into the role they would play indefinitely — that of a niche device and not a threat to the general retail industry. Yet this little flurry pointed to a revival in the coin-operated machine industry.[31]

Radio was important to the revival of jukeboxes in several ways. One way was by making the public more music conscious. Until radio arrived, the public had little variety in song selection and was forced to be satisfied with hearing a few songs over and over. The development of hit songs and song popularity itself in the days before radio was a slow proposition. As late as 1930, juke operators seldom changed a record until it was worn out. Radio changed all that. Within a few years during the 1920s, good music was transmitted to millions of homes. A tremendous interest was created for individual musicians, band leaders, singers, and so on.[32]

With radio came the achievement that gave the jukebox new life — amplification. To amplify sound was the single necessity the coin-operated phonograph needed to overcome many of its faults. Journalist Bill Gersh observed in 1937: "Without the fast and high development of radio the modern phonograph would never have come into being. It did not have the necessary sound qualities which amplification made possible. The industry borrowed technical advances which had taken place in the radio industry."[33]

Thus, by the latter half of the 1920s, the jukebox began to reappear in its new, amplified incarnation. In 1909, the National Piano Manufacturing Company was formed to produce automatic electric player pianos, which it continued to do until the late 1920s. Following several name changes, one of which was Automatic Musical Instrument Company, the abbreviated title of AMI Incorporated was adopted in 1946. AMI introduced the first fully automatic selective phonograph. Up to that time, some jukeboxes had offered a selective feature, but it was not fully automatic. Another innovation on this model was that it selectively played both sides of a record. Surprisingly, it was some 20 years later before this became a common feature on all boxes. A selective remote control box was developed and sold by AMI in 1932.[34]

Herbert Steven Mills and his brothers formed the Mills Novelty Company as they entered the field of coin-operated amusement equipment. Around 1906 they produced their first music machine and were soon competing with Wurlitzer and Seeburg for the player-piano market. Mills brought out its first jukebox in 1926, the "Dance Master." Bertie Mills, one of the brothers, recalled that first model did not offer a selective feature; it played the 12 selections in order. Afterwards he made it selective. Records in those days were not uniform — some played quite loud, some played quite soft. Mills installed a gadget that could be adjusted so all the records played at the same volume level. One of Mills's best known products around that time was the slot machine, a gambling device that was already banned in parts of America but was exported to Europe in large numbers.[35]

Seeburg retired from the business of making pianos and organs at this time and entered the field of new music machines. In 1927 Seeburg debuted its new juke, a nonselective unit. As demand and interest increased, Seeburg introduced its "Audiophone" in 1928. This model had an eight-selection mechanism that utilized eight individual turntables, mounted on a ferris-wheel device, which gave the customer a record-selection choice. Seeburg debuted its first wall box in 1936, a remote selector unit that put the jukebox's tunes within arms' reach of an even greater number of patrons. Installed in booths, on walls, and on counter tops in a position remote from the master juke, it offered the customer a choice of 20 selections.[36]

Of the five companies that would become the dominant jukebox makers, three entered the field in 1926–1927. Rock-Ola and Wurlitzer came a little later. Wurlitzer's story is intertwined with that of Homer E. Capehart. Aged 24 in 1921, Capehart went to work for the Holcomb & Hofe Manufacturing Company, maker of a variety of coin-operated machines. Four years later he was sales manager. In 1926 the firm entered the automatic music machine field with the Electromuse. Wanting to improve the product, Capehart found a way in 1927 — a better record changer, called the Simplex. He bought the invention on his own. However, Holcomb was not impressed and fired Capehart. After raising some money, he turned around and formed the Capehart Automatic Phonograph Corporation. In the spring of 1928 it began to manufacture the Orchestrope. It was capable of playing both sides of its 28 disks. As well, it was supplied with remote control wall boxes for use in restaurants. By July 1928, some 625 units had been sold at $785.50 each. Capehart's greatest influence at this stage lay in merchandising. Using techniques he had learned at Holcomb, he established a network

Seeburg's Audiophone juke (left) introduced around 1927. Just after World War II it introduced the Select-o-matic (center) which made the 100-selection box a reality. On the right is the 1967 Spectra.

of dealers throughout the country who would display, promote, and sell Capehart equipment to independent operators. In turn, those operators would place machines in locations on a commission basis. It was the introduction of this middleman that would help the industry to develop the way it did.[37]

Capehart gambled that the coming boom in the phonograph field would be in home use and his firm turned to concentrate on that area. However, the stock-market crash put an end to those hopes. In 1932 he was fired as president and general manager of the Capehart Corporation. Again, he scraped some money together to form his own manufacturing company in 1932. He would do little with it for nearly 15 years. Instead, in 1933, he approached Wurlitzer hoping to sell them on the idea of an inexpensive record player for home use. Having lost much of its market in the latter 1920s, Wurlitzer had financial difficulties by 1928. During his meeting, Capehart realized it wasn't a record player the company was after, but an automatic phonograph. Apparently Wurlitzer had heard about the success of the new jukeboxes and was beginning to wonder if it might not be a good product for his firm. Wurlitzer knew that the repeal of Prohibition was imminent. Seizing the opportunity, Capehart sold the company his Simplex mechanism and himself. He started his position as vice president and general sales manager with Wurlitzer in June 1933. Off to a modest start, Wurlitzer produced an average of 60 boxes a week in 1934, about 3,000 units for the year. For 1933, the firm manufactured just 266 of the 10-selection model.[38]

Rock-Ola Manufacturing Corporation was first organized by David C. Rockola in 1924. When people pronounced his name they often got it wrong saying "Rocks," "Rockla," "ROCKola," and so on. He inserted a hyphen in the company name to insure it was pronounced properly. Rock-Ola started not as a manufacturer but as an operator, acquiring 1,000 ABT pistol target machines and operating them under the name of Target Skill Machine. It grew until he and two partners had routes in Missouri and Illinois and also operated 5,000 weighing machines. As 1926 ended, Rockola knew all there was to know about weighing machines and decided to diversify. Thus was born the Rock-Ola Scale Company, which manufactured weigh scales. His first effort was called the "Low Boy," and he had no trouble selling it.

While making scales, Rockola found that soda straws were being used to avoid the necessity of inserting a coin into the machine. So he designed a coin chute that curved so the straw would not work.[39]

Between 1928–1930, the company moved into the amusement-game field, producing pinball games. While making his rounds, Rockola discovered some of his customers were getting a new coin-operated table game called "pinball." It was spreading rapidly and Rockola decided he would move into it in a big way. Over the next three years he made over 60 different

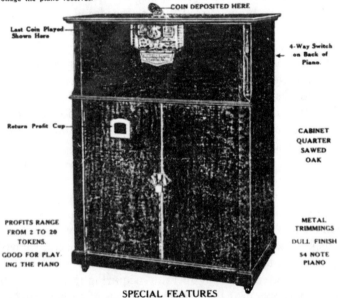
Rock-Ola's 1926 "profit-sharing" player piano. It was an attempt to pass off a slot machine as something else. Slots were then under heavy attack from communities. Soon thereafter, Rock-Ola abandoned the piano for the box.

games. Pinball games were then coming under increasing attack around the nation and were banned in some parts. Some manufacturers were making horizontal slot machines and calling them pinball games. There was a wave of righteous indignation over machines that "snatched pennies" from the poor and corrupted little children. Another black mark against the industry was that many racketeers had moved into the field of operating amusement games, after having been put out of work by repeal of Prohibition. Considering all these things, Rockola decided that pinball was not the soundest base for a growing empire. David Rockola said: "Prohibition had been repealed and bars were opening up all over. People needed cheap entertainment, and I got to thinking about music." Rock-Ola was the last major jukebox maker to enter the field. Its entry came in 1935 when the firm introduced the 12-selection "Multi-Selector."[40]

Although most of the major manufacturers had entered the jukebox field between 1926–1933, there was little growth in the industry. One reason was that other types of coin-operated devices were enjoying great success, primarily the pins and the slots, and were taking up much of the attention of the major established operators. Few could see an advantage in purchasing a jukebox that cost around 10 times as much as a pin game. However, those devices began to meet increasing legal problems. Experienced operators started to look for "something stable." The Depression also aided the growth of the jukebox industry. When the output of consumer durables dropped an average of 65 percent, record sales slumped by 94 percent and record-player sales by 96 percent. During those economic hard times, people cut back on luxury items. Records then retailed for about 75 cents, plus the cost of a record player. These were luxury items in the 1930s. In any case, they had radio, which provided plenty of free music. It was easier to splurge a nickel in the box every now and then than to save a pile of nickels to purchase home hardware and software. Probably the single most important element in boosting the fortunes of the jukebox was the national repeal of Prohibition on December 5, 1933. All over America, bars would spring up over the next few years. Bars were then, and would remain, the favorite location of jukes. Whereas speakeasies often avoided music machines because they feared losing such amenities if they were raided and closed, bars had no such worries after repeal.[41]

While radio provided plenty of free music, it focused entirely on the music of white, urban culture, shunning both country and black music. Because radio neglected this area, rhythm and blues was the only category that really avoided the catastrophic drop in record sales in the early 1930s. It is said, for example, that Bessie Smith kept Columbia records afloat at that time, and also, Brunswick and Victor began to emphasize their "race" records. For blacks too poor to buy R&B records, the jukebox was the only place to go. The radio was not an option, even if they could afford one. When electrically amplified jukeboxes began appearing in the late 1920s, two types of black locations were the first to welcome them — because they were a vehicle for their own music. One type of location was the shanty bar or café in poor Southern agriculture areas where blacks were allowed to party. The second type of location was in the North at rent parties held in private homes — they were not allowed in speakeasies. Meyer Parkoff, an operator of the time, recalled that before repeal Harlem was the main area on the East Coast for jukeboxes. "Rather than hiring a band, they would ask me for a phonograph which I would put in on the Saturday and take out after the weekend," he explained. "This gave them an additional source of income which helped pay the rent, because they didn't have to pay the band, and they made some money from the juke box. There was a lot of that in those days."[42]

The state of the coin-operated amusement-machine industry was described in an editorial in the March 12, 1932, issue of *Billboard*. A. C. Hartmann mentioned the recent convention of the Coin Machine Manufacturers' Association, which had been the biggest ever held. The industry, he said, "is flourishing today as it never flourished before." Factories, in some cases, were working overtime to try and catch up with orders. While there had been machines and games for years and years, he thought "they by no means can be compared with those in this machine age. The novelty of the whole thing, of course, is the automatic feature and it is novelty with merit that the public seeks in these times." Hartmann thought it only natural that coin-operated amusements should meet with popular favor "when the general public is financially embarrassed, more or less, and especially when one considers the great amount of fun to be had for such nominal charges." He predicted they would be around for years to come. Since Hartmann made no direct or indirect reference to jukeboxes, it would appear they were a very minor part of the industry overall. Within the pages of *Billboard*, coin machines, for the first time in the 1934–35 period, had their own section. Over that same period, the section jumped to regularly being 10 to 20 pages in length (much of it ads, of course) and even more in special issues.[43]

One of the first articles (perhaps the first) specifically on jukes came in the June 7, 1931, issue of the other major trade publication, *Variety*. This piece reported that it was unanimously agreed that the most profitable business in coin music was the "music machine" with small overhead, practically no upkeep, no advertising costs, and no losses. Not knowing what to call the device, it also used the term "music box." It estimated that the weekly gross "of the music boxes in speaks, candy parlors, restaurants and cafes hits close to $250,000." It also pointed out that "[P]ianos, once the

Wurlitzer's Tonophone (left), an orchestrion (center), and its 1934 jukebox.

big moment in the coin-operated music business, have gone the way of the zither concert and the town pump." With regard to tunes available on the machines, the article stated: "There's no such thing as classical music. It's strictly pop tunes that the nickel-droppers want." According to this account, there were three grades of jukes, "as standardized by the music box business." The nickel unit for the average place, the dime machine for the "ritzy mob," and the quarter units for the "suckers." Also, "In the speaks and femme flats, where the suckers have as much loose coin as they say they have, the two-bit route is the only road to music." Much of this account was probably highly exaggerated. As produced by the industry, jukes all played a selection for a nickel. While there were ways to increase the price, no other evidence indicated boxes in this period operated at a play price of more than five cents per tune, as this account said they did.[44]

Nonetheless, the jukes were becoming established. It is impossible to say how many were around in this early period. One source estimated that in June 1933, when Capehart joined Wurlitzer, there were about 25,000 in the United States. Given Wurlitzer's low production in 1933 of 266 units, followed by around 3,000 in 1934, that estimate could be high. That was likely a maximum number; perhaps there were a few thousand less. Whatever the number, they were little known as 1933 ended. However, before the decade was over, the jukebox would be a ubiquitous part of the American scene.[45]

3

Jukeboxes Spread Across America, 1934–1940

"There is a marked distinction between 'hot' records and 'rot' records." David Rockola, 1936.

"Paul Whiteman gets $5,000 a night to play in New York. You can hear him here for only a nickel — play our Do Re Mi." Grant Shay, Mills Novelty Co., 1936

"Thanks to the music machines phonograph recordings have become more important to the band leader than the radio...." Jimmy Dorsey, 1940.

Over the course of the relatively short period from 1934 to 1940, jukeboxes moved from being hardly visible to being a highly visible, pervasive part of the American landscape. As 1933 ended, there were perhaps 25,000 boxes in America, maybe somewhat less but not likely more than that number. Wurlitzer was responsible for just 266 of those, all produced late in 1933. The takeoff year for jukes was definitely 1934 when AMI, Mills, and Seeburg were turning out boxes as fast as they could make them. Their combined output for the year was around 15,000. Wurlitzer manufactured 60 boxes a week that year, adding another 3,000 units to the 1934 total. For the years 1935 to 1937, Wurlitzer produced annual totals of 15,000, 44,397, and 40,000 units, respectively. By the end of 1937, sources told the company that half of the jukeboxes in America were made by Wurlitzer, 105,000 out of the grand total of 210,000. In the late 1930s and through the 1940s, Seeburg and Rock-Ola would contend for the number two spot.[1]

The fortunes of the jukebox industry and the record industry became intertwined in this period. Sales of disks to juke operators boosted industry sales considerably while technological improvements in records, along with the 1934 introduction of inexpensive records, helped in the widespread, rapid growth of the juke industry. Sales of records in 1921 hit $106 million, a total that would not be surpassed until 1946. Over the years 1922 to 1925 sales declined to $92 million, $79 million, $68 million, and $59 million, respectively, due to the increasing appeal of radio. Then the industry recovered, posting totals for 1926 to 1929 of $70 million, $70 million, $73 million, and $75 million, respectively. When the Depression arrived, it caused a second record industry general decline. Yearly sales for 1930 to 1933 were $46 million, $18 million, $11 million, and $6 million, respectively. Following that came a strong recovery from 1934 through 1940 with respective yearly sales totals of $7 million, $9 million, $11 million, $13 million, $26 million, $44 million, and $48 million. Unit sales grew even more strongly as the public purchased more and more of the newly introduced cheaper records.[2]

Prior to 1906 the *Wall Street Journal* argued the phonograph "was considered a toy. Buyers refused to touch it; great artists refused to record for it." Record players were expensive, as were records, and both were of low quality. Then famed Enrico Caruso signed in 1906 with Victor. His records started to sell; other artists began to sign up with record labels. Many consider that event to have heralded the true start of the modern record industry. In 1913 a better quality record was developed. Production of both records and phonographs climbed sharply during 1920 and 1921, partly due to orders accumulated during World War I.[3]

Then came radio, with a vast improvement in sound reproduction. Beside it, the record player "sounded amateurish." By late 1924 and early 1925, record players — the tonal equals of the best radios of the day — were introduced. Sales of players and disks increased — then came the Depression. In 1929, Radio Corporation of America (RCA) bought control of Victor, thereby bringing the technical advances of radio to the phonograph field. Over the period 1929 to 1933, recording developed to a higher technical point, while by then the radio had ceased to be a novelty and commanded less public attention.[4]

1934 and 1935 were important milestones for the phonograph industry, with radio contributing substantially to the rebirth of records. Radio networks "began a musical education campaign, and, in the interest of public service, broadcast operas, symphonies, etc." Decca Records was formed in August 1934, with the goal of selling good music on a 35-cent record, compared to the then standard of about 75 cents for a disk. It was a huge stimulant to record sales, and within a few years Decca was the unit volume sales leader of the industry (but not in dollar volume). Swing music became very popular around 1935, giving records an even greater demand. Also, that year saw the introduction of record albums. These factors, coupled

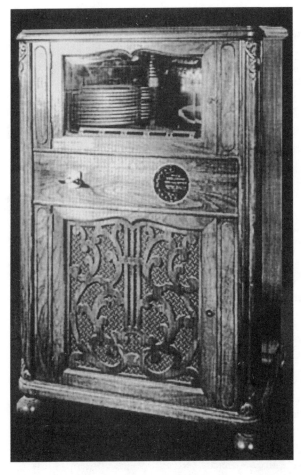

Wurlitzer's Debutante, 1934.

with the presentation of popular orchestras with the new tunes by radio and jukeboxes, all contributed to putting the industry back on its feet. Records were reborn as a home entertainment medium.[5]

Also noted in the *Wall Street Journal* citation was that: "In turn, sales of low-priced popular records encouraged the development of the juke box. Currently, coin-operated phonographs (juke boxes) are the largest consumer of records on a unit basis." In conclusion, the account stated: "These operators pay 21 cents [wholesale price] a record for popular music. What low-priced music on records has done for them can be seen from their growth in this country from 20,000 juke boxes a few years ago to the currently estimated 300,000 units of today [1941]." Reportedly, coin-operated phonograph operators did not gamble on music hits. Instead, they waited until a tune had become thoroughly popularized on the radio or elsewhere before placing it on their machines. "Nevertheless, juke boxes have contributed in some measure to plugging popular music."[6]

From almost the beginning, those operators had help in record selection, thanks to lists published in the trade publications, especially *Billboard*. October 12, 1935, was the date of the first instance of jukes getting their own section (one page in this case) in the larger Amusement Machines section (a section itself only about one year old) in *Billboard*. One feature on that page was the "10 Best Records" list. Separate lists for New York and Chicago were presented, with 10 songs for each city, from each of three record labels. Those titles represented the 10 best sellers for "automatic phonograph operators" reported that week by record firms. Such lists, in various formats, would be a regular weekly feature of this publication for decades.[7]

Readers of that issue were also advised to consult the Radio-Orchestra section each week and to scan the "Network Song Census" and "Sheet-Music Leaders" for information on the most popular tunes over the air and in the sheet-music field. From the Chicago list, the first listed songs for each of the labels were Bruns-

Rock-Ola Regular, 1936.

wick, "I'm Painting the Town Red"; Vocalion ("race" records), "Joe Louis Strut"; and Melotone, "I'm on a Seesaw" by Joe Haymes and his orchestra. Leading songs on the New York list were RCA-Victor, "What a Wonderful World" by Richard Himber and his orchestra; Columbia, "Cheek to Cheek" and "Top Hat" by Phil Ohman and his orchestra; Brunswick, "Cheek to Cheek" and "No Strings" by Fred Astaire, Leo Reisman, and his orchestra. One month later *Billboard*, for the first time, ran its best-selling list in box format. Apparently the list was now for the country as a whole. Tunes numbered one through ten ran down the list while the names of three record labels ran across at the top.[8]

As the years went by, the lists underwent several revisions. December

1937 saw *Billboard* introduce a new list feature, the week's best records, selected by that publication, from the latest recordings released. In the Sweet Music category one of the four picks was Guy Lombardo, "I'll See You in My Dreams"/"Summertime." From the Swing Music category one of two picks was "Free for All"/"Monsoon" by Art (not yet Artie) Shaw. In the final category, Vocal, one of three picks was Dorothy Lamour, "You Took the Words Right Out of My Heart"/"Thanks for the Memory."[9]

Less than a year later, *Billboard* stopped picking those tunes itself, relying, reportedly, on tabulations based on radio performances, sheet music sales, reports from music publishers, and information from "prominent" operators. The three categories then used (each containing four or five titles) were "Going Strong — Keep Them In"; "Coming Up — Better Stock Them"; and "Operators' Specials." In that latter category were records not yet hits but which gave "every indication of becoming successful."[10]

When its Record Buying Guide was less than a year old, in August 1939, *Billboard* boasted that the guide had climbed in popularity and operators were said to regard it as an outstanding editorial service. The three categories were then called "Going Strong," "Coming Up," and "Possibilities." In this August issue, the publication explained in more detail how disks were picked for the categories (each of which now had three to seven titles included). Each week representatives of *Billboard* in the 30 most important juke centers in the country contacted at least four of the leading box operators in their territory to determine which recordings were going strong, coming up, or going down. On the reports those representatives sent in were listed the names of the tunes as well as the orchestras or artists whose versions were most popular. On the basis of those reports, records were listed in the first two categories. The popularity of the tune — irrespective of the number of artists who recorded it — was the sole yardstick by which it was measured. For example, one title listed in "Going Strong" was "Stairway to the Stars," by Glenn Miller, Jimmy Dorsey, Horace Heidt, and Al Donahue. That is, four versions of the tune were in circulation. Regarding the last category, "Possibilities," the publication explained that in most cases listed titles would not as yet have appeared in jukeboxes. In selecting songs for this category, *Billboard* editors "not only rel[ied] upon their own experience and judgment" but also took into consideration the popularity of the tune on the radio and reports of sheet music sales and information from music publishers.[11]

When *Billboard* surveyed its weekly Record Buying Guide for 1939, results indicated the winner was Glenn Miller who garnered 132 mentions from 26 different tunes. His nearest competitor in the orchestra field was Guy Lombardo with 57 mentions on 16 songs. Actual runner-up to Miller was Bing Crosby, who had 78 mentions on 24 numbers. Next were the

Andrews Sisters with 55 mentions, then Artie Shaw with 53. A total of 84 recording artists were mentioned in one or more of the guide's three to four sections during the year, with that figure broken down into 66 bands, 8 vocal groups, and 10 individual singers. Twenty names of the 84 each achieved 20 or more mentions throughout 1939. The largest number of mentions scored by any artist on any one song was 16 — a tie between the Andrews Sisters' "Well, All Right," Glen Gray's "Sunrise Serenade," and Will Glahe and the Musette Orchestra with "Beer Barrel Polka." Based on these results, the publication declared that the contention, said to

Rock-Ola Imperial 20, 1937.

be firmly held by the majority of the music trade, that the country's jukeboxes at least equaled, if not surpassed, the importance of radio as a builder of both artists and songs, had been proved.[12]

Another trade publication that published similar lists for box operators was *Variety*, which had one called "10 Best Sellers on Coin-Machines." Songs were ranked in terms of their popularity from 1 to 10. They were reported by operators to *Variety*. Names of more than one band or vocalist after the title indicated, in order of popularity, whose recordings were being played. In this period it was common for several artists to each have a rendition of the same song out at the same time. A second sub-list in this publication was called "Tunes Gaining Favor." This was a variable number of songs directly below the top 10 in popularity but said to be growing in demand on the music machines and destined to be on their way to the top.[13]

Other parts of the coin-machine business were also booming during this period. The New York–based distributing firm Modern Vending Company set a sales record for the Wurlitzer Skee Ball game machine in October 1936, when it used an average of two train carloads of the machines every day of the month. Still, orders were backing up since Modern could not get enough machines to fill those orders. A couple of years later game manufacturer J. H. Keeney & Company was said to be so busy in producing its five games to the point that there were some delays in shipments due to the firm's inability to manufacture games fast enough to meet the demand.[14]

The case of Modern Vending illustrated how the sudden growth in jukeboxes affected the existing coin-machine industry. Prior to 1936, the firm had been handling most types of coin machines, but not boxes. After a 1935 convention of the coin-machine business, Modern changed its policy and began handling music machines. In February 1936, it placed an order for 1,040 of the new 1936 Wurlitzer Simplex machines, an order said to be the largest ever placed in the coin-machine industry. Yet four months later those boxes were all committed to operators, and Modern placed another order for 1,040 more units.[15]

Throughout this period the prevalence of coin machines that were slot machines, or slot-like in the sense that they delivered a payout, continued to decline. This was a factor that caused existing operators to turn more to jukeboxes for the stability they seemed to offer. A 1939 ad placed by Keeney for a pinball-type game called Pot Shot noted that it came in two different models (both one ball). One gave a free game, and the other model gave a payout. Initially pin games had mostly given out a cash payout, the same as the slots. The difference was that slots paid out purely on the basis of chance while the pins paid out, theoretically, on the basis of skill. Slots disappeared as they were banned in most places, except for the few jurisdictions that opened themselves up to gambling devices. Pins, on the other hand, evolved differently, giving up the cash payout completely and substituting free games. Thus, they were able to avoid the gambling label and to continue to exist almost everywhere. At this time, horse-racing games were also very popular, many of them also offering a cash payout. Chicago-based distributor Monarch Coin Machine Company placed a May 1939 ad offering, among other items, 18 different used payout games for sale. Many were horse-racing items, such as Turf Champ, Derby Day, Preakness, Photo Finish, Racing Form, and so on. Prices of these games ranged from a low of $12.50 for Winner to a high of $47.50 for Klondike.[16]

If the buying-guide lists in the trade publications were not enough for the operators, other features and articles appeared on an irregular basis to guide operators in record selection. Seeburg sales manager Earl Holland told of the importance of selecting records and programs on "automatic phonographs" by relating the experience of Simon Wolfe of Jacksonville, Florida, a man said to have long experience in the operation of "coin-operated musical instruments." In addition to the usual advice such as programming each location as a distinct entity, Wolfe added that the operator must "[t]hen educate the lessee to the fact that the operator is capable of selecting music to suit his location, at the same time leading him to believe that he is making his own selections...." It was also important to

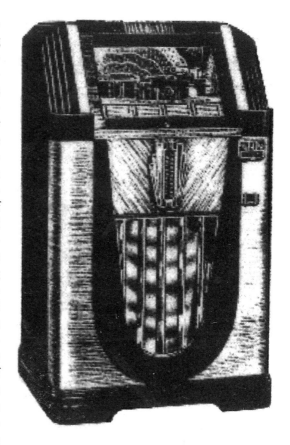

Rock-Ola Monarch 20, 1938.

educate the location owner that if he got tired of hearing the same tunes, the customers did not. Hits were good for two to six weeks of play and should remain on the box until their popularity had waned. Because of that, it was recommended that not more than half of the records on a box be changed each week. Wolfe advised that after his weekly visit to each box to make changes, "I find it most profitable to leave the machine tripped to play the entire program. Thus familiarizing the lessee with every number on the machine, thereby stimulating their interest to such an extent that they will boost the machine to patrons."[17]

One short-lived feature in *Billboard* was a column containing advice on record selection and programming from music operators across the nation who chose to write in and tell what tunes were hot "nickel grabbers" in their jukes. The column in the October 22, 1938, issue had seven different commentators. The most frequently mentioned artists were Bing Crosby,

Benny Goodman, and Tommy Dorsey. All these operators stressed the usual, giving patrons what they wanted, programming for local tastes, and so forth. But E. R. Carlstedt of Moline, Illinois, added: "In order to find out in advance what they will want I find the radio an invaluable aid. By this I mean that the songs usually requested by patrons of phonograph locations are usually the ones that are to be heard on the air-lanes of that particular territory."[18]

A later round-up article featured advice from 13 different operators. While the usual advice of programming specifically for the location, and its patrons, was almost never absent, it did not seem to have been followed very often. In this article, 12 of the operators mentioned *Billboard's* Record Buying Guide as an indispensable source. Three of them specifically mentioned the radio. Jack Moloney, of the Forth Worth, Texas, Panther Novelty Company, felt that 50 percent of all records would make some money for the operator, but only 8 to 10 percent would become big hits.[19]

The industry did not want to see numbers placed in its jukeboxes that could be considered off-color in any way. The smut issue was first raised in late 1936, and a flurry of interest lasted for about one year. The issue came up again in 1939 and stretched into 1940, although it was somewhat less intense than it was the first time. The first reference seems to have been a November 1936 article in which it was observed that box makers had taken serious notice of the growing use of a certain type of recording that was jeopardizing the "high reputation" of coin phonographs. They saw the tendency as a "grave menace" to the industry. At a gathering of operators in Chicago, David Rockola of Rock-Ola Manufacturing Corporation pointed out to them in no uncertain terms the necessity of upholding the music machine's "excellent" reputation. He said: "I am cautioning you to guard your good reputation with every means at your command.... I am naturally much concerned and frankly, much disturbed over the fact there is a certain trend toward the use of cheap, smutty recordings on automatic phonographs on location in barrooms and taverns."[20]

Explaining his reasoning, Rockola added: "But to publicize the use of suggestive songs and ditties, laying your business wide open to city-wide and perhaps state-wide criticism, seems to me the most foolhardy and disastrous step that a smart music operator can take. All of us know what happened to other types of coin-operated equipment in some cities where a foolhardy operator would place machines on location near schoolhouses ... we must maintain decency and use our utmost discretion in dealing with the general public." A further hazard was the fact that some locations had added extra loudspeakers that duplicated the recording to passers-by on the street or to another part of the establishment. According to Rockola, instances had been called to his attention wherein public opinion was rising against off-color records. Mom, pop, and kids were then patronizing neighborhood taverns. There was a time, said Rockola, when such types of records could go into every barroom without disturbing the public sentiment. In those days only men patronized bars. But times had changed, and with the advent of the cocktail lounge, a mixed crowd could be found at every bar, with little regard to age. That's why Rockola cautioned his audience "to avoid the use of questionable recordings."[21]

Not much more than a month later, Rockola was at it again. This time he cautioned a gathering of operators in his company's new Chicago display room that at that

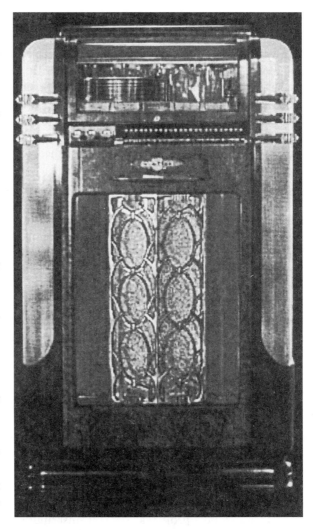

Wurlitzer 500, 1938. Note that early machines were plain, wooden units. Starting around 1938 boxes moved to plastic and neon as the luxury light-up era began.

very moment in various parts of the country local authorities were finding fault with various types of coin-operated machines. That included nearly all types of machines, except phonographs. He believed that authorities everywhere looked upon jukes as "real American entertainment" and viewed box operators as respectable businessmen. He felt suggestive songs and questionable ditties jeopardized the good, clean, well-established, and well-thought-of legitimate business of the operators. Families did not like to be subjected unintentionally to ribald words—instead of a popular number created by "real" composers, "99 per cent of whom compose their music and lyrics for the 99 per cent of the American people who are clean, decent and moral." The best evidence that a vast majority of people detested smutty records was the tremendous number of letters, observed Rockola, he had received since his first pronouncement on the subject. Apparently most of those letters actually came from operators—who promised they were far-sighted enough to be good. No one could dispute the fact, he said, that the real song hits of America were always those that were "uplifting and inspiring." Admitting there were also "swing" and "hot" numbers, there was a difference because they just had a snappy rhythm, but clean words. In almost every instance, they were just "fast" time, rather than with a "fast" set of lyrics. "There is a marked distinction between 'hot' records and 'rot' records."[22] Columnists soon joined in to condemn off-color material. Ralph Neal felt there were five essentials for juke profits. One was good records. Neal pointed out that in some locations, especially those patronized by a certain group "who are bent on their own personal pleasures," one could justifiably use the latest "hot-stuff records" for increasing profits. However, they had to be handled with care. Operators should not load all their machines, in public places where mixed crowds went, with records of that type. If that advice was ignored, there was a likelihood those patrons would react unfavorably against the operators. Don't kill the goose that laid the golden egg just for the sake of some extra profit, Neal warned. "Keep the records of this type in the places where they belong."[23]

Another journalist, H. F. Reves, drew a line between "filthy" records and those with "a few suggestive" words. The latter category was okay. Reves warned against off-color records because the whole industry got a black eye, not just the specific operator. As well, he worried that smutty records on jukes could lead to stringent local laws and regulations, or even the banning of jukeboxes.[24]

More and more people came out against smut records. Just two months after Rockola's initial caution, Arthur Hughes, a Dallas operator, publicly warned about the dangers of unseemly loud music emanating from jukes in residential or semi-residential locations. Mostly, though, he warned about smut. He argued that the logical market for off-color numbers—the red-light districts—were quickly becoming a thing of the past. "True it is that the bawdy houses of old had their coin-operated electric pianos." Another element he mentioned was that if a juke was used in combination with an outdoor loudspeaker (as was said to occur occasionally in out-of-the-way roadhouses) the chance passing of an individual or group who objected to the songs would undoubtedly "bring down their wrath and the law enforcement officials upon the unhappy owner of the resort." Hughes concluded that the chances of an objector hearing the off-color songs, wherever the box was located, were so great that they "are simply forbidden by the dictates of good business." And, he argued, risqué records were not that popular anyway.[25]

Six months later, leading juke operators in New York expressed their opposition to the use of smutty records, which some members of the fraternity had been using on their locations. Continued use of such records, they felt, would in time cause the industry to come into general disrepute. Operators using such disks were reported to be in the minority and were said to obtain those

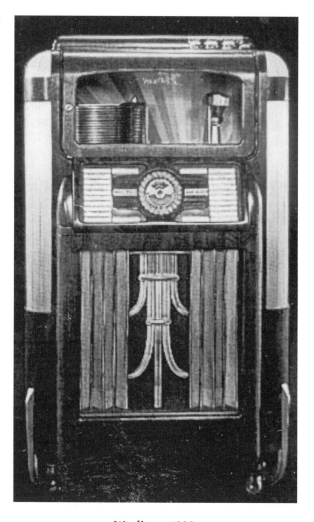

Wurlitzer, 1938.

off-color records in wholesale lots at prices higher than the cost of regular records. Prominent operators in New York stated this situation was but another factor that proved the need for an organization capable of controlling the use of such records. Unless some of the larger operators got together to form such a group, they feared the use of smutty records would continue to spread "until they attract the attention of law enforcement bodies who are apt to create a very unpleasant situation."[26]

Howard Kass, general manager of the phonograph division of the Newark, New Jersey, Major Amusement Company (an operator) sent a letter, in October 1937, to each of the location owners who had one of his jukes on their premises. It warned about risqué records and advised them to refrain from using them. Kass spoke about considerable trouble in and around New York City during the previous month. In several cases, machines had reportedly been confiscated and storekeepers arrested. He added that within the past two weeks his company had been notified by police authorities in northern New Jersey warning Major Amusement about the use of those records. Included in the letter was a clipping from a Newark newspaper reporting that in Union Township (just outside Newark) a plan had been set up to license all jukes in public places. Policemen were making the rounds of those locations, and if any machines contained "dirty ditties," then, said Kass, "out the window they go!"[27]

Beginning on September 27, 1937, in Union Township, New Jersey, said Councilman William Nothnagel, police were making the rounds of the 40-odd taverns with one object in mind — to eliminate suggestive records. What annoyed Nothnagel were reports about the musical adventures of "Little Audrey" and an unnamed "licentious Hawaiian melody." So he, in cooperation with Councilman F. Edward Blertuempfel, were setting up a plan to license all phonographs in public places.[28]

Using perhaps the strongest language to date against the off-color material was James Mangan, advertising manager with juke maker Mills Novelty, in a full-page guest editorial in *Billboard*. He opened by saying he wanted to show how the music operator "who uses the lecherous record is really nothing more or less than a bum sport." He said that cases were daily becoming more and more numerous where establishments had been closed, owners arrested, and licenses revoked because smutty records were played in those places. However, he presented no details regarding these incidents. Such records, he believed, were unfair to the location owner because the business could be shut down, unfair to manufacturers because the industry was threatened, and unfair to the operator because such disks tended to put the name "operator" in the class of "the moral leper, the blasphemer, the lecher, the outcast." Lastly, it was unfair to the public at large, a great many of whom had no desire to be subjected to such "filth." Mangan observed that we condemned the prohibitionist because he wanted to take away from us something we liked, but far worse than the prohibitionist "is the reprobate who tries to make us take something we don't want!" The greatest threat that faced the jukebox industry was, he said, "lecherous records." For Mangan it was not difficult to define a lecherous record: "A lecherous record is one you wouldn't want your 15-year-old daughter or your 10-year-old son to hear."[29]

Next to weigh in was S. C. Schulz, sales manager with Decca Recording Company. Operators were jeopardizing their entire business for the sake of a few nickels, simply by placing off-color disks in their machines.

Even if it was only one record in one machine, that record "has pressed into it enough damaging evidence to ruin the entire phonograph business." He, too, spoke of the difference in the saloons of 20 years earlier. They were spots for men only. Risqué songs were alright then. Even if the strains of bawdy songs floated outside the premises, it was taken as a matter of course by most passers-by. It was "[m]en having fun in a man's way." However, that saloon was no more. Although smutty disks "were sometimes highly profitable," it was not worth it. The biggest difficulty then facing the juke industry, exclaimed Schulz, was "the complete eradication of smut discs."[30]

Reporter M. Orodenker declared that the major record labels (Victor, Brunswick, Decca) had a self-imposed censorship on songs they recorded. Already, he said, law enforcement agencies in many states were confiscating boxes on the grounds that they contributed to the delinquency of both minors and adults. Again, no details were provided. So critical had this "diseased" condition become, the major labels had joined forces with the coin-phonograph industry "in waging a Carrie Nation campaign to stamp out the use of pornographic platters." Those record labels were said to have taken their stand against off-color material almost two years earlier, around the beginning of 1936.

Rock-Ola Deluxe 20, 1939.

Smutty records, agreed Orodenker, sold at higher prices than standard material. Also, they gave no composer or artist credits on the disk, only the title.[31]

On Christmas Day 1937, David Rockola lashed out again at the problem, in ever stronger terms, in a *Billboard* full-page guest editorial. Referring to the manufacture and distribution of smut records, he said it was "Truly music enemy number one!" For years the business of operating music machines had a "spotless reputation," he argued, and it was then under attack. He felt it was "only natural" that a location owner would make a request for off-color records if he knew they existed. "He must therefore be guided accordingly. After all, the avoidance of obscene records is for his protection just as much as for the operator." It was the "clean, inspiring rendition of popular music" that had brought phonographs into national popularity. Therefore, Rockola cried: "Let us keep them that way! Let us all co-operate to defeat the common enemy." As a starting point, Rockola wanted each person in the music industry to persuade every owner of smut records to destroy them. The next step was to get the jukebox associations in each city and state to boycott the use of smut records. And last, but most important, declared Rockola: "Let us learn how to answer the location owner who demands these records. Teach him the truth of the matter."[32]

Things seemed to quiet down for over a year until a February 1939 account announced that the juke industry was again being plagued with a "disease" that made its appearance "every year or so, the smutty record scourge." The New Orleans Association of Music Operators was said to be waging a fight against the use of smutty disks in that city. Complaints had reached the ears of the licensing board in Boston, and they had gone into action to suppress the use of off-color material. Trouble from such records had also reportedly broken out in New York City, but that city's Automatic Music Operators' Association was quick to check it by passing a resolution that forbade its members from using any disks on their machines of a suggestive or obscene nature. To make sure the resolution was adhered to, the association made it known that the group's legal counsel was forbidden to defend any operator who got in trouble through violating that resolution. Supposedly, there was then a small boom in the production of double-entendre records.[33]

In its Record Buying Guide in 1939, *Billboard* made it clear on more than one occasion that double-entendre disks were omitted from its lists.[34]

As 1940 began, Wurlitzer sales manager M. G. Hammergren declared that the more responsible elements in the industry were also aware of their responsibility to the public. Consequently, they would not furnish or permit suggestive and risqué numbers to be placed on their boxes. It was certain to demoralize the business if the public came to associate automatic phonographs with questionable records.[35]

Around the same time, a letter was sent to all jukebox operators by the Automatic Phonograph Manufacturers Association (APMA). It was signed by officers of the five manufacturer-members; the John Gabel Manufacturing Company, Mills Novelty Company, Rock-Ola Manufacturing Company, J. P. Seeburg Corporation, and the Rudolph Wurlitzer Company. The letter requested that operators refrain from using objectionable records or gambling attachments on jukes. Pointing out the good reputation of the industry, the letter added that APMA felt most operators realized how quickly the use of obscene records on boxes in the communities, or the use of gambling attachments, "would bring discredit to the industry and result, in many communities, at least, in prompt prohibition not only of the records or the attachments but of the phonographs as well." APMA's letter declared itself to be just a reminder to the operators to know APMA's attitude and to be aware that the use of off-color disks would be a serious threat to the industry and that the consequences could be serious. More ominously, the letter stated "that an operator who continues such use cannot continue to be a good credit risk." Since most operators purchased jukeboxes on credit with little money down, this amounted to a threat to cut off supply. People were urged by the letter to report any objectionable records that came to their attention. The letter closed with a final threat: "Your attention is called to the provision in most conditional sales contracts prohibiting the use of any gambling attachments, or attachments not supplied by the phonograph manufacturer."[36]

To keep off-color material out of jukes in Detroit, the United Electrical, Radio and Machine Workers of America, Local 737, established their own censorship arrangement. A business representative of the union told city officials that his union had found one record that was slightly "suggestive" and, in conjunction with distributors, his organization had the disk eliminated from machines supplied by a Detroit operating firm. Said the union spokesman: "We want to keep these machines acceptable to the public and we are doing our part to keep objectionable records out of the machines."[37]

At the end of 1940, in the wake of reports that smutty records would be appearing on the market in greater numbers, the Automatic Phonograph Manufacturers' Association said its members would do everything possible to discourage the use of records "that would bring the music box business into question." Group officials appealed to all operators to help protect the industry's good reputation, saying that the problem of obscene records was a "fester" on the growth of the industry that, if allowed to continue, would destroy it. Once again the group urged people to report smut users to local and/or state music operator associations, or to themselves: "This will help to protect the good name of the phonograph industry. It will prevent affronting public decency with dirty records."[38]

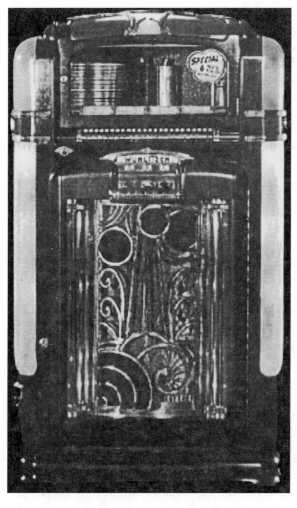

Wurlitzer 700, 1940.

Smut would be raised in the future as an industry issue, but only infrequently. Never again would it receive as much intense attention as it did in the late 1930s. Little evidence was presented that it was of much concern with a large segment of the general public or that many citizens were complaining. Rather, it appeared to be an over-reaction by the juke industry, a response to what might happen. At the time, slots and pins were under attack, but the jukebox industry worried that some of the bad publicity splashed over the entire industry. Jukebox people went out of their way to protect themselves and to try and keep their part of the industry above reproach because as cities and states began to levy license and tax fees on the industry, rates were set differentially for segments of the industry. For example, a vending machine could be assessed a very small annual fee while a slot was assessed a much higher fee. It was one way of punishing or eliminating the "bad" elements of the coin-machine industry. When the box revival began, the coin-machine industry was divided into two general categories: vending machines and amusement machines (this included basically everything that was not a vender). Jukebox people wanted to see their machines spun off as a separate, third category in order to lobby for lower license fees and to avoid any bad press that fell on the amusement machines. Due to their sudden popularity and huge increase in numbers, jukes did indeed soon become a third, and distinct, category within the coin-machine industry. Thus, it was important to the jukebox people that the music machines keep themselves pure and clean.

As the jukebox grew in popularity around America, operators were increasingly drawn to the new machines. Many were established operators who had other types of coin machines on location; many were newcomers to the coin industry. One of the former was Jack Eisenfeld of Washington, D.C., who ran the General Amusement Company. Eisenfeld started in the music business early in 1935 and like many other operators he bought a few different makes of boxes and set them out on location. He had been lukewarm on the music business until he met J. A. Darwin, a Wurlitzer representative. Then he signed up with them and discarded all his other operations, turning exclusively to music. His firm was able to take over locations that had been averaging $5 to $7 a week per box in revenue and build them quickly to the point where they reportedly produced $18 to $30 per week per machine. Those locations knew that every week the records would be changed. Locations producing better than average income could have their disks changed twice a week if desired, or as often as they thought necessary.[39]

Eisenfeld urged proprietors of various locations to maintain a good dance floor, even if small. One location owner reportedly was forced to tear out his $2,300 soda fountain, telephone booths, and all excess fixtures "to make room for the crowds the Simplex drew." For use in locations equipped with booths, Eisenfeld designed a "music menu." Wall boxes then barely existed. Eisenfeld thought his menu was important in getting nickels from customers "who will not go up to the instrument and personally make their selections of records." In each booth was placed a card listing the juke selections. Those cards measured 3½ by 5 inches and read, "The waiter will deposit your nickels and dimes and select your favorite numbers."[40]

Typical of the newcomers to the coin industry was Guy Constantini of Hopedale, Ohio. Early in 1936, he was engaged in the grocery business. Then he sold out and entered the music business. A little over a year later, he operated a route of 40 boxes and had just placed an order for another 25 machines. Constantini was said to be very enthusiastic about his music operation.[41]

Giving insight into route management was Babe Kaufman, president of Babe Kaufman Music Company of New York, an operating concern. Kaufman got into the coin business in 1931, starting with a distributorship from manufacturers for various games. In 1934, at a convention, she took an interest in the automatic phonographs that Wurlitzer had on display, and took a distributorship. Over the first 60 days she sold 800 jukeboxes. However,

A Wurlitzer trade ad, 1935.

to learn the phonograph business, she bought 200 machines to operate herself and soon thereafter she gave up distributing in order to operate fulltime. Near the end of 1938, she was one of the largest Wurlitzer operators in the East, with 750 jukes on location. A year and a half earlier, she entered the field of cigarette vending and then had 350 of those machines on location. Her firm employed 15 servicemen and collectors, using 12 trucks, to look after the boxes.[42]

When she started in the music business in 1934, Kaufman recalled: "Those were the days when you could place machines simply by calling tavern owners on the phone. Many times we placed 15 or more machines a day as a result of telephone solicitations. An $8-a-week net take per machine was just average, and we took the first $5 and split 50-50 over that with no trouble at all." Recently her firm had taken over a route of 106 music machines in eastern New Jersey. Taverns made up the bulk of those locations. All the boxes were Wurlitzers, each of them less than a year old. When Kaufman's collector went around the first week, he took the sum of $209 — less than $2 a machine — out of the cash boxes. Yet just a few months later each of those units was averaging $4 to $5 a week. Under the previous ownership, those jukes were generally not properly fixed when broken, they were covered with dust and dirt, burnt out light bulbs had not been replaced, needles were cheap and worn down, and mechanisms needed greasing and oiling. Also, records were not changed often enough. It had been the policy of the former operator to buy records just once a month. When some numbers were going well he would delay purchases another two weeks. The collector who had handled the route had been paid $25 a week to look after all 106 machines. That caused Kaufman to comment: "No wonder he didn't take a personal interest in his job! We immediately put him on a commission basis and his lowest salary to date has been $57, while he has made as high as $80 during a good week."[43]

Systematically, Kaufman laid out the route. She determined that 80 locations made a route. Each Kaufman collector made 16 calls a day — 30 minutes for each — for five days. Saturday was an unstructured workday and the collector was free to make goodwill calls, deliver special request records, look for new locations, and so on. Thus, this collector had 26 locations turned over to another route man. At the end of three weeks, with the machines cleaned and polished, new needles, new records, and new bulbs installed, the take jumped to over $3 per box. Not satisfied with that figure, Kaufman declared, "It didn't take us long to discover that one reason the take wasn't larger was that location owners had got out of the habit of shooting their own nickels into their machines."[44]

What that meant for Kaufman was that she and her employees had to start from scratch and resell those men on the importance of music to the success of their businesses. They pointed out to those location owners that without music "a tavern is dead." People came in for one drink, and if there was no music they left in search of a livelier spot. Where there was music, those same people would linger for a while and order two or three drinks instead of the one they would have purchased if there had been no music. Kaufman drove home the necessity of the location owner putting his own money into the machine to provide music for his patrons. "We got down to brass tacks and showed them that by shoving a few quarters into the machine — half of which they'd eventually get back — they could keep a crowd of say six or seven people at their bars for a half hour or more, during which time they might consume just one added round of drinks." If those people bought two rounds, then the owner would net $2, figured Kaufman. It must have worked, for at the end of seven weeks under Kaufman's operation, those 106 locations were averaging a gross of $4 to $5 a week per box.[45]

Trade organizations to lobby on behalf of the industry were forming within a year or so of the jukebox revival. By September 1935, when the Texas Music Machine Operators' Association held a meeting, it was reported that locals in San Antonio and Beaumont were organized practically 100 percent and affiliated with the state group. It meant that nearly every music operator in those cities was a member of the local. Similar activity was taking place in other cities and states. Such groups organized to fight fees and taxes on music machines, which some communities and states were already applying. As well, those groups tried to establish and impose uniform conditions on locations in their area by, for example, having each operator offer the same commission split to location owners. It was also hoped that such groups would eliminate, or reduce, the amount of poaching in an area. Poaching took place when an operator tried to convince a location owner to remove a box placed by an operator and replace it with one from the new operator. Inducements to do so often included offering a higher commission rate to the location.[46]

Not surprisingly, juke makers were very active in encouraging established coin operators, and industry newcomers, to take the plunge and become jukebox operators. R. G. Norman, Wurlitzer advertising manager, penned an article in November 1935 that included a full-page ad extolling jukes. It urged coin-industry people to diversify into boxes because good music locations were pretty certain to be good spots for other coin machines. The operator who supplied music stood the first chance at furnishing the other types of coin equipment that could be profitably operated in those places.[47]

When he analyzed locations, Norman felt that a good site had to be well patronized and that people had to be spending money. Dancing was preferable but not altogether necessary. Places where young people congregated or where working people gathered for food and entertainment were usually good spots. "Don't think you must have 'backstreet' locations only — music is definitely 'out of the gutter,'" he said. Norman added that if an operator did have backstreet locations "all the major record companies put out unlisted records which are just the thing for these places."[48]

Ralph Mills was the Mills Novelty Company vice president in charge of sales. He hyped his machines, and the industry, at the same time as Norman. Declaring the years 1935 and 1936 would go down in history as the great dance years, he said, "The reason is the coin-operated phonograph." Calling the tavern the best phonograph location, he explained that the juke

WURLITZER LEADS AGAIN!

MODEL 412—Handsome, massive cabinet of beautifully matched walnut veneers. Base and edge of top solid walnut.

MODEL 312—Outstanding, colorful modern cabinet. Striking color effect obtained with contrasting veneers.

Operators will clean up in Best Locations
with the WURLITZER-SIMPLEX *for* 1936

Again Wurlitzer leads the field! Again Wurlitzer produces what is unquestionably the finest automatic phonograph ever made—the greatest money-maker ever offered American operators!

The 1936 Wurlitzer-Simplex is basically the same instrument that has set the pace for the industry for the past several years. There are no radical changes that will make earlier models obsolete—only such improvements as experience has proved advisable have been incorporated. But every feature—from improved coin slot mechanism to simplified wiring is a real money-maker.

Unrivalled for Beauty, Tone, Volume

The new cabinet—created by one of the country's foremost designers—is bigger, handsomer, more impressive. The new spectacular blaze of color in the top compartment is the greatest attention catcher ever introduced in the automatic phonograph world.

The new Full-Range Sound System raises automatic music reproduction to entirely new levels. Its tremendous volume can fill a hall—yet it can be tuned down to a whisper without the slightest trace of distortion.

Big Money in Automatic Music

Improved business conditions put automatic phonograph operators in line for the biggest money they have ever made. Don't pass it up—and don't forget that the 1936 Wurlitzer-Simplex gives you the jump on all competition—enables you to gain and retain the biggest, best, most profitable locations in any territory—will make all other automatic phonographs obsolete. WIRE, PHONE or MAIL THE COUPON TODAY.

THE RUDOLPH WURLITZER MFG. CO.
North Tonawanda, New York

MAIL THE COUPON FOR BIG MONEY-MAKING PROPOSITION

The Rudolph Wurlitzer Manufacturing Company.
North Tonawanda, N. Y.

RUSH ME FULL DETAILS ON THE 1936 WURLITZER-SIMPLEX—ACCLAIMED THE GREATEST VALUE EVER OFFERED OPERATORS!

Name ....
Address ....
City .... State ....

A 1936 full-page Wurlitzer trade ad.

had been slumbering for a few years, giving way to a great extent to the radio while Prohibition was at its peak. However, as soon as it was repealed and the beer tavern opened, "in most cases the phonograph was the first fixture to be moved in after the bar itself." He claimed there were then 200,000 taverns in America. And because taverns were such good spots, it meant a juke could generate a revenue of from $10 to $30 per week. For those operators "who have never heard of the phonograph," he pointed out that current models were very different from the older types—they were technically advanced.[49]

By Mills's estimate there were around 2,000 juke operators in the United States, some with as few as five machines, some with as many as 300 or 400 units. "It is a certainty that phonograph operating is one of the most firmly established operating fields in the whole coin-machine business," he enthused. The phonograph was bigger than the average coin-operated game and the total price was also larger. However, an operator could buy on time with very little money down. Mills stated that all the boxes his firm had produced since it started production some eight years earlier were all still in operation. Net earnings to the box operator, claimed Mills, were $8 to $25 a week. Arguing that a jukebox was not just a background piece of furniture in a location but an integral aspect, Mills explained that when a deluxe phonograph appeared in any kind of location, whether that location was poorly decorated or perfectly decorated, something happened. That box "at once strikes the central decoration key of the whole location and very often causes the storekeeper to add new furniture and fixtures in order to complement the indisputable beauty of the phonograph."[50]

Journalist H. F. Reves noted that every night spot was a potential jukebox location. Also, good spots were pool rooms, cigar stores, drug stores, confectionaries, restaurants, and anywhere else people congregated occasionally for a little recreation and the attention was not centered wholly upon purchasing something. It was important that a potential spot be a place where people spent some time, where they lingered. For example, department stores would not be good potential locations. The ordinary restaurant was still awaiting exploitation, he felt, because most people liked music with their meals, a development that he linked with the arrival of the radio in most American households.[51]

Reves noted that the sudden change in the amusement-game field that turned all popular attention away from the older games, such as the animated football and baseball figures, to the pinball games was then paralleled in music. It all started with the end of Prohibition. Taverns, beer gardens, and cabarets sprang up overnight. Music came into its own as it had not since "canned music" appeared on theater screens across America in 1927–1929, with the arrival of the talking motion pictures. Reves told of a 1934 survey in Detroit that showed over 300 night spots reporting some kind of orchestra, but 90 percent of those locations had only a two- or three-piece band and paid low wages far below union scale. A low quality of music resulted with the public becoming disappointed. Reves concluded: "Customers had become accustomed to mechanical music and only demanded that it be good." Jukeboxes then, in 1937, were priced at $200 or so per machine.[52]

Locations were mostly in neighborhood bars and restaurants. Mainly they were down-scale establishments. Occasionally, during this period, they made their way into places they weren't usually found. In 1937, Howard Johnson was a chain of 56 ice-cream shops and restaurants in Massachusetts, Rhode Island, Connecticut, and New Hampshire. Each had a Seeburg Symphonola on site. Every time the chain expanded, the new outlet was equipped with a juke. In fact, space was provided for them in the plans and construction of each of their new outlets. Despite the fact that the chain served no liquor and there was no dancing in any of the outlets, those jukeboxes were reportedly "tremendous profit-makers in each of the fine dining rooms."[53]

Meanwhile, in New York City, one of Rock-Ola's operators was placing boxes in beauty parlors, with 14 having been sited. At one salon, the juke was placed in the reception room near the cashier's desk. A patron could send her request to the desk and the cashier played the machine. She kept a record of customers' requests, then when the patron paid her bill, she also paid for her requested songs. Supposedly, this experiment of placing machines in beauty shops was working very well; the boxes were played in the shops nearly all the time from 9 A.M. to 9 P.M. One shop owner felt the music increased the efficiency of her workers. Customers and employees no longer chatted because both listened to the music "and naturally they speeded up their work." Business increased at another salon because customers stayed longer "and were unconsciously more susceptible to sales suggestions for additional beauty work." Another owner explained she placed her phonograph near her large display window. Not only did people stand outside and watch but her customers, too, clustered around the unit to watch the record-changing mechanism. The owner believed that the music could be heard outside the shop and that it drew new customers inside.[54]

Up-scale locations, night spots or restaurants, were never very receptive to the music machines in the 1930s or in later times. When a machine was placed in such a locale, it was usually well publicized. A 1940 article datelined Philadelphia related that just a year or so earlier it would have been impossible for an operator to get a big night club owner "even to listen to the thought of spotting an automatic phonograph on his premises."

Just a year later a few boxes were so placed — installed not to supplant live music but to supplement it. Two reasons were said to be behind this trend. One was the ever-growing interest of the public in records and the "mechanical excellence of machines that enable them to blend harmoniously with night club appointments."[55]

One of those jukeboxes was located in Philadelphia's "swanky" Delmonico supper club where Harvey Lockman had sited a machine in his off-side cocktail lounge. Lockman employed an orchestra full-time, but during intermissions between dance and show sessions the box was available to patrons who liked their music continuously. At Frank Palumbo's Latin Quarter theater/restaurant two orchestras were employed. In addition, four phonographs were sited: in the night club, the banquet hall, the cocktail lounge, and in the downstairs restaurant. Many birthday parties were held in the establishment, said Palumbo, and all of them wanted to hear "Happy Birthday." Orchestras didn't mind playing that number once or twice during a night but balked at more repetitions. Palumbo left the jukes to the operator to program but did insist that each contain "Happy Birthday" and "Auld Lang Syne." At Jack Lynch's Tropical Bar night club on the roof of the Hotel Walton, two large orchestras played continuously. Other music was provided by singing entertainment, a person playing the piano, and one juke. Lynch explained that since it was impossible to expect musicians to be around every minute the night club was open, "the machine is that ever-present 'Johnny on the spot.'"[56]

Later in 1940, another account noted that for years the larger night clubs had been reticent about using jukes, but that sentiment was said to be dissipating rapidly as more and more of the better clubs installed machines. Roadhouses, small clubs, beer gardens, and taverns had long been good locations, and with the larger spots seeking the services of operators, about the only type of night club location still holding out was the bigger hotel. An example given was in New York where the generally poor summer business forced some night clubs to drop relief bands and to avoid running the main band into overtime. Therefore, some club managers had boxes installed to fill in the time when the band was not performing. In the larger clubs where the bar was partitioned off from the rest of the club, it was reportedly not unusual to see a latest model phonograph spotted near the bar. The volume of the box was usually toned down so that it could be played even when the band was playing.[57]

Still, siting boxes in swanky spots was a rare event. Nevertheless, the makers kept trying to find a way to crack that market. In 1940, Wurlitzer announced a new model, the Colonial. Designed for high-class hotels and night clubs, private clubs, exclusive restaurants, and other locations, Wurlitzer described it as follows: "It is devoid of large plastic panels and brilliant illumination, and is described as being more conservative"—in keeping with the surroundings of its intended exclusive locations. The cabinet featured a Governor Winthrop top, pewter finished hardware, spinning wheel grille, and was distinctly Early American throughout. Wurlitzer believed a market existed in those up-scale spots but worried that those locations may have felt the conventional jukebox appearance was not in keeping with their decor, which was often Colonial.[58]

One account broke locations down into five types—presumably the most important ones—and analyzed their differences. Operator Sam Lerner of Philadelphia's Stanley Music & Amusement Company discussed soda fountains wherein he felt the safest programming guide was to follow the current popular hits as listed in *Billboard*. It was the songs the kids sang, the sheet music they bought, and the records they requested on radio stations that determined their music machine selections. In most cases the particular band playing the song was a secondary consideration. Another tip he offered was to pay attention to the various radio programs broadcast over the radio stations in the operator's own town. Announcers on those programs could tell you "in a minute" the 10 or 20 most requested numbers. Lerner concluded, "You can't go wrong with the listings in The Billboard."[59]

College spots as a location were discussed by Charles Aitro, an operator with the New Haven, Connecticut, Yale Amusement Company. Yale always had a file in their office of the bands engaged for proms and various parties at the college. They also studied literature pertaining to nationwide college polls on favorite bands and vocalists. One thing they had discovered was that many college students did not care for many of the nationally known name bands. Rather, they preferred society orchestras playing swanky New York hotels—often visited by New Haven students. Hence, it was Yale policy "to use records by society bands currently engaged in the East." As well, the company sold many used records to students from their headquarters and kept track of such purchases as an index of popularity.[60]

Discussing "Negro" locations was Everette Johnson of New York's Interboro Music Company. He divided spots into two categories: those patronized by Blacks who had come up from the South, and those patronized by West Indians. That first group was further broken down into age ranges of 14 to 18 years, 18 to 25 years, and 25 to 40 years. Locations where Southern Blacks from 14 to 18 gathered were usually candy and ice-cream stores where dancing was permitted. For a record to be a hit there "it must be in the true jitterbug style." People in the 18 to 25 age group were said to be drawn to sentimental tunes, mixed in with hot swing, while those aged 25 to 40 usually gathered in beer gardens, where sentimental numbers had strong appeal. Blues numbers also were strong in the latter category. A good blues number would be successful in any Harlem location, except those patronized by Blacks from the West Indies, who preferred calypso music. In an ordinary location a quarter deposited in the machine usually meant five different records, said Johnson. But in Harlem, "it frequently means the same record will be played five times. Contrary to popular belief, double entendre records do not go in Harlem. We've tried them on numerous occasions but have yet to find them profitable." As a last piece of advice, Johnson mentioned to not overlook at Black locations that the favorite records of the waitresses were included in the machines. His firm had found that those women did "a bang-up job of getting customers to put nickels in the machine" when their favorites were among the selections.[61]

Taverns as locations were analyzed by Max Lipen of Detroit's Brilliant Music Company. He found a general trend in those spots to novelty music such as "Oh, You Beautiful Doll" and to sentimental music like "If I Didn't Care." Hillbilly tunes were often popular in taverns and usually needed to be included among the selections. If patrons included foreign customers then the best selection for their tastes were "polkas and similar numbers." Vocals in a foreign language were never used. For the average tavern, Lipen advised a balanced group of records. For example, a typical mix on a 24-selection box would be two Viennese waltzes, two hillbilly numbers, five popular dance numbers, four novelty records, four songs of the Bing Crosby, Dick Todd, or Tony Martin type, two polkas or international numbers, and five records selected especially to fit the individual tastes of a location's patrons.[62]

Cocktail bars were discussed by Louis Herman of County Amusements in Mount Vernon, New York. Operating in wealthy Westchester County, he declared that any spot where the society crowd gathered was difficult to program. Going by the Hit Parade alone as a guide was not sufficient. In such locations, swing records were taboo, he said. It was the soft, sweet tunes patrons of those spots wanted — the type of music that formed a pleasant background to their conversation. To a great extent, they relied on requests by the location owner. One practice found to be a great help was to closely follow the progress of bands playing at the Waldorf, the Rainbow Room, the Savoy Plaza, the St. Regis, the St. Moritz, and other leading night clubs and hotel rooms where Westchester residents went to dine and dance. When their patronage seemed to converge on two or three spots because of their preference for the orchestra or vocalist, "we lose no time in putting records by these artists in our machines," Herman said. Cocktail bars drawing an older crowd preferred Viennese waltzes, some of the lighter classics and similar standards. On the other hand, the younger country club set went more strongly for popular numbers done in sweet style by one of the currently reigning favorite bands. "But loud and blatant swing done in the true rug-cutting style — Never!" cautioned Herman. "Unless the spot is frequented by a jitterbug element, we forget about them."[63]

One problem that sometimes plagued jukes in locations was competition from other sources. Operator J. D. Leary of the Automatic Sales Company in Minneapolis sent a letter in 1937 to all his location owners after a man phoned Leary to say that he had been in a tavern that had a box operated by Leary. That man said no one could play the phonograph because the proprietor had a radio going at high volume. When the customer put his nickel in the box and the number started, the proprietor left the radio on. Leary's letter suggested that the issue was one proprietors should think about. He added: "There is no comparison between the quality of recorded music as reproduced by the modern phonograph and the general run of radio hodge-podge that customers too often are forced to listen to." That upset customer had asked Leary why a proprietor would want a radio on anyway, "when at best they are anything but pleasant to listen to, especially in a tavern."[64]

Regardless of where a box was sited, one problem that plagued them, and the entire coin-machine industry in the 1930s, was the problem of slugs. A June 1935 account told of the problem in New York City. The Independent Subway System had been receiving slugs in its system at the rate of 1,575 daily since the system opened in September 1932. It was estimated that in New York City about 10,000 slugs per day were deposited in turnstiles, telephones boxes, and other coin machines. The Interborough (subway) received around 1,200 daily and the BMT (subway) about 600, with the rest going into the Independent and other coin machines. So pervasive was the problem that New York State passed a law in September 1934 making it a criminal offense to make, distribute, sell, or possess slugs with "fraudulent intent." Despite that, slugs could still be bought openly in some stores, surreptitiously in many others. For the most part, the slug industry was said to be tied up with "the popular nickel pin-games industry." Jukes were not singled out for any specific mentions.[65]

Despite making no mentions of jukes specifically, that slug article caused a great deal of worry to *Billboard*. One article fretted that some sort of movement might start to ban pin games. Arguing that such a move would not eliminate or relieve the slug evil, it did admit, "It may be taken as true that the improper use of slugs has increased considerably during the last two or three years," and that "It is also true that pinball games have no doubt had a full share in increasing the circulation of slugs." Reporter Bill Gersh, in a separate article, worried that an entire industry might be forced to get out of New York City. He, and the anonymous author of the other article, urged coin-operation people to vigorously police themselves and the issue. Gersh said that a few hundred slugs could be bought for a few cents.[66]

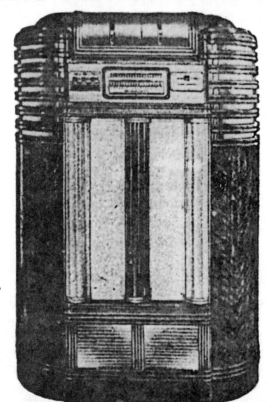

Seeburg Original

COMPLETE CABINET ILLUMINATION

THE CONCERT GRAND

Design and mechanical construction of Seeburg Symphonolas fully protected by patents issued and pending.

THE MERCHANDISING FORCE BEHIND
GREATER MUSIC PROFIT
20 RECORD MULTI SELECTOR SEEBURG SYMPHONOLAS
CONCERT GRAND—REGAL—GEM

J. P. SEEBURG CORP.
1500 DAYTON STREET
CHICAGO, ILLINOIS

A 1938 Seeburg ad.

However, before the problem got out-of-hand, technology put an end to it. Mills Novelty introduced a new model early in 1936. Among its features was a new coin-accepting mechanism, which the manufacturer claimed to be virtually slug-proof. As well, it was said to not reject worn coins, if genuine. As in previous Dance Master models, the machine accepted nickels, dimes, and quarters, giving one play for 5 cents, two for 10 cents, and five for 25 cents. If desired, the mechanism could be set to give six plays for a quarter. Later that same year, Seeburg announced that in a test its Symphonola model was fed 100 slugs. Of those, 92 were rejected, 8 triggered a play. Seeburg claimed this was the best rejection rate in the industry. Three years later, in 1939, Rock-Ola declared that its latest model, described as a "luxury light-up," had a 99 percent slug-proof coin mechanism. By the end of this period, technology had eliminated or reduced the slug problem to the point that it never again became a major issue.[67]

A much bigger problem operators had with locations revolved around commissions, that is, how much of the juke's weekly gross take should go to the location owner. Jack Eisenfeld of the General Amusement Company in Washington, D.C., complained, in 1935, of "chiseling" operators who offered 40 to 50 percent to the location but used poor machines, performed no upkeep, and changed records rarely, if at all. From that it appeared that Eisenfeld's company paid less, but no amount was mentioned.[68]

A larger debate on the issue was set off by E. C. Johnson, Seeburg's general sales manager, when he told of receiving a letter from an operator with 200 phonographs on location. For years that person had sited his boxes on one of two contracts. On one he took the first $4 and divided the balance 50/50. For the second he gave the location one-quarter of everything up to $10, one-third up to $20, and split equally any receipts over $20 a week. With those contracts, the operator said he was able to meet his obligations and to make money. However, he wrote, a lot of new music operators had entered the field and were offering locations a 50/50 split of all receipts. He wanted to know how he could successfully make money on that basis.[69]

Johnson replied bluntly that it could not be done, although he did add, "Music is profitable, more so in the long run than any other branch of the coin-machine business." He explained that in Seeburg's long experience of manufacturing and selling music machines they found that 75 percent of those defaulting on payments were guilty of giving too big a percentage to the location. In Dallas he said the standard terms then were one-quarter to the location up to $10 and one-third of receipts over $10 per week. Operators in Dallas were said to have agreed on those standard terms. Since they met monthly, any price cutting reported was "immediately corrected." At a recent meeting of the music division of the National Association of Coin-Operated Machine Manufacturers, the subject of percentages came up, explained Johnson. It was agreed that in the event operators in any territory got to fighting over the 50 percent concept, the makers whose machines were involved would send their representatives to that area, get the operators together, "and show them the error of their ways."[70]

Spartanburg, South Carolina, operator R. T. Thomason agreed that jukes could not be operated successfully on the basis of a 50/50 split — the location had to receive less. Noting that his area had experienced several percentage wars he said they had been resolved using "salesmanship" — arguing mainly that an operator giving a large percentage could not provide the latest and best records. In his area, a location owner was not convinced he was going to make a lot of money. Rather, he was told that Thomason would supply him music for the entertainment of his customers and that his commission would more than offset any increase in his electric bill. "We have found that the average location," concluded Thomason, "is perfectly willing to give everything that comes out of the cash box merely for the privilege of having music to satisfy his patrons." The use of a straight 50/50 revenue split was apparently fairly commonplace at this time.[71]

Journalist Ralph Neal declared, in 1936, that under "proper" percentages, 25 percent was the accepted location commission. In only rare cases should the percentage be more. Some operators took the first $5 in weekly receipts and then split any excess on a 50/50 basis. That was equivalent to 25 percent on a $10-a-week machine and a little over 35 percent on a $20-a-week spot. Neal warned, "Stay away from the straight 50-50 commission if you want to make a big success in the music business." He suggested extra money could be made by renting idle machines for special occasions. Lodges, clubs, fraternities, and so on were said to be willing to pay as much as $10 or more per night for phonographs.[72]

In Michigan, the Wayne County Music Operators' Association, in an attempt to abolish "unfair" trade practices, imposed an experimental moratorium in the fall of 1938 for one month on all location jumping by members of the association. It was agreed that no members would place a machine in a location in which another member had one, no matter how favorable the deal that could be arranged with the location owner. During their monthly meeting at the end of the moratorium, operators were said to be in favor of the experiment and to view it as a success — the few exceptions were said to be "accidents." However, majority opinion of those operators definitely favored a return to "normal" competition. Joining the group required an initiation fee of $5 to $100, plus monthly dues of $7.50 per 100 machines. Another agreement was put in place by this group whereby the organization members agreed to a standard payment rate for location owners. Under the new schedule a maximum of 50 percent to the location was established, but only after deducting a minimum sum each week to go to the operator as a service charge for record costs. That minimum was $2 on 12-selection jukeboxes, $3 on 16-selection models, and $4 weekly on boxes playing 20 or 24 numbers. Establishing this agreement was reportedly done to keep operating practices "in the realm of fair trade."[73]

The parent group of Wayne County was the Michigan Music Operators' Association. The secretary of that group, Max Marston, explained that he liked to meet new operators entering the field, to see what kind of operators they were going to be, and also to show them that they could not meet their machine payments if they offered locations a 50/50 split. Accordingly, this group said it had reached an agreement with the distributors in Detroit to direct their sales toward only group members and not to sell to new operators if the Michigan Music Operators objected to them for any reason.[74]

Wurlitzer sales manager M. G. Hammergren declared in 1940 that the quick-profit guys were out of the business and it was more stable. Although he used no specific numbers, he stated: "Today every successful music merchant knows that he can't give locations more than they should rightfully get and still remain in business; that it is far better to get acquainted with his competition and arrange things so both can make a profit than to engage in ruinous price-cutting tactics."[75]

A few months later, Seeburg vice president in charge of sales Henry Roberts spoke out about the "evil" plaguing the industry — the fallacy of percentage. In his view, too many operators were trying to eliminate and fight competition by offering too high a percentage. Locations were getting an asset for nothing. They should pay for it, but Roberts was resigned to the fact that they would not. Locations were after higher commission rates because some "chiseler" had been throwing large numbers around. Cooperation and education were the solutions. Cooperation among operators was needed to establish a definite percentage for locations "of not more than 30%." Locations needed to be shown how much of an asset they were getting. Roberts stated that the most successful operators were those who had never allowed a percentage higher than 40 percent, and that only in isolated cases. The problem of percentages troubled the industry throughout this period. It would continue to do so well into the future.[76]

Promotion and publicity were important to the industry in these early years. Early efforts were rudimentary and became more complex over time. As early as 1935, *Billboard* reported on the "widespread use" of various coin-operated amusement machines and venders in motion pictures as part of the background. It struck the publication that no stronger medium could be used to build up the industry and that automatic amusement should capitalize on that means of creating fashion, as clothing styles were so influenced by the movies. Of course, admitted the article, film producers had taken up the use of, say, pinball games, in their movies because of the great popularity the games had built up for themselves.[77]

Paramount's 1937 film "The Barrier" was filmed on location near Seattle, at Mount Baker. It starred Leo Carrillo, Jean Parker, and Otto Krueger. The Hart Novelty Company installed a new Wurlitzer in the lodge housing the entire Paramount company. Hart officials said the machine enjoyed enthusiastic patronage every night.[78]

Capitol Automatic Music Company was the exclusive distributor of Rock-Ola products in New York. In June 1936, they hired a taxi to transport a Rock-Ola Multi Selector model to the ocean liner *Queen Mary*, two hours before the ship sailed for the United Kingdom. Supposedly, a special squad of private detectives had been hired to assist the regular police department in clearing the way so the taxi could reach the *Queen Mary*. Lots of people were milling about due to the high level of general interest in the liner. It had all the markings of being a public relations stunt.[79]

Detroit's National Coin Machine company reported business was booming in 1936 with operators unable to keep a box for more than 24 hours before it was placed on location. Some 7,000 music machines were estimated to be on location in the Motor City. Patrons were said to ask location owners without boxes why they did not have one. National Coin Machine had installed its own special sampling device on its Mills Do Re Mi models. This device was set for 30 minutes and if nobody played the machine for that length of time, the juke automatically started to play and gave a full-length "sample" record without charge. Apparently that attracted the attention of the customers and usually drew business.[80]

John Winthrop suggested that every restaurant owner with a music machine should instruct his waitresses to suggest music frequently to the patrons. For example: "Would you like some music with your dinner? We have a beautiful phonograph and the very latest songs." Some restaurants called attention to their music machines on menus—but most did not. Additional printed material could be added to those menus, such as "Music adds to the pleasure of this meal. The latest in music from our coin-operated phonograph."[81]

Mills Novelty executive Grant Shay also advocated advertising on menus by adding something like "Paul Whiteman gets $5,000 a night to play in New York. You can hear him here for only a nickel—play our Do Re Mi." Enthusiastic about the idea that music had to be merchandised, Shay also advised operators not to overlook good spots, observing that big places did not always pay the best, and that sometimes it was the small taverns with "peppy crowds" that paid the best. He encouraged operators to leave a sheet of paper near the machine so customers could write down their requests for numbers to be placed on the box. Only a few years earlier, Mills Novelty used to send out separate mailings to the coin machine and to the phonograph operators, said Shay. But now Mills sent the same mailings to both because practically all coin-machine operators also handled jukes.[82]

Rock-Ola's Phonograph Division established itself as a clearing house, providing a forum for the exchange of publicity ideas among its operators. One Rock-Ola operator bought space in his local paper to advertise: "A new Rock-Ola phonograph has recently been installed in the well-known establishment of John Jones." Included in the ad was a description of the man's place of business. Another operator had advertising cards printed, outlining the features of a location and ending with "Come in and see and hear the latest music on our new Rock-Ola Multi Selector Phonograph." Cards cost $2 per thousand and another $2 to distribute that number. It was said to pay for itself from the increased plays. Still another operator used small checkbook-size blotters that he distributed directly to households. That blotter read: "Every time you visit a place of amusement (except the theater) ask the proprietor if he has Rock-Ola music. He can get all the latest songs for you on a Rock-Ola Multi Selector Phonograph."[83]

The Michigan Music Operators held a contest in the spring of 1939. One musical number, with no words, had been specially recorded and placed in every juke of every association member in the state. Patrons were to listen to the tune and write lyrics for a first prize of $500. Lesser amounts were awarded for spots two through five, and so forth. Lasting from May 3 until July 15, the contest dates were picked to build up play "during those slow summer months." Association secretary Max Marston explained that the contest would automatically increase play on the boxes, and it would bring a demand for member-operated phonographs in locations where non-members had machines when the public got interested in the contest. Some 5,000 machines were operated in the state by association members. Marston added, "It may be conceded that 9 out of 10 players may not bother to enter the contest — but at least they will drop a nickel just out of curiosity any way."[84]

Toronto, Canada, radio commentator Clair Wallace, who broadcast nightly over station CFRB, devoted one of her programs to jukes, after some listeners had put in a request for a topic talk on that subject. For her older listeners, she explained that a jukebox was an automatic phonograph while explaining to her younger audience that an automatic phonograph was a jukebox. Wallace added that the machines came in three sizes: 12, 16, or 24 selections. She explained they used ordinary records but used a special needle that played 4,000 times without being changed and that the average popularity life span of a record was one month. Finally, she said that on site a 12-disk machine was expected to be played at least 50 times a week while the largest, the 24-record size, "must play 1,000 times a week to pay its way." It was all good publicity, even if some of the numbers were wildly off the mark.[85]

Young and old, jitterbugs and sweet fans, they all love Artie Shaw, nabob of the nickel nabbers. Few musicians have woo so wide a following. Every coin machine needs such a "best friend" as Artie Shaw. Keep your machine on its toes with the newest Bluebird Records by Artie Shaw.

New Victor and Bluebird Records to Capture the Coins

ARTIE SHAW AND HIS ORCHESTRA

B-10430—Oh, Lady Be Good—F. T.
    I Surrender, Dear—F. T.
B-10412—Last Two Weeks in July—F. T. (V. R.)
    Two Blind Loves—F. T. (V. R.)
B-10406—Day In—Day Out—F. T. (V. R.)
    Put That Down in Writing—F. T. (V. R.)
B-10446—Many Dreams Ago—F. T. (V. R.)
    If What You Say is True—F. T. (V. R.)

It Pays to Use

VICTOR AND BLUEBIRD RECORDS

Victor Division, RCA Mfg. Co., Inc., Camden, N.J.
A Service of the Radio Corporation of America

Trademark "Victor" Reg. U. S. Pat. Off. by RCA Mfg. Co., Inc.

A 1939 trade ad tying Artie Shaw ("nabob of the nickel nabbers") to Victor Records and the jukebox.

By 1939–1940, publicity efforts were getting more sophisticated as the jukebox industry tried to identify itself more openly with the recording stars of the day and the theaters in which they performed live shows. Kemo Novelty Company of Milwaukee was the Wurlitzer distributor for Wisconsin. When the Lawrence Welk band played at a local theater, it tied up with Kemo in plugging Welk records in Kemo phonographs. That operating firm placed on about 350 jukebox backboards promotional material plugging the Welk records and the band's appearance at the local theater. Kemo head William Montrose explained that when they hyped a band coming to town it boosted its concert attendance, it increased record sales, and it put more nickels into the cash box. Kemo was active in keeping the public "phonograph conscious." Whenever a name band came to town, Montrose sent flowers to the orchestra with a card on which was written "With the compliments of the phonograph operators of Milwaukee." That resulted, said Montrose, in reciprocation by the orchestra leaders who might publicly thank the box operators, "and, incidentally, the public learns that automatic phonographs are appreciated by the band. Naturally, this adds to their prestige and helps to build phonograph patrons."[86]

At his 1940 stage show in

Chicago's Oriental Theater, Tiny Hill, billed as "The Biggest Orchestra Leader in America," utilized two Rock-Ola Luxury Light-Up boxes, placing one on each side of the stage. Two bandsmen would press buttons on the boxes while the orchestra played "Nickel in the Slot." Their record selection would then be announced, naming the tune and the orchestra. Then Tiny Hill and his aggregation would imitate the tune and orchestra supposedly selected. This bit of business was said to be a big hit with the audience.[87]

Increasing cooperation between artists and phonograph operators, for cross-promotions, came about because boxes could make hits, according to one account. "And with this realization artists have abandoned their former indifferent attitude to the music boxes, and are building a closer cooperation with operators." There was a mutual benefit with the artist increasing his music machine and box office draw while the operator increased his take. Guy Lombardo and his Royal Canadians were set for a

A 1939 ad linking Eddy Duchin and the music machines.

one-night show at the Tromar Ballroom in Des Moines, but before the date Lombardo effected a tie-up with local music-machine operators to promote his disks a couple of weeks in advance of the show. When he arrived in Des Moines, he played host to several operators. That personal touch solidified his relationship with them while Lombardo's subsequent gross at the ballroom was his best at that spot in two years. Plays of his records on boxes in that area doubled.[88]

Band leader Al Donahue had a special advance man, Henry Okum, whose duty it was to travel ahead of the band on its tours and make friends with the operators. It was, of course, those people who had the power to put certain records on their boxes or decline to place them. Okum's special record-promotion material helped operators and so did his promotion of closer cooperation between operators and local owners of theaters and ballrooms who featured artists giving stage shows. Orchestra leader Horace Heidt had a couple of people who got together with operators on every band tour, offering helpful selling hits. During Duke Ellington's run at the Denver (Colorado) Theater, house manager Bernie Haynes arranged a tie-in with Gibson Bradshaw, Denver's Rock-Ola distributor, to feature Ellington in 300 locations. His engagement was advertised on stickers placed in each machine, and his disks were played in the lobby of the theater on a new juke. Tiny Hill personally visited operators in every town he played, offering his services in any way he could. Lawrence Welk's cooperation involved the placement of a box in the lobby of the Riverside Theater in Milwaukee when he played that venue. With the agreement of the Riverside and leading phonograph men, Welk had cards distributed atop many jukes in the Milwaukee territory announcing his engagement. So successful was this promotion that Welk repeated it in other towns where he performed.[89]

Nor were promotions limited to orchestra leaders in advance of their stage shows. Night club owners, ballroom managers, theater managers, movie directors, musical comedy producers, and others had found many uses for boxes, generating a great deal of publicity. One film was 20th Century Fox's 1940 release "Private Affairs" with Roland Young. It featured a jukebox in a full five-minute scene. On the Broadway stage in the 1939 season, producer Eddie Dowling used one in "Here Come the Clowns" in a tavern scene. A newly released song was titled "A Nickel's Worth of Rhythm." Theaters by then made it a common practice to use a music box in the lobby to promote in advance the songs from musical shows coming into the theater, to exploit the band leaders announced as coming attractions, either in the flesh or on the screen, and to serve as a link between the theater, the operator's locations, and the retail record stores, which in turn advertised songs from the motion picture. Ballroom operators from coast to coast had

Bing Crosby and Wurlitzer combined in a 1938 ad.

boxes in their lobbies, filled with the latest records of bands currently playing or announced as coming attractions. Nightclubs used boxes to help furnish continuous music, filling in when live bands were on breaks.[90]

By late 1941, *Billboard* boasted that it was impossible for band leaders,
music publishers, recording companies, ballroom operators, band management offices, and theater owners to conduct their business "without
devoting a major portion of their activities to studying and exploiting the
automatic phonograph." Only in the past two years had those branches of
the entertainment industry recognized to any extent the potential offered
by the jukes. Record sales took a dramatic upswing the moment the phonograph entered its "streamlined" period; that is, between 1933 and 1934 when
the mechanically improved machines came out of the ice-cream parlor stage
into the newly opened cocktail lounges and taverns. Prior to that point,
band bookers and managers hardly ever bothered to include recording sessions in their percentage contracts with their bands because the money
bands were making from records was almost negligible compared to the
grosses they earned through theater, ballroom, and radio engagements.
Band leaders in particular started campaigning among the music-box operators in an effort to discover the needs of the latter and become better known
among the operators personally. Orchestra leaders made it a point to meet
and entertain the phonograph men wherever possible.[91]

Coin-machine conventions for the industry were well attended by the
band leaders with frontmen such as Tommy Dorsey, Orrin Tucker, Glenn
Miller, and others hosting special cocktail parties and get-togethers for the
juke men. Those band leaders wanted to know what the phonograph operators considered the right type of record for the boxes. When the bands
hit the road, many leaders also made it a point to visit local operators, talk
to tavern associations, and so forth. Some bands hired special advance men
to go on the road and effect promotional tie-ups with the theaters, ballrooms, and music stores to plug their recordings with the operators
throughout the country. All kinds of aids such as decals, placards, and fancy
title-strips were distributed to the phonograph operators by the band's promotional man. Some leaders reportedly spent a hefty sum of money each
year just sending sample records out to lists of operators. Publications such
as *Billboard* were another main expenditure for orchestras because the leaders had found that advertising their disks in those papers reached most of
the industry. Such ads were targeted specifically to jukebox operators. Theater managers first started tying-in with boxes by spotting them in the foy-
ers of the theaters, complete with records of the orchestra playing in that
venue.[92]

With all the success of the jukeboxes, the idea soon arose that advertising should somehow become part of the industry. First mention of the

At the Blue Moon nightclub (1940) in Wichita, Kansas, band leader Herbie Kay (left) posed for a publicity shot beside a Seeburg box and with Walter Rein of the firm Music Service Corp. Note that Rein is holding a remote unit.

possibility seems to have occurred at an industry convention held in January 1938 at Chicago. A plan discussed there was closer to reality by spring. The National Phonographic Network intended to sell commercial advertising by plugs on records used on automatic phonographs. Company president John B. Griffith said he planned to supply records to phonograph operators at little or no cost in order to promote the use of disks with commercial ads. Reportedly music licensing groups such as the Music Publishers' Protective Association and ASCAP (American Society of Composers, Authors and Publishers) were both prepared to negotiate a license fee with the firm. Griffith claimed the groundwork for his plan was already laid since he had contracts with about 4,000 automatic phonograph operators, with some 245,000 machines. Records to be furnished to operators would have 25 to 40 words of advertising about products salable in locations, such as liquor and cigarettes.[93]

Almost a year later, journalist Tom Murray reviewed the plan for placing short ads at the start of records. He thought the idea "offers national advertisers one of the best advertising bets they have ever had." Operators he had talked to mostly favored the plan, but they also felt that operators

During a 1940 concert tour stop in Indianapolis band leader Sammy Kaye (right) stopped for a publicity photo at Jock's Guarantee Distributing firm where he was greeted by Paul Jock.

should receive some sort of financial inducement; that they would not bother with the ad records just for the sake of free disks. Some worried that location owners would also expect some sort of cut if they had to listen to advertising over and over. A few operators opposed the idea because some of their location owners opposed the concept. Griffith's plan was never implemented, but the idea of advertising on jukeboxes would resurface again and again as time passed.[94]

Despite the growing popularity of jukes, it was not until 1939 that the boxes started receiving attention in the national news media. That year, in its September issue, *Fortune* looked at the revival of the record business and concluded that the largest consumer of disks, on a unit basis, "is the gaudy slot machine." Some record labels, presumably just a little ashamed of them, were said to have a weakness for underestimating the percentage of their output that went to them, but Decca was proud to say it "loves them dearly, and, in fact, claims credit for helping start their boom." Juke fans estimated 300,000 boxes and record consumption for 1939 at no less than 30 million disks, with prospects for 500,000 boxes and a 50 million record year in 1940. However, *Fortune* said a credible estimate for 1938 was 225,000 machines using 13 million records and a modest increase in store for 1939 and 1940. Seven manufacturers were producing units, but Wurlitzer and Seeburg were the biggest. Each box cost around $300. The business magazine concluded:

"The obsolescence is staggering because juke-boxes are constantly restyled, 'style' meaning the latest thing in raucous conspicuousness. The overwhelming majority of records in juke-boxes are the 35-cent disks; hence their share of dollar sales is not as large as unit sales. Juke-boxes, however, create interest in a lot of popular disks and are responsible for a large sale to ... record purchasers."[95]

That prompted the trade publication *Advertising Age*, in its September 11, 1939, issue to quote from the *Fortune* piece in its own article giving credit to coin-operated phonographs for reviving the record business.[96]

Just two months later, an Associated Press (AP) story appeared in newspapers all over the United States that dealt with the rise of automatic phonographs and discussed the importance of that industry to the music field. Customers dropped "frequent nickels into a brightly lighted music box — an automatic phonograph." The article mentioned that record sales in 1939 were expected to hit 55 million, a 20 million increase over 1938, and that the 200,000 boxes would use 10 million of them. In an editorial "correction," *Billboard* conceded the 200,000 figure could be accurate but challenged the 10 million number, noting that it would be less than one new record placed on each machine each week. "It is a well-known fact that some operators place four or five or more new records each week on a phonograph, depending on the income of the machines," argued the publication.[97]

AP's article went on to say that the jukes had made the reputation of half a dozen performers almost before the general public heard of them, citing Glenn Miller and vocalists Bing Crosby, the Andrews Sisters, and the Ink Spots. Yet the account later said, "In general, the popularity of a record in the music boxes whose repertoire is revised only every week or so runs considerably behind radio popularity." Numbers like "Moon Love," "Wishing," and "Over the Rainbow" began to be popular in the bars about the time they were slipping away on the radio." Also mentioned was that band bookers had allied themselves with the juke operators for local build-up campaigns through the phonographs in advance of touring bands. AP said there were half a dozen large manufacturers, boxes cost around $300, they were placed on location on a commission basis, "and may take in as much as $100 a week." That last comment caused *Billboard* to insert another correction pointing out that in a good location with a good crowd and if the box was played every minute for six hours for seven days a week the total would reach about $35 gross. In conclusion, AP's article stated: "Their locations are not confined to taverns. The fancier bars and restaurants, which at first snubbed the blatant machines, were finally convinced that even the silk stocking trade would pour in the nickels." With the exception of the *Fortune* article, none used the word jukebox — still an epithet to the industry.[98]

Manufacturers could hardly keep up with the demand for jukeboxes. Rock-Ola was running double shifts in 1936 and contracting out some of its work — wood for cabinets. It was then producing around 1,000 units per week at its Chicago plant. That factory then contained 14 huge conveyors, all but two of which had been installed within the previous 12 months. One year later, Rock-Ola announced that for the week ending July 17, 1937, the number of orders placed for the 20-selection Imperial model reached 3,750, the highest weekly total ever for Rock-Ola, for any model.[99]

Over the three years ending in the middle of 1937, Wurlitzer increased its office personnel by 600 percent. A second shift was added each day for bill posting. Every day Wurlitzer received 1,000 local and 150 long-distance phone calls, 200 to 300 telegrams, and 2,500 pieces of mail. Wurlitzer's factory ran two to three shifts a day for more than a year during 1935–1936. Their backlog of orders worth $4 million was the greatest total of unfilled orders the company had ever faced. September 1936 production was set to average 250 phonographs a day. Also, production of its amusement game, Skee-Ball, was again stepped up due to ever-increasing demand.[100]

Having established an industry structured in a particular way — sales only to operators who placed jukes on location on a commission basis — the makers were determined to maintain that structure. They would not sell a box directly to a location owner. Wurlitzer advertising manager R. G. Norman explained in 1935 that manufacturers' policies meant a lot to the operator in the selection of phonograph equipment. "Any factory that sells both to locations and operators is betraying the operators who buy its products," he added. "Not only is this an unethical practice but it is a most detrimental one and exceedingly harmful to the operators of America." It was only the operator who offered a "complete music service."[101]

Reinforcing the idea that boxes would not be sold to location owners was Wurlitzer district manager W. E. Simmons. In 1937, he reported that every month dozens of location owners visited the Wurlitzer office with the idea of purchasing a phonograph. Also, many letters were received every week from location owners requesting box prices. Each got a form letter from the company stating that Wurlitzer sold its product exclusively to operators: "We have found through experience with thousands of phonographs that the best results and earning power can be attained when machines are serviced regularly by an expert technician and by an operator who knows the public whims in music." Regarding in-person visits by location owners, Simmons related that each of them was "given a reverse sales talk on owning his own phonograph and a good argument as to why he should continue with the operator regardless of what make instrument is now on his location."[102]

During the summer of 1938, Wurlitzer executives embarked on a tour

A 1939 Wurlitzer ad which reinforced the idea that used machines it took back in trade would be destroyed and never sold directly to locations — where they might compete against operator-placed units.

that would hit 21 major cities from coast to coast and cover a total of 14,682 miles. At each stop a lavish banquet meeting was held for the firm's operators and distributors. Principal executive on tour was vice president Homer E. Capehart. At a stop in Detroit, he estimated there were 300,000 to 325,000 boxes on site in America, and reiterated Wurlitzer's policy of selling machines only to operators. Some 423 operators attended the July 6 meeting in Baltimore where Capehart announced that old jukeboxes would be taken in at liberal trade-in allowances and that those old phonographs "would be completely destroyed." The plan to destroy trade-ins was to prevent the market from being glutted and inflicting further hardship on operators. Additionally, it was to ease their worries that somehow those used machines might be sold directly to locations. Furthermore, Capehart declared that absolutely no new models would be introduced at the coming December coin-machine show. Increasingly a sore point among operators was that manufacturers introduced new models far too frequently, often more than once a year. Thus, they were pressured by locations to install the newest units when the current ones were fully useable and, more importantly, not yet paid for. Even at this early stage in jukebox history, new models were being introduced not because of any technological change or improvement, but merely for the sake of change and to try and increase sales.[103]

Keynote of the Wurlitzer trip was to crystallize the thinking of the American box operators towards stabilization of the industry. Reportedly, every one of those 423 operators at the Baltimore meeting signed the music operators' pledge, which promised "to consider the interests of my customers first and thereby be a credit to the industry as a whole, by keeping my phonographs clean and in good working order — always supplied with fresh needles and good records; To maintain the dignity of the music-operating business by offering my customers clean, wholesome records." As the pledge continued, it became much more mercenary and focused on the needs of the operator first, that is, to increase his share of the take: "To increase my share of the earnings from the phonographs I already have in locations; To place instruments in locations only on a basis that assures me fair returns and to maintain that percentage under all conditions; and, To stress the phonograph as a means of attracting and holding crowds that will increase the location's bar and food business rather than to emphasize direct profits from the instrument itself."[104]

One operator who suggested a solution to the new-model problem was Ralph Neal. He used new models to replace the "slightly obsolete" machines in the big-pay spots just as quickly as possible. The machines so removed were then located to the next best paying spots, and so on down the line. In the fair and not-so-fair spots, Neal recommended having your older

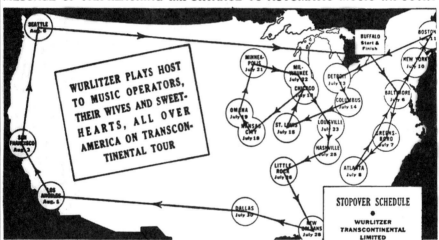

A trade ad for that 1938 wide-ranging Wurlitzer tour.

machines, which had undoubtedly paid for themselves several times over. By siting new models in the big-pay spots, an operator could forestall competition, which was more likely to try and poach the lucrative spots, more than the less lucrative locations.[105]

Michigan Music Operators' Association secretary Max Marston advised that for every machine an operator bought he should break up an old one. He praised Wurlitzer for recognizing the problem — by introducing its liberal trade-in policy. Marston felt these were the best ways to keep the market "clean." He was positive that new equipment would take in from two to three times as much money as would a two-year-old machine.[106]

When Capehart announced Wurlitzer's trade-in policy and that those trade-ins would be destroyed rather than sold to competitors, he went one step further to reassure operators. To emphasize his point, Capehart published trade ads showing workers at Wurlitzer's plant in North Tonawanda, New York, smashing traded-in used models.[107]

Walter Hurd was the Amusement Machine section editor for *Billboard*. In a 1938 editorial, he discussed the issue of publishing in his journal the price of used phonographs— both operators and manufacturers opposed the practice. Hurd observed that it had been the general impression that phonograph advertising had been free of prices, at least more so than for any other type of coin machines. Publishing prices of used machines caused difficulties in dealing with locations about commissions. Location owners who saw the low prices on used machines took the attitude that operators got all their boxes, including new ones, at those prices and should therefore pay higher commissions. What was true was that juke makers had all consistently refrained from publishing prices for new phonographs. Amusement game makers did publish prices for new units in their ads, even in the face of criticism from operators all over the country. Around 1933–1934, game manufacturers began publishing prices for new units when games were very low in price and quick volume was the goal.[108]

Advertisements annoying operators, said Hurd, were those for used jukes, placed by distributors, jobbers, or by large operators. It was to be expected since everyone in the business knew how the average distributor or jobber had reached the stage where he had to take in an old machine on practically every new box he sold. Hurd thought operators should not talk about the cost of machines with location owners at all. Those who did "are like the vending trade back in the golden days of 1929, which was always talking to locations about how vending machines would displace human hands." Jukebox operator associations forwarded their complaint letters to the manufacturers. They, in turn, wrote to *Billboard* to suggest that publishing prices of used machines was not a good idea. While a reader would never see the price of a new jukebox in an ad in *Billboard*, the publication was full of ads, with prices, for used ones, and had been since around 1935. On the same page as Hurd's article was an ad placed by the W. B. Novelty Company of St. Louis offering used boxes. Four Wurlitzer models were available, from $65.00 to $122.50; five Seeburg Symphonolas, from $69.50 to $115.00; a Rock-Ola Multi Selector at $75.00; and a Mills Dance Master for $39.50. It was typical of many such ads in every issue of the publication.[109]

Some new models introduced may have had no technological changes but many did. In its 1935 ads for the Simplex Multi Selector, Wurlitzer announced the machine allowed people to select from 1 to 12 numbers at one time and to play them in the order of selection. That feature was said to generate more money than machines that did not permit people to select more than one number at a time. The following year, Seeburg announced six new models for 1937. Features included the newly developed 15-record multiselector, in which records were played in the order selected and could not be canceled. If no definite records were selected, they would play in consecutive order, depending on the amount of coins deposited.[110]

Rock-Ola and its distributors conducted a nationwide survey late in 1937. They questioned operators, location owners, and patrons as to just how many selections a jukebox should contain. Results showed that 5 percent favored 12 numbers; 13 percent voted for 16; 79 percent opted for 20; and 3 percent favored more than 20 selections on a box. From this survey it was learned that the average person remembered between 17 and 20 song titles.[111]

Doing everything possible to help operators increase earnings, Wurlitzer engineers announced in 1936 they had developed a record-counting device that was adaptable to all Simplex boxes made by that company. This device could be installed or removed in one or two minutes. The unit was numbered from 1 to 12, corresponding to the number of selections in the machine. Since he would now have an accurate play count for each record in the box, the route man did not have to guess which records to change, nor did he have "to take the word of the location proprietor or a waitress when it comes to changing records."[112]

An electric coin slot that accepted a nickel, dime, or a quarter for one, two, or five plays was a new feature in the 1936 Mills Do Re Mi model. It was claimed to be slug proof. The machine could also be equipped with a radio coin box, a portable stand mounted on casters with no wire connection to the jukebox. Inserting a coin into this device caused the phonograph to play "instantly." In effect, this coin box was a miniature broadcasting station that sent a radio impulse to the receiving set in the phonograph. This device could be wheeled about in a location, for example, from table to table in a restaurant.[113]

Sometimes companies not involved in juke manufacturing entered the industry indirectly by producing accessories. Wall boxes for the music machines were an example. Chicago's ABT Manufacturing Company placed ads in 1938 for an "improved" ABT Wall Box. Measuring 13⅛-inches high, 6⅛-inches wide, 3-inches deep, and weighing 7.25 pounds, the cost per unit was $8.50 F.O.B. Chicago. The ad read: "People like to have things made easy — they don't go out of their way unless it is necessary." Each wall box had a blank program card, filled in with numbers 1 to 20, on which titles could be printed or typed. From 1 to 20 coins could be deposited in a wall box, each coin registering for a separate play on the machine. Operators were also assured "absolute protection for their earnings," as each unit came with a slug detector "plus 8 feet of special armored cable, making it impossible for players to short circuit wires by inserting pins, knife blades, etc. for free plays." The large coin box was said to hold up to $10 in nickels.[114]

While remote access units were available for most of this period, they seem to have enjoyed little popularity. Chicago's J. H. Keeney & Company was another firm that produced accessories for the industry. Keeney reported, in 1940, that its Keeney Remote Selector Wall Box for jukeboxes was experiencing a sudden rise in popularity. It was adjustable to suit a 12 to 24 selection box. Generally, though, it was after World War II before the remote selectors became really popular.[115]

Makers expanded their lines to include more and more types of models. Rock-Ola introduced its new Imperial 20-selection model in 1937 to a reported heavy demand. Following that came an Imperial 16-selection model. These were larger "full-size" units. A big demand still existed for its small, compact Rhythm Master model, which came in 12 or 16 number variations.[116]

Automatic Musical Instrument Company (AMI) announced at the start of 1941 that it would devote itself to producing a complete line of automatic music equipment, including jukes, wall boxes, floor and wall speakers. It was no longer in the operating business, after 28 years. The era of the gaudy models, the so-called light-up era, lasted from around 1938 until the late 1940s. Typical was AMI's newly introduced Singing Towers model. It stood 70-inches high and had five light-up panels that illuminated "the machine from base to ceiling with a new system never before applied to phonos." One feature of that illumination was that four different color combinations came on the model as standard equipment. The operator could pick the color he desired and freeze it, or he could have the color scheme change automatically with every song. Although the box had 20 selections, only 10 records were needed since the mechanism played both sides of a disk. This was still an uncommon feature.[117]

When David Rockola announced in 1938 that his firm would introduce

The 1938 trade ad for ABT's wall unit.

no midseason new phonograph models, hundreds of letters and wires of commendation for that policy poured into the Rock-Ola office. In response to operators who had been asking the company if it planned to bring out any more new models that year, Rockola stated: "Definitely no. There will be no mid-season models. It is our firm conviction that, for the good of the operator as well as the industry as a whole, new models should be introduced only once a year."[118]

One oddity of the time was manufactured by Economy Production of Philadelphia. Designed to be an accessory, the Phono-Mike was an attachment for phonographs that allowed the patron to sing or whistle while using the record playing as an accompaniment. Supposedly it could be used with any phonograph, could be installed in two minutes, and was certain to "pep" up locations. A separate charge of five cents was made for each use of Phono-Mike. It was an idea that sank like a stone and was never heard from again — at least for a few decades when it resurfaced as karaoke.[119]

The sudden and spectacular rise of the industry caused various writers to comment on that success and to try and explain it. Journalist L. Force said in 1936 that the juke first appeared on the scene in the fall of 1933, but in the beginning it was "scarcely worthy of notice from other branches of the operating business ... being careful not to intrude in the business dealings of Mr. Big Coin Machine Operator." It was obvious to him that the tavern of the time, which grew out of the repeal of Prohibition, was "the main spring of the whole business." The tavern owner soon realized he was not going to stay in business for long just by selling beer and that he needed some sort of device to attract the crowds and hold the patronage. Floor shows, entertainment, and dancing were as essential as the beer tap. Soon the tavern entrenched itself as a place for entertainment — a place to go and stay, drink a few beers, eat a sandwich, and dance and be entertained. Good places, said Force, could afford a floor show — an orchestra. But for every place that could afford an orchestra, there were 10 places that could not. Entering the picture was "the tavern owners' life saver, the automatic phonograph." Successful from the beginning, it was no exaggeration to say, he thought, that in many cases the profits from the phonographs were the difference between closing the doors and leaving them open. Increased demand for the machines came from a vicious circle wherein if Tavern A installed a box, then Taverns B and C felt they had to get one. Concluded Force: "Even the coin-machine operator who scorned it a few years ago when it first came on the scene is now getting into phonograph operating with both feet." Although he made no mention of the economic difficulties of the Depression, it was obviously easier for neighborhood taverns to provide, at no cost to them, jukeboxes to entertain their patrons than it was to obtain any type of live entertainment.[120]

A year later, *Billboard* editor Walter Hurd declared that music then had the most "optimistic note" in the coin-machine industry. The coin phonograph had found a basic place in connection with the modern tavern, the tavern having become "the meeting place of the American public." For Hurd, the industry had two problems. One was the too frequent introduction of new models, a costly event for operators. Second was the bitter competition among operators in the rate of commission paid to the locations. Operators of long experience with other types of coin machines were turning to jukes. He noted he was surprised "at the number of men who gained their experience years ago in operating slot machines who now say frankly that they are turning almost exclusively to music." Hurd declared that jukeboxes and vending machines were the two types of coin equipment recommended to all operators as a legal, stable area of the coin industry to be a mainstay for their business.[121]

Sometimes when someone praised the industry they got carried away and drifted into the realm of fanciful dreaming and exaggeration. One example was A. J. Demers, attorney for the Arkansas Music Operators' Association, who delivered an address at a meeting of that organization in Jonesboro, Arkansas, on May 29, 1938. That address, carried over radio station KBTM in Jonesboro, was an appeal to the public on behalf of music operators. Demers stated that phonograph operators could be considered "an important factor in keeping peace and happiness where ordinarily there would be gloom and unhappiness by placing phonographs in the small towns and villages where people would ordinarily be unable to hear music of their own selection, and for such a small amount of money." If it was not for jukeboxes, "thousands, yes, hundreds of thousands of merchants would be out of business." The Depression had made extra revenue a necessity. Demers went so far as to claim that if it were not for the jukeboxes, thousands of musicians would be out of work. His logic here was that they recorded for disks; the more records sold the more work for musicians. Mentioning the "trouble" then in the news over Europe and the Orient, Demers declared: "It is a well-known fact that in Italy, Germany, China and Japan they do not have the pleasures of the coin-operated music instruments because of ridiculous laws. I believe that if coin-operated music instruments were in operation in these countries like they are operated in the United States that the people would be thinking of happiness and good times instead of war."[122]

• That the rising fortunes of the juke segment of the industry came at least partly at the expense of the declining fortunes of the gambling machine segment was made clear by Walter Hurd as he editorialized over the industry's progress in 1937. He thought that year could be epitomized as the year of the payoff for the payout table games. Legal obstacles finally led to a serious decline in the market for those machines during the second half of 1937, and both manufacturers and operators felt the losses seriously. Games of chance provided quick money, and big money, for operators wherever such games could be run. The most important benefit of the payout types of machines to the coin industry itself, said Hurd, had been "this fact that operators could use them for quick money while investing in and paying for more stable machines such as the high-grade phonographs, vending machines, etc." Noting that both the juke and vendor divisions had often criticized the games of chance for damaging the reputation of the entire industry, Hurd stressed again that it was the "fast money" payout machines that made it possible for a large number of professional operators to invest in "high-grade music and vending machines."[123]

A common cry heard in the industry, from operators to the manufacturers, continued Hurd, was for something legal; that is, a game such as pinball, which met the legal definition of a game of skill. Over that year 1937, Hurd declared, it was the music division of the coin industry that was the most optimistic and generally successful branch of the industry. Expansion of the industry was due to the high quality of the machines, the work of the record companies in furnishing new records, "and to the more reputable nature of the business." Vending machines reportedly had a strong year, their first real comeback since the Depression blow of 1930.[124]

Emphasizing the success and popularity of the phonographs, and coin industry in general, was an account in *The Evening Telegram* of Superior, Wisconsin. An editorial observed that Nellie Taylor Ross, director of the U.S. Mint, reported the minting of coinage was running behind schedule: "And Mrs. Ross says one of the major reasons is the enormous increase in popularity of automatic phonographs and vending machines." She saw that as the chief factor in the coin shortage. It meant, thought the paper's editor, that it might be time to start taking the automatic phonograph seriously because "When any device throws the U.S. mint behind schedule it must be important."[125]

All observers agreed that the last half of the 1930s saw a huge rise in the growth and success of the box industry. Most of those observers also agreed on what the underlying factors were. One area of disagreement was over the relationship between the boxes and the record industry. Did the jukes make hits or follow popularity trends? What portion of disk output went to jukeboxes? Which was more dependent on which? Herb Allen was an executive with Columbia Records in 1936, and prior to that he had been with Brunswick Records. In his opinion, record manufacturing had been a precarious business, even in its peak years. A record was "strictly a luxury" in the home and could be dispensed with in time of need. In common with all luxury products, records desperately needed a stabilized market with an element of necessity in it. Six years earlier, he said, a few operators of coin phonographs, pioneers in a Prohibition-governed land, after being turned away by record labels and referred to retail dealers to buy their disks, built their routes to a point where their purchases could no longer be ignored. They became large enough and important enough to successfully demand a wholesale price on their record buys.[126]

When that point was reached, certain problems arose, continued Allen. First and most important was the question of the type of material that would make money for operators, compared to that which people would buy to take home. A basic difference here, he thought, was the conditions under which records were heard. For example, the "clever and sparkling arrangement" that sounded great in the glass-enclosed demonstration booth at the record store was totally lost in the "noisy and confusing atmosphere of the average location." On the other hand, the brilliance of performance that would get nickels often was "too blatant to be tolerated in the home." So records started to appear that were aimed directly at the operators' market. Artists were known as operators' or dealers' artists. At a later date, whole catalogs were devoted to one or the other market. Brunswick Records went so far as to set aside the Vocalion label [which featured only Black artists] for operators and to record for that label only such items as would be sure-fire money makers in phonographs. Artists such as Duke Ellington, Cab Calloway, Red Allen, Putney Dandridge, Wingy Mannone, and many others, some of whom were not known to the dealer and the retail record buyer, turned out disk after disk that went into thousands of units sold — to the box operator.[127]

Helping the operator to merchandise disks was the next step taken by the labels, said Allen. For the operator's "hit-and-miss" methods of presenting his program of records were substituted neat, printed program strips, giving the song titles and artists and supplied with each record. That alone had done much to increase the play on phonographs. Special lists were assembled to supply operators with weekly lists of new recordings and also lists of best-selling operators' records already released and tested. Contemplating the future of jukeboxes, which Allen saw as having much, much more growth, this record executive was made happy by one thought: the juke operator "must buy records."[128]

Billboard argued there was no doubt that the jukebox industry could claim a big share of credit for reviving interest in the record business and that industry had staged a strong comeback in the past few years after almost being destroyed by radio. *Billboard* agreed that radio had done a lot to cultivate a taste for, and an appreciation of, music; and that it had made name bands, but it could not give you your favorite song played by your favorite band "when you want it" like the phonograph could. That was why record sales in 1937 were "nearly five times" those of 1933, while the 1937 figure showed a "70% increase" over 1936. Actually, record sales for 1933, 1936, and 1937, were $6 million, $11 million, and $13 million, respectively.[129]

Nat Cohn, president of the New York-based operating concern Modern Vending Company, argued there had been an unprecedented rise in record sales, increasing steadily since the panic year of 1933. He attributed that rise directly to the fact that box operators were "selling" that music as fast as it was being supplied.[130]

Big-name artists of the time also acknowledged the power of the box industry. Bandleader Tommy Dorsey praised the operators, noting their power to make or break a record by putting it in their machines, or declining to do so. Dorsey described the operators as "a force not realized by the public and recognized only recently by the trade." Box operators were being showered with promotional material from the labels and artists "more than they realized ever existed. As a matter of fact, most of it never did exist until an analysis or two showed the powerful position of the operator in the industry." For his part, the leader said he tried to make contact with as many operators as possible in his travels, and for the prior two years had kept in touch with them through his promotion man, Jack Egan.[131]

Bandleader Jimmy Dorsey (brother of Tommy) gave a radio interview over station WDAS in Philadelphia in which he said, "Thanks to the music machines phonograph recordings have become more important to the band leader than the radio, which at one time was the all-important medium." He advised bandleaders starting out to go out and make a hit record because a band could play a hundred hotels from coast to coast and every ballroom in every town or present polished performances over the radio day in and day out for weeks and years and still be far from the top. However, if a band made a single record that was successful, it could become a sensation overnight. Dorsey also pointed out that in selecting tunes for recordings the wise bandleaders kept an eye out for the potential appeal of the record in music machines. However, he did not point out any specific characteristics.[132]

George Tucker, Associated Press staff writer, believed there were two major reasons why record sales in 1939 were 700 percent above those of 1933. Second reason was that young people were more interested in music and were buying more records. First reason was that across America there were "some 250,000 drop-a-nickel automatic phonographs which provide[d] a market for millions of records annually." At least Tucker had his numbers right. Record sales for 1939 were $44 million and only $6 million in 1933.[133]

Irving Mills was another record industry executive with an opinion. He pointed out the increasingly important role played by the juke "as the single greatest medium for talent." After pointedly observing, "It is not often that music men look kindly upon the automatic phonograph machines," he went on to agree with others, such as Jimmy Dorsey, that records played an increasingly important role in the creation of new star talent, especially in light of the dramatic increases in disk sales. Until 1933, that talent making was done mainly by radio, he believed. However, since then increased commercial time bought by sponsors diminished time allotted to aspiring artists on the radio. After 1933, radio was no longer interested in developing new stars; it took established stars from areas such as motion pictures, theater, and sports. Record reviews were then common in at least 100 daily newspapers and magazines. Mills stated, "there is a major factor in building a name through phonograph recordings: the automatic phonograph machine." Giving an estimate of 200,000 to 400,000 boxes in the United States, Mills went on to calculate that if a record was played only once a night in 10,000 spots and each had an average audience of 10 people and the record remained in a machine for two weeks, then the total audience was 1.4 million.[134]

In its November 24, 1939, issue, *Time* profiled bandleader Glenn Miller, the "New King of Swing." Miller declared that automatic phonographs were responsible for his rising to a top spot among musicians. The jukebox was reported to be the record industry's biggest customer. Of the 12 to 24 disks in each of the 300,000 United States jukeboxes, the *Time* account estimated from two to six were usually Glenn Miller's.[135]

Journalist Daniel Richman argued that record labels had to balance home sales and meeting the needs of "nickel-droppers." Certain artists and songs had universal appeal, but that output had to be augmented by disks designed specifically for the boxes, records that would have little in the way of home sales but which to a certain extent were the "lifeblood" of the phonograph field. "There are several artists recorded with only the machines in mind, and there is no question that the amount of hill-billy selections released is designed almost solely for the boxes," said Richman. In a bar, tavern, or restaurant, a record had to have a faster, brighter tempo. For example, a slow, dreamy ballad would lose out to something like "Beer Barrel Polka." As examples of a phonograph's ability to make hits, he cited "Sunrise Serenade" and "Begin the Beguine," each said to have become a leading sheet-music seller and radio song play only after initially becoming a hit on the boxes. "Beer Barrel Polka" was distinctly a machine-made hit while "I Cried for You" had been published and forgotten for 15 years only to become a hit after jukebox exposure.[136]

Jukes were also credited in one account for making people aware again of records and record players; they began to buy them for their homes. What happened was that "Every automatic phonograph [became] a sampling station where people [could] conveniently sample records they may not have heard ... eventually they will have a list of records to purchase at their music store." In a public place, a box was a "sort of co-operative enterprise" in that patrons heard not just what they had paid for, but, of course, the many other numbers selected by others. "And every automatic phonograph is a powerful sales station for all popular music and recordings.... They boost the entire field of popular music."[137]

Columnist Dorothy Killgallen stated, in a 1940 issue of *Cosmopolitan*, that the coin phonograph had supplanted radio as the primary maker of song hits. She argued that jukes were responsible for the initial success of "Sunrise Serenade," "Beer Barrel Polka," "Begin the Beguine," "My Reverie," "Oh, Johnny, Oh," and most of the Bing Crosby and Andrews Sisters numbers. If a song hit on the boxes then it hit "the popularity jackpot all over the country." Much of it was due, she said, to young people in high school and college who voted with their nickels. When Glenn Miller hit stardom with "Sunrise Serenade," Killgallen said there was no box in America that was not carrying that number, "and no jitterbug passed by without paying his nickel tribute."[138]

Eva Warner reported that the growing number of retail record stores and new record departments in larger stores in Buffalo was attributed to the "stimulating effect of automatic phonographs on the record business." In 1939, Buffalo had few record outlets, while just one year later it had 5 "important" record stores and 15 smaller establishments. A year earlier, most of the older record-selling outlets catered mainly to classical-music lovers. In 1940, those same firms had a 50/50 sales-volume split between popular and classical selections, which, they stated, was due to "the tonic effect of music boxes." Interviews with record retailers showed them to be almost unanimous in their favorable opinion of automatic phonographs. Retailers felt their sales were greatly influenced by boxes "because, almost invariably, when a number goes big on the music boxes it also becomes a top seller with them." More and more young people came into the stores and asked for numbers they heard on jukes: "They always insist on the recording that is going best on the music machines." Other proof mentioned by Warner was the rise of certain artists to big record sales long before they became well known through the radio networks, citing Glenn Miller, the Andrews Sisters, and so forth.[139]

The Buffalo Electric Company (distributor of Victor and Bluebird records) remarked that its sales volume was split 60/40 in favor of operators over retail record stores, operator purchases of a specific title preceded stores' buying by a "wide margin," and that a jukebox hit was sure to sell to retailers. A second Buffalo distributor (for Columbia, Brunswick, and Okeh) said his sales also split 60/40 for the operators with those people being the first to buy new numbers. Dick Levy, in charge of the record department for Buffalo department store W. Bergman Brothers, said there was usually two to three weeks between the purchase of a number by operators and the purchase of it by his store. Department store Adam, Meldrum

& Anderson established a record department over two years earlier but sales of popular records did not amount to much for the first year. Sears Roebuck opened its record department in the spring of 1940: "In fact, the added interest in records, stimulated greatly by phonographs on location, was the instigating influence that gave birth to this department." Neissner's downtown Buffalo department store installed a record counter in 1938 when the store was built. In the two years since that time, disk sales had increased three-fold. The record department at Grant's department store was opened in October 1939. Warner concluded that all record outlets testified to the important part the boxes had played in boosting record sales and that the jukes could "certainly determine music trends."[140]

Daniel Richman returned with an article about the jukes' power to make or break songs and artists because of sales to boxes and the juke influence on home sales. First, though, he looked back to see how a song became a hit in 1920, a period with strong record sales before radio and jukeboxes. Public performances were then the only way a tune could be universally presented to people. It meant people had to make up their own minds about which particular record to buy. Richman concluded, "It was more a case of individual likes, dislikes and tastes." That picture altered completely and, continued the reporter, the greatest single factor in determining what records a person wanted to have in his own home was the automatic phonograph machine. "It acts as a testing ground, a 'sampling station' for good and bad recordings, hits, near-hits, and flops." Richman apparently denied completely radio's role in hit making at any time in the 1920s or 1930s. He cited "Sierra Sue" by Bing Crosby, which was listed in the "Going Strong" category in *Billboard*'s juke popularity list in one week while the disk managed to make the retail sales list that week only barely, in a "poor ninth place." A month later, long after it had hit its juke peak, "Sierra Sue" slid into third place among retail top sellers.[141]

More national media attention came to the industry when Barry Ulanov wrote an article in the October 1940 issue of *American Mercury*. He mentioned, "You may never have heard the gaudy slot-coin phonograph machine, grinding out canned cacophony at a nickel per record" called by the name jukebox. By his estimate, there were 350,000 units in America and they took up 44 percent of United States production of popular records. The big bands that had reached stardom in the previous 20 months owed "their triumph primarily to these nickel-oiled behemoths." Continuing with his colorful description, Ulanov said: "The Juke is all-American, as star-spangled as the flag, as native as the hot dog ... these huge and garish purveyors of variegated rhythm dominate the popular music scene." According to his estimate, the industry grossed above $150 million a year. Credit the boxes, he said, for carrying Artie Shaw's "Begin the Beguine" to new highs in record popularity and for doing the same for a series of Glenn Miller numbers including "Moonlight Serenade," "Sunrise Serenade," "Stardust," "In the Mood," and "Tuxedo Junction." Not only did jukes account for nearly half of all record sales, but they acted as "a powerful impetus toward the sale of at least another 25 per cent" for home use. Referring to *Billboard's* juke popularity charts, Ulanov observed that the publication's predictions could hardly be anything but right "because Juke owners buy what it recommends."[142]

When reporter Harold Humphrey tried to analyze what made a hit record in the boxes, all he could do was generalize that past hits showed that "exceptional lyrics and vocal treatment, unique arrangements and pop artists of the moment are big contributing factors." Of course, that would be true in any medium. His list of the 10 biggest jukebox hits in recent years, in no particular order, contained "Marie" (Tommy Dorsey), "Begin the Beguine" (Artie Shaw), "Sunrise Serenade (Glen Gray), "In the Mood" (Glenn Miller), "Bei Mir Bist Du Schoen" (Andrews Sisters), "If I Didn't Care" (the Four Ink Spots), "Beer Barrel Polka" (Will Glahe), "Oh, Johnny, Oh" (Orrin Tucker and Bonnie Baker), "I'll Never Smile Again" (Tommy Dorsey), and "Daddy" (Sammy Kaye).[143]

Ben Katz owned the Gaiety Music Shop in New York where up until 1937 the biggest part of his sales were in sheet music. Although he sold a few records, "they were negligible compared to the volume of the sheet stuff." There was no mystery in that for him since he felt very few people then owned record players and so, naturally, had little use for records. Things then began to change with more of his customers asking for certain records and for specific bands and artists recording those numbers. Curious about the fact that most of those new record buyers knew exactly what they wanted, he asked them if they had heard those records, and if so, where. A few said they had heard them over radio stations, "But most of my customers explained that they had 'auditioned' the records by dropping nickels through the slots of the coin phonographs in their corner taverns." In buying records for his store, Katz found it necessary to watch as closely as possible what records were the biggest hits on the machines.[144]

By 1941, Katz was selling five times as many records as he had ever sold at any time of the sheet music. He believed that over 50 percent of his record sales were the direct result of the customer first hearing the number on a juke. Katz declared that if someone like Tommy Dorsey released a new record he could tell almost immediately if it had the stuff to be a big hit. When asked how he knew, he explained: "Well, there are many ways, and not the least is *The Billboard* itself. Through its many services, the record retailer, as well as the coin phonograph operator, is aided immeasurably in ordering the records to be stocked from week to week." By referring to those popularity charts in the publication, the whole situation became something of a self-fulfilling prophecy. Sales and popularity ratings flowed down from the chart lists to box operators and retailers, and finally to the customers, rather than flowing upwards from the patrons. The biggest reason behind the boom in record sales for the home, thought Katz, was the coin phonograph.[145]

Record production reached a low point of 10 million units in 1932. By 1939, production had reached 35 million, with the 1940 output at 55 million. Output for 1941 was estimated, late in that year, at 100 million disks. That was still short of the all-time high of 110 million, reached in 1929. Sales of classical records also reportedly gained steadily between 1935 and 1939. For 1941, the *Wall Street Journal* estimated jukeboxes would take around 22 percent of record output (22 to 25 million disks). *Billboard* took exception to that figure of 22 percent, believing that conservative trade estimates put the jukebox take of 1941 record output at 45 million. It did not dispute the estimated overall total of 100 million units.[146]

When American jukebox manufacturers looked abroad with thoughts of exporting their coin phonographs, the outlook was gloomy throughout this period. In 1935, reporter Helene Palmer took a trip to Europe to look for coin-operated equipment. She visited arcades, fairs, expositions, and so on in London, Paris, Brussels, and Holland. While Palmer reported seeing a large number of coin-operated amusement games, especially pins, in all those areas, she made no mention of looking for or finding jukeboxes.[147]

A survey of foreign markets in 1937 made by the United States Department of Commerce's Bureau of Foreign and Domestic Commerce concluded the foreign export of American-made jukes was not impossible but was subject to "great obstacles." Of all nations surveyed, the best markets were determined to be Great Britain, Greece, and Palestine. However, in Britain only a poor market was considered to exist in the big cities where "customers have not the time available to enjoy listening to music for very long at a time." The best places in the UK were thought to be those that served as holiday resorts in the summer. There were no jukeboxes then in Great Britain, but should they become established, it was thought it would be difficult if they operated at a price of more than one English penny (2 cents) per record. That was the usual coin used for amusement machines, and it was believed that any cost higher would be met with a strong degree of resistance.[148]

Greece already had its own version of a juke in the form of an itinerant musician who carried with him a record player with a large, old-fashioned speaker horn. Equipped with a few records, he set up his machine on café tables and played selections for a voluntary contribution of coins. Most of the middle- and upper-class restaurants in Greece had a live orchestra.

The high initial cost for a box made Greece a difficult market, but there were no legal roadblocks to the import of jukes, as there were in many nations. Palestine prohibited the import of coin-operated machines having gambling features but had no ban on boxes. A number of combined radio sets and record players had been sold for use in restaurants there, the majority of which were U.S. made. However, local dealers in record players and other musical instruments said they knew of no instance of a coin-operated phonograph in Palestine. Looking at foreign countries overall, the report stated that in most countries, public establishments such as restaurants and bars provided free entertainment in the form of music by radio or orchestra, and it was felt that the customers could not be induced to pay for something they got for nothing. The report noted that the few coin phonographs then in Europe were "of ancient vintage and have proved to be of unsatisfactory performance, so that it may be difficult to overcome the unpopularity resulting from their use."[149]

Journalist Hans Ullendorff spent three months in 1938 visiting eight European nations. He found lots of coin-operated vending machines, but reported the majority of them were of European origin. He found amusement machines to be scarce, concluding they were apparently not considered first-class entertainment abroad because "You could visit hotels of all classes everywhere in Europe and practically nowhere would you see a coin-operated skill game, a pin game or a bumper table." In his lengthy article, Ullendorff only briefly mentioned jukes. He urged the United States makers to try and export their machines despite obstacles such as import duties and currency restrictions found in some nations. Wondering why the sale abroad of U.S. jukes was so low, considering that no other nation made them as good as America did, he concluded, "The answer is simple: The prices are too high for the purchasing power in other countries." He saw no great increase in sales unless the manufacturers sharply reduced the cost of their machines.[150]

Otis Ferguson, in the April 5, 1939, issue of The New Yorker discussed a juke he discovered in Cristobal, Panama. It took an American nickel to play it, "And 5 cents is fairly important money among colored people down that way," he said. Reportedly, people were crowded around the machine in order to get their nickels into it.[151]

During an exposition of automatic machines held in Paris in 1939, the automatic coin-operated phonograph was demonstrated for the first time in public. French businessman M. Matry was enthusiastic, concluding his country was ripe and ready for the jukebox. He felt it could touch a clientele new and unlimited. Ladies waited in places where pin games were located while their escorts played those machines. That wait got irksome for them and soon player and lady left, he explained. "With the phonograph installed these same ladies will derive their pleasure in hearing their favorite music and allow the men to continue with the amusement game."[152]

One estimate was that Mexico had 3,000 boxes on location in 1940, all American-made. Two obstacles stood in the way of more exports. The low value of the peso made the jukes expensive to import. Second, it seemed that most locations turned the volume up as loud as it went, generating many complaints from neighbors. The government had to step in to tell operators that unless they kept the volume down to reasonable level, the machines would have to be removed. Operators were given six months by the government to find a solution to the problem.[153]

Six months later no solution to the loudness problem had been brought forward. As a result the government began to order phonographs to be shut off. An immediate problem for operators and location owners was how to raise the money necessary to gain an injunction to permit the boxes to operate. The consensus was that an injunction would be granted. Only the Federal District of Mexico was affected. However, they feared other parts of the country would take similar steps.[154]

Official figures on the export of jukeboxes first became available for 1939. Statistics were compiled by the Bureau of Foreign and Domestic Commerce. The U.S. Department of Commerce first recognized the importance of the music-machine business that year when it began keeping separate figures on the export of boxes for the first time. Prior to that, juke exports were lumped in with musical-instrument statistics. In 1939, importers in 34 foreign countries paid $640,974 for 3,589 music machines; the average price was $178.92, excluding freight. Fully 88 percent of those units were bought by coinmen in the Americas. Mexico led the way, buying 1,665 machines (46 percent of total exports) for $279,482 (average price of $167.86); Canada bought 1,092 units (30 percent) for $195,232 ($178.88). Sales to other South and Central American nations amounted to another 12 percent. Mexico was considered to be a good market because no mechanical changes had to be made in the equipment for it to operate on Mexican current, unlike Europe. Also, import duty was only 10 cents US per kilo. At that rate, duty on a Wurlitzer model 616 was about $13 (about 286 pounds). Europe took only 11 percent of total exports, but World War II destroyed any hopes for big sales in Europe. Great Britain took 189 machines, Finland, 37; and Sweden, 28. Another technical change exported jukeboxes had to undergo was to have the coin-receiving mechanism adjusted to the size of various foreign coins. The low average price paid in foreign countries indicated that the vast majority of exported units, perhaps all, were used jukeboxes.[155]

Attempts to determine how many jukeboxes were on location in America, how much the industry grossed, how much an operator made, and so on were always difficult to make and often contradictory. One early estimate, made in January 1937, put the number of boxes in operation in the United States and Canada at around 400,000. However, that was surely too high, at least at that time.[156]

The first effort to take a stab at estimating financial numbers for the industry appeared in the trade publication *Variety* in July 1939. It reported that an estimate made by the National Association of Performing Artists of the annual gross on coin phonographs was $175 million. That group checked numerous sources and concluded that a machine had to gross a minimum of $10 a week, stating; "At anything less than that an operator cannot afford to allow it to remain in a location." Also, ads in trade journals were said to cite average grosses at from $7 to $14 per box per week. Thus, a machine grossed $520 a year. Looking at the question of how many boxes existed, it was noted that four years earlier the manufacturers conceded a minimum of 250,000; "Even then there were estimates as high as 400,000." However, since the greatest growth in the industry had been in the past four years, for the purposes of this calculation a "conservative" estimate of 350,000 was used. At $520 a year 350,000 machines would gross $182 million. To be conservative that was rounded down to $175 million.[157]

One year later, *Variety* returned with revised figures for the industry, this time based on its own estimates. Now it argued that the yearly take was $150 million. Noting that estimates of the number of boxes ranged between 300,000 and 400,000 — with Mills Novelty saying 550,000 — *Variety* based its calculations on 300,000 machines. Each box in large metropolitan areas like New York, Chicago, Philadelphia, and Detroit had to take in no less than $12 a week; in less populated areas the figure was smaller, but it was never less than $7. Assuming $12 a week led to a figure of $187.2 million a year; if the $7 figure was used the total was $109.2 million. Striking an average, the publication declared the gross annual take of jukeboxes in America to be $150 million. An average box in New York reportedly took in $15 a week, and some took in as much as $50 per week.[158]

Looking at other aspects of the industry, *Variety* put the average price of a juke at $300. Assuming 300,000 boxes in total and a replacement rate by operators of 25 percent of their machines each year, it meant that $22.5 million was spent on boxes annually. Operators figured they had to spend 7 percent of a machine's income for new records, meaning that $10.5 million was spent each year on new disks. Four makers dominated the industry: Seeburg, Mills, Rock-Ola, and Wurlitzer. Usually the operators put their units in locations on the basis of a 50/50 split of gross receipts with the location owner. Machines cost operators about $150 for a table model, $190 for a deluxe table model, $350 for a standard upright, and $400 for a deluxe upright. When new boxes were purchased, operators were financed, in the same way as were buyers of new cars. That the life of an average juke was four years was as much from tax treatment as from fact, since 25 percent depreciation a year was allowed as a business expense. Manufacturers brought out new models each year and kept sending circulars announcing those new models to location owners so the latter would badger operators for those new models. Said *Variety*: "It is that demand, more than anything else, that accounts for 25% replacement each year." Old machines were either rebuilt or exported to South America, Mexico, and Europe.[159]

Variety also reported that the majority of jukes were owned by large operators who had strings of 500 or more. One in New Jersey had 1,600 units. Fifty boxes was said to be the minimum needed to generate a decent income. Each 50 jukes required one person to service them. Therefore, if an operator had 500 units, his firm usually had 10 servicemen, each with a car; two traveling repair men, one shop man; and two or three people employed in the office. Most boxes then held between 20 and 24 selections, with each of those records good for 125 to 150 plays. A usual menu on a 20-selection box had ten numbers from the Hit Parade, two or three novelties, four or five old-time favorites, and the rest pop standards. The biggest all-time hit on the phonographs was said to be "Beer Barrel Polka," followed by "Stardust." The favorite singer on the boxes was Bing Crosby; Decca was the leading label. Records that retailed at 35 cents were sold to operators at 19 cents, 50 cent disks at about 28 cents, and those that retailed at 75 cents went to the operators for 47 cents. Used records were disposed of by the operators to outlet stores for two or three cents each. In turn, those places sold them for nine or 10 cents. Boxes were serviced and collections made once a week. On each of those calls, five selections a week were usually changed, on a 20- or 24-selection unit. The modernness and efficiency of the jukebox industry, in 1940, caused *Variety* to recall that automatic music machines were nothing new: "Almost anyone can remember way back when every ice-cream parlor had an old Wurlitzer chute for nickels at each counter. There were no selectors on the early devices and a 5¢ piece might draw anything...."[160]

Around the same time, *Billboard* declared there were 400,000 boxes in use. For 1939, the five leading manufacturers were said to have produced and sold 70,000 machines valued at $21 million. According to their figures, the average operator owned 70 machines valued at $10,500. Thus, the country's 400,000 boxes had a value of $60 million and were owned by 5,700 operators. Fifty machines were said here, also, to be the maximum number of units one serviceman could handle. Observing that phonographs provided "some cash returns" to location owners, the account added, "However, the essential value of the music machine is its power to draw and hold customers." This report calculated that an average of 1.8 records were added each week to each juke, or, the operators bought 720,000 records per week for the 400,000 machines—37,440,000 records per year.[161]

At the other end of estimates was one by the financial editor of *The Buffalo Evening News*, which first appeared in that newspaper. Editor Hilton Hornaday said there were 300,000 boxes in America grossing $50 million annually. That would average out to only $3.21 per week per box. Hornaday also estimated 60 million records were sold annually and that 30 million went to jukeboxes. He added that the 3,000 jukes in Buffalo and Erie County took close to 6,000 records and grossed $750,000 a year, for an average of $5 per box per week. In reporting this story, *Billboard* was most annoyed that the Buffalo paper used the "unfavorable term 'juke boxes.'"[162]

Billboard clung tenaciously to not using the word "jukebox." However, the industry got much more national media attention in 1940 and 1941, most of it celebrating the industry, its successes, and achievements. All of them happily used the work "jukebox," as the other important trade paper, *Variety*, had already done. While *Billboard* would resist using that word for some time to come, it was a futile effort—the word was here to stay. *Newsweek* announced, "In an estimated 325,000 American bars, railway stations, drugstores, excursion boats, and roadhouses up and down the land, the jookboxes boom forth song." Note the unusual spelling of the word.

Wurlitzer was said to make more machines than all if its four closest competitors combined. Referring to the role the boxes played in the sales boom in records, *Billboard* went on to say that each machine used 275 records a year. Given their estimate of 325,000 boxes, it would have meant jukeboxes took 89.3 million new records a year—a figure that was far too high. People in the South liked hillbilly numbers on the phonographs, a large Swedish population around Minneapolis preferred Swedish folk dances; jitterbugs from coast to coast went for Glenn Miller, Artie Shaw, and other swing bands. James Broyles, president of the Automatic Phonograph Manufacturers Association, said in 1939 the big five makers sold 70,000 units, priced from $150 to $425, to 230 distributors, who in turn sold them to the 6,500 operators in America. Here it was reported that the average operator had around 50 boxes (ranging from 10 to 1,500). The most popular area in America for the machines was the Northeast. Some machines grossed as little as $2 a week, the best ones took in $25 and more. Concluded the article, "An orchestra or singer can be made overnight with jookbox popularity."[163]

Billboard's Walter Hurd used the 400,000 figure as his estimate. Then he went on to enthuse, "Phonographs are now almost standard equipment in these small places of business ... they are a modern necessity." Hurd related that the makers sold their machines to 146 established distributors (who averaged eight employees each). Those distributors sold the units to at least 15,000 operators. "The extra food and beverage sales made by locations is enormous," said the editor. "In fact, no small percentage of the locations would go out of business if it were not for music machines." Back in 1935, Hurd estimated that 120,000 jukes (priced from $250 to $400) were produced and sold. During 1934 to 1936 manufacturers sold as many boxes as they could produce because every place wanted one. Any establishment that didn't have a machine on site faced the worry that customers would just walk away. Thus, almost every one of the boxes produced in that three-year period went to a new location. There was no such thing as an obsolete phonograph. In the latter part of 1936 and into 1937, industry leaders feared a saturation point would be reached. However, mechanical improvements "and constant redesigning" became so extensive that the industry attained stability on "the same basis as the auto industry." Thus, for the years 1937 through 1940, the industry produced 70,000 to 90,000 units per year. But there was an important difference in where the boxes produced in that later period were destined: "These have not been placed in new locations as much as they have been used to replace old models. The older phonographs are either junked or in many cases have been shipped to other shores." Hurd was admitting a saturation point had been reached at the very end of the 1930s. However, the industry was saved from any serious decline in sales and production by introducing extensive model changes and convincing operators to buy new machines and replace existing ones, even when the latter were not in any way obsolete and the new ones contained no technological improvements. Junking or exporting those replaced machines was important since it limited the number of used boxes that could be sold directly to location owners. Such a move would have threatened the existing industry structure.[164]

A few months later when Hurd reviewed the year 1940, with regard to the coin-machine industry, he mentioned that box estimates ranged from 400,000 (by general trade sources) down to 250,000 (provided by the Phonograph Manufacturers Association) but that no one knew for certain. It was known that 14,000 machines were in use in Chicago and its suburbs. That year featured a great increase in the use of accessories such as wall boxes, bar boxes, wireless and wired speakers, and so forth; items that made it more convenient for patrons to deposit their coins. Also, the business was "disturbed or honored by a great amount of newspaper and magazine publicity during the year 1940." Much of it, grumbled Hurd, came from freelancers who did not know the business very well. The sorest point from that situation was that many of those articles listed "exaggerated" earnings for jukes, something that tended to attract taxing authorities. Another type of publicity that made the industry nervous during 1940, added Hurd, was the use of the term "juke box." The trade tried hard without success to promote the use of the term "music box." So the trade thought perhaps it should accept the term and make the best of it. Government agencies were asked to trace the origin of the word and see "if a favorable human interest story could be found. Reports indicated that it originated in Europe, perhaps Vienna, and that it has a very favorable and historic background." None of that, of course, was true. Phonograph manufacturers estimated box production at 53,000 units in 1938, 70,000 in 1939, and 48,000 in 1940.[165]

Writing in *Reader's Digest*, Geoffrey Parsons and Robert Yoder said of the juke, "Not only has it made every corner tavern and highway restaurant a poor man's night club but it is to be heard in dance halls, beauty parlors, filling stations, bus depots." The sudden rise of the phonograph was due in part to the fact that it would "play a command performance of anybody's favorite tune at any time of day or night — and without the interruption of radio commercials." The authors continued, "and its popularity helps explain why the United States speeded production at the mint last year to meet a shortage of small coins." Parsons estimated the box count to be at least 295,000. Noting that the boxes of the early 1930s were "unostentatious," played 12 selections, and cost about $250, Parsons said that next came the era of "luxury light-up" boxes. "The juke of 1941 is as big as a restaurant refrigerator, has a soundproof, slug-proof coin chute, and costs from $300 to $500. It plays 20, 24 or 40 selections, accepts nickels, dimes, or quarters, is plastered with translucent plastics and colored lights, and can be heard the length of a city block." While in the early days the operator took a majority of the box receipts, in 1941, with increased competition and poaching, "the location commonly retain[ed] 50 percent." In a good location a box took in $10 or $15 a week; in a very good location the gross was $35, and a few boxes even reached as much as $90 a week. "Stops with hostesses to coax, 'Put a quarter in the juke box, honey,' do particularly well." Year after year, said Parsons, Bing Crosby probably earned more money for the jukes than any other performer.[166]

Walter Hurd returned to report that by around the middle of 1941 somewhere from 10 to 30 percent of box locations had complete music installations; that is, a phonograph and the auxiliary wall and bar boxes and auxiliary speakers. In fact, that trend had brought at least three manufacturers into the field of producing auxiliary equipment. However, a war-related materials shortage was developing. One factory had scheduled production of 20,000 wall boxes and bar units over a period of a few months. Because of shortages in material it only produced 8,000. At this time there were six juke makers: Wurlitzer, AMI, John Gabel Company, Mills Novelty, Rock-Ola, and J. P. Seeburg. All but Wurlitzer (North Tonawanda, New York) were located in Chicago. Those firms all produced jukes as well as a full line of auxiliary wall and bar boxes, speakers, and so forth. Additionally, Packard Manufacturing (Indianapolis), Buckley Music Systems, and J. H. Keeney & Company (both in Chicago) produced auxiliary equipment. Estimates of how much the complete music installations increased the play varied from 10 percent to as much as 100 percent. Whereas operators had formerly planned to pay for a box in 12 months, it then required from 18 to 24 months due to higher prices and extra costs for the auxiliary equipment. "Many operators still use amusement games, when conditions are favorable, to make quick money to pay for their phonograph equipment." Hurd still estimated 400,000 boxes and 250,000 wall and bar boxes in use. He said there were 250 distributing firms, dealing with 7,000 music-machine operators. Record output in 1938 was said to be 33 million (15 million of them taken by phonograph operators); in 1939, 60 million (31 million); in 1940, 75 million (37.4 million); in 1941, an estimated 100 million (45 million).[167]

Hurd also presented some detailed area reports. With a population of 264,151, Birmingham had about 1,250 boxes, one for every 211 people. In Montgomery, population 78,008, there was one juke to every 156 residents, whereas the state of Alabama had 3,500 phonographs, one to 810 people. Birmingham had 15 box operators, none of whom operated jukes exclusively. Ten percent of Birmingham locations had complete music systems, which was estimated to have boosted patronage about 20 percent. Those operators bought an average of 1.5 records per machine per week. Minneapolis had a population of 489,971 and around 1,000 jukes, a ratio of one to every 490 residents. Twenty phonograph operators were located there, and eight of them operating music boxes exclusively. Only 5 percent of the locations had complete music systems. Operators bought approximately three new records per week per machine and their operating costs were estimated at $3.50 per box per week. Denver, population 318,415, had a box total of 800 and had one juke for every 400 people. With 2,500 machines in Colorado, the state ratio was 1 to 500. Thirty-five music operators called Denver home; ten of them operated jukes exclusively. About 25 percent of the locations had complete music systems, and some operators reported the boost in business from these systems to be as much as 50 percent. Operators purchased three new records a week per machine and sustained operating expenses of $1.50 a week for each jukebox.[168]

Another highly enthusiastic account came from Maynard Reuter who wrote: "Trying to find a town without an automatic phonograph these days would be something like trying to find one without some sort of baseball diamond…. For in the brief span of less than a decade the automatic phonograph has become as American as baseball. It ranks right up there with the hot dog, ice cream and other bits of Americana as part and parcel of our American way of life." He also used the figure of 400,000 machines as his estimate of the number of boxes on location in America — one for every 325 people in the United States. In New York City there were about 12,000 machines; 6,500 in Detroit; 750 in Miami; 1,600 in New Orleans; 400 in Greensboro, North Carolina; 3,000 in Baltimore; 1,250 in Birmingham; 7,500 in Chicago; 2,400 in Milwaukee; 1,000 in Minneapolis; 2,500 in Cleveland; 1,500 in Buffalo; 500 in Des Moines; 800 in Denver; 350 in Spokane; 1,000 in Seattle; and 4,000 in Los Angeles. In addition to the more familiar bars, grills, restaurants, and similar establishments, Reuter declared the boxes "essential furnishings" in an ever-growing number of night clubs, swank cocktail lounges, hotels, roller rinks, dairy bars, school recreation rooms, country clubs, drive-ins, bowling alleys, "and even in beauty shops."[169]

As recently as four years earlier, Reuter continued, the industry was approaching the saturation point. However, the economy picked up considerably as war work and preparations began, and hundreds of new locations sprang up to cater to the needs of the new workers. Engaging in more than a little exaggeration, Reuter concluded, "when historians at some future date record the contributions which inventive genius made to the social and economic betterment of this country during the 20th century they will do well to rank the automatic phonograph on the same level with the automobile, the airplane and all other inventions which have contributed so much to our progress." Jukes were that important because "when trouble besets a nation, whether it comes in the form of war, plague, flood or famine, music has always been a leveling influence to help people keep their feet on the ground and maintain a true perspective."[170]

Lewis Nichols, in the New York Times Magazine, wrote about the big rise in the juke industry and predicted, "Give it a couple more good seasons like last Winter and last Summer and it will be one of the nation's larger industries — like automobiles or the movies." He believed the box total to be 300,000 units and the industry annual gross to be $90 million. Industry profit was, officially, he said, "$10 to $15 per year per box, which was a five percent return on investment, the same as on "conservative railroad bonds." Unofficially, though, that profit was "more or much more." On the whole, he felt jukebox music followed the music on the radio and that jukes did not make hits but simply added to the sales totals of records made hits through other outlets. Nichols was one of the few writers to report on problems facing the industry. Three problems he found were taxation from various levels of governments; copyright, wherein jukes paid no royalties to artists; and "the expression juke box." He declared it a Southern term: a barbecue stand was known in certain parts as a jooke joint; in a jooke joint stood an automatic phonograph; therefore, a jooke box, a jook box, a juke box. "The trade considers the words as damaging and unpleasant, but an almost endless campaign to avoid it seems to be getting nowhere."[171]

Between 1934 and 1940, the juke industry enjoyed phenomenal success. Boxes moved from approximately 25,000 units all the way up to approximately 400,000 machines. The coin-machine industry as a whole enjoyed a similarly huge success. Considering all this happened during the Depression, when most industries were declining significantly, the feat was more astonishing. There were a few problems, however, looming on the horizon. One was the general reputation of the industry, one was the copyright situation, and a third was taxation at various levels of governmental jurisdiction. Mostly the amounts of tax, or license fee, were small, but an industry that revolved around nickels hated to part with even one. Taxing jukeboxes began early at both the city and state level. In the spring of 1935, both houses of the Texas legislature approved a bill providing a $10 annual tax per coin machine, on all machines operated by a one-cent coin up to and including a five-cent coin, and $20 per machine operated by a sum greater than five-cents. A provision of the bill provided for the confiscation of machines if the tax was not paid. Also, the machine owner was required to attach the tax receipts to the machine. Coin machines were defined, and Section 1A of the bill listed specific machines under that definition. "The following are expressly included within said term: Phonograph, electrical piano, electrical battery, graphophone, target pistol, miniature golf machine, miniature football machine, miniature baseball machine, miniature race track machine, stereoscopic machine, gum machine, candy machine, handkerchief machine, sandwich machine, sanitary drinking cup machine, marble machine, marble table machine, marble shooting machine or marble machine of any description." Gas meters, pay telephones, cigarette vending machines, and pay toilets were exempted from the tax because they already paid a tax, except pay toilets.[172]

Twenty-nine Texas music operators contested the legality of that bill. They argued that phonographs should not be classed, and taxed, as coin-vending machines but, rather, be defined as service vendors and therefore not taxed at all. That suit was heard by the 53rd District Court at the end of October 1935. Agreeing with the music operators, the court granted a permanent injunction against the imposition of the tax on phonographs. It was a short-lived victory as Texas later successfully imposed a tax on boxes.[173]

Another early effort was made in 1937 when the Pennsylvania legislature introduced a bill that called for a tax on each phonograph on location in the state; the fee amounted to half the price of a liquor license. Immediately, the Pittsburgh Phonograph Machine Operators' Association was busy lobbying against the proposal. This, of course, was one of the reasons operators tried from the earliest days to form local, state, regional, and national trade groups.[174]

Minneapolis enacted the Mechanical Amusement Ordinance in 1935, which was aimed generally at pinball games. Under that provision, the license fee was $25 a year and the machine had to be operated on chips with no cash value. As far as jukes were concerned, nothing happened for two years. Then suddenly, without warning, the Minneapolis license inspector's office detailed four men to go out and tell locations to disconnect jukes in their places and leave them disconnected until a license was placed on each machine. Apparently somebody in the office gave the ordinance a very thorough reading. Phonograph operators fought that change in direction by pointing out a box was not an "amusement device operated by a coin." Drafters of the measure were consulted. They agreed with the music operators, and the boxes were again left alone.[175]

In May 1938 coin phonographs were exempted from the Arizona state luxury tax as applied to coin-operated games in a decision by the Arizona State Supreme Court, reversing a decision by the Maricopa County Superior Court. The decision described the music machines as selling a necessity rather than a luxury and declared they were not games of chance. In the unanimous decision, the three judges said they were of the opinion the real intent of the Arizona legislature was to tax mechanical games that were operated by means of depositing a coin or token in a slot and not upon mechanical devices not in the nature of games "which furnish to the consumer something of value for a fixed price, whether that something be tangible or intangible in its nature."[176]

Hull, Quebec, Judge B. Bedard ruled that music machines could be taxed by the city on the same basis as peanut and chewing-gum vending machines and issued summonses for 26 shopkeepers who had automatic music machines on their premises. He declared that since music was a commodity in the sense that it satisfied a need, it could be sold. And the machines supplying that commodity could be called automatic vendors and taxed.[177]

Savannah, Georgia, city officials changed their minds and revised a city tax on boxes after meeting with a delegation of operators. Originally the city was to impose a $10 annual tax on each machine. Operators argued they were not objecting to a reasonable tax but considered $10 to be prohibitive and exorbitant. Due to the frequent changing of models, upkeep, changing of records, robbery from machines, use of slugs, and other factors, said the operators, it was important to realize that phonographs did not yield the "lucrative income popularly believed." They said the average weekly gross per machine was only about $6, of which the operator kept half. The coin men declared that the $10 tax, applied to the machine's location and not the box itself would subject an operator to paying $50 or $60 a year per machine as a box had to be moved on average five times or so a year. Machine operators presented an alternative tax proposal that called for a payment of $200 a year by an operator — regardless of the number of boxes owned — plus the issuance of a permit for location of a machine; the latter to cost $1 and be valid for six months.[178]

Two restaurant owners in Hartford, Connecticut, were charged with violating a Sunday law in that city when they allowed dancing, to jukes, after midnight on Saturday. However, Judge Edward C. Carroll of the East Hartford Town Court dismissed the accused when he decided that dancing in eating establishments after midnight on Saturdays was not a violation of the Sunday observance law when music was furnished by a phonograph and paid for by the patrons.[179]

Late in 1940, Chicago City Council legalized jukes after they had been silenced for a number of days following the discovery of a statute prohibiting entertainment slot machines. Chicago's mayor and council agreed that the general public wanted the music-box entertainment and were in no mind to thwart the desires of the "spending public."[180]

The Federal Revenue Act of 1941 imposed a tax on coin-operated amusement and gaming devices, among other items. The Internal Revenue Department ruled the measure did not apply to coin-operated phonographs. A 5 percent luxury tax was imposed on all admissions, cover charges, service charges, refreshments, and merchandise of roof gardens, cabarets, or any similar places furnishing a performance for profit. It meant that a location that provided an orchestra and also reserved floor space for dancing had to collect 5 percent of everything a customer bought. Locations that depended solely on coin-operated phonographs for patron entertainment were exempt whether nor not they provided space for dancing.[181]

All of these attempts, and the many others, to tax and license the boxes, and control or ban other parts of the coin-machine industry, appalled the trade. *Billboard* Amusement Machines section editor Walter Hurd argued that all the branches of the coin-machine industry had to ask for more liberal changes in some of the long-accepted views of business and public morals. "The price we must pay as an industry is to become out-and-out liberals in practice and policy." Hurd saw liberal awards on amusement games and fair value to the customer on all types of machines extending "to liberal views of the social and economic questions of the day." He went on to say, "There are members of the coin machine industry who ask the public to be liberal toward our business and our machines, and yet they themselves are reactionary on every modern question."[182]

Hurd pointed out that Homer Capehart had recently offered a watchword not just for the music division but for the entire industry when the Wurlitzer executive declared: "Poor people put money into your phonographs. Poor people have a right to the economical entertainment which you offer them. Poor people have a right to enjoy good music with their beer or their sandwiches. If we emphasize this great truth it may help to defeat unfair taxation and legislation." Hurd thought that was a bold statement of policy in favor of the masses. The phonograph and coin-operated games all offered economical entertainment to the common man. Therefore, if the industry seized upon Capehart's statement "as a slogan of public policy it could be developed into a real program of liberal social progress. It would be the strongest argument against the misguided form of paternalism which seeks to regulate and control the morals of the masses by law because 'they are poor.'" Also appealing to Hurd was that Capehart had taken a "courageous step" by urging operators to pay good wages. In the opinion of the editor, rather than antagonize labor or the masses of the people, it would be better for industries like the coin-machine trade to take a bold step "in favor of the mass of voters of good wages and better living conditions for them and for the most progressive issues of the time."[183]

While the copyright situation would bedevil the juke industry for decades, the music-licensing organizations were in a weak position in the 1930s and offered little challenge to the juke trade. Music boxes were also indirectly involved in copyright activity concerning record labels. In 1937, the Music Publishers' Protective Association was investigating an alleged practice among certain record manufacturers of leasing their product to the jukebox trade, thus avoiding the need to pay royalties. Under legal provisions, the record label had to pay royalties on the records it "manufactures and sells." By supplying the box industry with disks on a leasing basis, the record labels, felt the music publishers, may have been circumventing their obligations to the copyright holders of the music.[184]

Later that same year, the major record firms, including RCA, Decca, Brunswick, and Columbia, announced that henceforth their record information labels and sleeves (envelopes) would carry a label stating their records were only for noncommercial use on record players in homes and that the original purchaser agreed the disks would not be resold or used for any other purposes. Apparently that move was in response to vigorous protests from the American Federation of Musicians (AFM) who threatened to refuse to permit its members to make additional recordings unless the abuses complained of were corrected. However, the labels on the disks extended a free, non-exclusive license to use any of the records manufactured by it on coin-operated phonographs in the United States and Canada, "except in locations to which an admission fee is charged or where musicians were formerly employed."[185]

The real copyright battle, of course, was the one waged by the music-licensing groups to have jukeboxes come under coverage of the Copyright Act of 1909. Among other things, that legislation declared that any public performance of music for profit required a royalty fee be paid to the copyright holders. However, a specific exemption was granted in that act, which said, "The reproduction or rendition of a musical composition by or upon coin-operated machines shall not be deemed a public performance for profit unless a fee is charged for admission to the place where such reproduction or rendition occurs." Reporter Andrew Weinberger noted the contradictions inherent in the act when he observed that when a location owner had a juke on site to entertain his customers and stimulate patronage, he was indeed rendering a public performance for profit. That location owner would be held accountable under the law, if not for the exemption clause. If a location owner, said Weinberger, were to accept a coin from a patron and in return play a disk on a home record player he had brought to his bar that was not coin-operated he would be subject to intervention by the copyright owner, similarly if there was no receipt of money; or if the location owner simply played his home machine. Bills occasionally surfaced in Congress to alter the situation but then died, such as happened in 1940 when the Shotwell bill fell into limbo. Generally, such bills focused on one of two actions: removing the juke exemption clause and/or adding some special fee or cost on to each record played on a box or a fee on the box itself. Weinberger believed that no bill would ever be passed into action that brought a material detriment to the trade, since coin-phonograph operation was "too important an industry."[186]

In 1940 *Billboard* took a look at the groups arrayed against the juke trade in the copyright issue and concluded there was little to fear. One group was the AFM, who, because of loss of employment for its musician members, had a "venomous feeling" toward everything connected with automatic phonographs. However, the AFM had taken no action against the trade, or even tried to. First, the AFM would have to get Congress to legislate that the performing rights of the work were vested in the musicians who recorded it, similar to the way that the American Society of Composers, Authors and Publishers (ASCAP) controlled the performing rights of the people who created music and lyrics; that is, a new category of copyright holder would have to be created. For example, a song such as "My Way" had copyright vested in the people who wrote the music and lyrics and the music publisher. AFM wanted to see, say, Frank Sinatra's version of "My Way" vest the singer with the performing rights to the number for his rendition — similarly for every other singer who recorded "My Way." This would be in addition to the mechanical royalties every singer got for each copy of a number that was sold. *Billboard* believed there was no chance of that happening anytime soon or later. They were right.[187]

Only music publishers were allowed to be members of the Music Publishers' Protective Association (MPPA). Initially, that organization wanted to tax location owners a certain yearly sum per phonograph, say $1 a month or $10 a year, to use its material. That idea was dropped because it was thought unlikely it could be achieved. A second idea was to set up royalty payments on records in excess of what had been paid to publishers by recording labels since the disk industry started. All along, record labels had been paying music publishers, whose product they recorded 1.5 cents in royalties per side on a record retailing for 35 cents, and two cents per side on a disk sold for 75 cents. Whether the buyer was a citizen buying a record for his home record player or a juke operator buying it for multiple use on one of his boxes to generate income for himself and the location owner, that royalty fee folded into the price was the same. If the MPPA won, they wanted to institute royalties as high as 5 cents or 10 cents per disk side. Those publishers would not raise the royalty payments on records destined only for home use. *Billboard* thought they had no chance either then or in the future. Again, it was right.[188]

The third group discussed was Broadcast Music Incorporated (BMI), which had only just been formed as a music-licensing organization and was backed by the radio networks and radio stations. ASCAP supplied 98 percent of all music used by radio. The current five-year contract between ASCAP and radio (due to expire on the last day of 1940) called for radio networks and stations to pay 5 percent of their income (advertising revenue) to ASCAP in return for permission to play material from ASCAP's catalog. With renewal talks well underway, the networks balked at ASCAP's proposal, a sliding scale of royalties ranging from 3 percent to 7.5 percent. In an attempt to free itself from what it saw as dependence on ASCAP, the networks created BMI, which was attempting to build a catalog of music sufficiently strong so that the networks could indeed be freed. Agreement was not reached in renewal talks and a strike began in 1943, wherein ASCAP withdrew all its material from radio. That strike lasted about a year and most of the music aired over the radio were numbers so old that copyright had expired and they were in the public domain. BMI did survive, and over decades it would grow large enough — by then sold off and independent from radio — to rival ASCAP. However, in 1940, when it was only months old, *Billboard* considered it no threat at all to the jukeboxes.[189]

Much older, and thoroughly dominant in the music-licensing field, was ASCAP, which turned 25 as of October 1939. Still, survival had not been easy, and much of its energy and resources went into the fight to maintain itself. It had to establish itself legally in every state one by one. Most of the time that meant protracted legal action, since one or more opposition groups would fight on the ground that ASCAP was a monopoly and operating in restraint of trade. At this time, ASCAP had prevailed legally in 42 of 48 states. In those states having ASCAP laws in effect, an ASCAP license had to be taken out by every establishment using music in a public performance for profit. ASCAP, and other groups, were then active in seeking the support of Congress to remove the juke exemption from the Copyright Act or, failing that, to require phonograph owners to pay a special license for the right to use copyrighted music in public locations, say $10 a year per machine. While observing that all such past and present measures that had come before Congress were then dead or dormant, *Billboard* believed ASCAP could be a "potent threat," but not then, as war preparations were taking precedent.[190]

Despite that the coin machine industry was one of the very few that enjoyed tremendous growth — and increased employment — in the Depression 1930s, the industry was regularly slammed, at the general level and at the music division specifically, for creating unemployment. Walter Hurd admitted unemployment was real and widespread, feeling it boiled down to the pros and cons of the machine age. "You can't tell a man out of a job that there isn't something wrong with the machine age. He doesn't know what it is, but he knows there is something wrong." Still, part of the progress of the machine age was the prominence of coin machines. He felt the "vending machine and music divisions of the trade are most open to attack," and were most easily made the victims of "cleverly disguised propaganda." Any group opposed to them could easily develop material "which purports to show that such machines add to unemployment by replacing human beings with mechanical devices."[191]

Editorializing on the topic in 1937, Hurd recalled the super promotional days prior to 1930 when vending machines were given wide publicity. More than one manufacturer of vending machines, in his publicity, hailed the day "when automatic vending machines would displace clerks in stores, etc." All that was "foolish" publicity in the first place, and it stirred up organized opposition to vendors by organized labor. Automatic phonographs had only recently felt the cry of unemployed musicians, said Hurd, agreeing their problem was a real one. "But the only investigations that have been made so far indicate the automatic phonograph is not the real cause." The trouble, he thought, lay deeper, but in many cases the box "may be an aid to the musicians and the locations that employ them. In other words, it is a trying situation in which clever agitation might arouse strong public sentiment against the phonographs." Those broad statements by the editor contained no data or evidence to support the idea that jukeboxes aided musicians.[192]

Three years later, Ben Boldt, advertising manager for Rock-Ola, said that many of the jobs formerly enjoyed by musicians— in the pit of a legitimate theater, in cinema houses, on the stage of vaudeville houses, and so on — had disappeared. Then he went on to say the 300,000 jukes in the phonograph industry brought opportunities for musicians. Boldt offered no facts or details. The implied argument seemed to be it was because of all the records juke owners bought and caused to be bought for home use. Trouble with that was that musicians got a specific sum for participating in a recording, whether the disk went on to sell a thousand or a million copies. Jukes did contribute to unemployment for musicians, but so did a lot of other things. Their sole lobby group, the AFM, was, however, fighting a losing rearguard action and would soon become a spent force.[193]

Generally, jukes did not get much bad press in the early period of their history. The same could not be said for the coin-machine industry overall. It left the phonograph industry worried about spillover effects. A May 1937 *Billboard* editorial dealt with the subject of the "noise"—bad publicity—that was made at intervals about the "slot machine racket." A fear was that the average citizen might believe that where there was so much smoke, there must be some fire. "Many other types of coin-operated machines seem to have felt the effects of adverse publicity. It used to be the penny scales." One of the most bitter campaigns, recalled the account, had been launched in 1930 by a national labor organization against vending machines, while at the moment organized musicians opposed the phonograph. Cigarette vending machines had been recently banned from a large city, with the official explanation being that minors could buy from the machines. "But the real opposition came from chain and department stores, through the channels of the Better Business Bureau." Changing the subject, the editor lashed out to say the real "racket" in connection with the coin-machine industry was what could be called the "legislative racket," that is, prohibitive laws or excessive tax bills. "The proportion of such bills is outstanding. The adverse publicity given to games and slots encourages those items. Churches and reform organizations support such efforts." He thought much of the negative newspaper publicity was unfair because it did not distinguish between types of machines. As a result, merchandise vending machines, automatic phonographs, and legal games suffered by this "general misunderstanding. Pinball games are on the borderline between skill and chance."[194]

Fisher Brown, Dallas distributor and former president of the Texas Coin Machine Operators' Association, was asked by a reporter in 1939 what was wrong with the coin-machine industry. His reply was bad publicity, claiming that newspapers and radio networks were waging a consistent war against the industry, citing it as "rackets." To correct that wrong impression, it was necessary to secure "proper" newspaper publicity and to organize internally even more.[195]

What did arise were a few articles that spoke obliquely and indirectly about the influence of organized crime. In a later period such references would be aimed specifically at jukeboxes, although they applied to the industry as a whole. In Chicago in 1938, Homer Capehart, while on a large goodwill tour for Wurlitzer to meet distributors and operators, warned an audience that "outside influences" were trying to creep into the industry and "tell music members what to do." His audience was said to have recognized this "as a public reference to activities of organizations, apparently centering in Chicago, that have undertaken to control the supply of help for music operators."[196]

More detailed, but equally mysterious, was an article six months later. It told of E. G. Steffens, manager of the International Association of Automatic Electric Phonograph Owners (Chicago-based) who addressed, by phone, an association meeting of a group of Southern California phonograph operators. He was looking to get state and local groups to affiliate with his in order to stamp out the "seemingly insurmountable" obstacles of cutthroat competition and chiseling and unethical practices "so prevalent in the operating industry." That had been done, he said, in both Chicago and New York when operators had affiliated with him. According to him, his members controlled 98 percent of all boxes in each of those cities. In both cases the affiliation was with his group and with the International Brotherhood of Electrical Workers, all part of the International Association of Automatic Electric Phonograph Owners. Needless to say, it was unusual for box operators and the people they hired as employees to be part of the same organization.[197]

A year later, in 1940, a brief account appeared in *Billboard* that spoke of the "injurious publicity" given to the phonograph industry recently in Chicago by three of the city's newspapers. Those "racket headlines" applied to the industry were quickly picked up by newspapers and columnists in many parts of the country.[198]

In the face of the worst economic decade ever experienced, the 1930s were a remarkable period of growth and success for jukeboxes and for the coin-machine industry overall. Writing in *The American Business* magazine in 1937, George Crook praised the coin industry and urged storekeepers to get some machines. Not many years earlier, a slot machine, a penny-gum vendor, and a penny-peanut vendor "practically constituted the coin-operated machine field." But, in 1937, one could get Coca-Cola, candy, cigarettes, and self-posed photographs made "while you wait." Others dropped coins in machines for the purpose of gambling, to make a telephone call, to try a little target practice, to learn their weight, or to play a game. "Public acceptance of the machines has been universal and in many cases tinged with gratitude." Photographs were available in less than five minutes, 10 cents for one photo. Amusement devices selling intangibles such as music, games, or gambling were more lucrative than the vendors of tangible merchandise, said Crook, but their popularity was shorter lived. The greatest money maker was said to be the regulation slot machine. Those gambling machines were illegal and subject to confiscation in many states, but where they were allowed to operate they were tremendous money makers. For a $13 jackpot from the nickel machine, about $150 may have gone into the machine. "This mechanism is subject to regulation by the operator and the percentage of profit depends only on his inclination or his conscience," said Crook. Operators who installed pinball games usually paid location owners 50 percent of the receipts. A popular game could gross $2 to $15 a day. A penny-gum machine installed on a one-third of the gross basis could make from $2 to $4 a week for the store owner. A weighing machine kept all day just inside the door of a store could be moved out in front at night, properly secured, to increase its income from window shoppers. Large chains such as Sears, Woolworth, and Kresge were said to use that method. Crook definitely recommended store owners deal with a professional operator of coin machines. In fact, the option of a location owner buying a machine directly was not discussed at all. Although game machines were short-lived in popularity, a good operator would rotate them from location to location. "The purpose of automatic selling is not to replace salesmen. It is to augment their efforts or to go places they cannot reach," concluded Crook.[199]

Production of jukeboxes from Wurlitzer fell to 33,721 units and stayed at about the 30,000 mark annually up to World War II. Its driving force, Homer Capehart, bored and restless, resigned on January 5, 1940. He went on to a political career as a three-term U.S. Senator for Indiana. Wurlitzer remained the dominant box maker through World War II. Seeburg, looking for an angle to increase its sales, scored one in 1938 when it produced a box with translucent plastic panels, behind which were fixed, low-wattage bulbs that made the phonograph glow. Manufacturers had striven to give their equipment drawing power by using veneers, steps, and angles on the wooden cabinets. But this was the age of electricity and the "light-up" box was a breakthrough. When Seeburg's Symphonola was unveiled at a 1938 convention, it stopped the show. Rock-Ola, Wurlitzer, and AMI went back to the factories and restyled their 1938 models. Soon Wurlitzer was producing models that surpassed those of Seeburg in style and illumination. When boxes first started to become popular in 1934, models were mostly housed in plain wooden cabinets, boxy and large, much like home-radio sets from their early days.[200]

Historian J. Krivine wrote that in the Depression boxes were still playing jazz, but a whiter version as rendered by such artists as Vincent Lopez, Paul Whiteman, the Dorsey Brothers, and Benny Goodman. "The Music Goes Round and Round" sold 100,000 copies in 1936—that had not happened since the 1920s. Decca was putting its resources behind popular music and had signed up several of the performers who recorded for

Brunswick's 75-cent disks: Guy Lombardo, the Mills Brothers, and the Rhythm Boys (one of whom was Bing Crosby). By 1939, jukes consumed about 30 million records per year, while serving the double function of buyer and seller. Millions of records were purchased because they had been heard the night before on a box. In that same year, "Beer Barrel Polka," played on every juke in America, sold 300,000 copies. A Decca disk retailed for 35 cents; it wholesaled to box operators for around 20 or 21 cents. Thus, that inexpensive disk had an earning power for a box that could be as high as $10. Mostly the jukebox was considered suitable for family entertainment. Operators encouraged that tendency, as it was good for business and it gave them respectability. Ever since racketeers moved into the slot-machine business, the coin industry suffered with a bad reputation. If repeal of Prohibition was a major factor in the sudden increase in box sales, it also caused racketeers to begin operating coin equipment. Whether or not the bad reputation of the industry was deserved, the image was there. Seeburg and Wurlitzer both established sales agencies in England by around 1935–1936. Prior to 1937, it was estimated there were less than 100 boxes in England and most of those were secondhand. More interest was shown there in 1938–1939 and, for the first time, boxes were shipped there direct from the makers. War ended that and restrictions on the import of nonessentials into England were not lifted until 1955.[201]

In half a dozen years, the box industry had soared to undreamed of heights. That it took place in a time of economic depression made the achievement all the more impressive. Its future looked equally sparkling. A saturation point had been reached, but sales strategies to increase the replacement rate of old boxes kept sales up. Then, as the economy turned sharply upward as war closed in, new locations sprang up, increasing the potential for placements. The unpleasant specter of saturation could be forgotten, at least for a while. The industry had just about convinced itself that it was more important to the record industry than anyone else and that it was the most important factor in producing hit songs and popularizing vocalists. It was puffed up with its own importance. The juke industry left this period cocky and arrogant; it probably had a right.

4

Boxes Get Patriotic, and Curb Juvenile Delinquency, 1941–1945

Jukeboxes in America "can now become a great and timely answer to any despoilers of our ideals — of our liberty." Homer Capehart, Wurlitzer executive, 1940.

Using a light to register a coin is helpful because "[d]uring the interval between the disposition of the coin and the hearing of the music the patron will not be hammering your box off the wall or roller skating with the phonograph." K. C. Kline, Illinois operator, 1942.

"The juke box (without which any teen-age center is a total loss) works overtime from 2 to 10 p.m." The Detroit Times, 1943.

With the coming of World War II, jukeboxes made an extra effort to help the war effort and to show their patriotic side. Another major development of this period was the spread of teen clubs and teenage centers. Activity in those places revolved, of course, around the box. Jukeboxes presented and promoted themselves as protectors of youth, as a force in curbing juvenile delinquency. At the time, delinquency was much in the news. Families were split up with the war on, and the remaining parent was much busier and worked longer hours. All of this supposedly led to a rise in delinquent behavior. Happy to be involved in these efforts, the jukebox industry saw it as an opportunity to reinforce to the public that jukes were respectable, and that they were good citizens and model businessmen. They hoped this would help keep any bad reputation at bay.

As early as June 1940, *Billboard*'s Walter Hurd delivered a full-page

editorial about building public morale and patriotism in
that time of war. "In time of
fear and distress music is one
of the most helpful tonics
that can be found.... The
automatic phonograph and
the music operator have a big
place, along with all other
music channels, in helping
to keep up the spirit of the
American people." Reports
from Canada and England indicated the phonograph was
actually playing a significant
part in supplying cheerful
music to soldiers and to civil-
ians as well. "No doubt the
civilian population needs its
ration of music to keep up
courage more than the armed
forces." Hurd noted the juke
was among those forms of
music that could be had by
the patrons of public centers
at low cost. "If the whole
truth is told, the phonograph

Wurlitzer 750, 1941.

makes it possible for many citizens to hear good music at a price within
their reach." It was the masses of people who frequented the taverns, restaurants, and so on from which the armed forces were drawn. The good cheer
of those masses could best be maintained in trying times by "having popular music everywhere."[1]

Agreeing that the automatic phonograph was not the only means of
cheering up people, he added that the 400,000 machines, with from 12 to
24 selections per box, "do make an army for good cheer that is sure to serve
a useful and patriotic purpose." There were two groups, thought Hurd, that
wittingly or unwittingly put a damper on the good that phonographs did
in keeping public morale up. One was the group that would put "excessive"
taxes or fees on jukes. "This is a time for organizations and taxing bodies to
boost public spirits by being very fair in assessing taxes." The second group
was "otherwise" sincere church people who could destroy national unity
in times of emergency. That was because church people often proved to be

a "national handicap" by trying to regulate masses of people who did not belong to their groups. "This tendency affects a number of businesses and business locations that are contributing a great share to maintaining American courage and spirit."[2]

Later in 1940, Homer Capehart waxed eloquently when he declared: "Patriotic records in a great circuit of more than 350,000 automatic phonographs engulfing the entire United States mean bringing directly to every citizen of our country a clearer picture of what this great nation stands for. This is the most gigantic, most direct musical network ever created by man. It is also the most popular musical network ever conceived." He went on to add that the box network could then become "a great and timely answer to any despoilers of our ideals — of our liberty." Capehart wanted to see patriotic songs promoted and brought to the public. He urged every music operator in the country to install such music, "the music of Americanism," in his automatic phonographs. His hope was that a national organization would be created, one whose program would be "Americanism through music."[3]

Around the same time Capehart delivered his message, *Billboard* representatives conducted a nationwide survey that showed the trend toward "a patriotic record in every machine" was steadily increasing. Operators in the East and those on the West Coast used more patriotic tunes than those in other areas. Highest levels were seen in New York City, Boston, and Portland, Oregon. The most used number, by far, was "God Bless America" by Kate Smith, although some favored a version by Bing Crosby. Second favorite was "I Am an American" by Gray Gordon. All the operators using patriotic tunes said they were doing so not because they wanted to cash in on any wave of patriotism, but because they thought it was the right thing to do. Only one operator said anything negative. He remarked, "The patriotism that comes after the fifth pitcher of beer is not the kind the music machine industry wants to foster ... there is no need for such pseudo-patriotism."[4]

A February 1942 editorial in the New York *Herald Tribune* praised jukeboxes for promoting patriotic songs. Some selections then available on phonographs included "Remember Pearl Harbor," "Goodby, Mamma, I'm Off to Yokohama," and "You're a Sap, Mr. Jap."[5]

Another area jukeboxes were involved in was war bonds. Music operators in Michigan, and throughout the United States, were reported to be united in their campaign to sell war bonds, along with much of the rest of the country. Many operators had placed the record "Any Bonds Today?" on their machines. Newspapers devoted space to the tune and radio stations had plugged and played the number. As a direct result of that activity the phonograph operator in Detroit was said to be "respected as a business man doing his definite bit for national defense and not just a 'juke box' operator."

[This seems to be the first time that *Billboard* used that word as part of its own material. That is, not included as part of a quoted citation from another publication.] Another account offered the thought that the "well-known" roles of the juke in wartime included boosting the morale of both workers and fighting forces, "quickening the step of all who hear martial music," and selling war bonds.[6]

Manufacturers of boxes faced a growing shortage of materials during the latter half of 1941. On December 10th that year, the federal government stepped in when Donald M. Nelson, Priorities Director of the Office of Production Management, issued an order prohibiting the production of coin-operated gambling machines after February 1, 1942. Nelson told makers of jukes, and some other coin-operated devices, to curtail their output 75 percent by the same date. Jukes, penny weigh scales, and pinball games had to reduce production 25 percent that December, compared with average production in the 12 months ending June 30, 1941. Beginning January 1, 1942, production of those items had to be cut 50 percent. Makers of slot machines for gaming purposes had to reduce production 50 percent that month and 75 percent in January, with a full halt in February. Those moves marked the most drastic limitations yet placed on a civilian industry because of a shortage of materials needed in defense production. The industry trade group, the Automatic Phonograph Manufacturers Association,

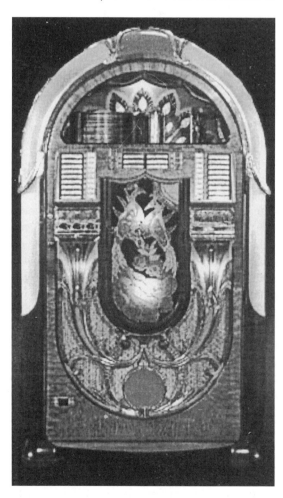

Wurlitzer 850, 1941.

fully backed the order. Not much later the government ordered the complete stoppage of the manufacture of automatic phonographs as of May 1, 1942. None of those box makers (then numbering five) suffered financially; all moved quickly into full-scale production on war work.[7]

As the war dragged on, boxes more and more became associated with soldiers. Over 24 USO centers and canteens were operating in Philadelphia in 1943, with more on the way. Music machines were said to be a "must" on those premises when it came to keeping men in the service entertained. Operators made sure all such places were supplied with both a machine and records. While all the clubs entertaining the servicemen also had the benefit of a radio set, "it is the juke box that is in demand. More than one canteen director had stated that the servicemen like the juke box best because they can hear the songs they like best." Many canteen directors were also reported to be frank to admit that apart from the evenings when night club and vaudeville entertainment was provided, it was the box that kept the servicemen entertained. "That the music machines are doing an excellent morale job for the servicemen on the home front is obvious on any look-in at any canteen in the city."[8]

Walter Hurd felt it was the men in the armed forces who, in the period 1942–1943, gave jukeboxes the "greatest wave of popularity ... the music machines have ever seen." Newspapers and magazines let the country know about it. Hurd thought that perhaps men had to get away from home to appreciate fully how much coin phonographs meant in everyday life. When men in the overseas forces began to write home, they often mentioned what they missed most while away, and newspapers published those letters. It soon became apparent that a lot of men were writing home how much they missed jukes, among other items. The Pepperell Manufacturing Company bought a large advertising space in papers in May 1943 to publish "A Letter from a Soldier." That letter was received from a former employee, then a soldier overseas. Among the things he missed were such everyday items as movies, hillbilly music, Coca-Cola, and jukeboxes. Soldiers in camps and military posts in the United States also gave abundant testimony as to how they liked the music machines. One example was in the June 26 issue of the *Saturday Evening Post* wherein a feature article on post exchanges contained a half-page illustration showing a group of servicemen gathered around a box. The caption was "The juke box is always a focal point of interest in any PX."[9]

When Hurd wrote his piece, the full ban on box production had been in effect for 1½ years. He said that the industry had been able to keep practically all of its machines in working order and in operation. If a machine became too old for use or was damaged, its parts were immediately salvaged and thus helped to keep other machines in operation. Hurd estimated there were 400,000 jukes on location in America and that the reduction, if any, in the total number, due to the production ban, "has been so small as hardly to permit any estimate of such decrease." A minor auxiliary industry sprang up to provide new cabinets for old machines. The mechanism was taken out of the old juke and installed in a new cabinet, giving the appearance that it was a new jukebox. According to Hurd, some machines were then being placed in "elite establishments which formerly did not accept them." Supposedly that was because the public had demanded such music at times when orchestras could not perform. It represented a breakthrough because "For some years during the development of the juke box trade, there was a tendency to keep them out of the best places, but that is no longer true." While many thousands of homes had not purchased a phonograph before the war curtailed so many manufacturing industries, "everybody comes in contact with a juke box and its recorded music in the daily routine of life in practically every town and city in the country."[10]

First Hamilton Service Men's Center in Brooklyn was a major embarkation and debarkation point with about 20,000 men at the center every month. Two music machines were in the center, side by side. One was programmed only with classics, including Corelli's "Sonata in F" for organ and strings, Gounod's "Ave Maria," and Johann Sebastian Bach's "Fugue a la Gigue." The classic box played at lunch and dinner while the standard machine, featuring Harry James, Artie Shaw, and so forth, was for use at evening dances. No nickels were required in either phonograph. Center director Jack Schneider said the base was a somber area; soldiers had tight nerves and wanted to relax. Many soldiers had told him that the sound of a hot trumpet or a three-minute drum solo put them on edge.[11]

Operators were still able to receive lots of advice in regard to programming their units. Jack Hudnall, of the Cincinnati-based Ohio Specialty Company, said that in his firm's "hilarious-type" locations, catering to a mix of young and old, "snappy tunes" were the must items. Each box also had one to two jitterbug selections and the same number of semi-hillbilly tunes. In those spots the best results were from disks recorded by Artie Shaw, Will Bradley, Kay Kyser (novelty tunes), Bing Crosby, Tommy Dorsey, and Fats Waller. For his secluded spots, those with high-back booths and soft lights, Hudnall declared that soft music was the proper stuff. Phonographs did well in such locations and wall boxes in those establishments had reportedly increased the take considerably. "Such locations are usually infested with the young lovers slyly holding hands." The best disks for those secluded spots were the works of performers such as Wayne King, Freddy Martin, Guy Lombardo, Sammy Kaye, and Bing Crosby.[12]

Another important spot for Hudnall were the high-school, jitterbug locations catering strictly to the teen element. In those spots the orchestra

A 1943 trade ad designed to convince operators to buy a new cabinet and install an old works, to give the appearance of a new jukebox. This was at a time when World War II restrictions had brought the production of new units to a halt.

leader rather than the tune was the thing. Among others, they liked Artie Shaw, Will Bradley, Benny Goodman, Tommy Dorsey, Jimmy Dorsey, Les Brown, Glenn Miller, and Gene Krupa. For locations frequented mainly by middle-aged people, Ohio Specialty's formula was to give them plenty of polkas and lively numbers, with an occasional "good old hillbilly ditty." For spots that were strictly "hillbilly," Hudnall gave them plenty of Bing Crosby, the Carter Family, Riley Puckett, Jimmy Davis, Bill Carlisle, Cliff Carlisle, and the Shelton Brothers. Also, he threw in an occasional Irish ballad. Hudnall reported his company had only two ways of selecting the disks they purchased. They knew which bands were most popular in their locations, but depended "almost entirely upon *The Billboard* Record Buying Guide" to find records that were going the best in the jukeboxes. His only other aid was the ad literature sent out by the record companies. Hudnall concluded that he could not stress the importance of the Record Buying Guide enough: "I don't remember ever getting one bum steer."[13]

Another operator offering advice was Fred Van de Walker of the Modern Automatic Music Company in New York. For their taverns, cocktail lounges, restaurants—any location where patrons divided their attention between music and drinking, eating, and talking—Modern stuck to "softly played melodious renditions." Vocals were also popular, as were "cute" novelties, if they were not "too noisy." What was important was to "Never, never, however, drown out their conversation with blaring music." When locations were ice-cream parlors and other spots where high-school students hung out, Van de Walker stated, "the impressiveness of a band's name means much." For locations in Harlem all good "colored" bands were popular. Blues numbers were tops in spots with an older crowd while hot, old-fashioned jazz did well among spots catering to a younger clientele. "Spirituals, especially when dressed up in new versions, are sure-fire hits." Van de Walker also heavily stressed the importance of using *Billboard*'s Record Buying Guide. It meant that list continued to operate as a self-fulfilling prophecy.[14]

Country tunes got a boost in this period as a result of several factors. One was the AFM strike that started in 1943 and lasted over a year. Since no new recordings were made, operators and retailers turned to alternatives. A second factor was a shortage of materials—shellac in the case of records—which resulted in fewer copies of all records being produced. Since retailers usually had their orders filled before box operators, the latter, again, looked to alternative material. Thirdly was a new and larger market for such numbers in heavily industrialized parts of America as the "hillbillies" moved in large numbers to these areas to take advantage of wartime employment opportunities.

In Philadelphia, until the early years of the 1940s, hillbilly records were considered "virtually the kiss of death." Music retail stores as well as box operators "always viewed the hillbilly disks as a sort of annoyance. It was rare to find a music shop with more than a dozen hillbilly records in stock and even rarer to find any such waxes in a music box." But now machines were picking up country disks with "unbelievably" good results. Such records not only led the local jukebox parade but had paved the way for music stores "to cash in on the hillbilly craze started here by the machines." Leading the way was Al Dexter's "Pistol Packin' Mama." According to this account the music operators had been "virtually forced" to use such material, due to the difficulties they then experienced in trying to find enough suitable material. It all started when one of the Philadelphia operators received a letter from his brother, in the Army and stationed at a Southern camp, to put "Pistol" in his machines, saying it was hot. Taking the advice, the operator had great success. Motor Parts Company, local distributor of Columbia-Okeh records (Dexter's label), said it was the first time country records led the sales list in Philadelphia. Also, radio stations were calling Motor for copies of "Pistol" because they were receiving requests. Rex Alexander of Motor remarked, "'Pistol' was getting more requests on the air than the Frank Sinatra sides." Alexander also "admitted that the onrush for the side was started by the juke boxes." Even the "high-class" record departments found in Wanamakers and Gimbel Brothers were hounding distributors for more copies of "Pistol." Other country records that had success in Philadelphia, after Dexter's initial inroad, included "No Letter Today" by Ted Daffan's Texans, Al Dexter's "Rosalita," and "The Honey Song" by Louise Massey.[15]

In Baltimore there was also a high demand for country tunes at taverns, restaurants, and other spots that provided jukebox music with food and drink to those who had moved to that city from West Virginia, Kentucky, Tennessee, and other parts of the country. Half of the selections played at those spots were country numbers. About 250,000 of those country people had settled in the area, lured by large wages at defense plants, and "hillbillies are good spenders."[16]

Minneapolis had some 1,100 boxes run by 25 operators. They could not get new records because of the AFM ban. Then some enterprising operators began putting back into boxes old tunes such as "Stardust." Labels started producing reissues. Everyone did well. Country songs were also doing well in Minneapolis with two favorites being "Pistol Packin' Mama" and "No Letter Today."[17]

Phonograph operators in Ohio initiated a program to adopt a hit tune each month. Members usually placed the selected hit tune in the number one tray on the machines. A special title strip and a display card were also used to boost the record. Selected for March 1943 was "Moonlight Mood"—then available in renditions by at least four artists: Glen Gray, Kay Kyser, Connee Boswell, and Glenn Miller. Operators reported that the average play per record (for the selected hit) was about 15 to 20 per week.[18]

Chicago's Century Music Company, an operator, used the national guides to pick disks for their machines. At headquarters a large chart listed the 24 disks in most Century boxes. The rest of the chart was divided into 12 columns, one for each route, plus a column for the grand total. Route men returning from their weekly calls would write in the number of plays for each selection. Each week the chart contained about 10 or 15 of the most popular selections current on the radio, in movies, or those getting a lot of advertising. It also contained several successful standards. Century had a library of 400 or 500 old tunes doing well on their second run. Like all operators, they had to deal with a shortage of new material. It was possible, thought Century, for a route man to help "put over" a number, especially one that was comparatively unknown, by getting the employees at a location to listen to a selection a couple of times, then setting the machine to play that song a few times after the route man departed. Then when customers came in and asked what was good, those employees frequently suggested the selection they had just heard. When it came to picking new songs, if Century had any doubts as to their potential for success, those records were first tried out on the firm's own route men and servicemen. If most liked it, the number was included in their boxes since "their taste [was] about the same as the general public."[19]

According to a survey for 1942, Glenn Miller was king of the jukes, then came Harry James, Tommy Dorsey, Kay Kyser, and Jimmy Dorsey. A year earlier Jimmy Dorsey had been on top. Among vocalists, Bing Crosby was "head and shoulders above" everyone else, then came the Andrews Sisters, Dinah Shore, Gene Autry, and the King Sisters.[20]

For six consecutive years, beginning in 1939, Artie Shaw's "Begin the Beguine" was the number one box pick at Shaner's, a neighborhood grill in Denver. Each week for all six years, the plays had run out the meter, which registered up to 70. An estimate by the location operator was that "Begin" received an average of another 35 to 50 plays in excess of the 70, or about 115 plays a week. Due to wear and tear, some 320 copies of "Begin" had been placed on the machine. From the time it was first placed on the machine, up to and including January 1945, it was estimated the number had been played 34,960 times. It was thought to be a record for a tune.[21]

When Metropolitan Opera basso Alexander Kipnis remarked casually in 1945 in Washington, D.C., that he hoped jukes would popularize classical music after the war, the Washington *Times-Herald* did a limited person-on-the-street survey. Results found everyone surveyed believed the idea had no chance, or very little. Respondents thought people wanted lively

A 1942 trade ad with the Clark firm offering to modernize Wurlitzer units.

music in places with dancing and drinking. They wanted the kind of music that got "the joint jumpin."[22]

For some people the choice of what record to put on a jukebox was simple — a silent one. Cleveland Mayor Frank J. Lausche was thinking about putting a special tax on the phonograph. With some 2,000 boxes in the city, he thought the city could produce revenue, perhaps in the hundreds of thousands of dollars. Lausche digressed to say: "They play so continuously that, in some cities, blank records have been installed for the convenience of persons who simply cannot stand another recording. For a nickel such persons may obtain several minutes of silence."[23]

Using a different method to obtain the same result was Justice Tom Fletcher of Civil Justice Court in Richmond, Virginia. Fletcher became annoyed when a phonograph was installed at his favorite luncheon spot that drowned out some of his conversations with his attorney friends during the lunch hour. To solve the problem he took to carrying with him a sign that read "Out of Order," which he hung on the box when he sat down for lunch. When he left, he removed the sign, depositing money in the machine to compensate for the loss so that others could have music with their meals. Said Fletcher: "It's a reasonable fee for peace and quiet."[24]

Sometimes the noise involved an entire community. A police drive in New York against noisy phonographs began in July 1945, after Mayor Fiorello La Guardia, in a Sunday radio address, told of complaints he had received about them. One month later, three Brooklyn tavern proprietors each pled guilty in court to having jukeboxes that played too loudly at times. Each was fined $5.[25]

Smut problems received only a couple of mentions. The Phonograph Operators' Association of Eastern Pennsylvania and New Jersey went on record in 1942 that they would not tolerate smutty records in their machines. For some weeks smutty records had been making their appearance in the area. Widespread use of such records five and six years earlier, said the account, gave the industry a black eye in that area, one that took several years to live down. Sentiment against smut was said to be so strong among operators there was no need to impose any fines or penalties on them for using it. Operators were determined that no such records find their way into their machines "regardless of requests of location owners." They also weren't "interested in the get-rich-quick appeal of such records." Association business manager Jack Cade remarked: "Such records are not legitimate. They might just as well expect the operator to lower himself by selling smutty pictures and literature. Such recordings are in the same class. They belong to the back alleys and degenerates."[26]

Around the same time, officials in Massachusetts decided to enforce a local ordinance to license jukeboxes for Sunday operation — it had been unenforced for some years due to definitions of some of the terms of the measure. According to an unnamed official in the Massachusetts Department of Public Safety, one of the reasons for beginning to enforce the measure was the use of suggestive records on some of the boxes. Operator W. E. Watkins said: "This is just one more statement to add to all that has been said against using suggestive records. The sooner such records are absolutely banned from all coin-operated phonographs, the better off we will be."[27]

J. M. Dalziel, an operator in Lake City, South Carolina, reported on the use of coin-operated phonographs in locations catering to Blacks, where the machines were sometimes referred to as piccolos. He used the term "jook" to refer to those spots. "The one-room shanty containing the piccolo may not be worth $25 for scrap, but it is a common thing to find one of the latest light-up models worth several hundred dollars in such a location and rolling in the nickels." Dalziel advised operators to let the "jook" owner select the records for the box. Three or four new records a month were said to be enough to keep the nickels flowing. "The jook man seems to prefer the 12-record model, since a larger number of records seems to confuse everybody and slow up the works." An average box in one of these locations contained three or four Hit Parade tunes, three or four "swing-eroos," an occasional country tune, and the rest blues numbers. A record that made a hit in these locations, such as Bing Crosby's "Blue Hawaii," was good for 8 to 10 months and was "sure to be played continuously to the exclusion of almost all the others."[28]

There was hope in this period that arcades would be revived and become a major place to site music machines. During the summer season arcades in the resort areas had been successful for a number of years. However, it was only in the early years of the 1940s that indoor arcades had shown a definite upward trend. This trend continued long enough at that time to show that indoor arcades were becoming a permanent amusement feature for the public in practically all cities. Some of those arcades were so successful as to be "almost unbelievable." One account felt that a number of established operators would bring in their machines off their routes and open arcades to save money by reducing the number of vehicles, and gasoline, needed to service routes. Centralizing machines into arcades also would reduce the number of employees an operator would need. The manpower shortage was a serious problem during World War II.[29]

One unusual spot for a juke could be found in Detroit, in the Ernst Kern Company, one of the city's three leading department stores. It was installed in the Seventeen Shop, devoted to 13- to 17-year-old girls. Sometimes there was a line-up of teens around the machine, listening and waiting for a chance to play it.[30]

Despite having supposedly slug-proof machines, slugs continued to trouble the entire coin-machine industry. So the industry rejoiced when it received the aid of a formidable federal weapon in its fight against the false coins. It happened in April 1944, when President Franklin D. Roosevelt signed an act making it a federal offense to manufacture, sell, or display tokens or slugs with the knowledge or intent that they might be used in vending machines and other coin-operated machines. It was an amendment to Section 168 of the Criminal Code. The new measure was designed to eliminate the wholesale manufacture of slugs "which, in past years, caused millions of dollars of loss to operators of vending machines and other coin-operated devices." Roosevelt's action was in response to industry lobbying for many years. That lobbying had been increased as a result of failures in the 1940s to gain convictions when a judge declared existing statutes should be supplemented by new federal legislation. That is, he advised the coin-machine industry to seek relief from Congress rather than from the courts.[31]

No matter where a jukebox was located, it could attract unusual customers. Rosiclare, Illinois, operator K. C. Kline learned that firsthand after one of his location owners told him about a patron. Every time the customer put a nickel in the box, he pounded it with his fist or slapped it with his hand before it had time to start playing. Kline spent a night at the location and saw some patrons who would knock the machine two or three inches down the floor every time they put a coin in the slot. He wondered why they did that since the mechanism worked perfectly and never did a coin fail to play. Perhaps, he thought, it was simply a habit carried over from earlier days, when machines often had to be "jolted" to start. Operators had learned that patrons would not tolerate a machine that would not play when they put in their coins. Let one fail "and it will soon get a lot of punishment." While the old-style cabinets would stand a lot of that treatment, the newer cabinets with more plastic soon showed the effects of rough handling. It cost operators a lot of money. Kline recommended one way to stop it was to put the box in a place where it could be seen by location management. Another tactic was to take the rollers off the bottom so that the machine could not be rolled. Kline had sometimes taken out slug-proof phonographs and replaced them with machines that weren't slug-proof. Or he removed the slug ejector from the unit, making it a straight coin slot taking anything in the shape of a coin. "It is easier, and less expensive, to get a few slugs than to travel 50 miles to unplug a coin slot." However, his best strategy was to place somewhere in the cabinet a pilot light that snapped on immediately when a coin was inserted and stayed on as long as the machine was playing. Kline explained this instant feedback for the patron was important so that "During the interval between the disposition of the coin and the hearing of the music the patron will not be hammering your box off the wall or roller skating with the phonograph." It was an especially good strategy for wall-box locations since he had "seen very few persons who failed to hit the wallbox when they put in the coin.... Anything that will let the patron know that his coin has registered will stop a lot of banging and pushing on the machinery."[32]

A very different patron and box interaction took place in late 1944 at a spot called the Broadway Orange Grove in Oklahoma City. Edwin Long and Theone Clifford met at the juke where they argued about who would put the next nickel in the machine. Apparently one thing led to another and, in January 1945, with the cooperation of the owner, the couple married right in front of the juke that triggered their romance. Removed from the box by the owner, just before the ceremony, were a couple of numbers thought to be inappropriate: "I'll Walk Alone," "Into Each Life Some Rain Must Fall," and "Don't Fence Me In."[33]

Teenagers, jukeboxes, and delinquency came together in the 1940s, in reality, in the media, and in the public consciousness. Most of this early uniting was put in a positive light, that is, jukeboxes were seen as a force in reducing delinquency amongst youth. One of the first, informal accounts to present this idea concerned Clifton, New Jersey, in 1939. Based on the complaints of parents, educators, and clergy, city officials ordered the police to stop local soda emporiums from purveying "hot" music to young patrons. In their defense, the soda-bar owners said the teens could not go to public taverns and were kept out of trouble on soft drinks and "swing phonograph music."[34]

That teens were major customers of jukes was evident by 1940. When Mills Novelty Company held an open house in Chicago in January of that year, one of its top attractions was a group of jitterbugs, who danced to the music of Mills phonographs. Company advertising manager James Mangan remarked: "There was a reason for having the jitterbugs at our open house party. First of all I believe that young folks are among the heaviest supporters of phonographs." He then quoted from an article by nationally known columnist Dorothy Killgallen that the swing set was the young set, and students voted with their nickels. "Therefore, we chose the jitterbugs as representative of the young, swing set which patronizes phonographs heavily."[35]

A May 1943 account described a nation that had become seriously disturbed in recent months about the problem of juvenile delinquency. Civic leaders in all parts of the country had expressed worry at the increase in the behavior and were also urging that the nation do everything possible at once to turn the tide. Many blamed it on war tensions, and thus, it was to be expected. However, others who worked with young people said the real problem was that of providing suitable places of amusement for the nation's youth. Much could be done, they felt, by establishing proper amusement

A 1943 Wurlitzer ad.

centers in cities and towns throughout the country as soon as possible. Cited as an example was an amusement center recently established in Burlington, Iowa. The Burlington Student Center, known as the Spider Web, was open to all high school and junior college students; it was seen as one answer to the "growing juvenile delinquency problem." There had been much talk in Burlington about the fact there was no place for students to congregate after school and evenings, except Burlington drugstore hangouts. Soon the Burlington Kiwanis Club got involved and set up the Web, which contained a dance floor, a soda fountain, a lounge, and more than a dozen booths and tables. It was open every afternoon except Sunday from 3:30 to 5:30, Monday nights 8:00 to 10:30, Friday nights from 7:30 to 11:30, and Saturday nights from 7:30 to 11:15. The age limit for members was 15 to 21 with dues being 50 cents a school year. Parents acted as chaperons. The center's centerpiece was, of course, a music machine. "A juke box never stops grinding out modern jive, and jitterbugging is popular." The music box took in $35 in nickels during the first couple of weeks it was open.[36]

During the course of 1943 a growing number of teen clubs were set up to combat juvenile delinquency. One was opened in Austin, Texas, another in Des Moines, Iowa, and several were established in Minneapolis. *Billboard* thought that if the juke industry was organized to lead in the establishment of these centers, they might appropriately be called "Juke Box Clubs." In fact, one center in Cincinnati was known as the "Juke Box Friday Night Club." All of these centers prominently featured music machines for listening and for dancing.[37]

Philadelphia's first teen club opened in June that year in the Germantown area. Self-imposed rules required that every fast record played be alternated with two slow numbers. Officials of the Germantown YWCA (where the club was located) were enthusiastic about the center's possibilities, while noting the spot's major attraction was the music machine. When teens first started pouring in, the first question asked was if there was a jukebox in the place. Those officials admitted they had not realized before "what great fascination the music machine holds for the teen-age youngster."[38]

During that summer in Philadelphia, amid suggestions of a city-wide curfew for teens recommended by a grand jury, civic and welfare groups expressed grave concern over the increasing juvenile delinquency in the city. Jack Cade, business manager of the Philadelphia Music Machine Operators' Association, stepped forward to offer a "timely and constructive solution to the problem that [was] getting out of hand." By way of providing "wholesome and diverting amusement" to the teens, Cade suggested to city leaders setting up teen centers throughout Philadelphia. As an example he pointed to the one in Germantown. Cade thought the delinquency problem was due to "carelessness" of parents, either through their own neglect or because they were working extended hours at war plants. Also, he pointed to the successful operation of the dozens of servicemen's canteens and clubs scattered all over the city, where music machines provided "the only medium of entertainment." What he deplored was that public and civic-minded individuals and groups "overlooked the tremendous appeal of the music box with its recorded popular music in devising means and ways in coping with the juvenile delinquency problem."[39]

Later that summer, Cade's group, in conjunction with the Community Council (made up of representatives of the various public welfare groups in the city), went on to set up a teen center in the Roxborough section of town, called the Community Canteen. The operator association donated a box, a "generous" supply of records, and a public address system. Open on Wednesday and Friday evenings, the center was declared a huge success, drawing 400 to 500 teens in the course of an evening.[40]

About two months later Helen McMann prepared a report based primarily on a study of the teen club set up by Cade and his partners. She undertook the project as a representative of the Philadelphia Board of Education. Her report placed emphasis on the important role played by music machines. For added diversion the center had a game room equipped with various coin-operated devices. That report supported the contention, long voiced by music-box industry leaders, that the teen clubs, with a full complement of music and amusement machines, were "strong enough in appeal to help Philadelphia's youngsters who are 'losing their bearings' in a topsy-turvy wartime world." McMann's report recommended to the board of education the establishment of a city-wide chain of teen clubs. Making that less likely was the report that some officials of the school system were still "prejudiced" against setting up such teen clubs because "their appeal is based principally on coin-operated devices." However, it *was* felt that press and public pressure would eventually make the board "see the true light."[41]

As the teen club idea spread, *Billboard* editor Walter Hurd reported that the movement then had a momentum much greater than ever before. It was an idea he believed promised to become a permanent civic movement in America. Spreading fast and receiving such strong public support, it was an idea "worth careful study by the coin machine trade, particularly the music division of the trade." Newspaper stories about the clubs, and there were many, mentioned the juke as a necessary part of the equipment. "This certainly is the most favorable publicity ever given to the juke box industry, and for that reason the trade should find a way to give full support to the movement." In less than a month, the number of teen centers in Detroit had recently moved from 0 to 130 clubs in operation. Large and small communities were equally affected by the phenomenon.[42]

Thinking about the future, Hurd commented that emphasis was then placed on those teen clubs for their value in entertaining young people during the war emergency "but the juke box trade should begin at once to make the teen-age club idea its permanent civic project." Each division of the coin-machine industry, he felt, had long needed some charitable or civic project it could sponsor as a means of cultivating public favor through the performance of useful services. Because of the wide use of music machines in the teen clubs, it seemed to be a natural for the juke industry. While it was highly probable that civic leaders would devote much attention to the club concept for the duration of the war, Hurd worried that when the stress of war was past that interest would falter and die. "The juke box trade should keep this in mind and make plans for a permanent organization of some kind to maintain these clubs for years to come." Hurd thought there could be nothing better for the juke industry itself than to set up a national board with state and city chapters "for the sole purpose of sponsoring teen-age clubs, or, at least, supplying the music for these clubs—that is, the juke box and records could be furnished by the industry."[43]

A teen club in Kalamazoo, Michigan, drew as many as 600 young people on Friday nights. Every student aged 15 to 19 was eligible for membership. Open four nights a week, the club charged 10 cents admission on Mondays and Wednesdays, 30 cents on Saturday nights, and 40 cents on Friday nights, when a live orchestra played for part of the evening. Sunday afternoons the center opened with free admission.[44]

Reports continued to pile up on the founding of youth clubs to combat juvenile delinquency, with the box always reported as the center's showpiece, its main attraction. The Cleveland Phonograph Merchants' Association arranged with J. Kemeny, city recreation director, to have boxes installed in the seven municipal recreation centers. A story in *The Detroit Times* said, in part, "The juke box (without which any teen-age center is a total loss) works overtime from 2 to 10 P.M." The *Des Moines Register* devoted a full page to a teen club in Fort Madison, Iowa, where the music machine took in $90.35 in September 1943.[45]

At their regular meeting the members of the Missouri Amusement Machine Association pledged to donate one jukebox for each teen center organized by local schools. All area schools were reportedly planning to establish such clubs.[46]

Margaret Wells wrote a detailed account of the teen clubs in March 1944. She felt kids who became problems were innocent victims of the times and in many cases, the victims of a lack of parental supervision. When school let out for the day, the students often had no choice but to go to "questionable" places of entertainment or to hang out on the streets. Taverns and the liquor industry received their share of criticism with respect to teenagers because, it was said, those youngsters insisted on going into taverns in order to listen to jukeboxes. The tavern operator did not want such trade, "yet keeping it away presented problems." Wells agreed that an essential part of the equipment of any such club was a box, and music was one of the main magnets for drawing youth to these centers. Also, in smaller centers, teens may never see a name band or entertainers in the flesh. Most kids preferred, thought Wells, hearing records by good bands to the amateurish efforts of a school group or mediocre professionals.[47]

When a teen club was organized in Moline, Illinois, by high-school students, it was given wide publicity. In the first 10 weeks of its existence, more than 1,000 teens joined the Moline club. A 1944 survey by *Billboard* found operators in over 100 cities and towns who reported such clubs in their communities, with all but five clubs equipped with jukes. Some 66 of those operators said they had donated one or more jukes to these centers. Many operators reported they were servicing machines for free. Some of the larger cities had dozens and dozens of clubs. As a result, operators and distributors had received a lot of favorable publicity. That publicity, said Wells, "has helped to remove some of the stigma which has been attached to the music boxes." The rise of teen clubs was a boon for the coin-machine trade because many people criticized any place using a box and were prone to classify them, good, bad, and indifferent, as "juke joints" and to claim they led young people astray. However, concluded Wells, "By putting juke boxes in youth clubs, the entire industry is bound to be benefitted."[48]

Club Mohican, a teen center in Gardena, California, was described as a place where the music machine "is, quite naturally, the most popular thing in the club and it blares without ceasing from the time school is out until we fold up at night." For extra amusement the center had such coin-operated games as skee ball, Shoot the Jap, Western Baseball, and others. Average daily attendance was 200 to 300. Also at the club was a fully equipped soda fountain and soft-drink bar. On average, each teen at the club consumed three Cokes and a hamburger. The 537 members were aged 13 to 21, and paid $1 every three months for a membership.[49]

When the 30th National Conference of Catholic Charities met for four days late in 1944 in Brooklyn, one of the assertions made was that teen centers "with their wholesale entertainment facilities of juke boxes and snack bars, are a means of saving a lost generation of youth."[50]

A nationwide survey in 1945 by the recreation division of the Federal Security Agency found there were 3,000 teen canteens in America, and more than 2,200 of them centered around jukes. Those clubs were said to be more popular in smaller cities and towns. Additionally, the survey said that the specific opening of youth centers had meant a decrease in juvenile delinquency, at least in some areas. Echoing that view was a report that same year from the Federal Bureau of Investigation that commented first on an "alarming rise" in juvenile crime. It went on to add that in many towns across the country, the opening of a youth center "has resulted in a downward trend in juvenile delinquency." Chicago juvenile authorities declared that "a wave of crime by teen-agers and bobby-soxers now is sweeping the country."[51]

Wurlitzer 1943 ad.

A probation director who worked with a Connecticut juvenile court said that "a juke box, a soda bar, a lounge, a chance to gather with the crowd and an opportunity to smoke, a place to dance and say hello to a girl are almost necessary for the modern youngster."[52]

Although most accounts joined teens, boxes, and youth clubs in a positive light, a factor decreasing juvenile delinquency, there were a few reports that took an opposite position. One 1943 account observed there was a recent trend by reform groups to criticize music machines as having something to do with the current wave of juvenile crime that was "serious in all parts of the country." *Billboard* sharply declared the charge false and that it could do great damage. The publication tried to explain that it was the availability of liquor in some locations which was to blame, if there were any problems in fact. At the same time, the paper urged the establishment of teen clubs since, "Experts in the field say this is the best way to solve juvenile delinquency."[53]

Memphis, Tennessee, made the jukebox situation a public question when it passed an ordinance to license the machines and to limit the number to one in each location. When that system went into effect, small operators complained the police department was favoring large operators. Soon the issue was in all the newspapers and "reflected an unfavorable tone concerning the trade." Columnist Clark Porteous of the Memphis *Press-Scimitar* looked at the positive and negative aspects of the music machine before he declared, in a three-column headline: WE PROTECT OUR CHILDREN FROM JUKE: OTHER CITIES PROTECT THEIRS WITH IT."[54]

In San Francisco, the board of supervisors decided, by a margin of one vote, not to turn control of jukes in the city over to the police force, as had been proposed as a measure to curb juvenile delinquency. That action followed weeks of controversy between the police and the juke operators over the proposal for the former to attack delinquency through phonograph licensing. It was a measure proposed by three members of the board, at the suggestion of Police Chief Charles Dullea, which provided that machines be licensed. Had the measure passed, supervision of the boxes would have been transferred from the city's electric department over to the police department. Operators argued against the measure claiming the ordinance was discriminatory; that it would drive small businessmen out of work; and was "un-American in that it attempted to penalize an innocent occupation to give police more control over taverns."[55]

Members of the city council in Minneapolis brought up a motion to license jukes at $10 per year and also to place an 11 P.M. curfew on such music. That marked a revision of a previous draft ordinance that called for the banning of boxes within 300 yards of a school or church.[56]

During the war, promotional and tie-in efforts by the juke industry were much less intense than prior to the war, but they were by no means abandoned. Some Hollywood studios promoted songs from their musical films in conjunction with box operators. Paramount used advertisements and direct mail for operators to place recordings of tunes from its release "The Fleet's In," starring Dorothy Lamour and Jimmy Dorsey's orchestra. Twentieth Century Fox boosted its musical "Sun Valley Serenade" in a drive that saw operators working in concert with exhibitors to hype the film. In Jacksonville, Florida, and in Cleveland, Ohio, machine operators featured Glenn Miller recordings of "Sun" tunes coincident with the showing of the movie in their territory. They also used special title strips and placards praising both the records and the film, causing a "heyday" at the theater box office. When Fox released "Song of the Islands" it sent a press book to exhibitors all over America. Within that book were cited the number of "Islands" records and the opportunity those provided for "juke box displays and song-plugging handouts in all spots handling machines."[57]

Spike Jones and his band the City Slickers left Hollywood in August 1943 on a tour of a number of Eastern and Midwest cities. Jones sent his "press angel" June Bundy ahead to contact music-machine operators and to arrange parties for them in each town where he was to play. Bundy stayed about a week ahead of the band and was in direct charge of coin-machine promotion on the tour.[58]

Famed singer Marian Anderson commented that the modern jukebox music, be it ever so sentimental, was furnishing "raw material for truly great American music."[59]

Panther Novelty Company of Fort Worth, Texas, one of the city's leading juke operators, sponsored a weekly radio program that aired every Sunday evening over station KFJZ. Hosted by a local media personality, the show was called "Jack Gordon's Weekly Record Round-Up." Launched in 1941 on a trial basis, the program proved popular enough that it was still going strong over a year later. Each week, about 24 hours before broadcast time, Gordon and two Panther executives selected the tunes to be featured on the show. In his chatter between records, Gordon urged listeners to go to their favorite tavern or café and enjoy the latest records on the coin-operated phonographs. Listeners were told which selection number on the jukes was connected with certain hit tunes. "In fact, every tune offered on the radio show is given an exact selector number on the phonos for the listeners to remember."[60]

Wurlitzer presented the 30-minute radio program "Abe Lincoln's Story" on February 12, 1945, on over 100 Mutual Network stations. This was the first time in coin-machine history a juke maker had sponsored a coast-to-coast radio program.[61]

Band leader Jimmy Dorsey became the latest appointed member in good standing of the "Fraternity of Distinguished Gentlemen of the Juke Box," late in 1945. Additional members were appointed to the fraternity each Tuesday night in a segment of an NBC coast-to-coast radio show called "Johnny Presents," sponsored by Philip Morris cigarettes. As a continuing part of the show, the idea behind the fraternity was to introduce popular band leaders whose records had become hits by way of the jukes.[62]

Buffalo, New York, operating company Mills Amusement conducted a newspaper campaign that focused on the fact the firm operated phonographs in a chain (unnamed) of 37 restaurants located throughout the city. Six weeks into the campaign, Mills executive B. L. Kulick declared it had already proven itself to be an unusual success. Mills ads appeared over the name of the restaurant chain indicating that each outlet had jukebox music available. Blow-ups of the ads were also produced and placed in the windows of all the locations. Kulick stated that the campaign had greatly increased the patronage in all of the restaurant outlets.[63]

Placing advertisements on jukes continued to be an idea that surfaced from time to time. The Phonograph Operators' Association of Eastern Pennsylvania and New Jersey went on record in 1942 that they blacklisted advertising records in their machines despite the fact that advertising records weren't then being actively pursued by the industry.[64]

However, that changed toward the end of 1945 when a device for opening the nation's jukeboxes to commercial advertising was being demonstrated by its Tennessee inventors. S. D. Wooten, chief engineer of radio station WREC at Nashville, and Bill Trotter, program manager at Knoxville station WNOX, came up with the idea. They emphasized the possibilities of advertising products usually sold on the premises of establishments that were likely to be home to a box — beer, soft drinks, candy, and so on. The Wooten/Trotter appliance would cost about $10 per unit if sold singly. However, if it was mass produced in a high enough volume the cost could drop to $4. Each commercial ad went on an individual disk that replaced a regular record in the box. An ad could be any length up to the capacity of the record. Most boxes then held 20 to 24 selections, and with at least a couple of selections on each machine that were never played it was argued that one or two commercial records would not interfere with business. The inventors' device functioned to regulate the sequence in which the commercial disks played. For example, an advertiser might want his message played after each regular record, or after 3, 4, or 10 records had played. A customer would always get the selection he paid for, but the advertisement would play for free at fixed intervals. Box operators were said to feel that their weekly take for running an advertising record should run from $1 up, depending on location.[65]

With all the juke makers out of box production due to the war, the problem of those manufacturers selling machines directly to locations did not come up. Nevertheless, that problem did surface. Members of the Philadelphia area operators' association, following group action taken two months earlier, made individual pledges to see that no machines fell into the hands of a private individual. Some distributors and operators, outside the association, were reported to have sold reconditioned boxes for home use. One operator was accused of selling used jukes to location owners. That particular operator, whose business tactics moved the association to action, had advertised boxes for sale in papers reaching the tavern trade. Causing even greater concern was the fact that his selling plan allowed machine collections to go toward paying for the machines, which was criticized as "virtually an installment selling plan." Association business manager Jack Cade declared that the future of the industry depended upon control of jukeboxes by regular operators and was jeopardized by permitting machines to fall into private hands. Cade also pointed out that there was always the danger of a private owner taking a machine purchased for private use to his place of business. The association, he said, had kept a close check on virtually all machines sold to private individuals and had found that the majority of them had been bought by people who operated a place of business that was actually, or potentially, a regular box location. Fumed Cade: "The commercial juke boxes were never intended for home use. After the war the public has been promised home jukes—automatic record players. But the machines today are meant to be solely for commercial operation in public places." One of the checks placed by the association on those selling jukes to private individuals was freezing the sale of parts to them (obtaining parts was often difficult during the war). Association members pledged not to cooperate with such operators or distributors (who sold boxes to private individuals) when the former were in need of any parts or materials.[66]

Understandably, there were no technical changes in boxes during this period. One thing that did happen was the spread of remote units such as wall boxes, bar boxes, and so on. According to Baltimore operators, the use of wall boxes assumed a new importance in the field of box operation. When wall units were first introduced a few years earlier, they said: "Some operators looked upon them with skepticism. They looked upon their introduction as but another means of manufacturers to boost their sales for new or additional equipment." The lack of new equipment allowed wall boxes to eliminate from the restaurant, tavern, or other location "the steadily growing shabby appearance of the aging music box. Through installation of wall boxes, the aging machine can easily be removed to a basement spot or backroom location outside the view of patrons." Another significant aspect of the situation was the fact that the owner of a location equipped with wall boxes was more hesitant about changing operators. That owner would think twice before requesting an operator remove all his equipment in order to have another operator enter the location.[67]

June 1945 saw the announcement of a new process, "music in color," wherein colors were flashed on a screen to accompany music, matched in some way to reflect the music. This idea's potential power as an attention-catcher was a major selling point. It was hoped the new device might enhance the effect of the illuminated plastic panels and other decorative devices already in use on the boxes. The jukebox industry, observed an account, had long been confronted with the problem of obtaining a device "which would attract attention to the box and still allow it to maintain a certain dignity of appearance." This "music in color" idea was not heard from again.[68]

While there were no technological changes in jukeboxes themselves during the war years, two ideas did surface that involved different uses for the boxes. Both phone music and soundies had their birth shortly before the United States officially entered World War II. Writing in *American Mercury* in October 1940, Barry Ulanov mentioned the beginnings of a system of jukes wired to a central studio and supplying records by telephone control. He said it was a system that would give customers a choice from thousands of numbers instead of a "measly dozen or two."[69]

A few months later *Billboard* editor Walter Hurd wrote that telephone music received considerable attention and enjoyed widespread newspaper publicity near the close of 1940. This system had a central board or studio with leased telephone wires extending to music outlets in 10 to 30 establishments. The central studio had one or more attendants and from a few dozen to hundreds of popular records that could be placed on record turntables and piped to the point where the music had been requested. Customers spoke into a microphone to request a record and also deposited their coins. Juke operators met the new idea by fitting standard boxes with microphones, to be used in the telephone music system. If the new system failed, the standard juke could remain in the location. Hurd felt the phone music idea would have only a limited appeal.[70]

Writing around the same time in *Reader's Digest*, Geoffrey Parsons, Jr., and Robert Yoder discussed a system they called an "automatic hostess." A customer stepped up to a cabinet, which featured the picture of a pretty girl, selected his song from a list that might offer as many as 600 selections, dropped in his nickel, and was rewarded with a friendly voice saying "Selection, please?" He was talking to a girl in a central studio connected with the various locations by leased telephone wires. The hostess had a helper to find and play the records. For 25 cents the hostess would dedicate a number to anyone the customer wished to honor. Parsons declared, "Enthusiasts proclaim this the juke box of the future."[71]

Jukebox operators in the Philadelphia area were fully involved in the telephone music system just a little over a year after the idea was first mentioned. Play-a-Tune, representing members of the Phonograph Operators' Association of Eastern Pennsylvania and Southern New Jersey, was organized by the association. All Philadelphia members were represented in Play-a-Tune. In February 1942, a studio of 30 turntables was set up in an office building in Philadelphia, which also housed the association. Plans called for another studio using 20 turntables to open soon in North Philadelphia to serve that area. Within six months Play-a-Tune hoped to have 100 turntables in operation.[72]

Telephone music systems as described above, with live hostesses and so on, quickly died only to reappear in a slightly different format. Headquartered in New York, Personal Music Corporation started in 1940 but made few installations of its telephone music system. The firm was inactive for several years before starting up again in May 1945 to make and operate entirely new equipment. Personal Music maintained studios where music from dual automatic record changers was piped into locations over telephone wires. Locations were provided with small eight-by-eight inch speaker cabinets that were placed along counters or in booths. Upon depositing either a penny or a nickel — depending on the type of box installed — customers received either three or six minutes of uninterrupted, nonselective music that could be heard only in the immediate vicinity of the speaker — perhaps two or three people near a counter speaker, and only the people in a booth. Personal Music was said to be then in the process of installing equipment in New York's Grand Central Station, in all United drugstores, including Rexall and Liggett, and the coast-to-coast chain of Mayflower Doughnut shops. The company placed either a penny or nickel box in a location after it conducted a "careful canvass" to determine which was best suited. For example, a location near a university, patronized mostly by students, might get a penny machine since students were likely to be on limited budgets. With regard to its selection of music, it was observed: "While the customer has no choice of the recording he is to hear, the firm makes a careful selection of disks designed to please a wide variety of listeners. Response from locations tells whether or not the choices are good." Grandiose future plans by the company included operating its own equipment in 33 major cities and selling franchises in other communities. Hoping to provide a balanced 24-hour-a-day program, Personal Music purchased the same recordings for all of its studios, "so that the program in each city is identical."[73]

Telo-Tune was formed in Chicago in 1946 to operate coin-fed music equipment using telephone lines to transmit recorded music from a central studio to various locations. Named Musicale, the system featured several

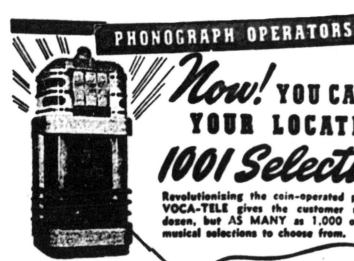

A 1940 trade ad for one of the telephone music systems trying to get established. None did.

variations in phone-music wall boxes, chief of which was a selectivity element. Before each selection was played, a short announcement piped in from the studio "sells" the song through every box, but the number itself was audible only from those boxes in which customers had deposited coins. Thus, the customer knew what tune would be played and could take it or leave it. Telo-Tune equipment had supposedly then been in operation for two months at 10 Washington, D.C., locations, including Ford's Restaurant and Blue Bell Waffle Shops.[74]

Simultaneously with, but independent of phone music systems, the story of "soundies" was unfolding. Barry Ulanov wrote about Phonovision or Talkovision, a "slick combination of the standard Juke box and miniature movies." In preparation for an anticipated rush of orders the Phonovision Corporation of America had hired a large staff, appointed a former producer of movie shorts to supervise its three-minute productions, and started producing jukes that could be seen as well as heard.[75]

Walter Hurd enthused that these new movie machines were the ultimate in coin-operated entertainment. Already a dozen or so firms had announced developments in that field, including a juke manufacturer. He felt the real issue hinged on the production of suitable and attractive films. Hurd argued that an entirely new type of film would have to be developed for these new movie machines. "Current development during the year tended to be simple illustrations of musicians in action, giving what might be called an illustrated recording. The possibility of musical shorts and musical comedy stunts was suggested."[76]

Geoffrey Parsons observed that there were many competitors in the field but that a likely candidate to lead the pack was Jimmy Roosevelt (President Franklin Roosevelt's eldest son) with "Soundies, a glorified juke box giving a three-minute sound movie for a dime." Even more optimistic was Parsons's conclusion: "Always looking ahead, when movies and music and automatic hostesses pall, the juke box man plans a super-super-juke box with television."[77]

Heading his own company, Jimmy Roosevelt had signed a contract in 1940 with the Mills Novelty Company to manufacture the movie coin machines. However, wartime restrictions on the use of materials severely limited the new venture.[78]

Progress of the jukebox movie industry was almost completely on hold by 1943 because of the war. Some 28 firms had announced they would produce films for the machines and/or manufacture movie machines. However, only one was then actually in business—the Soundies Distributing Corporation of America (an affiliate of Mills Novelty), headed by Roosevelt. Soundies had 4,500 machines (called Panorams) on the market, of which 1,500 were operated by its own organization, Soundies Operating Company. An additional 1,500 machines were located in schools and war plants for educational purposes. Soundies produced its own pictures and bought all it could from independent producers. "Original talent budgets have been trimmed to the bone to conform with the small income from the limited number of machines." Virtually all product was furnished by William F. Crouch, Soundies publicity director, who had been placed in charge of production. "Crouch contributes the majority of shorts, using unknown talent, and playing up, primarily current song hits. In addition, he shops around for movie machine shorts which have never been shown, as well as musical sequences from old movie features which are adaptable for movie machine use." In mid–1943, the AFM was in the midst of a long musicians' strike that lasted all of 1943 and well into 1944, which taxed the ingenuity of producers of those musical shorts. Unable to use musicians, they were forced to buy old musical tracks and devise suitable action or concentrate on vocals only. "This condition has made the use of old musical shorts very popular."[79]

According to Soundies, the operator did not complain about the age of the short as long as it furnished entertainment. Many musical sequences from British-made films, never released in America, had been sliced out and presented on the machines "under suitable titles." Soundies planned to continue its current sales schedule for the duration of the war. That meant it would release a reel of 8 three-minute shorts a week, among them six new subjects and two reissues. "While originally Soundies went overboard on the use of well-known performers, the reception given them on location did not warrant the high salaries paid them. The company will, henceforth, concentrate primarily on good, unknown talent." Reportedly, these movie machines had introduced many newcomers to films who had gone on to be picked up by major film producers and given lucrative contracts. Cited as examples were Dorothy Dandridge, Jean Porter, Marvel Maxwell, Grace McDonald, and Alan Ladd.[80]

A report late in 1945 indicated that Soundies might be redesigned and adapted for commercial use, such as presenting sales films in dealer showrooms, advertising films in hotel lobbies and transportation terminals, and so on. However, Soundies, along with telephone music, were dead. Nevertheless, the concept behind Soundies would reappear in the future.[81]

Within the record industry it was estimated that 75 percent of the 120 million records likely to be sold in 1943 would be of popular music, 20 percent would be classical, and the remaining 5 percent would be children's disks. Popular records still retailed at 35 cents each, with sales of that group expected to be 35 percent of the total in 1943, down from 50 percent a couple of years earlier when the industry faced neither a manpower nor a materials shortage. With those shortages, labels devoted more of their resources to higher-priced disks (50 cents, 75 cents, and $1). For the past several months, the record industry had been getting just 20 percent of the shellac (a key disk ingredient) it received in 1941. That would have meant practically an industry shut-down had it not been for the development of "extender" substances and reclaimed shellac gained from a scrap-record campaign. At first, extenders led to poor quality records, but further improvements had supposedly led to technically much better extenders.[82]

Little was said in this period about the power of jukes to make hit records. One of the few comments in that area came from RCA-Victor general manager J. W. Murray, who said that coin-operated phonographs in public places were helping to make "popular selections become hit tunes more rapidly and create a specific demand for recordings which appear in these juke boxes." Predicting that there would be many more jukeboxes on location after the war, Murray concluded, "The juke box is doing and will continue to do a valuable pre-selling job for popular disks."[83]

Results of a questionnaire answered by over 100 members of *The Billboard* Operators' Advisory Committee gave record labels information on what type of music was not being recorded that would do well on jukeboxes. Some 25 percent of those operators said more country tunes were wanted (by Roy Acuff, Ernest Tubb, Tex Ritter, Al Dexter, and Bob Willis—in that order). More waltzes (Wayne King) were wanted by 22 percent of the operators while 16 percent wanted South American numbers, 10 percent wanted Hawaiian, 9 percent voted for more novelty numbers (Spike Jones), 8 percent wanted vocal quartets, and 6 percent wanted more foreign tunes.[84]

That same Operators' Advisory Committee responded to a nationwide survey of industry record buying habits in 1945. Respondents reported operating a total of 5,044 boxes and that during March that year they bought 44,042 disks, a little more than 8.5 per machine. Operators made their purchases as follows: 25,499 from the big three labels, RCA, Columbia, and Decca; 9,084 disks from other record labels; 6,580 from retail stores; and 2,879 from other sources such as ads in newspapers and second-hand shops.[85]

Even though a war was underway—with its resultant shortages of materials for civilian consumer goods—record sales went up dramatically. In millions of dollars, sales of records from 1940 to 1945 were, respectively, $48, $51, $55, $66, $66, and $99. An even more spectacular jump took place in 1946 when record sales reached $198 million.[86]

As was to be expected, there was much less foreign trade in jukeboxes during the war years. Private Irving Bader was home on leave in June 1943, after service in Australia and the South Pacific. Formerly an employee of a Cleveland operating firm, J. C. Novelty Company, Bader reported there were no jukeboxes whatsoever in Sydney, Australia. A more detailed report on conditions there came two years later from George Davidson, a juke operator in Sydney. Like England, Australia had no coin-machine imports since the start of the war in 1939. In all of Australia he estimated there were only 200 boxes. First American-made machines arrived in Australia in early 1938, but official figures showed that few shipments were made. One result of the shipping lanes being closed in 1939 was that the latest model jukes available on location in Australia (in late 1945) were 1938 vintage, or older, and were "barely hanging together." When the music machines were first imported they created little stir. Operators felt they were not profitable while the public regarded them as merely novelties. Not until American soldiers began to arrive there did the machines catch on. When those soldiers left, there was some drop in play but it was still said to be twice as high as in prewar days. Standard equipment in arcades was two boxes, one at each end, played loud to attract attention. Other good locations were restaurants and milk bars (like soda fountains), which drew a lot of teens. Australian liquor laws prohibited jukes where liquor was sold.[87]

In Mexico, operators said the best places to put machines were in cantinas (saloons), small cabarets, beer parlors, and restaurants. Many towns with a population of 10,000 or less and without running water and electricity, nevertheless, still had boxes. Usually a location owner received 20 percent of the gross receipts from the operator. Operators estimated that Mexico City had 1,000 to 1,500 machines on location. Favorite American singers in Mexico were Bing Crosby and the Andrews Sisters.[88]

Figures compiled by the United States Department of Commerce showed that a total of 7,233 coin machines of all types (valued at $552,119) were shipped to 25 foreign countries in 1945. That export business was less than half of what it was in prewar days. For example, in 1940, 15,668 machines ($1,248,692) were exported to 47 nations. The United Kingdom was out of the picture entirely during 1945, but they had in 1939 purchased 10,224 machines valued at $432,591. During 1944, 5,870 machines ($766,689) were shipped abroad — 2,544 of those were jukes ($560,346). In 1944 Mexico bought 1,921 jukes valued at $385,233. The following year Mexico purchased 799 boxes ($194,237).[89]

Industry figures indicated that in 1940 the six box makers produced 49,000 units and about 39,000 in 1941. The total number of boxes in operation was estimated at 400,000, as of January 1, 1941. As well, there were about 250 distributors and 7,000 operators. Record production for 1938 was said to be 33 million disks (15 million used by jukes); 60 million in 1939 (31 million); 75 million in 1940 (37.4 million); and 110 million in 1941 (45 million). General industry data as of December 31, 1941, indicated there were 1.15 million amusement machines in operation — 300,000 phonographs (which contradicted the above number) and 3.43 million vending machines. Within the latter category were 3 million penny venders, 126,500 cigarette venders, 250,000 five-cent candy bar vendors, and 28,000 beverage machines.[90]

Information on profits from operating music machines continued to be sketchy or nonexistent. Baltimore's Alpha Vending was registering a highly satisfactory volume of business, despite help shortages and mechanical problems, according to Alpha head George Andoniades. Best results, he said, came from locations in the war plant area, where wages were high. Alpha operated many types of coin machines but received its best collections from jukes. While collections on pinball games and other nonmusic machines were fairly satisfactory, varied and spotty results were normal. "Not so, however, with music boxes, where collections are holding up well and showing a fine upward trend," commented Andoniades.[91]

High praise for the industry came from the pen of Glenn Dillard Dunn, music editor of the Washington *Times-Herald*, when he extolled the merits of the juke as the most powerful means of forming the musical tastes of the nation. Calling the box "America's most influential music educator," Dunn went on to point out that the industry made "handsome donations to the military camps and hospitals and to civic philanthropies such as Washington's Junior Police and Citizens' Corps when they staged soft drink dances to get teenagers off the streets." Dunn argued that phonographs formed or deformed the likes of millions in those "impressionable years" when musical tastes are fixed. He called the radio and the cinema mere "extensions" of the juke. It was the box that made American music "the real music that the public loves and will pay for — the music of the mob." If Americans were ever to love music of higher artistic worth, he said, "it must derive from the juke box idiom. There is no other source for a nationalistic expression, and unless fine music is nationalistic, it never is accepted by the multitude."[92]

This period was mostly a very positive one for the juke industry. No new machines were manufactured, but otherwise the industry thrived. Negative aspects were not absent but relatively minor. One thing that irritated the industry was that the passage of laws restricting or banning the boxes and measures taxing the machines continued to be passed. Massachusetts had an older law that prohibited public entertainment on Sundays. However, certain entertainment could be licensed in locations where admission or other valuable consideration was charged. The cities issued the licenses, which then had to be sent to the state Department of Public Safety for its approval. A flat fee of $2 for each Sunday license was fixed by statute. In 1934 the counsel for the City of Boston gave an advisory opinion that the statue applied to locations containing a jukebox because of an implied admission charge. Then licensing was applied to box locations in a few cases in a few cities. However, in 1937, the Massachusetts attorney general gave an opinion to Public Safety that the statute did not apply to box locations because no admission or other valuable consideration was charged in fact. On that opinion, juke licensing was stopped. Nonetheless, in 1942 the Department of Public Safety advised the cities that it believed the phonograph locations should be licensed. Such licensing started in Boston and spread to other cities in the state. Apparently reports that some jukes in the state contained "suggestive" records triggered the move.[93]

A proposed city ordinance in Charlotte, North Carolina, would have established a nightly curfew on music of all kinds in liquor locations and would also have placed a ban on box operation for the entire day of Sunday. That move followed suggestions made by the chief of police when public criticism began to accumulate concerning conditions in some locations. Jukes were reportedly operated in homes in the "colored district," and those homes had been converted into "regular dens where liquor is sold and other irregularities" took place. However, the Charlotte City Council gave the police department suggestion the cold shoulder and voted to ask the city administration to completely revise the ordinance so as to omit the attack on juke music. The council said the original proposal was decidedly unfair to reputable merchants and stores in the city.[94]

On another front, Special Circuit Judge C. P. Rouse in Frankfort, Kentucky, upheld the right of the State Alcoholic Beverage Control Board (ABCB) to enforce regulations in rural taverns that would ban jukeboxes, dancing, pinball games, and other forms of amusement. Kentucky law imposed that ban unless the population of a city or town was sufficient to provide for a regular police force. In a special opinion delivered in advance of formal orders, Judge Rouse refused an injunction to enjoin the ABCB from enforcing its new anti-roadhouse ruling. After the ABCB was created by the 1944 General Assembly, it issued a regulation denying licenses to any place commonly known as a roadhouse in counties not maintaining police patrols. A roadhouse was defined as "any public place outside an incorporated city or town patronized by the public for the purpose of amusement such as dancing, the playing of music, juke boxes, pinball machines, slot machines or games of any kind."[95]

One of the few taxes the juke trade accepted without objection was a special federal excise tax of $10 per year on each music machine levied in 1942 to aid the war effort. That law divided coin-operated machines into two groups: vending machines that were exempt from the tax and amusement and music machines. Although the tax was levied on the location, it was understood that the taxes would be paid by the box operators, as was the case with the pin games.[96]

When Oklahoma governor Robert S. Kerr signed into law a proposal that would take 10 percent of the gross receipts from jukes in that state,

Billboard complained that Oklahoma "took the lead in the setting up of juke box grab plans ... Juke box grab plans of various kinds have been suggested by many agencies." All of those various grab plans were based on the theory, fumed the publication, "that juke boxes are regular mints." Oklahoma's House of Representatives first passed a bill for 15 percent of the gross, but the Senate killed it. Later, though, the measure was revived when Kerr explained that "the church people wanted the bill passed." As far as *Billboard* was concerned, that indicated anti-liquor forces were the real force behind the passage of the bill. The journal declared the measure to be one of the most serious laws yet passed affecting boxes "and has all the earmarks of a real political grab plan." Income from the tax was estimated at from $150,000 to $360,000 a year.[97]

When the Massachusetts legislature debated a proposal to impose an annual fee of $10 on each box, bill sponsor Representative Enrico Cappucci (D., East Boston) estimated Massachusetts would gain $2.5 million yearly. That, of course, would have been impossible since Massachusetts had nowhere near 250,000 machines. Walter Guild, managing director of the state Automatic Music Association, testified against the measure and exaggerated in the opposite direction. Guild estimated there were 10,000 to 11,000 boxes in the state before the war, but by 1943 the number was 6,000 to 7,000. He argued the highest weekly take from jukes was about $10, split 50/50 with the locations and that the maximum yearly profit was about $25 per machine. Therefore, he felt the tax, which would generate $70,000 in revenue for the state in the first year, was too high.[98]

San Francisco, in 1944, rejected a proposal that would have raised a box tax from $1 a month to $2 a month. With around 1,800 machines in the city, revenue generated from the existing tax was $23,364 per year.[99]

In a May 23, 1945, decision, the Illinois Supreme Court declared the Chicago juke tax was too high, although the city had the legal right to pass a license tax. Chicago's box tax was passed in December 1943, at a time when city council was looking for all possible sources of new revenue. An annual tax of $50 was placed on juke locations. Two other coin-machine license fees were passed at the same time: one covering arcade amusement machines and another covering target guns. Operators of those two types of machines accepted license fees, but box operators and location owners at once began to contest the measure. Chicago's tax was not only a cause of worry for local operators and locations, but the high tax received newspaper publicity all over the country and the worry was that it would inspire high juke taxes in other areas. Agitation for a tax in Chicago first began in 1940. Through the long period of agitation for a juke tax, tavern owners played an important part in fighting the proposals and were credited with causing many delays before the law was passed. Two appeals were taken against the tax. One was by the operators and the other was by the Amalgamated Beverage Congress, representing location owners. The city of Chicago appealed that decision, asking for a rehearing of the May 23rd decision. However, that appeal was rejected at the end of 1945.[100]

Lansing, Michigan, passed an ordinance that licensed jukes and amusement machines at a rate of $25 annually per machine. As well, it imposed a $1,000 business license fee on the operator. It was invalidated by Circuit Court Judge Leland W. Carr, who declared the business licensing provisions of the ordinance "unconstitutional and discriminatory." A Miami, Florida, measure attracted national attention because it set up a standard to limit music machines to one machine for every 265 people living in the city. It, too, was declared invalid. During the fight over the measure it was reported that about 800 jukeboxes were operating in the city. A court decision in Springfield, Massachusetts, removed phonographs from the Sunday ban on music, part of a general law in the state. A newly enacted license law in Philadelphia — with about 3,300 machines there — held up in court. Detroit also passed a box license law, applied to the city's estimated 5,000 machines. Operators there did not contest the measure after it passed because they had fought a vigorous defense in hearings before council and obtained a fee they considered "fairly reasonable."[101]

Problems with copyright and unemployed musicians surfaced briefly. In 1943 ASCAP filed two lawsuits in United States District Court, New York, against two New York tavern owners claiming copyright infringement of ASCAP controlled songs on jukebox records. According to ASCAP, the two Manhattan taverns once used live musicians and held ASCAP licenses. When those businesses revised their policies, substituting jukes for musicians, the permits were canceled, but the owners still benefited from the use of ASCAP material. In its view, the exclusion of coin machines from the 1909 copyright law occurred because the current juke situation, which had replaced live musicians in many cases, could not have been envisioned at that time.[102]

A January 1945 editorial in the trade journal *The Musician* declared that the music machines were "fast becoming a national nuisance." Stating that the city council in Duluth, Minnesota, had legalized boxes in 99 liquor and beer establishments while banning the use of live musicians in those places, the editor complained the government exacted an amusement tax from hotels and restaurants that employed live music — but not on jukes. Acknowledging that so far interpreters of the law had ruled it was the public that played the records in those machines, the editor argued that records made for home use should not be placed in jukes in public places because it enabled box owners and location owners "to earn from the use of the records a profit to which they are not morally entitled — and the musicians who make them thus literally play their own selves out of hundreds of jobs."[103]

Bernard B. Smith wrote an article in *Harper's* in December 1942 that was sympathetic to the plight of musicians losing work to the music machines. Smith argued the boxes should be made responsible for unemployed musicians within the context of technological unemployment. He proposed the formation of an organization called the National Foundation of Musicians that would collect a percentage from jukeboxes in all locations, say 20 percent a year. That would amount to $20 million annually from a juke take estimated to be $100 million and be used to help unemployed musicians. In reply, *Billboard* said that Smith did not take into account that federal, state, and local governments were already taxing phonographs "and that the government should have preference over any organization that may be set up or has already been set up." It added: "These taxes should come first, before any charitable organization of any kind begins to dip into the juke box earnings, which seem so fabulous to certain people." A second basic weakness in Smith's case, bristled *Billboard*, was that the federal government had already set up a social security plan "which has in it the greatest and the most sensible methods yet devised for solving unemployment problems in any industry." Proposals for organizations such as Smith mentioned were "rather futile when compared with what the government is doing, and will do in the future to meet all unemployment situations."[104]

Other types of coin machines continued to draw heat from the public. In Oregon City, Oregon, Women's Christian Temperance Union (WCTU) and other religious groups combined to attempt to get a referendum on the ballot as to whether to allow pin games in the community. For technical reasons, the measure failed to get on the ballot. Speaking for the trade, *Billboard* cautioned there should be no cash payouts by the machine and that minors should be kept away from them. Calling gambling "an evil," the account went on to note that machines were clearly marked "For Amusement Only" and were intended to automatically give free plays for winning or tokens were delivered to the winner for the purpose of replaying the machine. However, in most locations the winner could cash in his tokens for money. He was not obligated to do so but invariably did.[105]

Mentions of organized crime involvement also appeared on occasion. When a Chicago grand jury was investigating organized gambling in 1943, the Chicago Crime Commission urged the grand jury to investigate the jukebox trade, claiming that prominent politicians were involved with organized crime in the music-machine industry. An industry supporter lamented, "The incident is one of those unfortunate things that occur in various cities at intervals..."[106]

An otherwise brief and innocuous account in *Billboard* on March 13, 1943, reported that two men were taking over the Wurlitzer distributorship in New York, New Jersey, and Connecticut. At a trade gathering, several company executives presented Meyer Lansky and his associate Ed Smith to Eastern box operators. Said Wurlitzer official Mike Hammergren: "We know that in Meyer Lansky we have a man who is liked and respected by everyone ... we are confident that as Wurlitzer's new distributor in this territory he will make many new friends." When questioned about his plans, Lansky intimated that "he would much prefer to have his actions speak for him." At that time Lansky was one of the top figures in America's organized crime world and had been so for many years. Known primarily as the mob's chief banker, he was also involved in the formation of organized crime's assassination department — the dreaded Murder, Inc. Lansky's name may not have been well known among the general public, but his connections to organized crime could hardly have escaped the notice of *Billboard*, the juke industry in general, and Wurlitzer.[107]

As World War II ended and America readjusted to civilian life, the juke industry was optimistic. All over the United States, boxes were rapidly aging and in need of replacement. The end to hostilities held the promise of opening many lucrative foreign markets that had been closed for years to American-made music machines. Forgotten for the moment was that the industry had almost hit the saturation point back around 1938. As 1946 began it seemed as though there was nothing but good times ahead for the industry, for as far as one could see.

5

The Nickel and Dime War, 1946–1950

"Since five-cent-a-tune music is the music of the masses, it will remain the emphatic policy of this company that Seeburg phonographs will continue to present music for a nickel." Marshall Seeburg, 1946.

"You can't pay $1,000 for a juke box with nickels." James Fitzpatrick, operator, 1950.

"Most jukebox operators don't fear tele[vision] is threat to their industry." Variety, 1950.

Predictions for the juke industry in the postwar period tended to be rosy and overly optimistic. One account estimated that in 1941 there were 8,000 operators with 300,000 machines on location with each of them taking an average of 112 records that year. A 1944 survey indicated that each operator would want 75 new phonographs in the immediate postwar period, for a total of 600,000 units. Using the 112 records per box as a standard meant the 600,000 new boxes would need 67.2 million disks. Plus, it was thought, not all the 300,000 units then on location would be scrapped.[1]

Some hoped that the fast-spreading cocktail lounge would become a profitable new type of location for music machines. Detroit then had 168 such establishments, all reported to be doing well. There was supposedly a rapid growth in this "new type of high-class tavern" in most cities, especially in larger communities. Those 168 Detroit spots employed cocktail combos, or groups of musicians ranging from high-priced solo pianists to a trio or quartet, sometimes in shifts. While the box trade always aspired to have a higher presence in the high-class establishments, it was never very successful in that regard.[2]

More cautious in tone was an estimate that the present stock (in 1945) of rebuilt boxes on location would have to last longer than the average operator anticipated, and that it would be at least three to four years following the end of war before sufficient equipment would be available to fill all needs. At the same time, the export business in used boxes was steadily increasing and orders and requests from South American operators were much larger than could be supplied. A number of the larger New York area distributors anticipated that the export trade would absorb all the used equipment available "and that everything and anything that works will be bought up as soon as more shipping space is to be had." Exports to countries such as Brazil, Colombia, Nicaragua, Ecuador, and others was expected to double or triple as soon as the war ended. This was a positive development with respect to selling more new units in America since it indicated that no glut of used boxes in the United States would arise and possibly slow the sales of new machines. It also decreased the likelihood that such used units would be sold directly to location owners.[3]

Surveying the situation, *Business Week* declared, at the start of 1946, that "rejuking" the nation meant replacing the 400,000 boxes of 1942 vintage and older "now beaten to pieces." A typical operator was said to keep for himself as much as $25 weekly per machine from top locations and as little as $2.50 a week from poor locations. That difference accounted "for the not infrequent connection between juke boxes, precinct politics, and strong-arm squads." Included in the established juke industry, returning to box making, were six firms: AMI, Gabel, Mills, Rock-Ola, Seeburg, and Wurlitzer. Three other major firms had announced they would enter the field: Aireon Manufacturing Company of Kansas City, Kansas; Bally Manufacturing Corporation of Chicago; and Packard Manufacturing Company of Indianapolis, headed by jukebox veteran Senator Homer Capehart. With regard to Capehart, the business publication noted, "His efforts to bejuke a saloonless nation in the 1920s were less than spectacularly successful." Bally had long been involved in the production of pinball and other coin-operated amusement devices. Most of those manufacturers, established and new, were hoping to get out their new models throughout the spring and early summer of 1946. Aireon was heavily touting a new electronic volume control on their units, wherein a microphone hung in the "noise center" of a room and automatically turned the volume of music up or down to a preset level. Its music machine was said to be wider, lower, "and less garishly lighted than most prewar models."[4]

With regard to the problem of deciding which records to put on boxes, Norman Weiser argued that programming was one factor often overlooked by veteran operators who entered the business when the machines offered as few as 12 to 16 selections. It was then comparatively easy to pick a best-selling disk. Even when box capacity was increased to 20 to 24 selections, programming was still a "minor" issue. Only with the coming of economic hard times for the juke trade in 1948, thought Weiser, had the importance of programming become apparent. The music publisher was important because he, above all others, determined whether a song would be a hit. And that was determined by the promotion the publisher put into a song. Also important was the volume of records released by a label and the methods of promoting those disks (through trade ads, placards, mailings, and so on). Weiser said those factors "may well determine whether or not it will find public favor on a large enough scale to make it a money winner for the operator." With operators spending about 10 percent of their gross receipts on new records, Weiser deemed it imperative that they keep close tabs on charts, the Hit Parade, record reviews, and *Billboard* listings. One operator advised that at each location the box should contain at least one favorite record of the owner and/or staff. No matter how well programmed a juke was, it was all lost unless the phonograph was operating and attracting the attention of patrons.[5]

Another person who favored placing an owner's favorite disks on a box was operator Robert L. Johnson of the Panama City Music Company in Florida. Contrary to the opinion of some operators who believed that "putting the bartender's favorites" on the phonograph was a mistake, Johnson felt the major portion of his off-season profits were due to "putting three house records on the box" at every location. Panama operated 140 music machines and 100 pinball games through the Northwest Florida Gulf Coast resort area. The peak collection period ran from May 1 until the end of August, when lots of tourists were in the area. Instead of accepting the usual slump in sales after September 1, Johnson began to go after the location owner. It was an automatic rule with the firm to allot three records "to the house" on every box, whether it was a 100-selection or a 24-selection model. Said Johnson: "We do not even care whether the public likes the number which the location owner chooses." By programming the owner's favorites, Panama had found the owner was likely to spend a lot of his own money playing the juke.[6]

Regardless of what was programmed on the machines, the noise level continued to be a nuisance in some areas. Irvington-on-Hudson, New York, police chief Bernard McCall announced in July 1947 that he was ordering an 11:45 P.M. curfew on the playing of tavern music machines. McCall explained that he had no special power to order such a curfew but would attain enforcement by arresting violators for disturbing the peace and by submitting reports to the State Alcoholic Beverage Control Board. Dance-band music and crooning from the jukes could be heard several blocks away on summer nights with windows open. Such noise had been emanating from some taverns until 3 A.M. Four tavern proprietors conferred with McCall and reportedly agreed to cooperate fully.[7]

Around the same time a wave of unfavorable publicity aimed at noisy jukes arose in Chicago. Because both operators and location owners recognized the problem and took the necessary steps to control the situation, that publicity was said to have disappeared within a few months. Evidence for that came from the increased requests from locations for remote control units to make volume regulation simple. The most popular form of that type of control was a regulator placed below the bar in a tavern or behind the counter in an eatery. Most operators said they rigged up their own remote unit from standard regulator parts. Remote control regulators were most popular in bars, hamburger stands, and ice-cream shops where it was often difficult to regulate music machines except from behind the counter. In such establishments the control units were installed upon the request of the owner, but a few local operators were actively promoting them. Installation of regulator units could be made for a cost of about $2 and took around one hour. Still, less than half of the area jukes were so equipped. The second best way to meet the volume-control problem, according to operators, was with properly located auxiliary speakers. Box and auxiliary speakers could then be controlled in one of three ways: together, separately, or the auxiliary could be switched on or off as an extra.[8]

Unacceptable at any volume level, in any machine, were smut records, which received at least one mention in this period. Location owners joined with Chicago box operators in 1947 to head off and stop the use of off-color disks on any of the city's music machines. Ray Cunliffe, president of the Illinois Automatic Phonograph Owners' Association, reported that members of his group had contacted his office with reports of questionable releases. As a result Cunliffe directed a letter to the association membership warning them against such records. It said, "the popularity of such [off-color] records is always short-lived, and the profits from their use are certainly not large enough to justify the irreparable damage that could be done to the standing of the business." Martin Moran, representing the Illinois Tavern Owners' Association, joined Cunliffe in the drive against smut platters, saying his group favored "anything that will keep the tavern business on a high plane and eliminate anything of a suggestive nature taking place in such establishments." A survey of Chicago operators revealed that every one contacted opposed the use of off-color material for the good of the industry. Operators reported that some location owners, principally tavern proprietors, had requested that certain "questionable" records be placed on their phonographs.[9]

Some locations were seriously affected by a shortage of beer in the immediate postwar period. In turn, that led to a dramatic drop in juke play.

When the United States Department of Agriculture granted a 15 percent increase in grain allotment to brewers in the fall of 1946, it was hoped that such problems were coming to an end. In Philadelphia, local bars were required to close one day a week in addition to the Sunday closing required by law. Lack of beer was blamed by tavern owners for the shut-down that resulted in a 50 percent drop in coin-machine use in that city. The same situation was reported in Milwaukee. Jukes took the heaviest losses, but other coin machines such as nut venders also suffered big decreases. Many tavern owners in Chicago were obliged to resort to rationing beer in order to insure fairness. Tulsa, Oklahoma, beverage dealers were forced to reach an agreement to close on Tuesdays. Coin-machine usage fell from 25 percent to 60 percent in cities such as Baltimore, New Orleans, Dallas, Fort Worth, Detroit, and Richmond due to the shortage.[10]

A 1947 survey of Chicago operators on the question of marginal locations disclosed that from 10 to 40 percent of some operations consisted of marginal stops. Reporter Fred Amann noted that the majority of routes contained about 20 or 25 percent of such locations. Also disclosed was that most of the larger routes fell into the 20 to 25 percent group while the medium and small operations included from 25 to 40 percent marginals among their locations. Most operators agreed that marginal locations served as a sort of "safety valve." By permitting the use of older machines, the marginal stops served to work off such equipment with a profit. Older machines were defined here as equipment no longer usable in top-play locations, not "aged" boxes in the true sense of the term. Marginal locations also offered the operator the opportunity to reduce overhead by keeping older machines active instead of lying idle in the shop or selling them at a loss. Many times the amortization of a machine was only realized by placing it in a marginal location, operators claimed.[11]

Amann identified four types of juke locations; the marginal location ranked third, following the high-play spot and the mediocre location. Trailing in fourth place were the no-profit locations, which operators grouped among an ever-changing collection of failed choices. Although they were at the bottom of the profitable operation ladder, marginal locations were nevertheless an important part of every route. According to the survey, the majority of marginal stops were found in the neighborhood tavern off the main thoroughfare, with restaurants and "school stores" (small candy and school supply stores near high schools) ranking second and third as predominantly low-income spots. Guarantees, or front money paid by locations to operators, in the Chicago area (in marginals) were found to range from $6 to $9 a week, with an average of $7, depending upon the type of machine used. In a few instances, location owners were willing to pay as high as $18 a week to have a new model installed in their marginal location. Here, after

Salsbury Café, Vancouver, BC, 1946. A typical type of café for a box. *Vancouver Public Library, photo #26953.*

the first week or two, play dropped back to what it was before the new box was installed, indicating to Amann that a marginal stop would remain marginal no matter what type of unit was installed. The main reason a spot became marginal (outside of being in a poor district) was, said Amann, the "negative personality of its owner." For example, owner interference in setting the volume level too low. Besides keeping machines active, marginal stops provided a means of keeping the operator's name before the public by the prominent display of service cards on the boxes. Such cards had resulted in other location owners contacting operators wanting their own installations. It proved to the location without a machine that the operator was willing to site a box in other than a top-play spot. Lastly, location owners in marginal stops were said to be "easy to please."[12]

A different survey in 1948 found that Saturday was the best financial day for jukeboxes nationwide. Operators also generally agreed that Sunday was the worst day; there was no agreement on the ranking of the other days. Herman Duenisch operated a string of music machines through Du Page County in Illinois, near Chicago. He rated Saturday at least 20 percent ahead of Friday, which rated second best. Wednesday was third with Sunday far below average and Monday only slightly better. There was no doubt, said Duenisch, that adults were better spenders than the teenagers who comprised "the greater number of juke box daytime patrons." William Nyland, manager of the Chicago-based Western Automatic Music, rated Saturday first with receipts running 35 percent ahead of his next best night, Friday. Monday was third best for Nyland; Sunday was worst. Floyd Johnson, an operator in Prince Georges County, Maryland, also rated Saturday first with receipts one-third ahead of an average day and three times the take from the worst night, Sunday. Cities like New York, Chicago, and Los Angeles, where Friday was usually fight (boxing) night, had found that the advent of televised fights had a profound depressing effect on what used to be the second best jukebox play night. Floyd Pedrone, of Chicago's Little Amusement Company, ranked Saturday as his best day and Thursday his second best. Rating a good location at taking $30 a week, Pedrone said the average take on a Saturday would be about $10 while the Thursday income would be between $5 and $6. Thus, half his receipts came from the two best days. In a spot where the total take was lower, Saturday income would be $5 to $6 with the take on Thursday being $4. Sunday was his worst day. Pedrone thought Thursday ranked second because in his area shops were open that night. Oklahoma City operator Angelo Dominick reported Saturday to be his best day. Friday was next, then Wednesday and Thursday, about the same but slightly below Friday. Sunday was practically nil while Monday and Tuesday showed only slight gains over Sunday figures. Charlie Bernoff, of Regal Music Company, New York, said Saturday was his best day. If a juke took in $20 a week, about $6 of that came from Saturday play.[13]

Commissions paid to locations again became a hot topic as operators tried to find ways of increasing their incomes. Reporter Dick Schreiber believed all the cost burden was borne by the operators while the locations took only the "expense of a light bill and the mental torture of listening to a popular hit a thousand times." A 1949 survey of 4,562 operating firms yielded a total of 561 companies responding and 477 of them completed the section of the questionnaire dealing with commissions. A total of 435 of those operators (91 percent) admitted that all or part of their equipment was put on location with a 50/50 division of receipts. But nearly half of the operators pointed out that they used two or more types of commission payments; over half agreed that commission schedules in their territories could be changed. The survey left no doubt that operators disapproved of the 50/50 arrangement despite the fact that competitive reasons forced most of them into paying such commissions on all or part of their route. With 42.9 percent of the operators reporting they used two or more commission

Rob Roy Café, Burnaby, BC, 1949. Unidentified proprietor stands beside the increasingly popular remote jukebox unit, or wall box. *Vancouver Public Library, photo #28046.*

arrangements, it was revealed that most of them combined the 50/50 split with some form of first or front-money agreement. In response to the survey question "Do you think the commission schedule could be changed in your territory?" Fifty-two percent said yes, 47 percent said no, and less than 1 percent of the respondents were doubtful. Surveys conducted over the previous three years had repeatedly shown that operators thought the commission schedule could not be changed. Apparently the increasing use of first and front money deals, especially with new model equipment, convinced the average operator the commission arrangements could be adjusted if the sales approach was "built on a solid presentation of cost involved."[14]

The survey showed that operator opinion on commissions was unified only on one point — that the 50/50 arrangement, except at the route's best stops, was "financial suicide." One fact to be considered was that most of the music operators also handled pinball and other amusement games. A typical operator with both types of machines had a location giving a high weekly average on games for the past two years. He then installed a juke there on a 50/50 basis. Over the course of 1948 the juke grossed only $233, an average of $4.48 weekly. Said the operator: "The one-balls [games] make this a profitable stop, so we do not argue about the music commission." Operators who used a 60/40 split (in their favor) widely on their routes said they sold service rather than commissions. Many reported they would simply let a location go if that spot demanded more than 40 percent of the gross. One Kansas firm claimed they had locations on a 60/40 split who were content with that arrangement "until some other operator came along and offered them 50-50." Of all the responses to the survey, only one suggested using a sliding scale of commissions, depending on the gross of each machine — a method widely used in the vending-machine business. For example, if a spot grossed over $40 it would get 50 percent, if it was below $40 it would get 40 percent; if it was below $25 a week for two weeks in a row it would get one-third of the gross. A sliding scale was said to encourage location owners to try and reach the 50 percent mark. All agreed that a principal difficulty in changing commissions rested in the average operator's fear of what competitors would offer. Those 477 survey respondents paid commissions as follows: 1) 60/40 (in favor of the operator), 2.4 percent; 2) 50/50, 50.7 percent; 3) 40/60 (to locations), 16.8 percent; 4) 50/50 with front or first money to operator, 19.2 percent; 5) other commission arrangements, 10.9 percent. When asked what commission schedule would they prefer to use, responses were: 1) 60/40 (to locations), 9.3 percent; 2) 50/50, 1.2 percent; 3) 40/60 (to operator), 37.6 percent; 4) 50/50 with front money to operator, 41.4 percent; 5) other commission schedules, 10.5 percent.[15]

That survey drew comments from industry people who argued that the commission issue was more of a problem than the cost of new equipment, the cost of records, or salaries paid to route men and mechanics. Most operators felt they had been giving away too much of their gross receipts. Albert Denver, president of the newly formed national lobby group Music Operators of America (MOA), declared that music-machine operators had to make location owners aware of the increased costs in phonograph operation and the value of adequate service if they hoped to achieve and maintain favorable commission arrangements. He told a meeting of MOA members that they should act individually as public relations men in their dealings with locations. Denver explained that nothing could be done about the decline in juke revenue over the previous couple of years because the causal changes — general economic conditions and free television in taverns — could not be altered by the box trade. Therefore, he argued, the one practical way the operator could increase his income was by securing a larger percentage of the gross receipts. In order to get locations to accept smaller commissions,

A 1948 photo taken at a distributor launch in Vancouver, BC, for Wurlitzer's model 1100 box. The show was for operators and potential operators. Individuals are not identified. *City of Vancouver Archives, photo #CVA 1184-2689, photographer: Jack Lindsay.*

the operator had to discuss his problems on a "man to man" basis with the proprietor. The location owner could be shown, said Denver, that operating costs had skyrocketed and that good service cost money.[16]

Facing what they called a "business crisis," a group of Denver, Colorado, major music-machine operators agreed, in 1950, to request the owners of small establishments to accept less than the standard 50 percent split. Those operators had, in many instances, already cut payments to 25 percent and proposed to discontinue percentages altogether in locations where any such payment meant the difference between a profit and a loss. One operator said he would rather have the machines in his warehouse than "costing him $7 to $8 a week to keep them on a location." According to this account it was estimated that a third of Denver's 1,200 boxes on location were being run at a loss and would have to be pulled unless commission payments were cut.[17]

When a customer became overly enamored of a single juke selection, problems sometimes occurred. For a solid hour on March 1, 1948, Josephine Ostoloco fed quarters into the music machine at the Arco Bar & Grill in New York City and listened to a selection titled "Civilization." Another customer, Filipe Torres, also listened. He didn't like it and began to mutter over his beer. Finally, when Ostoloco changed a $1 bill and was about to replenish the juke for another hour, Torres rose from his table, aimed a few epithets in her direction, and then drew a pistol. He fired two shots at her and two more at bartender Nemesio Calasen, who had intervened. Both were seriously wounded. Torres fled the bar but was later arrested by pursuing police, who shot and wounded him.[18]

Leonard Eilers, 23, of Milwaukee was a devotee of local boxes. Because of his overpowering yen for the Frankie Laine number "Mule Train," he also became a public nuisance. Eilers was haled into court after he had played that song 481 times, a total expenditure of $24.05, which he had "borrowed" from his roommate. Placed on probation by Judge Harvey Neelen, Eilers promised not to play "Mule Train" any more when he visited his local juke location.[19]

All of the attention devoted to the effect of jukes on teenagers and delinquent behavior in the World War II period almost completely disappeared in this period. It was close to a forgotten topic. One exception was James Andrews, principal of Bloom Junior High School in Cincinnati. At a service club lunch meeting he explained that in schools a difficult time of day occurred during the noon period, especially in the winter months when the students were unable to go outdoors. Without giving specific details about the difficult time, Andrews declared the noon-hour problem at Bloom was solved by installing a juke in the auditorium.[20]

The cost of new boxes rose significantly in the postwar period. When

At that 1948 distributor display in Vancouver, an unidentified man showed the insides of the Wurlitzer 1100. *City of Vancouver Archives, photo #CVA 1184-2692, photographer: Jack Lindsay.*

an average music operator purchased a new machine in 1947 and 1948, the cost ranged from $800 to $1,000. About 18 months were needed to amortize that cost. In the case of larger operators, sales were outright and did not usually involve trade-ins. If they did trade in equipment less than two years old, those larger firms hoped to be able to amortize their newer purchases in 12 months. The larger operator who could afford to replace his equipment without trade-ins sometimes found himself in a position where he could resell his 18-month-old units to smaller firms, getting more for them than he could on a trade-in. Meanwhile, such a transaction provided the smaller operator with a cheaper and newer replacement for some of his prewar equipment that he had to date been unable to replace.[21]

Faced with escalating costs, some juke industry people turned to boosting private jukebox rentals as a profitable auxiliary business to add to profits. Chicago firm Walter Oomens & Sons had conducted a private juke rental section since 1933. One advantage of a rental business was that the smaller, lighter machines (the only type Oomens used for rentals) taken off regular locations when new equipment was installed would continue to bring in returns. In turn, the older of those rental units could be traded in on new machines when such machines were purchased as replacements for smaller boxes being retired from regular locations. However, Oomens' regular practice was to maintain a fairly stable group of rental machines and not use them to any great extent for new machine trade-ins. In any city of 100,000 there were said to be always 50 to 100 small parties and social functions going on every Saturday night, with each being a potential box rental. Oomens said he entered the rental business after repeated requests from friends and neighbors for use of a juke during a party. When he first started renting in 1933 he had no old machines to use so he rented out new ones. In 1947 the 10 boxes he had available for rental ranged from 1936 to 1940 models, representing just about every make on the market. Most of those machines were 1940 models. They held 12, 16, 20, and 24 selections. In those early days of his rental business, Oomens' practice was to give the person who rented the machine a key so he could replace or turn over the records in the unit to gain a greater variety of music. The renter could use his own disks or extra ones supplied by Oomens. However, that led to heavy repair costs, as the average renter inadvertently damaged the unit's changing mechanism. Now, boxes were delivered locked and only those records in the box were available for the customer to play. Of course, a choice of records was given to customers. The leading number requested in 1947 was "Beer Barrel Polka."[22]

Oomens reported that weekends were the most popular times to rent a box and the most consistent, year-round calls for rentals came from weddings; general parties were the next biggest occasions. With regard to holidays, Christmas was the best holiday for rentals, followed by New Year's and Halloween in that order. Rentals dropped off after the end of July and picked up again in early October. Private homes took 40 percent of the rental boxes, and halls and hotels took about 30 percent each. Rental prices varied with the type of machine desired, distance the unit was transported, and to what floor it had to be carried. Oomens would haul a machine no more than 3½ miles. If he received rental requests from outside that distance he referred them to another operator. For a Saturday night affair in a private home, the box was delivered Saturday afternoon and picked up the following Monday morning. The average length of time for a rental was one evening and the number of plays per rental unit ranged from 100 to 200. A fee of $12 to $20 per rental was charged, the lowest figure for a 12-selection machine delivered to a first floor or a basement address. No machine was ever delivered beyond the third floor if no elevator was available. In the case of manually carrying a juke above the first level, only 12-selection machines would be delivered by Oomens.[23]

The first national trade group for the juke trade was the Music Operators of America (MOA), formed in 1949. Its inaugural convention was held the following year with the desire that music operators segregate themselves from the coin-machine firms. Previously they had formed a part of the more encompassing coin-machine conventions. Music operators felt they were legitimate business people, but as reporter Robert Chandler observed: "They realize, however, that the public doesn't think so. And so, while they declare that they will cooperate with other coinmen, they are withdrawing into a separate and distinct organization." Thus, that first convention took on the aspect of a seminar in public relations. MOA wanted to set up a body that would have as its task informing the public that the music operators were a group apart from other coin machines

Rock-Ola 1422, 1946.

and that they were a respectable outfit. One of the first tangible steps in that direction was an executive committee resolution, passed before the convention, backing a bill in Congress that would have outlawed the use of obscene records. Aside from active support of the bill, MOA was determined to use all forms of moral suasion possible on its individual members to keep smutty material off their boxes. A feeling articulated at the convention was that the value of jukes was underestimated by artists and publishers as a means of making hits and stars. Moreover, music-machine operators believed that a prevalent feeling among artists was that they benefited the juke industry and not the other way around. As would be expected, the MOA convention also resolved to vigorously fight any Congressional attempts to subject boxes to copyright laws.[24]

Despite the huge number of boxes on location in America, the procedure for placing them in establishments was mostly informal. A 1946 estimate indicated that in Chicago only about half the jukes were placed on location under a written lease — bigger operating firms were more likely to use them than were small companies. The other machines were placed on a simple oral understanding with the location owner. Leases in the Chicago area usually ran for one year, as they did in New York, although some New York leases ran as long as three years. Covered under leases were items such as the commission rate, repair and installation of equipment, and how often new models would be placed. One large Chicago operator included in his lease that the location owner was required to see that aisles and passageways to the jukebox "shall not be obstructed in such manner as to interfere with the accessibility of the equipment by patrons of the premises."[25]

Wurlitzer 1100, 1947.

Box operators continued to be adamantly opposed to locations directly owning their own music machines and vigorously opposed any moves in that direction, no matter how slim any evidence might be to support such an assumption. They were firmly committed to the existing structure with operators alone buying units from the distributors. Reports from several sections of the nation in 1947 indicated there were an increasing number of jukebox sales direct to locations despite the fact that all "legitimate" makers, distributors, and operators had taken "a definite stand against such practices." Cities named as particular trouble spots were Milwaukee, New York, and Chicago where sales had been made, believed operators, by firms who had found the going too tough through regular sales channels. According to reports, there was a "sell or place" attitude among a few "wildcat" distributors for whom selling to established operators came first, but if that failed to bring in the necessary income then they resorted to direct sales to locations. However, a general consensus of opinion was that the main source of direct sales came from operators themselves and not from distributors. Some operators, "naturally, not bound by contracts to do otherwise," and with an excess of equipment, had resorted to selling to location owners. Operators who were leaving the business permanently were said to be among the greatest offenders.[26]

In most cases the equipment sold directly was apparently outdated and in poor condition. The net result was that locations got stuck with a machine that was initially a "discredit," without the "care" of an experienced operator, and a machine that became "a definite black mark to the entire automatic phonograph industry." Sale of outdated units was one concern but so was the sale of a number of postwar boxes. Manufacturers, without exception, said they were 100 percent in favor of sales to operators only and that any sales to locations were made without their approval. Reportedly there had been a few cases where distributors were dropped by makers for making location sales. They argued that location sales not only eliminated the particular location from the list of operator possibilities, but if the box was improperly serviced, it caused an "unfavorable public reaction," which could reflect on their own established locations. Direct sales to locations were a problem since the first days of the juke industry "and the fact that no more than between 5 and 10 per cent of locations have ever maintained their own juke boxes establishes its impracticability." One operator argued that if location-owned boxes were profitable, "our business would have folded up long ago." A majority of spots owning their boxes were described as locations assessed by operators to be marginal, or worse, spots that were avoided by operators. Not discussed in this passionate defense of a no sales to locations policy was what locations were supposed to do if they were indeed passed over by operators.[27]

An editorial response by *Billboard* to the problem produced another passionate defense of the maker/distributor/operator system stating that "the location-owned juke box has been the most complete failure of all ... the location-owned phono becomes a blight to the industry." Operators were urged to work through their associations, or individually, to do their utmost to stamp out location-owned equipment in their own territory.[28]

Location-owned jukes were voted down by Chicago tavern owners after they were surveyed in a check that included 50 taverns in the city and suburbs. Of the 50, only two owned their own machine. A third had owned its own box but after a short period had called in an operator to take over. The two taverns owning machines were described as "obviously" in the marginal or "red" group of spots. Both had ancient 12-selection machines "that had long ago lost most of their play-appeal." And of these two, one admitted that self-operation was a losing proposition for any tavern owner who could not make repairs on his units. The second one stated he had operated his own juke for the past eight years and that many of his patrons voiced objections to the out-of-date equipment. A recurring theme from the average tavern owner seemed to be that he was not willing or qualified to assume the operation of a box. Points against a location owning its box were 1) responsibility of servicing the machine; 2) not knowing how to pick the right records; 3) expense of equipment replacement; 4) no familiarity with "music engineering"— how to place wall boxes, how to determine the need for extra speakers, and so on; and 5) an entirely different business than tavern operation.[29]

Rock-Ola 1428, 1948.

From its earliest days, the jukebox price was a nickel per play. In this postwar period no issue dominated, and divided, the industry more than whether the price of a juke play should be raised to a dime. Despite the enormous amount of discussion, pro and con, that took place in this period, no final decision was reached. It would take a long time before the issue was fully resolved. Prior to 1946 there was only a brief mention or two about dime play. A 1943 story from the Omaha, Nebraska, *World Herald* discussed decreasing profits for box operators, due to increased costs, and went on to note: "Some operators have considered going to dime-per-play. Some have done so, but other machines can't be changed to dime operation without new materials, so that's out." While there were some boxes that operated on dime play prior to 1946, they were rare and isolated locations.[30]

Around the beginning of 1946, jukebox operators' associations first began to formally propose the idea of increasing jukebox revenue by raising prices from a nickel a play to 10 cents per play (three for 25 cents). Operators across the nation differed widely on the issue. Tests were run in California early in 1946 to determine just what would happen if juke play prices were hiked from 5 cents to 10 cents. Results were that gross receipts were increased, but the number of plays took a 40 percent nose dive. Over a period of time when a nickel box would have been played 100 times (grossing $5), the same machine converted to dime play received only 60 plays (grossing $6).

Wurlitzer 1250, 1950.

Many operators opposed the idea of an increase, feeling it would cut badly into plays, especially where employment was off and the economy bad. A price increase, they felt, would do more harm than good. Others favored a price increase because, pointing to the California results, it raised the gross take. Still another group of operators felt that tavern locations might be able to tolerate a price increase while insisting that machines in other locations should remain at the nickel play level.[31]

Over the last three months of 1946, the debate became extremely intense. A concerted movement to up the price of juke play from 5 to 10 cents (unless otherwise noted this option always involved one play for 10 cents, three for 25 cents) was launched in Chicago early in October by the box maker AMI. The firm was prepared to tee off the drive and expressed the hope that other manufacturers would join distributors and operators everywhere in making the changeover. Reaction to AMI's announcement was mixed. Faced with increased costs for initial investment, upkeep, and daily running, box operators had been looking for ways to increase profits. Three alternatives usually suggested themselves: 1) adopt the practice of taking first or front money; 2) make adjustments in the commission split to provide a higher percentage to operators; and 3) keep commissions as they were, but increase the price per play. While all three methods had been tried at least briefly by some, there was no unanimity of opinion as to which worked best. Many felt using the first two methods would lead to hard feelings between operators and location owners since the income of the latter would be revised downward — leaving only the third alternative. *Billboard* speculated that even if the number of plays fell 25 percent — and there was no reason to believe it would — gross receipts would rise 50 percent. For example, 400 plays at 5 cents each would gross $20, while 300 at 10 cents would gross $30. Making such a change, though, would require a broad educational program since "[t]he five-cent habit is a difficult one to break." In that regard AMI was prepared to take two steps. Firstly, it was ready to supply the necessary hardware to convert the company's boxes to dime play. Secondly, AMI would mail out literature to promote the idea both among operators and location owners.[32]

Close on the heels of the AMI announcement, it was reported that, generally, most operators would favor dime play. Proponents of the idea were in two groups: one maintained the switch had to be universal and the other maintained the type of locations should govern the price. Wurlitzer indirectly entered the debate when it changed the slogan it had been using in national advertising for general circulation. The company's full-page ads had been appearing in such publications as the *Saturday Evening Post* and had in the past contained the slogan "America's Favorite Nickel's Worth of Fun." Deferring to the fact that many in the industry were vocal about the need for an increased play price, Wurlitzer changed its slogan to "Musical Fun for Everyone." Operators with reservations about an increase felt that all firms within a given territory had to take the change together if it was to succeed. Some thought the price of a juke play could be variable, as it then was for soft drinks. A bottle of a well-known brand of soft drink ordinarily sold for a nickel, but sold for anywhere between 10 and 50 cents "in the plushier locations." Opposing an increase were some West Coast operators who thought nickel play should remain but that one-third of receipts (representing running costs) should be taken as first money with a 50/50 split of the remainder. Still other coast operators favored a retention of nickel play, but a 70/30 receipt split in their favor. One machine in Santa Maria, California, had been switched over to dime play during the war and never switched back. Even though it was surrounded by nickel boxes (owned by the same firm), play was reported to be holding up on the dime unit.[33]

Even though there was no unanimity of opinion on the merits of an increase, a few operators here and there, acting individually, made the change themselves. In a few cases the changes were permanent but mostly those increases were rolled back. Tim Crummett, partner in Kansas City, Missouri's, Central Distributing Company, reported that the trend among operators in the smaller towns of Missouri and Kansas was to dime play. However, his estimate was that about 10 percent of the operators in the smaller cities in the Kansas City territory had converted all, or most, of their machines. Jerry Wilson, Missouri salesman for Central, said that some operators who had converted found their income doubling. Crummett also remarked that one operator in his territory had his music machines, located in spots with dance space, on dime play for almost a decade.[34]

Late in November 1946, the Albany County Restaurant and Liquor Dealers Association (New York) adopted a resolution opposing any increase in the cost of playing a jukebox, from 5 cents to 10 cents.[35]

Just a few days after that, the Rudolph Wurlitzer Company formally announced its abandonment of the five-cent standard in favor of dime play. Company vice president H. M. Hammergren said the changeover of Wurlitzer machines would start at once but that it would take some time to complete the job.[36]

Ten days after that, early in December, a further illustration of the conflicting views on the issue became apparent when Marshall Seeburg, president of Seeburg, announced his firm was opposed to changing the juke play cost from the long-established nickel standard. Furthermore, Seeburg declared it was doing away with yearly model changes of its machines as part of a two-year plan unveiled at the annual distributors' meeting. The 1947 and 1948 models would have only minor cabinet changes, so the owner of a 1946 model could bring his equipment up to date without discarding a major investment. Thus, the operator who then owned a 1946 unit had three years to amortize the cost, which would lower his costs and allow him to be better able to maintain the five-cent play level. With regard to the proposed price hike, Seeburg said of his industry: "Our success is definitely tied in with the success of our operators. It is of primary importance that they operate at a profit and this can only be done if they retain the good will of the public. Since five-cent-a-tune music is the music of the masses, it will remain the emphatic policy of this company that Seeburg phonographs will continue to present music for a nickel." When the topic of the price hike came up at that Seeburg distributors' meeting, they unanimously adopted a motion that the policy of the entire Seeburg organization would be to maintain the nickel play cost. Speaking of nickel juke play by children and teenagers, Seeburg remarked: "We feel that such clean fun is a good influence and is a deterrent to child delinquency. We are opposed

Keep faith

with

the Public

MUSIC MUST REMAIN AT
5 CENTS A TUNE

See us about Seeburg's
2-year plan to aid operators

SHAFFER MUSIC CO.

COLUMBUS • CHARLESTON • WHEELING

EXCLUSIVE **Seeburg** DISTRIBUTORS

1907 • DEPENDABLE MUSIC SYSTEMS • 1946

Above: A 1946 trade ad by Seeburg against dime play. *Opposite:* A 1947 trade ad by Wurlitzer in favor of dime play.

It's a problem of making—

BOTH ENDS MEET!

The problem that faces the operating end of the commercial music business is a problem that practically every industry has faced...and solved...by increasing the price of its product.

It's the problem of making both ends meet!

In the case of the music operator, the cost of everything he buys, from labor to lamp bulbs, from phonographs to records, has been hiked to new highs.

Simultaneously his earnings are down from the wartime peak.

Ordinary horse sense should indicate that something must be done. Wurlitzer is doing it. Advocating an industry-wide change to quarter-dime play.

No business enjoys being forced to increase its prices. Yet the policy is so necessary and has been adopted so generally by *all* business that to challenge it from a standpoint of being unessential or unethical simply won't hold water.

It's to *your* interests as a Music Merchant that Wurlitzer has paved the way for quarter-dime play.

Analyze your problem. Consult your business records and your better judgment.

They will testify to the urgent need of "3 for 25¢—1 for 10¢" play. The Rudolph Wurlitzer Company, North Tonawanda, New York.

SURVIVAL TODAY CALLS FOR... uarter ime play

to the 100 per cent increase in the price of their pleasure." Looking ahead to what might happen generally, he added, "Raising the price of phonograph music will tend, we believe, to create a buyers' strike and operators will find their equipment sitting idle." He believed the answer to increased costs had to be found in increasing the number of plays per box and in eliminating yearly model changes, giving the operator a longer time to amortize the capital costs of his investment.[37]

Kansas City, Missouri's, biggest operator was Music Service Company. President Frank Murray said that 15 of his firm's units had been converted to dime play. All of them were in locations he described as "class spots." Additionally, his company had converted 75 wall boxes to 10 cent play. Collections, he said, showed an average increase of 10 percent for those converted machines. Howard Silverman, of Silverman Brothers Music Company in Kansas City, said his firm had converted four of its machines in county spots to dime play in the previous month. All were new jukeboxes and all were sited in night spots that featured dancing.[38]

Those box conversions taking place in Kansas City, few as they may have been, did not escape general public comment. News of dime play made page one of the *Kansas City Star* (Missouri) twice during one week in December 1946 as news stories, while also drawing comment from one of the paper's columnists. Front page stories also featured the price change in St. Louis.[39]

Before the end of 1946, *Billboard* conducted a nationwide survey of 3,204 operators on the question of a price hike. Results showed close to an even split: 1,532 favored an increase, 1,452 opposed it, and 220 declared themselves as neutral and offered other suggestions on how to overcome the problem of rising costs. Most of those 220 suggested that changes in the commission structure might be the best answer. Strongest support for a price increase came from operators in the Southern states while strongest opposition came from the Midwest states. The breakdown by region was as follows: Southern states (489 operators in favor of an increase, 234 opposed); Eastern states (350, 336); Midwest states (328, 474); Western states (285, 248). Of the majority of the 220 neutral operators who wanted commission changes most of those wanted to see a 60/40 division in their favor. Some also suggested some form of first or front money; for example, the first $5, then a 50/50 division. Operators opposed to dime play were convinced that an increase would hurt play in the long run while those in favor admitted play dropped initially but then leveled off, leaving the box with a higher gross.[40]

Perplexed by the results was the *Billboard* editor who noted the industry was a long way from reaching consensus on the issue. He also observed that a few months earlier some operators converted a few boxes to dime play "heard loud complaints from location owners and watched their play fall off. They quickly switched back to the nickel, convinced the dime was a mistake." But others, at the same time, found they could convert equipment in many locations "without losing play or incurring the public's ill will." Unable to offer any direction to the industry, based on that first national survey of the issue, the editor declared the question of whether to raise the price was squarely "on the shoulders of each individual operating firm."[41]

One group that did operate collectively was the Mobile chapter of the Alabama Music Operators' Association. All the members in that city converted all their boxes to dime play in a price increase that took effect in November 1946. In a letter to location owners explaining the changes, the Mobile operators said that with regard to income splitting the box owner would take $3 in first money (first money had not been part of prior agreements in the area) with the balance divided as per prior agreements (presumably that would have been 50/50, but it was not stated). While the letter pointed out the new arrangement meant a loss of $1.50 a week to location owners, it argued that it would be made up "to some extent" by the increased cost of a juke play. In justifying the new arrangement, the group pointed out that in the past year salaries to its employees had increased 75 to 100 percent, the cost of records had moved from 22 cents to 65 cents, and the price of new music machines was up 125 percent.[42]

Bob Barry, who conducted an inquiring reporter radio program "Man About Town" over station WAAT in Newark, New Jersey, asked his sidewalk interviewees on December 16, 1946, what they thought about dime juke play. All who were quizzed said dime play would not work in Newark. One of them happened to be a box operator.[43]

Around the same time Nancy Hendrick, a feature writer for the Sunday *Herald* in Bridgeport, Connecticut, wrote an article about the debate over 10-cent box play. She thought if the price hike went ahead it would destroy the industry. Hendrick said, "Upping the tariff to 10 cents may be the crusher that will send the gaudy piccolos—they're also called that in some quarters—into the oblivion occupied by miniature golf, flagpole sitters and other phenomena that once caught the public's fickle fancy."[44]

When phonograph operators met in Worcester, Massachusetts, to organize the Worcester Automatic Phonograph Operators' Association, their first order of business was an immediate vote to change all machines to 10-cent play.[45]

So hectic was the price issue in 1946, *Billboard* issued a summary report in its first 1947 issue that stated most jukebox firms were willing to wager that dime play would never become national. Once operating costs could be trimmed and play stimulated, most operators felt "the nickel price will hold. How much of a hold dime play will get on the industry will depend largely on the country's general economic conditions."[46]

E. R. Wurgler, Wurlitzer general sales manager, came out publicly to address the idea that raising the price of juke play might increase juvenile delinquency because of the inability of teenagers to meet the increase. Calling that idea far-fetched, Wurgler argued that even if there was any truth in it "experience demonstrates that at three for a quarter, a teen age crowd can raise a sufficient number of quarters to keep the juke box going much as it did before." He also said there was a general misunderstanding regarding the amount of money contributed to jukeboxes by teenagers "when in reality only a very small percentage comes from this class." Fifteen percent, at most, was the figure he used and felt that should be kept in mind by any operator who might hesitate in changing to dime play because he had overrated the importance of the teen market.[47]

When reporter Robert Seals summarized the situation, he said that while the controversy still raged, a majority of operators were holding off on any changeover in hopes of seeing a decrease in operation costs. Many newspapers had featured the story with space allotted for each side. Some of those papers had taken editorial positions in favor of a price increase, and some were opposed. Practically all of the pro-increase editorials, however, noted Seals dryly, "have followed the line that such an increase would tend to silence juke boxes in general." Among the makers, AMI and Wurlitzer remained in favor of the increase while Seeburg continued to publicly oppose such a move. Both AMI and Wurlitzer had begun to distribute promotional material and make public relations efforts to sell locations, operators, and the general public on their position. Among those opposed to changing nickel play were found many with novel suggestions. One operator mentioned closing the nickel slot so the box would not operate for less than 10 cents but would deliver two tunes per dime. Another suggested that two nickels or a dime be required for a single selection, but that a quarter would still deliver five songs. A third wanted to see six for 25 cents but 10 cents for one selection. Yet another suggestion was to charge 10 cents a tune for best-selling hits and artists, while still charging a nickel for less popular tunes.[48]

Six of Chicago's operators conducted an experiment in play prices in late 1947 in an effort to increase profits by increasing the number of plays while still only charging a nickel per play. The experiment consisted of converting boxes to operate on two plays for a dime or five for a quarter, eliminating the single play for a nickel. An earlier attempt to interest local operators in dime play in 1946 failed to gain the support of the operators, but that proposal called for one song for a dime, three for 25 cents. As a compromise, the current experiment simply encouraged heavier play of the box and did not increase the play price.[49]

A 1946 Wurlitzer ad aimed not at the trade, but at the general public.

Around the same time, six plays for a quarter was an idea being tossed around by some operators who hoped the concept would stimulate play. A survey of Los Angeles and Chicago operators revealed that 35 percent of those contacted voted in favor of converting to six-for-a-quarter play, 35 percent said no, and 30 percent were undecided. One reason in favor of this plan was said to be that after the sixth successive record was played and the juke fell silent, customers were more apt to "hear" the absence of music and, having had their musical appetite whetted, wanted more. Negative aspects included the cost of installing conversion devices and the fact that wall box installations would not lend themselves to such conversions. Chicago operator Jack Morgan, Jr. commented: "I had some machines fixed for a 'free' record at intervals when the juke was silent and it proved to be a good play boost." Against the idea was William Nyland, manager of Western Automatic Music, who said there was little quarter play on the boxes; most people put in nickels and dimes and an extra record would not entice more quarters. "Anyway, records are too expensive and wear out too quickly to spin for free," he added. A majority of the Los Angeles operators turned the idea down.[50]

The idea that dime play had arrived seemed to be slowly slipping away. Reporter Norman Weiser noted there were instances where 10-cent play was not only possible but actually in effect at an increased profit to the owner. However, he added that the general opinion, based on past experiences, throughout representative areas of the trade was that dime play was "ill-advised at this time" and that areas such as New York, Philadelphia, Los Angeles, Chicago, and other large cities were "definitely opposed" to its introduction. Basically, most operators felt conditions would not warrant an increase in the box play price: "Many point to the experiments along these lines a year or so ago, when tests ended in a rout, with many of those operators involved chalking up heavy losses." Many agreed the time to have made an industry-wide attempt to hike the price to 10 cents was during the war years, when most locations had heavy transient trade and regular customers were making and spending more money regularly. As far as operators were concerned, competition was the overriding factor. Unless all boxes in an area were running on a dime basis, individual operators would not attempt the price increase. In some cities where operator associations were strong enough (due to a high proportion being members) to bring about almost 100 percent cooperation in a move such as a price hike, the associations, in most cases, were opposed to the increase because of the current business conditions. In Los Angeles, operator Bob Baird charged a dime in transient spots during the war and got it "without a whimper." However, he reverted to nickel play at war's end because, as he said, "music is like a package of gum, they don't expect to pay more than a nickel for it."

Ray Eberts, one of the largest operators in Los Angeles, said he went to dime play a few years earlier but had to go back to a nickel because locations claimed the 10-cent policy drove patrons out of those taverns to others across the street with similarly priced drinks but cheaper music. Over the course of 1947, dime play had been introduced by a number of operators in Boston, by some in Nashville, and by a few in Philadelphia. In all cases the experiment failed and the operators were forced to revert back to the nickel standard.[51]

Weiser returned a week later, after checking with juke trade associations, to report that a majority of the associations and operators surveyed agreed that for them, or their members, 10-cent play "was not in the cards at the present time." All agreed that the problems of the industry could be cured by other means, such as reduced equipment costs and a reduction in the high cost of living in general. It caused Weiser to declare that as an industry-wide proposition, "10-cent play at this time appears doomed ... unless it is all-inclusive, it can never succeed because of the highly competitive nature of the music machine business." In New York, the idea of dime play was pronounced dead. Said Al Denver, president of the Automatic Music Operators' Association: "The worst thing we can do in the face of competition by television is to raise play to 10 cents. Several operators tried 10-cent play here about a year and a half ago. The experiment was short-lived. A check of the Utah Music Operators' Association found that nearly all the operators favored a price increase but that none would hold to dime play in the face of nickel competition."[52]

One location owner in Des Moines, Iowa, was adamant in his opposition to dime play. He had even removed the former operator when that person tried to raise the price to 10 cents. Explaining the situation to the current operator, the owner said: "I like my music, and I put most of the money in that juke box. At a nickel a toss I don't mind, but I'll be gol-darned if I'll pay a dime for a record in my own place."[53]

At the beginning of 1950, box operators in Chicago were moving toward the goal of eventually removing the nickel slot from their machines. So far operators had taken the first step toward what they called "public education of the dime-a-play" by giving customers two selections for 10 cents and by doing away with the nickel hole completely. Some 25 percent of the city's music machines were already converted to that standard. The recent hike in the cost of a call from a pay telephone to a dime in key cities was a main impetus for the juke move. While the public's ready acceptance of dime phone calls led the operators, all agreed that the "straight dime per selection policy is still a long way off." Still, the new Chicago policy would not be imposed at spots where the patrons were mostly teens: "As it stands now, most ops here feel they can get away with the two-for-a-dime play at pubs and restaurants, but are unwilling to test the kiddies as yet."[54]

At the Music Operators of America 1950 convention the subject of dime play came up in unofficial talks among operators. The consensus was that dime play on new machines placed in top locations might work, but local factors would have much to do with the final outcome of such a test. Costs had risen until, more from desperation than an attempt to test dime play, some new machines had been equipped with 10-cent chutes and placed on location. Results, as reported by those operators who tested the higher-priced play, ran the gamut from total failure to increasing a $60-a-week spot to $128 per week, and maintaining the higher level over a period of several months. Promoting juke play by building goodwill through civic promotions was suggested as one way of maintaining grosses at a profitable level. Finally, operators agreed that a myriad of factors peculiar to the area would have to be overcome before the dime-play tests could even be started.[55]

As 1950 ended, despite an economic squeeze on boxes in New York City and northern New Jersey, it signaled no early abandonment of nickel play in that area. Rather, operators became more intent on further adjusting income splits in their favor as the most practical policy. While few, if any, would hesitate in moving to dime play if others in their immediate area initiated the move, fear of competitive inroads by holdouts restrained even the more aggressive from taking the plunge. It was generally agreed the switch had to be all or none, which didn't mean a price hike would not be imposed "later this year or the next." Meanwhile, several operators in New York City and northern New Jersey reported they had been able to raise gross receipts by plugging up the nickel chutes. Those machines accepted only dimes and quarters for multiple play at the rate of five cents a tune. Joe Madden, of Old Reliable Music Service, claimed that plugging the nickel slot had increased income on some of his machines by as much as 30 percent. He added that patrons spent no more time picking two numbers than one and there were "no more Canadian nickels in the cash box." In this area most machines were operated on deals giving the operator a larger portion of the weekly income. Trade insiders placed the number of boxes no longer on a straight 50/50 split at about 75 percent of the total, with the main holdouts being machines that were either at the bottom or the top of the income ladder. Revenue from marginal spots, usually with pre–World War II equipment, if not divided half and half would leave too little for the location. Top spots, grossing over $60, would be too vulnerable to competition if the commission split was revised downward. Commission patterns in New York City then had operators receiving from $9 to $10 in weekly guarantees on early postwar machines to as much as $20 on late, 100-selection equipment. In an average spot with a Wurlitzer 1015 model, the operator took $10 off the top of about a $14 weekly income, leaving the rest to the location owner. In New Jersey the commission pattern in most cases had the operator getting

$5 weekly front money on early postwar equipment with the remaining receipts split 50/50. On newer machines the front money went as high as $10 weekly.[56]

A rather bizarre offshoot to this issue was a movement by the juke industry to get the United States Congress to adopt a bill to mint fractional coinage such as 2½-, 7½-, and 12½-cent pieces. This would, of course, allow box operators to more easily increase the play price and avoid a 100 percent increase, which they feared would generate public opposition, by charging 7½ cents per play. It was a movement with wide support not just within the juke industry but throughout the coin-machine industry as a whole. At a meeting of the Iowa Automatic Music Operators' Association in Des Moines, the group came out in support of the proposed 7½-cent coin bill. Said Leo Miller, president of the group: "Try and buy a nickel cigar. The juke box operators are still getting the same revenue while all of their cost have skyrocketed."[57]

At the Music Operators of America 1950 convention, juke operators came out strongly behind the proposal for new coins and saw the 7½-cent item as the answer to their prayers for increased revenue. Some 350 delegates attending MOA's first national convention unanimously endorsed a five-point program aimed at mobilizing American public opinion behind a movement to persuade the government to mint those new coins. The program was outlined to the convention by Edward Walsh Mehren of Beverly Hills, California, chairman of the American Institute for Intermediate Coinage and president of the Squirt Beverage Company. One of the Institute's contentions was that minting the fractional coins would permit pricing closer to value and allow convenience. Pricing closer to value, it argued, would free $8 billion then overexpended on commodities and services and would enable the consumer to spend that money for an additional supply of goods and services. The fifth point of the program went as follows: "That a song telling what coinage of a 7½ cent piece would mean in reducing the cost of living be composed and produced on records as soon as possible and placed in music (juke) boxes and broadcast by radio."[58]

A Connecticut newspaper interviewed two area operators on the question of fractional coins. Chester Morris pointed out that at a nickel a record, boxes were being run at a near loss: "A lot of the boys are on their way out. We're licked unless something can be done. This 7½-cent coin may be the answer." James Fitzpatrick complained, "You can't pay $1,000 for a juke box with nickels." Three local teens were also quizzed on the use of the proposed coin in jukes. All were vehement in their answers, stating that if it cost more than a nickel to play the boxes, they would not patronize them at all.[59]

At hearings held before the Senate Banking and Currency Committee

There's a Witchery
to WURLITZER MUSIC

Musical Fun for Everyone

Call it magic, witchery or what you will...Wurlitzer Music has a way of making any occasion a bigger occasion. More fun, More life, More laughter. Remember it the next time you're out for entertainment. Go where they have Wurlitzer Music. Sweet or swing, vibrant or mellow, the musical pulse of America is at your fingertips. The Rudolph Wurlitzer Company, North Tonawanda, New York. • • • See Phonograph Section of Classified Telephone Directory for names of Wurlitzer Dealers.

Above and opposite: More ads from Wurlitzer aimed at the public in the late 1940s.

Always the Life of the Party

Musical Fun for Everyone

Start the New Year right by having fun! Get your group together. Head for a place that has Wurlitzer Music. Along with you goes a tuneful promise of a grand and glorious time.

Nothing like these gay music makers to pace the life of the party. Hit tunes. Top entertainers. Laughter and fun galore.

You'll leave with a new resolution . . . a promise to spend more fun-filled hours in '45 where they have Wurlitzer Music. The Rudolph Wurlitzer Company, North Tonawanda, N. Y. • • • See Phonograph Section of Classified Telephone Directory for names of Wurlitzer Music Merchants.

The Sign of the Musical News acknowledges places where you can have just phonograph a Wurlitzer.

THE NAME THAT MEANS Music TO MILLIONS

The union of Wurlitzer pianos, microphones, commercial phonographs and electronic organs is heard 'round the world. The Rudolph Wurlitzer Company is America's largest manufacturer of pianos all sold under one name . . . also the nation's largest, best known producer of juke boxes and accordions.

on the minting of fractional coins, the juke industry argued that young people could not afford dime play and operators could not continue at five cents a tune, so a compromise at 7½ cents was the answer. One who testified was Edward H. Renner, general manager of the Northern Virginia Music Company of Alexandria, Virginia. His company ran 110 machines in northern Virginia. Renner said that before the war a new unit cost $440 while the same type of machine in 1950 cost from $995 to $1,100. Records that used to wholesale at 21 cents had moved to 49 cents. He added that when teenagers were gathered around a jukebox "parents don't have to worry where they are and what they are doing. They are entitled to musical enjoyment at a reasonable rate." Needless to say, nothing came of the movement to mint fractional coins.[60]

Another major issue that threatened the industry, and surfaced at this time, was the effect of television on juke play, especially in bars and taverns. It began to have an impact as early as June 1947, when *Billboard* conducted a survey of tavern television in New York and Chicago. Results revealed that such operations, on the whole, were not cutting box play. At the same time television set manufacturers and stations indicated the current rapid growth of tavern television was temporary. They were said to be predicting that as soon as home television ownership increased enough, television would no longer be a novelty for tavern locations and the sets would fall into the same category as radio as far as a trade stimulus was concerned.[61]

The Chicago check revealed that a total of 987 taverns had been equipped with sets in the city and 96 in the suburbs within a few weeks. The total number of taverns licensed inside the city limits was 9,688 and the total number of television sets in the entire city was 3,500. Thus, only 10 percent of taverns were equipped with a television, yet about one-third of all sets in the city were in taverns. The story told of New York operators was more pessimistic in tone than that reported in Chicago. New York box operators said that juke income was affected in locations with television, especially during afternoon baseball and evening boxing telecasts. Television, of course, had only a few broadcast hours each day in 1947. In Chicago most operators said box receipts dropped as much as 50 percent during the first week after video was installed but slowly rebounded until it was back to normal by around the fourth week. The Chicago picture also showed that television was not considered by the music men to be the major threat to juke income that they at first thought it would be. Telecasts were broadcast in the afternoon when baseball was the most commonly broadcast program and in the early evening before the juke really got "wound up" in such spots. Operators also called attention to the fact that locations would most likely have had their radios turned to the game.[62]

Locations claimed that business increases in taverns with televisions amounted to 30 percent, compared to spots with no video, in most establishments. Chicago operators reported that from 10 to 30 percent of their tavern locations had installed television. A number of those music men compared their problem with television to that of radio and records. Radio cut record sales to almost nothing when it first arrived on the scene, they said, but only a few years later the sales of home record players, and records, soared. Television could not compete with the jukebox because people liked to select their entertainment themselves, and television, like radio, did not permit that. Also revealed was that about 65 percent of the television locations in and around New York City also had jukeboxes. Telecasting time averaged about three hours daily and was seen in taverns principally during the afternoon and early evening.[63]

Most pessimistic was Ray Cunliffe, president of the Illinois Automatic Phonograph Owners' Association, who believed tavern television posed the number-one location problem for Chicago operators. According to Cunliffe there was no doubt that box receipts, in some locations where sets had been installed, had dropped under average grosses received before the video sets were installed. With only one station broadcasting, the problem was less acute than in New York, where taverns had a choice of four stations. Still, it was a headache for Chicago, with box-receipt decreases occurring mostly in the "middling" establishments—locations which were neither good nor bad.[64]

Los Angeles music men were reported, later in 1947, to be divided on the question as to whether television was reducing the juke receipts. But most thought that if video was decreasing juke play it was only temporary, pointing to the initial effect of radio. After the novelty wore off everything would revert to normal. Those operators felt the juke selling point was "Music you want, when you want it."[65]

By the middle of 1948, operators were troubled by competition from location television in 18 cities. It was a number growing rapidly with more than 60 stations in 40 different cities expected to be on the air by the end of 1948. As the first television sets in a new video town usually went into bars and taverns, music men could expect a drop in grosses for at least the first few months of video operation — until the novelty wore off. However, it was admitted that actual results showed that even after a few months, telecasts of events such as baseball and football games continued to affect the juke play.[66]

Telecasting of sports events was clearly the biggest worry for jukes. There was more baseball coverage on television in 1949 than ever before. Also, a record number of night games were aired, with most teams involved. Those night games offered the greatest headache, since they cut into the best hours of the juke day, from 8:00 through 10:30 P.M. Football coverage the previous fall had been the heaviest in history, "taking up valuable" Friday night, Saturday afternoon, and Sunday juke play time. Boxing matches were also starting to detract from box receipts.[67]

Early in 1947, with the release of new television sets in quantity, taverns and restaurants became the logical "showplaces" for this new medium, and heavy sales drives were directed at this market. In a matter of weeks those few cities where stations were telecasting were blanketed with video, and the results on boxes were felt immediately. In New York, for example, operators awoke one morning shortly after the start of the 1947 baseball season to find their grosses had fallen as much as 80 percent. Philadelphia and Chicago noted drops from 30 to 80 percent; in California receipts decreased 40 to 75 percent. Generally speaking, business in the first half of 1947 was still good. Where drops were similar, as in Philadelphia, Chicago, and California, it was found that an average of 80 percent of the juke locations had installed video. Most of them were made prior to the April baseball season start, but irregular programming had kept the hours of operation to a minimum. With the baseball season commencing, sets started operations at about 1:30 P.M., thus killing off practically all afternoon juke business on a seven-day-a-week basis. Thus, the stage was set and, as other sports commanded more and more time within the locations, the box grosses continued to drop. It was soon obvious that the plush financial war and early postwar period for the boxes was over, and by early 1948, as business in general at the average tavern started tapering off, the music-machine trade faced one of the most trying periods in its history.[68]

Regarding the impact of location television on juke take, the general pattern reportedly was that for the first six months of operation grosses dropped 80 percent. After 12 months receipts were off 50 percent — as sales of home sets grew and viewing interest began to level off, boxes started to pick up some of the lost revenue. Following 18 to 24 months, grosses were off 35 to 40 percent with taverns due to decreasing interest, sometimes removing sets entirely or turning them on only upon request. Also, taverns objected to the slowed-down bar sales while patrons watched the sets. After 30 months, juke receipts were off 25 percent. At the end of three years (with the city usually fairly well covered with home sets) the loss in juke revenue, due entirely to television, was estimated at a maximum of 20 percent. Taverns themselves, by 1949, had experienced a 25 percent drop in their business and were said to then value juke income even more with the result being they focused more on the box and less on the video. One suggestion for operators was to convince location proprietors that television and the box could be run simultaneously by simply regulating the volume on each instrument.[69]

At the MOA 1950 convention, operators bravely declared they mostly felt television was no threat to their industry. First, they said, tavern proprietors favored jukes over video because the latter was not a source of income while the former was. Further, customers drank more slowly while watching television, but listening to music did not affect their rate of consumption.[70]

While the impact of video on the trade was being assessed, the juke industry was exploring the possibilities of controlling some form of coin-operated video on location, perhaps in conjunction with a phonograph. One of the earliest attempts came in the fall of 1947 when the Videograph Corporation of New York announced it was introducing a new coin-operated television/juke combination as well as a new wall box that would offer video, two-channel radio, and music selectivity. Videograph president H. F. Dennison said his firm would advocate a minimum guarantee of $30 weekly front money for the operator handling his equipment. He emphasized his company would make every effort to establish that guarantee then while that phase of the industry (coin-operated video and combination video/juke) was new, so that location proprietors would not be broken in to expect a straight division of the receipts without a minimum guarantee.[71]

Around the middle of 1949, the General Electric Company and AMI announced jointly that an experimental jukebox television system was in operation in a luncheonette in Hoboken, New Jersey. Manager of GE's specialty division George F. Metcalfe declared, "We want to see if John Q. Public will pay five cents to see three minutes of television served right in his own booth at a café or restaurant." At the request of AMI, GE had constructed a special unit through which wall-mounted sets in booths were operated by a "master control unit," which could handle up to 20 wall sets. Location proprietors determined whether the system was set to deliver music or video and, with respect to the television aspect, "Patrons may regulate volume of sound, but the proprietor selects the program."[72]

Operators at the MOA convention, while declaring they did not see video as a major threat, said what they really wanted to know was how soon they could take over the marketing of television in restaurants and taverns. Optimistic about the prospect was MOA executive Hirsch de la Viez who said: "To control the picture and sound both, by dropping a coin in the slot gets a little too complicated. But what does look feasible is to let the picture go on without any sound. No sound would be heard until the coin was dropped in the box. Coin slot machines could be placed in each booth of a restaurant or taproom."[73]

Quickly throwing cold water on that idea at the same convention was MOA national chairman George A. Miller who felt the situation had reached the point where the public was so accustomed to free video in taverns and restaurants that they would refuse to pay for it. Sidney H. Levin, MOA national counsel, pointed out that he had conferred in New York with video set makers but despite intensive discussions was unable to reach any practical scheme of operation of a coin-operated television. Levin agreed that the trend toward free video in taverns had gone beyond the point where it could be stopped. Miller and Levin were right.[74]

When it came to promoting jukes during this period, the methods used in the past were continued. Samuel Abrams was with the Ohio Advertising Agency as well as being director of publicity for the Cleveland box operators' group, the Phonograph Merchants' Association. He related, in 1946, methods used during a five-year plan of advertising, public relations, and promotion of jukes. In Cleveland, all forms of advertising had been used since 1940. Basically, the paid advertising had promoted the hit tune of the month, a plan used until the war-time record shortage caused it to be halted temporarily. Under that plan, on the 20th of each month, members of the Cleveland association voted for a tune they believed had the possibility of being a hit. The selected tune was backed by newspaper ads, radio plugs, special title strips, and display cards on phonographs. It was said to be a successful program. By placing the selected tune in the number one spot on the box, it easily became the top pick on the juke and before the end of the month it became popular on the radio, was played by local bands, and even sales of its sheet music increased. A 15-minute radio program, featuring the top five songs on the music machines as well as interviews with band leaders was sponsored weekly by the association. When the circus came to Cleveland, the group had an elephant carry a banner publicizing the hit tune. The full cost of all the public relations work was paid for by a small assessment per phonograph. Some operators liked being in the public eye, assuming that with each endeavor they gained good will; some preferred to avoid the public eye, fearing exposure might increase the likelihood the industry would be highly taxed. In Cleveland and Ohio there were then no taxes or fees assessed against phonographs. Cleveland's juke trade was also involved in charitable and civic endeavors such as the Red Cross, the March of Dimes, and selling war bonds. As well, the industry cooperated with local movie theaters in promoting musical films, stage shows featuring recording artists, and by often temporarily placing boxes in the theater lobbies. Every time a recording artist came to town a luncheon was scheduled by the association in his honor. At those affairs "opportunities" presented themselves to discuss the types of records the operators desired. Among artists honored by the Cleveland group were Gene Autry, Tommy Dorsey, the Andrews Sisters, Duke Ellington, Jimmy Dorsey, Frank Sinatra, Benny Goodman, and Lawrence Welk. Additionally, the association studied all juke locations, continually checking them for appearance, selection of tunes, and quality of performance of the machine. Printed title strips for all records were supplied by the association to its members, eliminating the need for handwritten and typewritten title cards.[75]

To help promote a new tie-up between the Cleveland Phonograph Merchants' Association and RCA Victor, the record maker furnished hit tune records to 75 percent of the boxes in the city. The deal was between RCA and Cleveland Radio Electric, the label's distributor for the area. It was a tie-up that granted the label the exclusive promotion of a Victor record by the association operators for four consecutive months, beginning with November 1946, which was devoted to promoting Vaughn Monroe's "Racing with the Moon." This deal represented a revival of the old hit tune of the month program, in a somewhat altered format. Operators were requested to use special title strips featuring the song and to place the item in the number one position on the box. After careful consideration, the association decided to continue the use of streetcar advertising as the basic medium. Under the hit of the month concept, it was argued that juke plays of a song stimulated record sales of that number for the home.[76]

Apparently that experiment did not last too long because in 1947 the Cleveland association had changed to a different format. In July that year they held their fourth monthly Hit Tune Preview. Sponsored by the Phonograph Merchants' Association in cooperation with *The Cleveland Press*, the preview was conducted between acts of the final performance of "Too Many Girls" at the Cain Park Theater, Cleveland's open-air summer theater. An audience of 3,000 had the five songs in contention introduced to them and then played on a Rock-Ola jukebox on the Cain Park stage. After the records played, ballots were marked and collected. The winning song was slated to have the number-one spot on some 3,000 boxes throughout the Cleveland area during August. The overwhelming audience choice as Cleveland's Hit Tune for August was "I Wonder Who's Kissing Her Now."[77]

The Hit Tune party had its origins in Cleveland back in February 1941, when the Hit Record of the Month advertising campaign sponsored by the association was launched. Integral to the success of the original idea were hit tune ads that appeared in Cleveland papers, tie-ups with local department stores that publicized their record departments on the radio and in other media. All tunes selected in that early phase, before it was halted by the war, were picked by the balloting of association members. For practical purposes, the debut of the postwar revival of the Hit Tune party came on March 28, 1947, when some 3,000 record fans jammed the Cleveland Public Music Hall to pick the winning song for the month of May. An intensive one-week build-up was given to that party by *The Cleveland Press*. Tunes were played on a jukebox model, the name of which had been drawn out of a hat the previous afternoon.[78]

A "click" record of the month promotion, similar to the Cleveland

Max Mink, manager of Cleveland's RKO Palace Theater, beside a box set up in his theater, in 1948, to promote a monthly jukebox hit tune pick.

program, was launched in the Philadelphia area by the Phonograph Owners' Association of Eastern Pennsylvania. That group had also launched a full-fledged campaign aimed at teens. To that date, the 65 members of the association had donated a total of 15 boxes to various teen centers in Philadelphia.[79]

Following the same trend was the Michigan Automatic Phonograph Owners Association that decided in June 1949 to resume the monthly Hit Tune parties, which were suspended several months earlier and to reinstate a mass jury of teens to pick the Hit Tune of the Month. At least 5,000 teens were expected to attend the June party at the Eastwood Gardens, East Detroit. Tickets to the event were distributed free, but only on request, through local disk jockeys who were cooperating in the selection of the hit tunes. In addition, tickets were distributed individually by the jukebox association members, mainly through requests from their various locations. During the few months' hiatus in the teen selection parties, Hit Tunes were still selected, but by the association members. Selected for June as the Hit Tune was "Room Full of Roses" by Eddy Howard.[80]

Reporter Norman Weiser observed, late in 1949, that just one year earlier the phonograph business was emerging from one of its most financially disastrous summer seasons. With autumn and its usual increase in juke play, operators were more optimistic about their financial futures and more

Students from six universities, members of the College Fashion Board, pose around a Wurlitzer in the fashion shop of San Francisco department store O'Conner, Moffatt & Co., 1946. These students were on hand to advise student shoppers on fall fashions.

were getting involved in promotion. Hit Tune of the Month promotions were going strong in such cities as Cleveland, Detroit, and Cincinnati, in the spring of 1949 similar programs were launched simultaneously by five state, and one city, associations: Minnesota, Wisconsin, North Dakota, South Dakota, Iowa, and Philadelphia.[81]

Sherfick Music Service, a large operating firm near Columbus, Indiana, contracted for three 15-minute programs weekly over station WCSI-FM. As sponsors of "Top Tunes of the Day," Sherfick aired songs chosen by patrons of their music machines. The evening show, expected to promote play at locations, was scheduled to run for 52 weeks.[82]

When the Iowa Automatic Music Operators' Association met in Des Moines in 1949, the operators discussed and approved promotion deals with name band leaders that would see those artists supply the operators with records that were thought to have the potential to become hits. The operators maintained that if the band leaders furnished them with the records during visits to ballrooms in their area it would help stimulate business, not only for the box owners but for the ballroom proprietors and the band leaders. Several operators pointed out that in recent years the band leaders supplied only a small number of records to be placed in their machines. They argued that a larger supply of these free disks would be more beneficial because a small supply was hardly sufficient to "create much of an impression on the public."[83]

In 1950 Wurlitzer produced two television ads that they distributed free to their distributors around the country. Within a short period of time, distributors in at least six cities — Milwaukee, Pittsburgh, Dallas, Boston, Louisville, and Minneapolis — had purchased video time and put the one-minute spots to work plugging the coin phonographs. Patrons of taverns, and home viewers, saw a close-up of Wurlitzer's new Model 1250, showing its illuminated plastic top and the 48-selection record changer. The audience of most direct interest to Wurlitzer, though, was the tavern proprietor himself. It was hoped he would be sold on the unit after seeing and hearing it in operation as he probably had an out-of-date box on his premises. At the end of the commercial a brief period of soundless time was provided for the live announcement of the local distributor's name and address. Any inquiries would be passed on to local operators as active leads. The second ad provided by the firm was a 20-second station-break spot. Wurlitzer's campaign was thought to be the first time a major manufacturer tried to stimulate sales and box plays by way of television ads. It was all due to the fact that free video in taverns had cut seriously into jukebox revenue.[84]

Journalist Fred Amann declared, early in 1950, that location promotion had been receiving more attention in recent months and played an important part in the gradually rising box revenue of the previous six months. Charles Wiloth, of Tri-County Music in Chicago, designed a promotion to increase play that was said to be adding 15 to 18 percent to the normal weekly grosses. Wiloth, or one of his servicemen, selected an old record (one without vocals) and placed a corresponding title strip on the selection panel with the words "Mystery Tune" instead of the song title and artist's name. The same mystery record was not placed in more than one location at a time. Patrons were invited to fill out cards with their guess of the title. Wall signs and placards called attention to the mystery record and to the fact the winner received cash. After four weeks at a location the mystery record was removed and another one substituted whether the first one was identified or not. A cash prize of $1 the first week was increased by $1 each week the tune was not identified, to a maximum of $4. On the jukebox association level, members of the Washington Music Guild, in D.C., were plugging a local disk jockey and his pick of the "top tune" of the month, along with posters listing the top 10 tunes of each month. The disk jockey selection featured a picture of him, a well-known local figure. His choice of hits were said to be usually good for strong advance play even before the song made the big time. In return, the jockey plugged the city's boxes on his programs and featured a once weekly "top 10 records" program as taken from the jukebox selection panels. With this program, the Hirsch Coin Machine firm reported an average $8 per week increase in some locations.[85]

Another association-sponsored promotion program was run by the Amusement Machine Operators' Association of Greater Baltimore. Every week, each member operator selected three songs he believed would catch on. Those selections were then turned over to a panel of judges who chose, from the approximately 200 titles, the songs to be plugged for the week. A disk jockey tie-in was also used with the jockey promoting the hit of the week on his program and mentioning it as a juke selection. Operators followed through with their own location promotion by placing the record in the number one spot on the selection panel and placing placards at the location. Biddison Music of Baltimore used a scheme that revolved around the visits, for local engagements, of name singers and bands. Checking in advance on such appearances, the firm featured the tunes, past and current, made famous by the visiting artists. An idea in vogue in some areas was the pairing of a pop/country version of the same title. It was a gimmick said to work well in both country and noncountry locations. A variation of that idea by A&M Music Company, of Chicago, was known as the "double nickel deal." It involved placing two versions of current top hits in pairs on the same machine, such as "Jealous Heart" and "Room Full of Roses," encouraging many patrons to play both versions.[86]

One idea that seemed to surface during every period was that advertising should somehow be placed on the jukeboxes. Those ideas invariably vanished without a trace. After about six months of testing and experimenting, Chicago's Sar Enterprises reported at the beginning of 1949 a tie-up between Canadian Ace Brewing Company, as the advertiser, and Chicago operator Century Music wherein Sar's new phonograph device had been installed in boxes operated by Century in nine locations. The device included a timer and allowed a recorded advertising message to be played by the box at set intervals ranging from one to eight times an hour. In the initial field test, the Canadian Ace jingle, then featured on the radio, was played once every hour in the nine locations, all of which served the sponsor's product. While this was a new advertising gimmick, *Billboard* admitted it "has been tried in various forms in music machines for the past 15 years, but never successfully." Supposedly, Sar's plan would allow an operator to increase his weekly gross by $1 to $8, depending on the rate charged the advertiser. That income was to be divided between the operator and location owner in the same ratio as the existing commission split agreement between the two parties. In those locations where the Canadian Ace jingle was being played, location owners claimed there was a general increase in juke play as a result of the ads because patrons, after hearing the box turn on automatically and play the 10-second ad, produced a coin to play a number.[87]

From a technical standpoint not much happened within this short period. Mainly the industry concentrated on producing boxes that held a greater number of selections than in the past. In the fall of 1947, Wurlitzer held a press meeting to display its new model 1100. Adding excitement to the occasion was "an actor in Buck Rogers's fantastic 25th-century clothes who climbed atop an equally fantastic-looking contraption and proclaimed it worthy of the future." It was the only 1948 model produced by the industry. "In garishes, the supreme measure of jukeboxery, model 1100 was a knockout. By its side, previous models looked like church organs." Wurlitzer was following the proven industry formula that "the gaudier the machine the more nickels it would gather." Still king of the industry, Wurlitzer supplied about 60 percent of the total output, or 30,000 units annually, at $1,000 per machine. An estimated 400,000 jukes taking in $1.5 million per week were on location in America in 1946. However, the era of the extremely gaudy box, the luxury light-up age, came to an end for the industry around 1948. The novelty was wearing off and, more importantly, the industry was not so healthy as it had been and was less able to absorb yearly, or more frequent, model changes that involved little more than alterations in plastic panels and neon lights. Jukeboxes would always remain somewhat flashy, but the overboard-on-glitz period from about 1938 to 1948 was coming to an end.[88]

Things looked so promising for the industry immediately after the war that several new manufacturers entered the field. With the promise turning to illusion fairly quickly, most of those new makers made an early exit from the trade. One of those was the Aireon Manufacturing Company of Kansas City, Kansas. Aireon began producing boxes in the middle of 1946 and before the end of that year, just six months after its first juke was completed, it celebrated as the 10,000th box rolled off the assembly line. However, early in 1950, after operating for two years under trusteeship, Aireon closed permanently. The firm's facilities were offered for sale by the Reconstruction Finance Corporation.[89]

Dick Schreiber reported on a survey of the jukebox buying preferences of 561 operators scattered across the nation. Results showed that 46.9 percent of those operators felt they should replace 16 to 25 percent of their equipment every year. When they bought those replacement units most operators said they would have preferred to deal directly with the manufacturer rather than through a distributor. Prior to the war, when equipment prices and operating expenses were considerably less, the average operator set up schedules that enabled him to replace one-quarter to one-third of his equipment annually. Reductions in the replacement rate began to be noticeable as early as 1947 when higher costs began to reduce profits. Since all but one of the makers in the phonograph field, in 1949, marketed their production through established distributors, the question on buying preferences was important only as an indicator of operator feeling. Packard and Aireon revamped their selling set-up in 1947 to sell direct to operators. By 1949 Packard had discontinued production while Aireon, destined to be out-of-business within a year, had gradually appointed new distributors in key areas to supplement its direct selling. Homer Capehart led the brief, unsuccessful attempt to revive Packard. Ironically, it was Capehart who was one of the major forces some two decades earlier in establishing the system whereby makers sold only to distributors. When he revived Packard, dormant for years, he had no established network of distributors. Hoping to avoid the time and expense of setting up such a network, he tried to bypass it completely by selling directly to the operators.[90]

Schreiber felt the key to an operator preference for dealing directly with manufacturers could be summed up in the comment made by one operator. He said that one big problem operators had in their territories was competition from distributors who were able to buy machines for their routes at a better price. "This price advantage enables them to offer locations a more attractive commission which the rest of us have to meet." The only other explanation for the preference was that music men believed direct purchasing would mean a lower price. One question on the survey asked what percentage of equipment should be replaced annually. Results were 1–9 percent (8.4 percent of operators); 10–15 percent (36.3 percent); 16–25 percent (46.9 percent); 26–30 percent (6.9 percent); and over 30 percent (4.5 percent). Thirteen percent of the respondents favored direct selling from the factory to the operator; 41.6 percent favored selling through distributors, with their parts and shop departments; and 45.4 percent favored direct selling from the factory, with parts supply houses and repair shops in the territories.[91]

Within the record industry, jukes continued to be a major customer for disks. One 1946 account estimated there were 400,000 to 500,000 jukes in America with the record labels expecting the box industry to buy from 15 to 25 percent of the 300 million disks expected to be pressed that year. Expansion plans for labels were said to be based to an important degree on the expected doubling of the number of jukes within the next few years. Labels said that if they had the facilities they could sell 400 to 500 million disks in 1946, instead of 300 million. Record companies continued to concentrate on producing records that retailed for 50 cents rather than those in the 35-cent bracket.[92]

Over 900 operators throughout the nation were surveyed to assess their dealings with record companies. Results indicated that music men preferred to do business with record labels as follows: RCA Victor (813 votes), Capitol (517), Decca (432), Columbia (378), Majestic (159), and King (63). According to the survey, the best-wearing records were produced by RCA Victor (573), Columbia (516), Capitol (336), Decca (285), Vogue (222), De Luxe (123), MGM (87), Majestic (60), Signature (58), and King (51). In terms of which label operators purchased the most product from, the labels were ranked as follows: RCA Victor (2,678), Decca (2,469), Columbia (2,235), Capitol (1,708), Majestic (759), King (372), Mercury (341), MGM (133), Sonora (99), and Signature (84).[93]

One of the increased costs facing the juke industry was the rising price of disks. In the fall of 1947 distributors for several labels, including RCA Victor and Capitol, announced that wholesale prices had been increased by 6 to 10 cents, moving the price from 39 cents to either 45 cents or 49 cents.[94]

With the juke trade being so important to the record industry, some of the labels led by Decca, RCA Victor, and Capitol were competing for the box trade business with variations of direct sales tactics. Under the new pattern the fundamental source for label contact was the local jukebox operator association. RCA Victor had designed a special package announcing coming material that was being sent directly to 150 associations and 500 leading operators. For several months Capitol had also been taking steps to sell its products through local jukebox associations. Pressured by those moves, Mercury and Columbia also designed direct sales methods for the industry. A key reason for this new tactic by the labels was said to be the finding that the operators bought the first available version of a tune with hit potential. As a rule, competing versions to the original release had only a remote opportunity of drawing any business from juke operators.[95]

Sales of records, in millions of dollars, moved from $99 in 1945 to $198 in 1946, a staggering increase. For the rest of this period sales were flat and then decreased. The numbers for 1947 to 1950 were $204, $172, $158, and $184, respectively.[96]

One technical change in record manufacturing late in this period would turn out to be a boon for the industry, although it was feared in the beginning. From the beginnings of the record industry through the end of the 1940s, disks were relatively large, fragile, and easily warped or broken and played at a speed of 78 rpm (revolutions per minute). All that changed in 1948–1949 when Columbia introduced the 33⅓ rpm disk and RCA Victor brought out the 45 rpm record. Initially it was portrayed as a winner-take-all battle; one would survive while the losing speed would die. Eventually, both found a place in the record market as they supplanted the 78s, with the 45 becoming the speed for single-tune (per side) disks while 33⅓ became the speed for long-play albums (containing 10–12 songs in total). Other advantages of the new disks were that they were more or less unbreakable, lighter in weight, much easier to transport, and retained their playing quality for much greater lengths of time. As the 1940s ended, both RCA and Columbia were locked in a major advertising and promotion battle to sell their new speed records and record players for home use.[97]

Writing about this development, reporter Norman Weiser reassured his trade audience that any effect on jukes from the speed change was a long way off. Record availability would be sketchy until the public had accepted, or rejected, the new systems. Also, juke makers' problems in conversion to new speeds were said to be vast and costly. As of April 1949, only two manufacturers, Wurlitzer and Seeburg, were definitely interested in the 45 system and had a number of conferences with RCA officials. The other makers, AMI, Rock-Ola, Aireon, Filben, and Evans, had shown little interest to that point. Only RCA and Capitol were then committed to press on 45s the pop tunes making up the bulk of the records in the music machines. Columbia and Mercury were then the only labels committed to do the same thing on 33⅓ disks. Before makers would convert, thought Weiser, other labels would have to produce the new speed records. Until the public had passed judgment that would not happen. All of which meant, said Weiser, "for a long time to come the basic 78 rpm mechanisms used in the present-day machines will be retained." Even with some 2 million 45 and 33⅓ home record players on the market, that figure was only a fraction compared to the more than 15 million home players (78) then in use. Also, box manufacturers would first have to turn over the new systems to their experimental and research departments, resulting in the start of another lengthy program.[98]

In February 1950, Wurlitzer debuted the Model 1250 phonograph priced at $759.50. The 48-selection box was designed to play any speed. The most important mechanical change was the Adapta-Speed record changer that offered 48 selections on both sides of 24 records. This unit, for less than $10 in cost and 30 minutes of labor, could be adapted to play 45 or 33⅓ disks. Although it handled more selections, the new model used current Wurlitzer remote control equipment. Instead of employing a single tone arm to play the top side of the records, the new unit used two arms to play the selections on both sides. Wurlitzer said the Model 1250 would not make the present remote control equipment obsolete, which would play the 24 selections on the top sides of the records. Kits were available to convert wall boxes, and two new wall units played all 48 selections.[99]

Many operators who purchased conversions with new Model 1250s installed them only on one or two units, preferring to make location tests before putting out such units in larger numbers. Operators worried about such matters as record availability, wearing quality, reproducing quality, artist and hit tune availability, and whether the needle would hold the grooves of the new 7-inch plastic disks. Those tests were reportedly successful. Wurlitzer was the first maker to introduce a converter whereby their phonograph could handle either of the two new speeds. Its conversion kit sold for $8.75. As of May 1950, it was the only manufacturer to have done so. Seeburg had displayed a new unit to play 45s, but it was not being produced and would be released "if and when" the 45 rpm disks became a factor. AMI had also developed a conversion unit that could be used on any of the firm's three models. It was not then in production, but when the demand for such a unit was felt, it could be produced in "short order." Rock-Ola was also reported to be working on a converter but had been concentrating more on producing a model that could handle all three speeds. H. C. Evans, the last of the makers, announced it would also be ready to meet the demand for new speed units when the time came. No matter what happened at the maker level, operators generally agreed that current units with their standard 78 rpm disks would "be the mode for several years to come." And that if, and when, they were replaced by new speed units, that replacement would be done gradually and over period of two to three years, because of the existing large libraries of 78 rpm records.[100]

A few months later in 1950, there was still a reported pitched battle between Columbia, promoting the 33⅓ rpm speeds, and proponents of 45s, mainly RCA Victor. During this phase of the battle, the 33⅓ disk was 7-inches, the same physical size as the 45. When the competition finally ended, the 33⅓ survived by becoming the larger, long-play album and giving up any attempt to compete in the singles market against the 45s. However, at this point labels and box makers jockeyed for the best position.

Wurlitzer entered into an arrangement with Columbia Records whereby if the operator purchasing the Model 1250 allowed conversion on his machine, Wurlitzer supplied the $8.75 converter and Columbia provided 24 of its 33⅓ pop records, listed at $16.56, both free of charge. Labels were anxious to get their new speed records into boxes for the effect it would have on the public. That the public would hear and see the records in the jukes would go a long way toward increasing popular acceptance of the new speeds. An even more significant development was thought to be the effect this would have on the record label Decca. Considered to be the top label in terms of jukebox sales and plays, Decca was the only major label that had refrained from adopting either of the new speeds. If a lot of new speed disks started to show up in boxes, it might have caused Decca to see a threat to its market and to then commit to a new speed. With public acceptance of the new speeds in the pop field still undecided between the two, it was thought that a decision by Decca would probably swing the battle one way or the other.[101]

Seeburg announced, in October 1950, that it was adding the 45 rpm Select-o-Matic 100 to its product line and would continue to keep both speed jukes in production "as long as the record companies continue their policy of announcing simultaneous duplicate releases at both speeds." It was about a year earlier that Seeburg said its 45 rpm unit was ready to go when 45s became a factor. That came only days before Seeburg's announcement, from a decision on the part of all leading record labels to release popular tunes and single classical selections on 45s and to make simultaneous releases on 78 rpm disks. The battle of the speeds was over.[102]

Before 1950 ended, conversion to the 45 rpm speed was proceeding so rapidly that operators anticipated that 45s would be used almost exclusively in boxes by the end of 1951. Box makers were then all marketing new machines to play 45s and converting old boxes. Operators were buying the 45 records as quickly as possible primarily because of the economy in working with the 45s. Hit hard by the widespread installation of television sets in spots where boxes were formerly paramount, music men had found that conversion to 45s partially offset those losses. Slower speed disks virtually eliminated the breakage problem, formerly an expensive problem, and simplified servicing the boxes. The latter advantage stemmed from the long-wearing quality of the 45s, which made it unnecessary for the operators to buy two or three copies of the same song for each machine. The only drawback with the 45s was the lack of a library diverse enough to satisfy all preferences. Labels that produced mostly folk and country numbers still pressed mainly 78s. Sales of 45s during November 1950 rose to about 30 percent of the total market, a sharp increase over their previous 15 percent share. That dramatic rise was attributed to a huge Christmas promotion campaign devoted to 45 rpm home-record players and the disks themselves. It was a promotion at all levels of the industry, from the manufacturer to the retailer.[103]

With World War II over, the box makers once again eagerly looked to the foreign market. During 1946, U.S. firms exported a record total of 14,396 coin machines valued at $2,655,078 or nearly double the 1939 prewar high, with jukes accounting for 71 percent of the value of all machines shipped in 1946. Rock-Ola set up a coordinated system for handling foreign trade where it sold only new coin-operated equipment to distributors appointed in each of the foreign nations that Rock-Ola dealt with. Company assistant sales manager Lou Sebastian explained it was done that way because people in foreign lands, "while not objecting to Americans being on the business scene, preferred to do business with fellow natives." In most cases distributors sold to operators, except in countries where operators were nonexistent and the only feasible way of handling coin machines was by direct sales to the location. Among the problems in exporting were the crating and packaging of equipment for shipping, converting of coin chutes and mechanisms for foreign coins, and adapting of electrical systems. Sebastian observed, "It is a matter of record that in Southern countries with warm climates the people are naturally music lovers and like to hear music all the time." While the average American patronizing a tavern was more likely to order his drink and then play the juke to increase his enjoyment, those people in the Southern countries would invariably play the juke first, then have the drink as an addition to the music. In other words, Sebastian explained, "if they had to make a choice between music and the beverage they would be content to have only the music."[104]

The most popular coin machine in Mexico in 1947 was said to be the juke. Each play was priced at 10 and 20 centavos (two cents and four cents) depending on the type and locality of the establishment. By far the greater number of machines were owned and operated by location proprietors, with few actual operators having a route. The top box locations in Mexico, as in America, were in taverns and eating places.[105]

Music machines in the Union of South Africa were said to have a bright future, with high costs and difficulties in getting good records as the chief limiting factors, according to Alfred Jordan, a Capetown operator. He had been there for one year, after stints as an operator in both Australia and England. In South Africa, boxes in restaurants, cocktail lounges, and other locations similar to those common in the United States, were just catching on in 1947. Prior to that, the best spots, as in Australia, had been in arcades. When Jordan launched his firm in Capetown, it was unheard of for cafés and restaurants to feature jukebox entertainment. Two prewar 12-selection machines constituted the city's box total. Favorite locations were the verandas of the hotels, meeting places for guests, and indoor hotel lounges.

Records then retailed in that country from $1 to $1.25, leaving the operator cost at about 75 cents. Adding in other expenses, such as ocean transport, led Jordan to believe that dime play would prevail in his country. South African operators had been importing mostly used phonographs, at high prices, but also some new machines. Conversion of coin mechanisms to accept local coinage was done in Jordan's own shop. Popularity of juke music was said to be growing rapidly, although most of the locations opened to that point were patronized by the white population. With regard to the mixed race segment of the population, or coloreds, Jordan observed, "This class has its own eating and drinking places, and the few juke boxes which have been installed in them have been so popular that almost unmanageable crowds collect." No mention was made of the Black population. The largest areas for juke growth were the cities of Capetown, Durban, and Johannesburg. In arcades, which boomed during wartime convoy days, the juke was at first used as a free entertainment device, set to play without coin insertion, as an attraction for the amusement games.[106]

Exports in 1948 totaled 14,183 coin machines with a value of $2,309,581. By type of machine the breakdown was 3,894 jukes (with a value of $1,623,978); 6,437 vendors ($332,059); and 3,852 amusement games ($353,544). That represented a huge drop from 1947 totals of 26,542 machines, valued at $5,120,102, sent abroad: 12,379 jukes ($3,967,859); 6,785 vendors ($471,234); and 7,378 amusement games ($681,009). It was a business decline due to various embargoes. Canada, Mexico, and Argentina together imported 19,941 coin machines worth $3,061,042 in 1947, but due to restrictions in effect in 1948 were able to spend in total only $188,248. Jukeboxes, the traditional leader in the coin-machine export area, accounted for 70 percent of the 1948 dollar volume.[107]

Wurlitzer introduced the jukebox to Switzerland in 1949. Geneva representative of the firm, Eric de Stoutz, said: "I didn't expect them to be a success at all. I was afraid of the colors—so American looking! I was astonished to find that many Swiss thought them beautiful." At first Swiss people regarded the boxes with curiosity but came to realize the tone "was better than anything they had heard." He admitted that about 10 percent of the café customers complained about the music machines, calling them "ugly and tasteless" and saying they injured "the beauty of our country." So far, de Stoutz had installed 71 boxes in Geneva, Zurich, and Basel. German-speaking Swiss liked polkas, marches, and country songs while French-speaking Swiss preferred American jazz and French tunes.[108]

Laws, taxes or fees, and copyright continued to be issues that dogged the industry, but only to a minor extent. In 1946 the Town Commission of West Orange, New Jersey, considered an ordinance that would have prohibited the use of any coin-operated amusement machine or jukebox by a minor under the age of 16. Proprietors of establishments would have to verify ages by birth certificate whenever they doubted a patron's age. At the end of that same year, the Common Council of Syracuse, New York, passed an ordinance that all boxes in the city be licensed at a yearly fee of $15 per machine. That measure also made it illegal for the music machines to be played after 3 A.M.[109]

Also at the end of 1946, the Alabama Alcoholic Beverage Control Board (ABC) rejected a request by Birmingham attorney, Tom Skinner, to permit certain types of juke music in places where alcoholic beverages were sold. At the same time, Birmingham police commissioner Eugene Connor cited a city ordinance forbidding mechanical music in taverns. Canned music in retail licensed establishments throughout the state was at that time prohibited by the ABC Board in a ruling issued some four years earlier. Skinner was a close associate of Governor-elect James E. Folsom, who had been quoted as saying he would allow music machines in Alabama when he took office in January 1947. Acting apparently under the belief that jukes would soon be legalized, many locations in Birmingham had already installed phonographs with the coin slots sealed with tape. Connor declared that regardless of what happened to the state ban in January, the city ordinance would still be enforced.[110]

Tavern proprietors and juke operators in Alabama were officially notified late in 1947 that the ABC Board had issued an order lifting the ban on music in places where alcoholic beverages were sold. It meant that jukes and dancing would be allowed in public establishments selling liquor for the first time (effective December 15) since the administration of ex-governor Chauncey Sparks imposed the ban in February 1943. Official figures showed there were 2,868 retail locations with alcoholic beverage licenses in Alabama in 1947. The regulation change followed a declaration by Governor Folsom that he intended to see that "the little man in Alabama gets his juke box and beer." Permits were to be issued by the ABC Board allowing various types of music as set out in the regulation.[111]

However, on December 10 the ABC Board changed its mind and decided to suspend consideration of permits until there would be "proper compliance" with the regulations. Board members, seeing those already installed (but not working) boxes in many spots, claimed operators were "jumping the gun" and postponed any definite action on the permits. Several cities had already passed legislation prohibiting jukes in places where alcoholic beverages were sold, and others were reportedly considering such action. County governments, though, would not be allowed to prohibit the use of jukes in taverns. Fed up with what he regarded as stonewalling by the board, Governor Folsom, in February 1948, ousted the entire three-man ABC Board because it failed to come to a satisfactory decision regarding the use of boxes in state taverns. With a new board quickly installed, the first permits to allow jukes were issued in the middle of March 1948.[112]

Mobile, Alabama, was one of the communities that exercised the right to enact their own bylaw to ban coin-operated boxes in places selling alcoholic beverages. That law was skirted by Mobile operators who had closed the coin chutes and were renting their equipment for free play in the locations. It meant that many of the bands and piano players who formerly furnished live musical entertainment in Mobile spots selling liquor had disappeared. Operators were getting $10 per machine per week in rentals, and the locations bought their own records. Locations were said to not be complaining at an average $18 weekly cost, as they had been paying out anywhere from $15 to $50 per night for live talent. Units on location were run entirely within the law, simply because the coin chutes on the boxes were sealed with adhesive tape and the machines were run on a completely free-play basis. Said Mayor Charles Baumhauer: "The city of Mobile has no intention of issuing juke box licenses, but if the machines are giving music without charge the city cannot interfere." A survey made of spots that had replaced live music with free-play boxes reportedly showed the gross revenues of those spots had increased as much as 300 percent since the switch was made.[113]

When Youngstown, Ohio, imposed two separate city taxes on jukes, the industry fought back, getting one struck down and the other modified. One was a $25-a-year excise tax; the other was a $10 city-license fee. The excise tax was invalidated by the Court of Appeals of the Seventh District of Ohio because the city's charter contained a provision that no excise tax could be levied on a business without approval by a popular vote — no such vote had been held. When juke industry lawyers showed the city was put to little or no extra expense for inspection or policing of boxes the court, calling the $10 License Fee "exorbitant," reduced it to $5. A legal principal involved was that a license fee was imposed to cover the cost of regulation or inspection, and not for revenue-raising purposes. Operators declared they would not fight the $5 license fee.[114]

The Chicago City Council passed an amended ordinance in October 1946, that reduced to $25 the original $50 annual license fee established in December 1943 but which had never been collected due to legal challenges. Operators lobbied for a $15 fee but finally agreed to the $25 figure, promising there would be no legal contests. With an estimated 6,000 boxes in the city, Chicago hoped to generate $150,000 annually in revenue from the measure.[115]

New York City was thinking of imposing a juke license fee of $10 to $25 yearly. Chicago, Buffalo, and Syracuse were cited by Benjamin Fielding, New York commissioner of licenses, as places that licensed music machines.

Fielding revealed that a survey of New York City showed there were 9,165 boxes in the city.[116]

In Canton, Ohio, in February 1947, the Court of Common Pleas upheld the city ordinance placing an annual license fee of $15 on jukeboxes. A temporary restraining order had held collection of that tax in abeyance since it was passed in June 1945. Owners of several hundred boxes, who had secured the restraining order, argued the measure represented an illegal use of the city's police powers and that the fee was excessive. However, the court ruled the fee was not excessive when the expenses of administration and inspection were considered and that the licensing of music machines had been generally recognized as valid by the courts.[117]

A general article on legislative action planned for boxes argued that some measures may have been the result of unfavorable publicity received by the industry. Cited as examples were California, Illinois, Michigan, and New York. With regard to "unfavorable" tax proposals recently introduced in New York and California, the article commented, "it seems pretty certain that unfavorable newspaper publicity may have led to the high-tax proposals. For the bills seem to be definitely intended to injure the business and not to raise revenue."[118]

Bloomington, Indiana, city council placed license fees on coin-operated machines in 1947. The new measure taxed jukes $15 per machine per year, pinball games $20, and cigarette venders $12 per machine. Under a city ordinance Council Bluffs, Iowa, imposed a $100 license fee on box distributors while phonograph operators were assessed a $10 annual tax on each machine. Pinball operators paid a $50 fee per unit.[119]

Shifting of tax responsibility from box owner to location proprietor was adopted in 1950 by the Los Angeles city council when a new license fee of $7.50 per machine was set. The new measure specified that the fee had to be collected from the location proprietor. Under the old ordinance, the tax was collected from the box owner, which proved impractical according to the city clerk's office.[120]

Actions by music-licensing groups to eliminate the exemption jukeboxes enjoyed from copyright laws continued in this period. At the beginning of 1947, ASCAP had the support of radio broadcasters, Broadcast Music, Inc. (BMI — its rival performance rights society), and possibly the motion-picture business in its upcoming attempt to gain revenue from the performance of its music in coin machines. That assurance of support was reportedly given ASCAP within recent weeks and the former was counting on it in laying plans for its attempt to get legislation introduced by the current Congress for a law permitting ASCAP to collect from the music machines. Speculation about the reasons for the support focused on the idea that if ASCAP gained such a law it would benefit in the amount of

$3–$4 million annually. That money, added to ASCAP's other revenue, would make the society less tough to deal with in regard to its income from radio and motion pictures. That the juke industry was already fighting back was evident in an offer recently made to BMI wherein it was told if it would help the box industry successfully fight ASCAP then all records of ASCAP material would be barred from jukes, and BMI's used exclusively. BMI rejected the offer.[121]

Commenting on the long-running battle, *Billboard* noted that year after year bills were introduced as Congress met, and worried "there is always the prospect that one of these times the bill may pass." Also noted was that at the same time one or more anti-ASCAP bills showed up in state legislatures during every legislative year — usually on the ground of monopoly. While a few states passed such bills in 1945, the publication admitted they all lost out and were invalidated by state supreme courts. Despite that, *Billboard* took comfort in those bills, arguing that their appearance had only one meaning and that the public was widely opposed to the idea of paying special fees to organizations like ASCAP.[122]

Later in 1947, hearings were held before the House Judiciary Committee to determine if the 1909 copyright law that exempted boxes from paying royalties should be amended. Well-known artists such as band leader Fred Waring and composer Gene Buck testified that it should be changed. Arguing that no change was necessary, the box industry claimed it was largely responsible for the present wide sale of records and that, far from exploiting artists and composers, the boxes actually boosted their earnings. ASCAP declared the industry grossed $230 million a year, a figure disputed by the industry. Sidney Levine, operators' counsel, said, "There are 10,000 operators in the country who employ another 20,000 helpers— and nobody is getting rich." He added that the industry bought 20 percent of all records sold and stimulated the sale of others. Once again, nothing came of this attempt to bring jukes under copyright laws.[123]

Samuel Rosenbaum, trustee of the American Federation of Musicians (AFM) music performance trust fund, with the support of AFM general counsel Milton Diamond, urged the federation to find a way of collecting revenue from motion pictures and from jukeboxes. AFM president James Petrillo replied that it was too late to collect from the movies— they should have acted in 1927 — because the movie industry was then too powerful. As for jukeboxes, Petrillo said there was little the AFM could do to gain revenue from boxes. "What do you want me to do?" he asked. "Burn down the taverns that use juke boxes? That's against the law."[124]

Stories linking crime to the music machines continued to surface, now and then. Two Chicago daily newspapers simultaneously ran stories in 1946 about "juke box rackets." One paper stressed the alleged gangster connections of the trade — gangsters getting 50 to 75 percent of the take — while the other one emphasized an FBI investigation into alleged restraint of trade activities by distributors and operators.[125]

Industry information became a little more available with the release of more operator surveys. Writing in the New York Times, journalist Murray Schumach estimated that in 1946 there were about 280,000 boxes in America taking in $232 million annually, an average of $16 per music machine per week. He said the industry "is set for the biggest boom in its history." Some months later, Variety reported those same numbers as its estimates, citing "some authorities" as the source.[126]

The Census of Manufacturers revealed that 99,000 boxes were produced in 1947, with a value of $49,819,000. No breakdown of juke numbers was available for 1939, but the value of both coin and noncoin electrical phonographs produced that year was $19,055,000. The large number of boxes produced in 1947 represented catch-up for an industry for which no new product had been manufactured for a number of war years. A lot of older units needed to be replaced.[127]

Results from a comprehensive survey of 561 operators were released by Billboard in June 1949. One question asked the operator's average weekly share of the gross receipts per machine over the previous 12 months. Fifteen percent of the operators said $5.99 or less; 40 percent said $6 to $8.99; 37 percent said $9 to $14.99; and 8 percent said $15 and over. The average weekly gross for an operator was $8.82. Another question asked the average weekly operating expenses per machine (excluding depreciation). Twenty-four percent of the operators replied it was $2.49 or less; 41.7 percent, $2.50 to $4.99; 23.2 percent, $5 to $7.49; and 11.1 percent, $7.50 and over. Reporter Dick Schreiber observed that bookkeeping was sometimes inaccurate because in comments operators pointed out they could not always distinguish between amusement game and music expenses, since the two types of machines were often run as a unit — with the music machine installed to protect a good game location.[128]

Another part of the survey asked how many route men were employed: one employee (44 percent of the operators); two (37 percent); three (13 percent); four (2.5 percent); five (3.5 percent). Percentage of operator weekly gross spent on salaries and wages was 10 to 15 percent of gross (27.2 percent of operators); 16 to 20 percent (18.4 percent); 21 to 25 percent (24.8 percent); 26 to 30 percent (10.4 percent); 31 to 40 percent (13.6 percent); and over 40 percent (5.6 percent). Average weekly wage was $66.35. Such a wide fluctuation in money spent on wages seemed to again indicate a lack of knowledge of the true costs. Most of the operators surveyed (360 out of 561) ran both amusement games and boxes and used route men interchangeably on both types of equipment. A majority of the 561 operators

had music routes of 100 or fewer jukes; only 13.4 percent said they operated more than 100 boxes.[129]

A little over a year later, results were released from the second annual
music operator survey. It showed that the operator share of the gross take
per machine was $12.44, compared to $8.82 a year earlier. The breakdown
for number of machines operated was less than 50 (48 percent of operators); 50 to 99 (30 percent); 100 to 199 (13.5 percent); 200 to 299 (3.5 per-
cent); 300 and over (3.5 percent); and no answer (1.5 percent). Sixty percent
of all the boxes operated by the respondents were described as post-war
models, up 11 percent over 1949. A heavy majority of respondents ran both
music machines and amusement games. While a few also ran vending
machines, there was still a sharp line between amusement machines and
vendors. The sharp increase in operators' gross weekly receipts was thought
to perhaps be due to a concentration on the more profitable locations and
the elimination of marginal spots. Average weekly operating expenses
(excluding depreciation) per box were given as $4.78, about the same as in
the previous year. Operators spent about 22.2 percent of their weekly gross
on salaries, similar to 1949. A straight salary was paid to employees by 76.9
percent of the operators, straight commission by 7.7 percent, and salary
plus commission by 15.4 percent. On average a route man was paid $64.51
per week. Operators employed an average of 2.14 route men and 1.74
mechanics each. However, 81 percent employed two or fewer route men,
13 percent had three, and the remaining 6 percent had four or more. Surprisingly, only 27 percent of the operators were members of an active jukebox trade association. There were an estimated 400,000 music machines on
location in the United States.[130]

Up to this period the juke industry had enjoyed almost unlimited success. Stoppage of new production of boxes in the war years did not hurt the
trade. Operators thrived with increased business and decreased costs since
they did not have to replace boxes. Manufacturers all made profits by turning to war-related production. Other problems such as copyright issues,
taxes and fees, and stories linking organized crime and the industry were
more minor irritants than true problems. However, in the 1948 to 1950
period, for the first time, articles appeared in the trade press dealing solely
with the problems plaguing the jukebox industry.

During 1947 and 1948 box makers estimated that nearly 200,000 units
were produced, compared with an average yearly production of 72,000 units
between 1936 and 1939. This became a problem for distributors in the last
half of 1948 as they tried to move their inventory. One result was more
changes in the system than in the past, with an average of five distributor
changes per month as local franchises were awarded to other firms. As a
kind of climax, Packard Manufacturing (in a short-lived return to juke

manufacturing) announced that starting on January 1, 1948, it would revert to selling practices not used since the very earliest days of the industry, and then only briefly. All Packard distributor contracts expired that day and in their place the distributors were offered new contracts, at reduced commissions, which made them sales agents. Under the terms of the new Packard contracts, those sales agents merely took orders for equipment and then turned them over to Packard, which then shipped direct to the operator. Service, formerly provided by the distributor, was rendered through a number of regional service agencies. Packard's changes lowered the cost of the firm's boxes. Formerly listed at $1,000, the price of the Packard Manhattan dropped to a cost of $625 cash to operators or $695 on a payment plan that gave operators two years to pay off the price of the equipment.[131]

Distributors in general found themselves to be operating machines more than they ever did before. Dissatisfied with their sales figures, some distributors started their own routes when the phonographs consigned to them on a quota basis began piling up in their stockrooms. Other distributors, who sold machines on time payments with little or no cash down payment, found themselves having to repossess machines. Rather than turn the equipment over at a loss, some simply kept the repossessed routes intact and took over operating them. One observer argued that when a distributor could no longer make distribution its main function, but had to turn instead to operating, "something is wrong." With jukes no longer in the novelty stage they were being hurt by newer novelty entertainment, such as television. Some smaller locations that could have been box sites were opting instead for a Muzak system, which also cut into business. Despite the need for a price increase to a dime, and pressure from some parts of the industry for such a change, nickel play held firm. "There was no mass movement to experiment with the dime price since operators said they were largely convinced that the business could only continue at a nickel price."[132]

Norman Weiser gave a long report that solicited opinions from distributors as to how to increase operator income. All agreed such an increase was needed and how that could be accomplished was the number one problem in the industry. Suggestions covered the usual items such as front money, more favorable commission splits, and so on. A couple of distributors commented that a net of $15 a week was the minimum amount an operator had to have. Another argued that manufacturers could take a lot of trimmings off a machine and bring the price down as much as $300.[133]

When *Billboard* studied the situation at the beginning of 1949, the publication declared 1948 was "perhaps the roughest year in the history" of the coin-operated music business: "The war years and their resulting lush grosses are definitely a part of the past." Drastically reduced incomes to operators resulted in makers seeing production lines slowed, or even stopped. Fewer new models hit the market. Wurlitzer closed its production line in April 1948 to allow distributors to dispose of some of their growing inventories. What was reported to be a one-month shutdown extended through the balance of the year. Late in that year Wurlitzer's phonograph division was blamed for an almost $2 million loss; the price of boxes was reduced and distributor contracts were revised. Rock-Ola slowed its production line while AMI came out with smaller, cheaper models. New firms that entered the industry, Aireon, Packard, and Filben, all experienced difficulties and soon expired.[134]

For distributors as well, 1948 was a bad year. Prices for jukes were too high, inventories were too large, and there was a lack of credit. Most manufacturers canceled a large number of distributing contracts to appoint new sales representatives. Distributors changed lines; some simply closed their doors or went into other lines.[135]

Many operators who were solely juke owners had added pinball games along with cigarette machines, in response to increased operating costs and the constant inroads of television. However, even there competition was fierce. J. P. Manning, a wholesale tobacco firm in New England, had re-entered the field of selling cigarette machines. Manning offered machines direct to locations for $60, plus service and cigarette supplies at prices that gave the location more profit than regular operators were able to offer to proprietors.[136]

With the rough period of 1948 to 1949 behind it, and some resultant changes in the industry, the juke trade was reported to have more confidence in its future in 1950 than it had at anytime since the "lush months" of 1946. Production was now closely geared to sales, equipment prices were steady and consistent with earnings, and distributors and operators were in sound financial condition. Manufacturers had not relaxed their sales efforts, but high-pressure tactics and sales without down payments had "virtually disappeared." Makers who pressured their distributors with monthly quotas that were impossible to meet without such high-pressure tactics as sales with no money down had revamped their production goals and scrapped sales programs that pushed operators beyond their financial limitations. That changing attitude, forced on the industry after two years of overproduction and nearly two years of leveling off, was credited, said reporter Dick Schreiber, with putting the industry on its soundest footing since the end of the war. He doubted there would be an appreciable increase in the number of jukeboxes on location — estimated at 400,000. But the replacement part of the market still represented a large amount of business. Operators estimated, in 1950, they would buy on average nine boxes each. With a replacement rate in the area of 12 percent, it meant the makers could expect to sell in the neighborhood of 48,000 new units in 1950. Those makers conservatively estimated 1950 sales of new machines at 45,000 units. Schreiber thought there were 5,500 operators, each with an average of 72 boxes. Each purchased an average of 156 records weekly; 858,000 per week in total, 45 million annually. Some 64 percent of music operators also ran pinball games; 14 percent also operated cigarette venders; 39 percent also ran amusement games other than pinball; and 16.5 percent also operated venders other than cigarette machines. Overall Schreiber's account was very optimistic. But he neglected to discuss some of the obvious difficulties that would continue to affect the future of the trade.[137]

6

Jukes Have One Final Fling,
1951–1959

"Keep juke boxes out of Mexico." Sign at Juarez, Mexico, demonstration, 1953.

"In many cities boxes are largely the preserve of the underworld, with mobsters dictating who gets one, how the take is split and, often, what crooner you'll swoon over." Lester Velie, Reader's Digest, 1955.

"Such partisan attacks on the performing rights societies [ASCAP] … shed no light on the problem and only reveal the dog-in-the-manger attitude of the jukebox industry." Emanuel Cellar, House copyright hearings, 1959.

"We didn't like it, but we had to sell juke boxes to [Chicago gangsters]." Milton Hammergren, Wurlitzer executive, 1959.

As the 1950s began, the jukebox industry was full of renewed hope and optimism. In many ways it was a good decade for the trade. More boxes were exported than ever before as the foreign market compensated for a slow domestic one. Dime play was embraced and finally became the standard. Although the industry continued to enjoy copyright exemption, it never came under as much pressure on that issue as it did in the 1950s. Organized crime's involvement in the industry received widespread and lengthy national attention in the latter part of the decade. Thus, the 1950s ended on a sour note for jukeboxes with the industry largely unaware that the best years were over. From then on it would be all downhill.

One of the optimists was James L. Lennon, sales manager of the Coin Operators' Association, who felt, in 1952, that the industry stood on the threshold of what could be the most profitable period in its history. Several developments were responsible for that situation. One was the very recent debut of boxes that could handle 100 selections. Equally important was the introduction of the 45 rpm record that offered exceptionally strong service advantages—compactness and simplicity, nonbreakable, more durable, and easier to store, handle, and ship compared to the cumbersome, breakable 78 rpm disk. The industry had come a long way since the days of Edison's machine, "when listeners first put their money in a slot to hear screeching, parrot-like noises through a speaking tube." Analyzing the impact of television, Lennon made an unusual argument. Speaking of a recent federal government order to unfreeze license granting for some 2,000 additional television stations, he declared that move would herald a new era of expansion for the juke industry. Lennon reasoned that all those new stations would generate a new interest in records and that large viewing audiences would become increasingly aware of the new songs and new artists and, stimulated by seeing them on television, would want to hear those new artists again and again on records. This would all lead to more juke play. "With the new television era, the introduction of the 45s to coin ops and the new 100-selection machines, the industry is in a new period of expansion with far-reaching results."[1]

Less enthused about video was operator Jim Wickman who recalled back in the late 1940s when television first appeared in force in locations that "Juke box plugs were pulled in taverns during the busiest hours so as not to distract television viewers, and juke box play fell from 30 to 40 percent below normal." Many marginal locations were dropped altogether. Later when the price of television sets dropped, causing them to be found in more and more homes, juke collections began to rise. Still, Wickman added that it had been estimated that video "directly or indirectly reduces long-range juke box collections from 10 to 14 percent." Mostly the scare articles about the negative effects of video, so prevalent in the trade press in the late 1940s, were absent in the 1950s. It was not because television had no effect on juke play; it did decrease box receipts. However, the industry survived the worst of the decrease in the early phase when video was a novelty mostly seen in commercial spots. Then it bounced back a bit when the novelty of video waned. Also, as the industry came to accept a situation it was powerless to change there was less reason or need to discuss the matter.[2]

Programming guides and advice continued to be a major feature of the trade press. Standard guidelines changed little from the past, emphasizing such things as programming the box for the location. With jukes holding more and more selections, one piece of advice was that regardless of what tunes were chosen to be placed on a machine, they should be grouped by type so that they could be easily found. Also, in recent years, most operators reportedly turned over the record buying to their route men. The average operator spent from 10 to 15 percent of his gross receipts on new records.[3]

Jim Wickman returned to declare in print that American music patrons, who played an estimated 26 million tunes a day on the nation's 450,000 boxes, were finding increasing variety. Before the arrival of boxes that held 80 to 120 selections— only a few years earlier when boxes held an average of just 12 to 48 selections— there was little opportunity to offer more than a very limited variety of songs. Large capacity machines meant programming was more difficult. One operator said, "We have to program from 50 to 60 records for each of our machines, make sure that all the top current hits are featured, as well as the up and coming hits and all the customer's favorites in each location." According to Wickman, music men then relied on at least a dozen sources to assist in their record buying. Trade paper charts, editorial features and ads, and their personal opinion ranked first through third respectively. Other important aids were location requests, juke play meter counts, current artist popularity, and advice from one-stop outlets (places that wholesaled all, or most, record label disks). Seventy percent of all operators scheduled disk buying at least once a week, with box consumption estimated, conservatively, at 60 million yearly. Title strips on the machine listing artist and title were also said to be important. They "serve more than as a juke box menu. Salesmanship via title strips has become a major programming consideration."[4]

The need for a blank disk placed on machines was still expressed from time to time. Carleton Smith, National Arts Foundation director, urged box operators in 1953 to "please include a blank disk in all boxes so that listeners can buy five minutes of silence." Smith argued that quiet had become an expensive luxury in America. Not only was quiet good for the nerves, but it was also "necessary to enjoy music." He also asked for wider use on boxes of "music which nurtures the soul instead of merely assaulting the ear drums."[5]

A couple years later, reports came from the Bavarian Hotel & Restaurateurs exposition in Nuremberg, Germany, extolling the virtues of a silent record. Not just a hope, this item was a new product from the well-known equipment firm Siemens. In all respects it resembled an ordinary disk and was inserted in the juke along with the normal records. Any beer-hall patron desiring a brief respite from the music dropped a 10-pfennig coin (4.8 cents, the same as for a regular record) into the machine. The silent disk then dropped onto the turntable and ground away in silence for three minutes. For an hour of quiet beer-drinking, all the customer had to do was stuff 20 coins in the slot at one time.[6]

More or less at the saturation point, the juke industry constantly searched for locations beyond its mainstays of neighborhood bars and mom-and-pop diners. It rarely succeeded. Willens' Music Systems of Detroit started up in 1952 with the express goal of placing coin-operated music in drugstores. Two years later Willens had 25 locations in which it maintained hideaway phonographs (the box itself was out of public view, in a store-room or basement, and so on), carefully placed speakers, and remote selection boxes. All but 4 of those 25 outlets were drugstores. The others included a country club, a barbecue, and two drive-in restaurants. Owner Sam Willens observed: "We have opened a new field of business here in the large drugstores. These are all new accounts." Willens picked his drugstore outlets with considerable care; they had to have a soda fountain and a high traffic count. Remote selection boxes were always placed near the soda fountain. As a rule of thumb he installed one remote unit for every 4.5 stools at the soda fountain. One of the obstacles Willens encountered was the objection that the installation of a phonograph might turn the soda fountain into a hang-out for teens. Said Willens: "We sell the idea that the music system is put in solely as a convenience for the customer at the time he is shopping." With the large number of selections and good programming, he felt he was getting customers who had never played a juke before — older people who liked instrumental pieces and music that was soothing and relaxing. In some locations, he explained, women 40 to 50 years old came in who would never have given a thought to playing a box. "But when they hear the soothing music they want to know where it comes from. The clerk will tell them and before long they are putting in a nickel to hear their own selection."[7]

With regard to picking songs for his drugstore boxes Willens had no absolute rules, but he felt the operator who went after that kind of business should stay away from anything "too loud, too abusive or too rash" and "avoid what is out of the ordinary." Most of the drugstores Willens serviced had a machine that contained 20 semi-classic numbers, 20 to 25 pop tunes (instrumentals were preferred over vocals), 10 country numbers, and the remainder old favorites. About 15 percent of each unit's weekly gross went to record purchases. In July 1954, most of his installations were set to play one tune for a nickel, two for a dime, and six for a quarter. Since an average installation cost $1,400, Willens required drugstores to sign a three to five year contract with a $20 weekly guarantee to the operator. Some of his machines were installed on a straight annual rental basis with the rental amount determined by a survey of the traffic count in the store. Annual rentals ranged from $300 to $500 and any income over that was divided equally between the operator and the drugstore.[8]

A *Billboard* survey of operators in 1957 revealed more information about locations. When asked in what location did they have the greatest number of boxes, the responses were taverns, bars, and cocktail lounges, 69 percent; restaurants and cafés, 23 percent; ice cream parlors and snack bars, 8 percent; and private clubs, less than 1 percent. When asked which type of location was the most profitable, 41 percent said taverns, bars, and cocktail lounges; 45 percent picked restaurants and cafés; 9 percent said ice cream parlors and snack bars, and 8 percent picked private clubs. Of the total new locations added to routes in 1956, 43 percent were in taverns, bars, and cocktail lounges; 47 percent in restaurants and cafés; 7 percent in ice cream parlors and snack bars; and 3 percent in private clubs.[9]

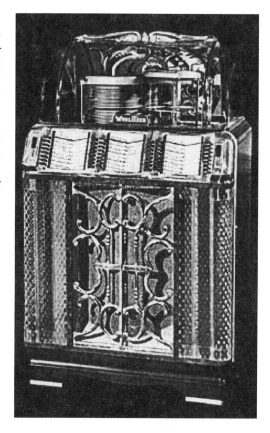

Wurlitzer 1400, 1951.

The main reason for the popularity, and profitability, of restaurants and cafés as box locations had to do with their longer hours. There was more time available for juke play. The 24-hour café was the most fertile source for an operator. These outlets were credited with more transient trade; and therefore a wider market. The length of time they were open placed them ahead of other limited-hours spots, which might nevertheless receive greater play while they did remain open. Cafés usually did not have the peak volume found in some taverns but maintained a steadier record of receipts over the long haul. Another point in their favor revolved around the "archenemy," television. Those 24-hour cafés did not seem to be as dependent on the video sets as did lounges, taverns, and bars. Eating seemed to lend itself more to music than watching television, whereas in a tavern, unless dancing was allowed, the "greater interest potential" of a television set seemed to take over. Operators did not have more music machines in cafés than taverns due to availability. There were not enough 24-hour cafés to go around. Considering what was a good spot in another context, opera- tors were almost unanimous in picking smaller neighborhood beer joints over the plushier lounges. Higher-class establishments often had live music on their busiest nights limiting the juke's potential. An operator in Michi- gan commented: "common people who congregate in local taverns and bars are your biggest market. People in high-class locations don't seem to spend as much money in coin-operated equipment." Spots catering to teens were also liked by music men, but play was not steady enough to rank those places high in profitability. A good teen spot was described as a very likely location for other amusement games, and by diversification a box operator could make the location a good source of revenue.[10]

Things got a little out of hand at Sheedy's Bar & Grill in Hicksville, Long Island, New York, when Dayton Hibbard dropped money into the box to play "Allegheny Moon." Three other patrons at the bar, Cornelius Gal- lagher, Gerald Janickey, and George Tappan, took offense because they were Elvis Presley fans. So every time Hibbard put money in the juke, the trio stomped hard on the floor, causing the machine to reject the record. Then, according to witnesses, a free-for-all broke out with the trio breaking two peanut vending machines, a chair, and bar stools before leaving. Later the three local youths were found guilty on malicious mischief and assault charges. Janickey was sentenced to 60 days in prison while Gallagher received a sentence of four months.[11]

Some New York City operators earned extra revenue during the holi- day season by renting music machines to private parties. The going rate for overnight rentals ranged from $30 to $50, depending on the condition of the equipment, with delivery and pickup included in the price. Because few operators had extra boxes, demand was said to be greater than supply. A lot of rentals were to employee groups of department stores, banks, and offices. Juke distributors should have been in a better position to rent as they had more units around, but they did not have any records. Operators had plenty of records, but they usually had few or no extra boxes. Outside of Manhattan, the going rate for a one-night rental of a phonograph was $25, but calls for such rentals were much fewer than they were in the city.[12]

The placing of boxes on location was still a largely informal matter. A 1952 survey of operators disclosed that only 17 percent of the respondents used written contracts when they sited machines; 83 percent did not, rely- ing on oral agreements. Asked if they believed written contracts should be used, all currently employing them said yes. Of the 83 percent who used no written agreements, 37.5 percent said they should be used, 22.5 percent said no, and 40 percent were undecided. Within the 17 percent group who used written contracts, only one operator covered all his locations that way. By contrast, one operator had only 5 percent of his sites on written contracts;

Wurlitzer 1650, 1953.

the group average had about 45 percent of their locations covered that way. A similar nationwide survey of operators in 1955 showed a significant shift as 40 percent of respondents said they used written contracts in at least some of their locations.[13]

Controversy continued in the nickel- or dime-play debate. An early 1951 account was pessimistic about the benefit of moving to 10 cent play after looking at a statistical breakdown of one week's income from a route segment of 56 locations in New York. During the test period 21,040 plays were registered for a gross of $1,052. Nickel plays were 7,954 for $397.70 (37.5 percent); dime plays (two for ten cents) totaled 7,576 for $378.80 (36.25 percent); quarter plays (five for 25 cents) equaled 5,510 for $275.50

(26.25 percent). Of that $1,052 gross income, $661.15 (62.85 percent) was retained by the operator — some locations were on front money deals. Following a change to 10 cents, no more than 4,512 plays (22 percent) could be lost if the operator was to gain revenue. Since dime play also offered the option of three tunes for a quarter, it was argued that the actual revenue per selection would average close to eight cents. It meant that 13,150 plays would be needed at the eight-cent level to generate the same gross ($1,052) as 21,040 plays at a nickel. Under those conditions, just to retain the status quo on income, no more than 7,890 plays (37.5 percent) could be lost following a switch. The question of how many plays would be lost after a changeover still remained unanswered. According to this account the argument that an operator could stand to lose 50 percent of his plays and retain the same revenue was invalid. Dick Steinberg, a Music Operators of America (MOA) director, argued for keeping the nickel standard, remarking that inflationary trends had not softened the public sufficiently to take dime play in stride, "The consensus is that the service would be over-priced at 10 cents." He reasoned that dime play would meet strong customer resistance and that a sizable percentage of players would stop using the music machines. Instead, Steinberg suggested that public relations and merchandising techniques be refined so that the base of play could be broadened further at the nickel rate while, at the same time, changing the commission split more in favor of the operator.[14]

Around the same time, operators in Chester, Pennsylvania, and surrounding Delaware County were in the seventh week of a sustained conversion to dime play and reported results to be "highly favorable" to that point. Half of the estimated 2,500 machines in the county had already been switched and the remainder were to be converted as fast as servicemen could be assigned to the extra duties. Box owners stressed the switch was not an experiment and that they looked at dime play (unless otherwise mentioned dime play always included the option of three selections for 25 cents) as permanent. In locations that had been switched, operators maintained that play levels were about the same as before the conversion. A typical pattern was for play to decrease for the first few weeks following the increase, and then build until it reached the old level. A strategy for making the switch acceptable to locations and patrons was to blanket a specific area with machines converted to dime play. If strong opposition was met in an area, it was bypassed and an adjacent section was converted. Later, the operator doubled back on the nickel "island" finding it by then softened to the idea. Many locations were on first money deals with revenue split 50/50 after the front money was taken. In order to increase both the box play and his income, the storekeeper became a "live music salesman" plugging the phonograph among his patrons. Places catering to teens had the most single-play patrons while the better spots had the highest proportion of quarter spenders. Cost of conversion was said to be minimal. However, the labor and time involved, especially in locations housing multiple wall boxes, was considerable. That slowed the conversion process, with change-over work scheduled in between regular route duties when time permitted.[15]

Journalist Norman Weiser reported in 1951 that operators in Philadelphia, Denver, Chicago, Detroit, Cleveland, and other urban areas were engaged in an organized test of 10-cent play. None of those tests were yet conclusive because they had only briefly been underway. In most cases operators worked with other operators so that no competing nickel juke "interferes." Operators remained outspoken in maintaining that dime play could only be successful if it was implemented by all box owners in a given area. While the volume of play had dropped in some of those test areas, in most cases, reportedly, the gross receipts had increased.[16]

By the end of May 1951, some 90 percent of all music machines in Chicago had been switched to dime play. However, customers were not feeding in dimes fast enough. Especially hard hit were the smaller locations, one of which reported its $15 weekly gross down to $1.75 in the first week of the price increase. One operating firm said it was breaking even in the more upscale pubs, but "taking a beating" in its smaller outlets.[17]

Just 10 days later a story in a different publication gave a different summary of the Chicago situation. Reporting that 98 percent of the city's boxes were converted, it went on to observe that general operator and location opinion was in favor of the switch. Changeover costs ranged from zero for new equipment to $6.36 each for certain wall boxes. Average dollar grosses were up over those from straight nickel play machines. Experience indicated that in the week following the conversion a machine's take would fall off $2 to $3, but thereafter revenue would increase. In top locations (high volume, transient patrons) the weekly gross increased from an average of $30 to $40 or $45. Spots that had been in the $15 per week range, had moved, in many cases, to $21 to $28. Marginal spots (smaller neighborhood taverns with mostly repeat customers) were the only type of location to raise major objections to the price change, but on the whole "finally agreed to the common-sense economics" of the increase. In such marginal stops, however, juke play had dropped 50 percent or more to give the same weekly gross, or one of $1 to $3 less.[18]

Important factors in conducting a successful switch to dime play were said to be promoting 10 cent play prior to actually converting boxes and the need to utilize an intelligent approach to the location-education phase of the switch over. Just as newspapers were quick to play up the demise of the five-cent cigar and the nickel Coke in many parts of the country, so did they publicize the passing of the five-cent box play. Operators in some areas had found that such publicity could be used to their advantage. For example, Illinois Amusement Association executive Lou Casola arranged for a feature story in the local papers explaining the price increase. The story stressed the rising costs of doing business, the higher salaries being paid, and the increased price of equipment. That same type of story had been printed in papers in at least a dozen other cities across the nation around the same time. Equally important to success was educating the location owner to the need for the increase. Newspaper publicity helped, but a more concentrated type of promotion was needed. In Chicago, for example, special

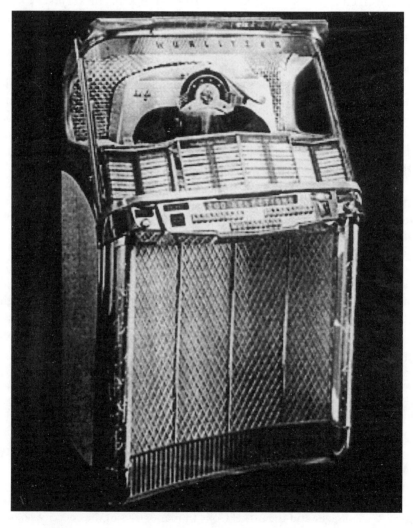

Wurlitzer 2100, 1957.

promotional pamphlets were given to the owners or managers in person, prior to any actual conversion. Those pamphlets explained in detail the reasons for the increase, noting such advantages as higher income, better programming, and top servicing.[19]

Late in 1951 one observer analyzed the play price situation, at the end of a year in which there had been much activity in trying to install dime play. It was reported that those tests of 10-cent play produced a wide variety of results, ranging from completely successful in some areas to failure in others. In many large urban areas there had been no attempt made to test dime play; while in others it was reported that all operators in the vicinity were testing hand-picked locations. Arguments in favor of dime play were summarized as follows: 1) higher gross receipts despite fewer plays; 2) fewer service calls and less supply costs; 3) more play stability; 4) inflation — everything else was going up in price, including pay telephone calls; and 5) longer life for phonographs and records. Arguments against an increase were: 1) public resistance to a 10-cent tab; 2) lower gross receipts registered in tests ranging from a few weeks to several months; 3) location resistance to increased juke prices; 4) time and cost involved in converting large routes, especially those involving many wall boxes; and 5) an increasing cost of living in general which was already cutting amusement spending by a large segment of the public. Other methods discussed and/or tested for increasing play at the location level, regardless of the cost of a play, were guaranteed money contracts, various promotion programs, and special programming.[20]

Things then quieted down as the price increase was not that successful. At the end of 1953 *Variety* reported that the nickel — a victim of inflation in subway turnstiles, phone booths, and other coin machines—"is still very much alive in the juke field." Despite sporadic movements by some operators to experiment with dime play, "the nickel is still standard in the jukes, with little likelihood of it being displaced in the near future." In the main cities of the East, "where 5c jukes are virtually universal," the operators were said to be showing a profit despite competition from television in the same spots. In some areas, notably Chicago, the 10-cent machines were being used without any adverse financial effects. Despite the good results in Chicago and some other smaller cities in the Midwest, most operators were in favor of maintaining the nickel standard. One factor in stabilizing the five-cent machines had been the introduction of the 45 rpm record, which had reduced replacement costs.[21]

Some more time passed with relatively little activity and then another major push toward dime play came in 1955. In March of that year some New York City operators began converting to dime play, as did music men in the Lake Okeechobee area of Florida. Also making the switch, with no public resistance, were members of the Eastern Massachusetts Music Operators' Association. Worcester had about 30 percent of its boxes converted while Springfield and Boston each converted about 10 percent of their boxes.[22]

Around that same time a nationwide survey of operators revealed that about 35 percent of all respondents had at least some portion of their equipment set for dime play. Nearly half of the 65 percent with all nickel equipment indicated they would probably begin to convert before the end of 1955. Since the start of that year cities like Detroit, Boston, New York, Cleveland, Hartford, Des Moines, and Akron had moved to the dime ranks with Omaha and Minneapolis scheduled to soon join them. Without exception respondents reported the first step toward dime play was securing inter-industry cooperation, the support of other music operators in a proposed dime play area. Another method was to increase the price on new equipment only, rather than changing the whole route at one time. Approximately 70 percent of the survey respondents not then on dime play said the only thing stopping them from switching over was a few operators in their area who were not convinced and planned to remain at a nickel. However, since 100 percent cooperation was hard to achieve, many music men bypassed that obstacle as best they could. For example, in Detroit operator cooperation was about 75/25 for dime play when the switch began. Of those with dime equipment about 65 percent of the machines were also set to give three plays for 25 cents, about 30 percent gave four plays, 4 percent provided five plays, and 1 percent gave six plays. Public reaction to the increase was the same wherever dime play was imposed. Its first reaction was negative, usually lasting for a week or two. However, the public had been conditioned to the vanishing nickel in other areas of daily life, such as the pay phone and a cup of coffee. When all operators converted at the same time, the public presented less of a problem. In Chicago, one of the first major cities to go completely to dime play, the public quickly accepted the move without being forewarned or "treated with kid gloves." In other areas the story had been different.[23]

AMI announced that starting in mid–April 1955, its model F phonographs and wall box equipment would come off the assembly line set for dime play. In areas where 10-cent play was not yet underway operators were told they could convert this new equipment "easily" to nickel play. This move was thought to make it easier for operators to impose the price increase if they could show locations that the factory set all new equipment for dime play. AMI's motto was "Factory Set for 10c Play — and worth it!" Wurlitzer declared that as of May 1 all phonograph equipment shipped from its factory would be set for dime play — and also set at three or four for a quarter. With AMI units a wide variation of plays could be set for a quarter. Rock-Ola announced it was considering the move while Seeburg declined to comment.[24]

Still, conversion dragged. The switch over in Minneapolis-St. Paul got underway at the start of 1956 but a couple of months later opposition to dime play by some operators in the area had caused the switch to "drag its heels." Meanwhile, music men in Peoria, Illinois, who had made several unsuccessful attempts to switch to 10-cent play in the previous two years, were trying again. Hopes were higher since this time the Peoria *Journal Star* had cooperated with the operators by publishing a favorable article about the need for a price increase. By the spring of 1956, a poll revealed that 70 percent of responding operators had at least some of their equipment set for dime play. However, well over half of that 70 percent ran fewer than 50 percent of their routes at a dime; over one-third ran fewer than 25 percent of their boxes at the higher price. This meant that the proportion of boxes at dime play, within the 70 percent group, was likely about 45 percent, not much over 30 percent when all the operators were considered.[25]

A second survey a few weeks later asked operators what percentage of their phonographs were on dime play. Responses were: under 25 percent of equipment (24 percent of operators); 25 to 50 percent (7 percent); 50 to 75 percent (11 percent); 75 to 100 percent (32 percent); and no machines on 10-cent play (26 percent of operators). Based on the two polls, this account concluded that although 70 to 74 percent of the operators used dime play, "approximately just 35 to 40 per cent of the nation's machines are operating at a dime." Two primary factors involved in successfully converting or operating at a dime, according to the operators were; relations among operators and relations between operators and location owners. Public resistance was considered a minor problem. Conversion to dime play could be successful in the face of nickel competition if the relationship between the location owner and the operator was solid; that is, if the location proprietor got better equipment, service, and higher income, understood the economic reasons for a price increase, and had been sold properly by the operator. If that happened then "the likelihood of the dime play operator losing the location to another operator who offers nickel play is minimal."[26]

Denver music men turned to the daily press in the summer of 1957 in an effort to pave the way for dime conversion in the area. It was estimated that only about 25 percent of the city's boxes were then on 10-cent play. The Colorado Music Merchants' Association was trying to remedy that with a newspaper campaign to educate the public as to why "the nickel has to go." Those ads detailed the cost increase to operators over the prior 10 years.[27]

Elmira, New York, began its conversion around the same time as Denver. It was the last bastion of nickel play in the state. Two months later, about 75 percent of the boxes were on the higher price. Elmira operators followed few rules in their campaign. No publicity was generated as to why the conversion was necessary; no public relations agency was employed to explain the operator's plight. Not one cent was spent on newspaper ads. Machines were not always upgraded. Operators in Elmira simply converted their boxes. They met no resistance of any kind. On July 4 there were no boxes in the city on dime play; by late August 70 percent were converted. By sometime in September the nickel machine was expected to be only a memory.[28]

That ease of conversion in Elmira marked 1957 as a turning point when the industry finally moved to a majority of higher priced machines. A poll of 53 major cities in the summer of 1957 revealed that over half of those cities had dime play on a majority of their boxes. Leading the way were seven cities at the 100 percent mark: Chicago, Memphis, Omaha, Gary, Little Rock, Hot Springs, and Pine Bluff. Forty-nine percent of the cities had 10-cent play on 75 to 100 percent of their machines; 21 percent of the communities had converted 50 to 75 percent of their boxes. That meant that 70 percent of the reporting cities were over the halfway mark in switching over. Nineteen percent were in the 25 to 50 percent range. Only 11 percent of the communities had less than 25 percent of their equipment converted to the higher price. Basically, the fight was over at this point. Only a few more articles would be devoted to the issue. As of 1957 dime play had won out. Remaining nickel machines would disappear rapidly and without much notice or protest.[29]

Industry promotion became quite different in the 1950s compared to earlier periods. Gone were the major promotions by single operators, or local associations, such as hit tune parties or publicity blitzes when name artists came to town. Television was changing the face of the entertainment business as it entered every home. Big band tours disappeared. Jukeboxes were still enjoying a successful period but less and less were they focal points. *Billboard* launched its own celebration in May 1953 to mark the 65th anniversary of the juke industry. Their choice of a beginning point was the time when Edison and his rival were temporarily unified as the North American Phonograph Company in May 1888. The publication devoted a great deal of space to the anniversary, although the number itself was unusual for a lavish fete. Normally splashy celebrations were held for the 50th, 75th, or 100th anniversary but not the 65th. When the 75th and 100th anniversaries were reached they were hardly noted. It was a situation that reflected the position of the jukebox within American society. In 1953 the box was still riding high; 10 years later it was well on the road to irrelevancy. As the importance of jukeboxes waned, so did the amount of space they received in the media. In fact, *Billboard*'s issue of May 23, 1953, was a special issue dedicated to the juke's anniversary. Also, the publication prepared a complete promotional kit that operators could use to obtain local publicity for the celebration. Jukebox associations and thousands of operators nation-wide were expected to build a solid, grassroots public relations event based on the anniversary. As part of its publicity efforts, *Billboard* prepared model news releases operators could use with their local newspapers, a fact sheet that would be helpful in interviews with disk jockeys, and a model speech for those operators and distributors who arranged to address local civic or fraternal clubs. Disk jockeys would participate in the celebrations by featuring recordings of some of the all-time juke box favorites. The publication contacted newspaper and magazine editors, and television and radio program directors to call their attention to the event.[30]

Within two weeks of announcing its campaign, *Billboard* had received more than 1,100 direct requests from various members of the industry for promotional kits. Those were in addition to 7,500 kits mailed already to top operators, associations, and disk jockeys at the start of the campaign. Local events to mark the anniversary included a proclamation by Arkansas governor Francis Cherry who declared the week beginning May 24 as National Juke Box Week. The Common Council of Detroit also proclaimed the week of May 24 as National Juke Box Week.[31]

A year later jukeboxes throughout the country were set to celebrate their 66th birthday with June 20 to June 26 as "Play Your Juke Box Week." To make the event a success, the entire industry, along with newspapers, record retailers, record labels, and record artists put their efforts behind the public relations campaign. Millions of Americans were to be made conscious of the promotion by radio, television, newspapers, and even roving sound trucks. In a combined effort, those groups placed posters in thousands of locations announcing the event, enlisted the aid of disk jockeys across the country, made arrangements with record labels and retailers to get their help in the drive, and enlisted the media in the concentrated effort. Through *Billboard*, operators again received kits to help in the promotion. Similar to the previous year's kits, they contained sample press releases, model speeches, industry facts, letters suitable for mailing to location owners, and a list of 139 All-Time Juke Box Favorites. The goal of "Play Your Juke Box Week" was to provide a reason for telling the public about the music-machine business.[32]

Local box associations still engaged in some promotion on their own, but in declining numbers. Promotional tie-ins with radio and television stations were the most popular PR programs with operators because they involved an exchange of services between music men and stations and cost the operators nothing. A typical example was a program launched in 1955 in Chicago by the local association, the Recorded Music Service Association, and radio station WAAF. Operators promoted the station by placing decals on their 7,000 boxes throughout the city that called attention to

to the juke box operators of America

One of many 1953 congratulatory ads on the juke's 65th anniversay. This one from band leader Guy Lombardo.

WAAF. As well, each month they programmed one tune in the number one spot on their machines. Selected jointly by an operator panel and the station's disk jockeys, the number was labeled Chicago's "Hunch Tune." WAAF, on the other hand, featured a daily disk jockey show, "Juke Box Matinee" from 3:30 to 4 P.M., which publicized the operators and their association, calling attention to the variety of jukebox music being offered throughout the city. Cooperative efforts with stations in civic events was also viewed as a rewarding PR plan for operators. In Detroit, for example, the United Music Operators of Michigan achieved radio, television, newspaper, and civic official cooperation in its battle against juvenile delinquency. The association, sponsoring a series of weekly teen dances, had the full cooperation of nine local radio stations. On a rotating basis, a disk jockey from each station emceed the event each week, with the others promoting the work done by the music men during their broadcasts.[33]

Another program was initiated in Peoria, Illinois, by the Music Operators of Central Illinois whereby they furnished local disk jockeys with all of their juke programming. That was said to have led to better public relations and a synchronization of radio and jukebox music. On the national level the Music Operators of America (MOA) sponsored a weekly radio show, "National Juke Box," over the ABC network from 9:30 to 9:55 P.M., starting October 15, 1955. That program featured the top regional box favorites of the week, as reported by MOA officials on each broadcast. On the first show, Al Denver, head of the Music Operators of New York, introduced two juke hits from the East. Newspaper advertising was another forum for promotion. In Pierre, South Dakota, Gordon Stout, president of the South Dakota Automatic Phonograph Operators' Association, informally discussed news events in an operator's life, in a breezy newspaper column. Operators who had run ads in local newspapers for a specific reason — to explain the reasons for dime play — sometimes decided to continue to advertise periodically for general reasons.[34]

Eighteen months later reporter Bob Dietmeier observed that the juke business was down, mainly due to declining tavern business. People were spending more leisure time at home with the television. Suburban growth also kept people more distant from drinking spots and with more bills to pay. Because of this, promotion had taken a different angle. Colorado operators said they were then giving employees at bars, restaurants, and cocktail lounges anywhere from $2 to $5 a week in dimes to keep the boxes playing whenever customer patronage fell off. One operator went so far as to give those dimes a greenish tint; the better to tell if they did indeed get played in the box. That was not a new idea, but the amount of money given and the heavy concentration on that method over a period of time was new. More generally, operators tried to draw location owners into the business by encouraging them to leave television sets turned off, even on fight nights, and to emphasize the jukebox instead.[35]

Once again the idea of joining advertising with jukeboxes appeared. Rodney Pantages, head of the Hollywood-based advertising agency Pantages Maestro, presented his idea to the MOA executive committee in the summer of 1954. His plan involved contacting national advertisers with material submitted for use on boxes to be selected by a special committee of MOA members. Money collected from the venture would be split evenly between operators and location owners. The approximate cost of advertising would be 10 cents per record played. With four records on each machine and one played every 15 minutes, the estimated revenue per machine was $3.20 for an eight-hour day. Pantages would charge advertisers for his service the same as any other ad agency. His payment would not come from the 10-cents-per-play amount. Those advertising records would be played automatically by a hidden timing device. Records would be furnished to operators without cost and would be labeled as to the type of location in which they were to be used. For example, a record with a beer ad would not be placed in drugstores. Before the day was over the MOA executives voted unanimously to adopt the program.[36]

Nothing much happened with this plan until April 1955, when Pantages made a presentation before a business session of the MOA convention. Commercials would be in the form of two-minute records and would be "tunes that are catchy and that do not grind out everyday commercials." Arguing that his plan was a way for operators to increase their revenue, he explained that it was his intention to see that the ad records submitted were as good or better "than the disks now being used on many machines." The final decision on whether a record should be used as a commercial on a phonograph would still be decided by a special MOA committee. At this presentation he talked of an advertising record playing every 30 minutes instead of every 15. He also argued the commercials would increase normal juke play by making customers conscious of the machine when it would have otherwise been idle. According to Pantages, a survey to estimate the average number of people who listened to a juke in New York found that number to be 200, based on an eight-hour day.[37]

Nothing happened with this plan for another year, until the 6th annual MOA convention in 1956. At that meeting MOA president George A. Miller told the gathering that MOA members were split 50/50 over the Pantages plan. As a result, the plan was abandoned.[38]

Changes within the industry itself were most noticeable in the number of selections jukeboxes offered and in the disappearance of some smaller manufacturers, most of whom had tried to enter what appeared to be a long-term growth market after World War II. Aireon and Packard both ceased to exist early in this period. Most surprising was the demise of Packard, since it was headed by jukebox legendary pioneer Homer Cape-hart. After leaving Wurlitzer in 1939, Capehart bought the old Marmon (auto plant) in Indianapolis and was just getting the company (Packard Manufacturing) going when World War II arrived. During the war Packard suspended box production to concentrate on ordinance work. In 1944, Capehart sought and won the Republican nomination for the Senate from Indiana; he was re-elected to a second term in 1950. At war's end Packard resumed production of phonographs and accessories, introducing its last model, the Manhattan, in January 1948. In April 1949, Packard announced it was suspending production until the cost of manufacturing jukeboxes declined. Apparently it never did, for in September 1951, Packard sold the assets of its phonograph division to Wurlitzer. With that sale Capehart officially left a business he had helped pioneer and devoted himself to his political career.[39]

The entire phonograph division of H. C. Evans & Company was sold for $200,000 in 1955 to two Mexicans who announced they would ship all the equipment and inventory to Mexico City where they would set up facilities for continuing the production of the Evans juke line. It would be the first box manufacturing plant in Mexico. Other divisions of Evans, the games and carnival lines, were sold to Four Aces Distributing Corporation. Although Evans was not a major box maker, it had been a long established firm in the coin-machine industry.[40]

A landmark was reached in the industry in October 1952 when Rock-Ola announced that it would put a 120-selection box on the market that month. All the major juke manufacturers then had neared, reached, or topped the 100 figure — most of them since the spring of that year, and all of them over the generally hearty objections of operators everywhere. Despite a three-year gap between the first and second maker reaching that mark, the trend proved to be unstoppable once it got started. The luxury light-up era was replaced by the large capacity period. Seeburg was the first to release a 100-selection model in December 1948; in November 1951 AMI unveiled its 80-selection D-80; in February 1952, Evans debuted a pilot model of its Century machine; Wurlitzer unveiled its 104-selection 1500 in April 1952; Seeburg released the third model of its 100-selection Select-o-Matic in May 1952; Evans released its 100-selection Century model in September 1952; then Rock-Ola displayed its Fireball the following month. Looking back, Wurlitzer started with a 12-selection model, jumped to 16, then to 24, 48, and finally to 104. Seeburg moved to 40 before its final step to 100. AMI moved from 20 to 40 and then to 80 selections. Evans went from 40 to 100 and Rock-Ola jumped from 20 to 50 before its move to 120. Those increases were not always well received by operators and distributors. With the larger number of selections came higher costs for machines, records, wall boxes, and other equipment; more service problems; and higher overhead all around. On the other hand, greater selection also brought higher receipts and greater public appeal.[41]

Jukebox production was as follows: 1946, 75,000 units; 1947, 99,000; 1948, 30,000; 1949, 35,000; 1950, 40,000; 1951, 45,000; 1952, 49,000; and 1953, 59,000. Of the total 1953 output, about 52,000 units were for domestic use and the rest were for the export trade. A pent-up demand for phonographs— the result of the war-time production stoppage — spurred production to 75,000 and 99,000 in the first postwar years. Eight firms were making new machines in 1946–1947. Production in 1947 quickly outstripped real demand. No down payment deals and high-pressure selling to new operators, as well as established firms, were the vogue in that period. By the end of 1947 boxes were backing up in distributor showrooms, and operators were having difficulty meeting their payments to finance companies. The blackest year in juke industry history came in 1948 when some makers shut down and distributors and operators were in a precarious condition with many going into bankruptcy. That same year music men in cities such as New York and Chicago felt the real force of competition from television. After that a slow comeback took place. Juke makers believed the domestic market should absorb 50,000 to 60,000 new boxes annually. With trade estimates at 450,000 for the total number of units on location, and a yearly replacement rate of 12 to 15 percent, replacements alone would sustain that volume. Over the period 1946 to 1949, the bulk of the units exported to foreign lands were used boxes that operators had retired from their routes and traded in to distributors. In 1953 foreign buyers took slightly more than 11 percent of new machine production. One juke manufacturer expressed an opinion privately that he expected his overseas business would equal his domestic trade within the coming 10 years.[42]

An estimated 61,000 units were manufactured in 1954 with around 51,000 for domestic use. The remainder, 16 percent of the total, was for the foreign market. The dollar volume of 1954's total output was in excess of $50 million. In 1955 about 63,500 units were produced (10,000 to 11,000 of those boxes were exported); in 1956 production was 61,000 (13,000 to 14,000 exported). Machine capacity continued to expand and 1957 was the first year all four remaining makers produced 200-selection boxes throughout the year.[43]

Relations between the juke and record industries remained strong. As the number of higher capacity boxes increased, the number of records sold to the juke trade by the record industry was estimated to have passed the 50-million-a-year mark, as of the start of 1952. Record labels claimed that at least 15 percent of their single records were sold for coin-machine use.

Dancing at the beach, Panama City, Florida, 1950. *Florida State Archives.*

Labels continued to provide special services for the music men. For example, Capitol and RCA Victor had a special sampling service for operators. Decca had produced disks like Grady Martin's "Slew Foot Rag" with coin machines specifically in mind, while RCA Victor told the operators that Pee Wee King's "Ragtime Annie Lee" was aimed at the jukebox market. More labels and record distributors were turning out title strips especially for the coin-machine business. Another strong indication of record labels' attitude toward the phonograph industry was their opposition to a bill before Congress that would have removed the juke copyright exemption. Reportedly, 150,000 of the first 200,000 copies of Tony Bennett's "Because of You" were sold to juke operators. Any increase in record sales to the trade came mainly from the increasing use of high capacity boxes but also from operators who stuck to the industry guideline of spending 10 percent of their part of the gross receipts on new platters. The move to dime play, and an increasing number of first or front money contracts, tended to raise the gross receipts.[44]

Discussions on the importance of the juke trade to the record industry were more muted than in previous periods. There was much less talk of how jukeboxes "made" hits and artists. Still, the box industry tended to exaggerate its own importance. In a 1953 account an unnamed record company executive was quoted as saying that for a record to become a big smash "it's necessary to get on the boxes … to have a 1,000,000-seller, you have to figure on the disks being on 300,000 boxes." Operators were also said to be traditionally averse to putting a second version of a hit tune, or potential hit, on their boxes; they also tended to turn their backs on a potential hit version of a tune they already had adequately represented on the flip side of a disk already on their machines. For example, Eddie Fisher's "I'm Walking Behind You" was the favored version. Because of that interest lagged in Vic Damone's "April in Portugal" and Frank Sinatra's "Lean Baby" as both had "Walking" as their B-side. On the B-side of "Walking" was "Just Another Polka." Since "Walking" was heavily purchased, sales of Jo Stafford's and Richard Haynes's renditions of "Polka" lagged (although favored by juke customers) because the number was on the B-side of the Fisher disk.[45]

Another account that same year argued that record labels and artists knew that both the radio disk jockey and the juke operator were important in putting over a new disk: "Most will agree that the jock usually starts the disk on its way, but they have found out that it is the juke box that sustains the new disk and helps build it into the real hit category." In other words, the disk jockey and the operator complemented — and were necessary — to each other. While radio furnished the music to those at home or in a car, the box supplied the music in most other places. A disk jockey played a new record once, and if there was no reaction to it he laid it aside. However, to place a record in a music machine meant a cost to the operator, which was why operators were often late in picking up a disk. They waited to see if it looked to be a success. Operators only began to buy a new platter in quantity after disk jockeys started playing it and its public appeal had been established. However, it was argued that the record took off much sooner than it would have if its only exposure came from disk jockeys.[46]

Journalist Is Horowitz reported in the early 1950s that the juke industry purchased 60 million records annually, which was 15 percent of total label output and 30 percent of singles output (excluding albums and children's material). Collectively, operators added a valuable measure of stability to the manufacturing process since labels, from year to year, could estimate with reasonable accuracy how many disks would be absorbed by that market. On a technical level, operators acted as a constant check on acceptable levels of quality because if labels turned out records that wore out too quickly the operators would complain. Horowitz also observed there had been a strong pressure from music men over the years to reduce the playing time of records: "All other considerations being equal, the alert operator is almost certain to favor the shorter side when filling his record needs."[47]

During 1959 Senate committee hearings on another matter, juke industry insider Herm Schoenfeld testified that coin machines played only a minor role in the hit-making process. Once the ball was rolling on a specific number, the boxes could help keep it going, "but the boxes have never been able to launch a hit under their own steam. The disk companies, however, occasionally give away disks to the jukes in order to guarantee exposure on 'nervous' hits."[48]

Record sales, in millions of dollars, for the period were as follows: 1950, $184; 1951, $191; 1952, $202; 1953, $205; 1954, $195; 1955, $227; 1956, $331; 1957, $400; 1958, $438; 1959, $514; 1960, $521; and 1961, $587. Despite its statements, the juke industry became less and less important to the record industry as the 1950s progressed. From the beginning the sale of single disks was by far the dominant transaction for the labels. The sale of albums began to rapidly increase in the late 1950s. And jukeboxes did not buy albums. The sale of single records moved from 81.2 million to 92.1 million from 1960 to 1961 (a 13.4 percent increase), while for the same period the number of albums sold went from 51.8 million to 67.9 million (a 31.1 percent increase). Each album, of course, was much more expensive than a single disk.[49]

One bright spot for the industry was the growth in the export business. A main factor in the postwar redevelopment of exports was the surplus of used units in America in late 1946 and through 1947 and 1948. Since the foreign firms were anxious to get equipment to replace their worn-out machines operated since before 1939 and preferred used equipment because of lower prices, much of that equipment started to move into foreign markets. Tom McDonough declared that the value of the music machines in paving the way for other coin machines was inestimable. Typically, foreign distributors began by importing a few jukes. Later the sales to those same firms increased. Then many of them tried out either some games or vendors, or both. Vendors had appeal as a product dispenser in the foreign cities while the games were used to complement the diversion offered by the phonograph. Once vendors and games got a hold on the public in one city in a foreign land, they usually spread to other cities. "But in most instances it is the juke box which has opened the door for other coin equipment," concluded McDonough.[50]

A large increase in exports in 1951 probably reflected the return of Canada as a market, and the continued high imports of the "historical" markets of Central and South America, Venezuela, El Salvador, Colombia, and Cuba. In November 1947, the Canadian government, faced with an acute shortage of dollars, imposed an embargo on the importation of all luxury goods, including jukeboxes. Beginning in 1950 the Canadian government started relaxing controls, with all controls abolished in 1951. Those first two postwar years were good ones for exporters but soon other countries

A Wurlitzer 1500 unloaded from a jeep in 1953 in Honduras. It was destined for the mountain community of Lepaera.

besides Canada found themselves with acute dollar shortages and imposed embargoes on the importation of coin machines. Those sanctions accounted for much of the drop in exports for the years 1948 through 1950. Exports for the years 1946 to 1951 were, respectively: 6,170 units (with a value of $2,075,936); 12,379 ($3,967,859); 3,894 ($1,623,978); 2,954 ($1,260,659); 4,332 ($1,872,732); and 8,442 ($3,058,749). The average price paid for an exported box over the full period 1946 to 1951 was $362.16 per unit. That was well below what American operators paid for new equipment (roughly $800 to $1,000) and indicated that most of the exported equipment was used.[51]

A 1952 survey of juke manufacturers showed that all found the export market for phonographs a lucrative and important adjunct to their domestic business. One continuing problem was the suddenly imposed embargos in nations that found themselves with currency problems. Importing fully assembled jukes into Mexico was then prohibited. No cabinets were allowed to enter the country. It reflected Mexico's policy against allowing imports of materials representing work local labor and industry could supply. In this case the mechanical insides of the box could be imported into Mexico, but then local arrangements had to be made to build the housings in Mexico.[52]

Wurlitzer's distributor for Mexico was the company Casa Riojas, owned by Jose Riojas. Established in 1939, the firm had sold 6,000 to 7,000 machines up to 1951. Annual sales for 1951 were said to be about 1,200 units, of which 75 percent were new. Some 5,000 boxes were then estimated to be on location in Mexico City with 25 percent of them operator owned. The usual commission rate paid to locations was 20 percent of the gross. Boxes were generally sold with no down payment if the buyer had a good credit rating. Otherwise it was with a down payment of 25–35 percent with the balance due in 12 to 18 months. Jukes operated on a 20 centavo coin (2.33 cents). Operators paid 3½ to 4 pesos (41 to 46 cents) for a record from RCA Victor, Capitol, Columbia, and similar labels.[53]

With few exceptions, Canada and Central and South America accounted for a majority of the total box exports for every year from 1946 through the middle of 1952. Besides Canada, those major importing countries included Venezuela, Mexico, Colombia, Cuba, Guatemala, Panama, and El Salvador. The exceptions included Belgium, South Africa, and the Philippines, which had figured prominently as importers. Cuba was among the top five importers for every year from 1946. South Africa and the Philippines dropped from the export picture when both nations, facing a dollar shortage, placed embargoes on luxury items. Belgium had been a consistent importer of jukes when it became almost the sole free European market after the war.[54]

American-made jukes were reported to have scored a big hit with the Japanese public in 1952. The price to import a new 100-selection Seeburg machine into Japan was $2,300, tax paid, while a 12-record Music Mite cost around $680. Part of the high price was tax, which on coin machines was 83 percent of the invoice value. Unlike America, the jukebox was not placed in Japanese beer halls, drug stores, or confectionery parlors. All the boxes were placed in large department stores such as Takashina-ya and Matsuzaka-ya,

Two young boys flank a juke somewhere in Burma, 1956.

which were comparable to Macy's and Gimbels. Those department stores sited the units in their main entrances where they proved to be a public attraction. Prospects for expansion in Japan were limited by a lack of coins. There were then only two coins in circulation, a one-yen coin and a five-yen piece (0.25 cents and 1.5 cents).[55]

Rock-Ola executive vice president J. Raymond Bacon returned from a one-month vacation in Europe in 1952 with the opinion that the overseas market remained largely untapped by the juke trade. According to Bacon, the biggest obstacle was a lack of familiarity with the jukebox music idea. He felt sure that it would take a widespread promotional and educational campaign before boxes achieved broad appeal among Europeans.[56]

Juke exports in 1952 reached 10,901 units valued at $4,138,884. In all, a total of 69,036 games, venders, and jukes worth $7,621,879 were exported in 1952, setting both new unit and dollar volume record totals. The previous all-time high was recorded in 1951 when 29,764 coin machines valued at $5,121,806 were shipped abroad. One of the key factors in the increase of juke exports was the growth in the use of 45 rpm records. More compact and much lighter in weight, 45s had lowered the cost of shipping records over great distances. As well, there was relatively no breakage in shipping compared to 78 rpm disks. Also, several nations, particularly in South America, imposed tax on incoming shipments based on weight as well as on value. For 1951, 61 percent of coin-machine exports were music machines, games were 30 percent, and venders were 9 percent. Those figures in 1952 were, respectively, 53 percent, 33 percent, and 14 percent.[57]

Venezuela topped the list of juke importers in 1952, taking $1 million worth of boxes out of the $4.13 million in total shipped overseas. It marked the fourth straight year that Venezuela topped the list. Reporter Steve Schickel said there were many reasons for that situation, "but foremost of these is the fact that it [Venezuela] comes as close to the 'American way of life' as possible. The people are fun-loving as a rule and get a big kick out of juke boxes and amusement games."[58]

Such a large increase in coin-machine exports caused *Billboard* to analyze the reasons behind it in an editorial. First on the list were inventiveness and dependability. No other country had ever matched the United States in its "genius" for building coin machines that were both attractive and profitable. Next on the list was coin machines' "universal appeal." With a great deal of exaggeration, jukeboxes were said to be as popular in Tokyo and Johannesburg as they were in Jersey. Third factor was an honest, sustained sales effort. There was a time, admitted the editor, "when the foreign market was generally regarded as an excellent place to dump out-moded equipment. Games, vendors and phonographs, long past their earning and mechanical prime, were shipped to unsuspecting buyers in Europe and

South America." However, the editor reassured his readers that the day of thinking of the export market as a dumping ground for worn-out equipment "is long since passed," mainly because many foreign buyers limited their purchases to new machines, while those who bought used equipment were "choosy."[59]

Not every country welcomed American jukeboxes with open arms. One theme of a 1953 May Day parade by 10,000 workers in Juarez, Mexico, was to express displeasure at the situation. Typical of many signs carried by the marchers was one addressed to Governor Oscar Soto Maynes of Chihuahua: "Two thousand musicians support your administration. Keep juke boxes out of Mexico."[60]

Juke exports for 1953 were 14,089 units valued at $6,317,533, up 50 percent over 1952 and 100 percent over 1951. The average price of a box leaving America was $445 in 1953, up from $350 in 1951 and $300 in 1947. Just five nations imported $100,000 or more worth of jukes in 1952 whereas in 1953 the number reached 12 countries. The top five importing nations accounted for 70 percent of the overall total in 1952, down to 59 percent in 1953. Venezuela led the way for the fifth straight year, spending $1,263,096 that year, compared to $238,442 in 1947. That country's 1953 purchases set a new record. Canada held the previous record at $1,233,213 spent on importing music machines in 1947. West Germany spent $209,573 in 1953, up from a meager $1,210 in 1952. France imported $381,425 worth of boxes in 1953; $46,562 in 1952; and nothing at all in 1951. Embargos were falling everywhere. Such strong growth caused journalist Robert Dietmeier to enthuse that the best was yet to come.[61]

A group of unidentified men pose around a box in 1956 in Malaysia.

As of late 1954 it was estimated that West Germany had 3,000 boxes on location, most produced by America's big four makers. But the German juke industry, then less than a year old, accounted for about 10 percent of all units on location. German-made machines sold for about $1,000, considerably less than the price of American boxes after duties and shipping costs were added. Because of the high cost of music machines, commissions to locations were seldom paid, with the operator simply paying for the electricity. However, in some areas where competition for locations was becoming a factor, commissions of 10 percent of the gross were paid to locations. Three years earlier all Germany money was of the paper variety, making the running of boxes much more difficult. Cost of a play on a box in Germany was mostly five cents, though it was 2.5 cents in many locations.[62]

Six months later an account said the cost of an American-made box in Germany was about $1,500 (including a 22 percent import tax) for a new 50-record, 100-selection juke. A German-made box sold for about $800. While initially operators were reported to have been content to pay the extra because of the "superior quality" of the U.S. product, in recent times the improved quality of the German box made the local product more competitive. Most music machines in West Germany were sited in coffee houses or in low-priced taverns selling wine and beer (Gaststattes). Here it was reported that restaurant owners did not buy the machines outright but leased them for a 24-month period for about $2,000 to $2,500, including record changes and service. Since those eating places had no other form of entertainment, the installation of a phonograph was usually seen as a profit-making move because it increased the overall business. Records in the music machines were a 50/50 split between pop tunes sung by American artists and German light classics.[63]

As of early 1955, Paris reportedly had some 1,250 boxes on location with about 600 more in the rest of France. Most of those jukes were American-made and operated on a 20-franc coin, worth about six cents.[64]

In 1955 American jukeboxes were in at least 40 foreign nations. Reporter Ken Knauf observed that in many foreign lands the box was more than just an entertainment: "In these countries, it represents the American people and their way of life, and through the juke, these people are able to enjoy part of that way of life — the pleasures of recorded music." United States tourists and American Armed Forces personnel overseas had done much to "sell" the jukebox. Throughout South America electricity was rare outside major cities and music machines were usually sold together with small electric generators. About 20 percent of Mexico's phonographs were operated that way. While a big potential market existed in most South American countries, a problem was finding enough money to pay for the machines. Jukes in Argentina were limited in number because they could not be imported from the United States or Germany. With coffee prices then falling, Brazil and Colombia imported far fewer units. Outdoor dancing to box music was the rage in San Jose, Guatemala, where fiestas lasted from Friday through Sunday night. The "dancehall" consisted of a landscaped area fenced off by shrubbery, where about 50 couples could dance. The music machine was placed behind the shrubbery and hooked up to a generator. About six such fiestas took place in San Jose every year. Couples paid a dime a dance to collection men who operated the juke concession.[65]

Knauf went on to report that Denmark had joined Germany in having a local juke industry. Most of the machines exported then to Germany were shipped disassembled. Under a new trade agreement 80 percent of the phonographs had to be broken down in that way. Boxes were similarly shipped to Belgium where they were assembled, stocked, and sold to Germany, France, and other European countries as a Belgian product. Most Belgian locations owned their own machines; the jukes were not regarded primarily as revenue producers, but as business stimulants. In many clubs— the types that would have bands in the United States— dancing was to jukebox records. With freight and duties, the European operator paid a lot more for his equipment than did his American counterpart, yet the average price for a box play was only 2 to 2.5 cents. In the Far East the Philippines stood out as the best market. Complete phonographs were no longer exported there. Instead, the parts were shipped and assembled in that country and placed in a Philippines-made cabinet. Freight for one pound of 45 rpm disks (about 15) was $3. Prior to World War II there were only about 40 music machines throughout the Philippines— and those were all destroyed in the war. By the middle of 1954 some 500 units were on location in the nation.[66]

Dollar volume exports of jukes, games, and vendors were as follows: 1946, $2,655,078; 1947, $5,120,102; 1948, $2,309,589; 1949, $2,008,064; 1950, $3,076,546; 1951, $5,121,806; 1952, $7,621,879; 1953, $11,370,188; and 1954, $14,941,649. Jukebox exports in 1954 totaled 21,683 units worth $10,655,504, 71 percent of overall coin-machine exports. West Germany purchased 3,044 boxes in 1954 ($2,120,248), up from 348 units ($209,777) in 1953 and up from 20 machines ($1,210) in 1952.[67]

Statistics for the export of American-made amusement games only were: 1946, $459,935; 1947, $681,009; 1948, $353,544; 1949, $295,482; 1950, $701,971; 1951, $1,519,422; 1952, $2,613,007; 1953, $3,960,181; and 1954, $3,188,087. More than 40 countries imported U.S. games in 1954. Figures for the export of U.S.-made coin-operated vendors only were: 1948, $332,059; 1949, $451,923; 1950, $501,843; 1951, $543,635; 1952, 38,350 units ($1,073,708, average price of $28 per machine); 1953, 16,122 units ($1,093,474 —$68); and 1954, 20,014 machines ($1,098,058 —$47).[68]

In Lima, Peru, a local restriction prohibited the playing of jukes after

11 P.M., a situation that seriously affected business. Boxes in Peru operated on a 50-centavo piece (2.5 cents). Locally produced records sold for between 65 cents and $1; imported 45s sold at $1.25. A city ordinance in Bogota, Colombia, which became effective on May 1, 1956, banned the use of jukes in about 3,000 bars, cafés, and other public places between the hours of 6 P.M. and 6 A.M. daily.[69]

Back around 1950 the United States exported only about 950 boxes to Europe, both new and reconditioned. Just five years later 11,350 were shipped to Europe, retailing there at between $1,400 and $1,600 each, compared to $1,050 in the United States. The 1955 estimate was that Europe had around 50,000 boxes on location, little more than one-tenth of America's total. According to *Business Week* the big four makers saw the overseas market then as a "necessity for stabilizing domestic sales. It is important particularly as an outlet for used jukeboxes." Belgians imported about 15,000 boxes — most of them secondhand — between 1947 and 1952 and re-exported them to the European market. Britain cut imports of U.S. machines from 77 in 1951 to only three in 1955, so AMI set up a subsidiary there. Wurlitzer shipped parts to its West German distributor, Gustav Husemann, who assembled the final product using some German-made parts. There were then about 35 Western European producers in the field. Since 1953 around 43 jukebox models — both American and European — had been on the market. In 1953 Germany rescinded Adolph Hitler's 1934 decree forbidding the operation of coin machines. That gave operators the green light to dust off stored amusement machines and move into the juke business. One German importer estimated that new U.S. boxes accounted for only 35 percent of the total. On the other hand, American makers claimed they had 90 percent of the market. Jazz and American-made hit parade numbers were popular on European phonographs. In Hamburg, Germany's, harbor area, for example, music machines carried 60 percent American music and 40 percent German and other European numbers. But in quieter cafés much of the music was local. Of the 24,372 jukes exported in 1955, half went to Canada and Latin America.[70]

Austria had a reported 3,500 boxes on location at the start of 1957. A heavy import tax added $500 to the cost of a new machine. As well, a premium of the same amount had to be paid to obtain the necessary foreign currency. A national group equivalent to ASCAP, the Austrian Society of Authors & Publishers, benefitted from juke play, receiving a license fee of between $2 and $8 monthly per box depending on the classification of the location. In most European countries the local performing rights group did receive a license fee for making its catalog available to jukeboxes, unlike the situation in America.[71]

Paris was said to have 8,000 phonographs on location in the middle of 1957, which indicated they were an important part of the café scene. First introduced to Paris in 1947, the boxes played second fiddle to table soccer games for some time. Then came political attacks on the machines, and Coca-Cola, by the Communists, as a form of "American colonization" of France. "This silly premise was soon shown up, but it had held up imports and gave the French a chance to begin to make their own boxes, though most are still U.S. brands (Wurlitzer leading)."[72]

During 1956, 24,600 American-made phonographs (worth $13,940,453) were exported. Six German makers produced boxes for the home market and for export to Japan, Australia, and Venezuela. Germany was believed to have 12,000 jukes on location in mid-1957, up from 1,000 in 1953. A licensee in England and one in Denmark manufactured an American juke line for domestic and export sales. One maker was then in production in Mexico—the firm that had purchased the phonograph assets from the H. C. Evans concern. Minting of coins had opened up Japan as a market while the spread of electric power did the same in the Philippines. In Japan a 10-yen coin (2.8 cents) was minted in 1954. Soon thereafter a 50-yen piece (14 cents) was brought out. Before coins were in common use, machines had to be operated by tokens purchased from the cashiers, "and the Japanese people didn't develop the juke habit." In the Philippines the giant Ambuklao hydroelectric plant put into operation early in 1957 opened up outlying regions and even areas in parts of Manila. As one Manila distributor said, "The additional power coming from the Ambuklao plant has improved the sound of juke box music, before this, Frank Sinatra sounded like Doris Day." A machine that sold for $1,000 in America cost as much as $3,500 in the Philippines. Nations then with outright bans on the importation of complete U.S. boxes included South Africa, Colombia, and the United Kingdom. Countries with tight restrictions included Australia, France, and the Philippines. Belgium, Venezuela, West Germany, and Canada had consistently been major importers of American boxes since 1953. In 1956 those four took more than half of all exported phonographs.[73]

Hungary had just one jukebox in the country, as of July 1958. Owned by the Hungarian state, the American-made box was located in the Casino night club in Budapest. For a cost of one forint (four cents) a customer could take his choice of classical or pop tunes, often the previous year's rock and roll hits. The machine was operated by a woman guard who accepted the coins and selections of the teens who patronized the state-run club. There were so many requests on the nation's only music machine that it was booked hours ahead.[74]

Mexico had an estimated 50,000 boxes as of the summer of 1958. A music machine imported from America cost about twice what it did in the United States, while a Mexican-made unit (the 200-selection Wurlitzer made under license) ran around $1,600. Despite the high price, the cost of a juke play remained 20 centavos (1.6 cents). In a very few of the top cabarets the price was 50 centavos (four cents), but such locations were rare. Of the 5,000 machines in Mexico City, about 70 percent were location owned with 20 operators servicing the other 30 percent. Outside of Mexico City, location ownership was almost total. "While most people consider the juke a No. American phenomenon — and its influence as an indication that people are adopting the 'American way of life' — in Mexico it is nothing of the sort," wrote journalist Aaron Sternfield. Boxes were not found mainly in the plush hotels and restaurants built for American tourists but "in native cantinas, in roadside soft drink stands, in the public squares of remote mountain villages, in the places where the poor people eat, drink and shop." Wealthy Mexicans and U.S. tourists patronized spots where top quality live entertainment was featured. Said Sternfield: "For the owner of a café or restaurant catering to Mexicans of the working class, a juke box is a must. If he doesn't have a juke box, the people will take their trade to an establishment that does. It's as simple as that." In such places domestic beer cost eight cents while soft drinks (Coca-Cola and Pepsi-Cola) went for two cents.[75]

In 1959 the United Kingdom lifted the dollar import license restrictions on jukes. Some insiders were then talking about a boom in business, perhaps tripling the 15,000 machines then in the country. Germany had its best year as a music-machine exporter in 1958, selling 6,000 phonographs worth $3 million. Britain was Germany's second-best customer, just behind Switzerland. Lifting of the dollar currency import restrictions applied to jukes and vending machines — but not to coin-operated amusement games.[76]

During the summer of 1959, some Mexicans were still unhappy with the music machines. Members of the Mexican Musicians Union sent an official protest to the federal government in Mexico City asking for an "official regulation of jukeboxes." Their contention was that the boxes were displacing at least 50 percent of the musicians in cantinas, clubs, and so forth. Musicians wanted a federal law enacted that would permit jukes to function only until 10 P.M. in areas where the unemployment problem was acute — obliging owners of those places to use live music. If the government failed to act and regulate the boxes, said union press secretary Francisco Montes, other measures were being held in reserve to combat the inroads of the "mechanical musical monsters."[77]

Later that year the Mexican government did enact a law that jukeboxes were to be shut off at 10 P.M. — most clubs operated until 1 A.M. The musicians union was at least partly responsible for that measure. There was also a belief that phonographs tended to keep young people away from home too late at night.[78]

At the end of the 1950s, reporter Omer Anderson wrote about a juke "boom" sweeping Communist Europe, said to have started around the time Russian leader Nikita Khrushchev made a much publicized visit to an American exhibition in Moscow in the summer of 1958. East Germany was said to have imported 100 machines from a West German maker in a single shipment to go along with another 900 units they had obtained from other sources. East Germany's state trading trust set up a juke operating division that requisitioned locations wherever it pleased — the trust also operated all the stores, cafés, and so on. By the end of 1959, Hungary had upwards of 3,000 boxes, Poland about 500, and Czechoslovakia maybe 1,000. Albania had a total of three, two of them in the capital city of Tirana. An estimate for the Soviet Union put the number at around several thousand.[79]

Taxes and license fees imposed on jukes at the state and local levels of government became more pervasive. However, the industry raised less and less of a fuss as it apparently resigned itself to the inevitability of taxation. A 1956 survey of 47 states and 32 cities found that music operators in the 21 tax-paying states were paying an average of 38 percent more in taxes and licenses that year than paid by operators in the 15 tax paying states in 1946. The average annual per-machine license fee of those 15 states in 1946 was $8.30; in 1956 the average from the 21 states was $14. Just one state — South Carolina — had an annual per-machine tax greater than $10 in 1946 ($15); whereas in 1956, four states had taxes exceeding that. Average per-machine annual license fee among the 32 fee-imposing cities was $13.75. Examples included Wisconsin (no tax), Milwaukee ($100 annual operator license and a $5 annual machine tax); Illinois (none), Chicago $25; Georgia (none), Atlanta $30 license; Louisiana ($10 tax), New Orleans, operator fee of $10.25; Tennessee ($5 for nickel machine, $10 for dime play units); and Nashville, annual $5 license, county fee of $11.[80]

Two years later, in 1958, a much larger survey of 802 cities, towns, and villages was conducted. Cities surveyed ranged from the largest such as New York and Chicago, down to the smallest, such as Council Grove, Kansas (population 2,800) and Susquehanna, Pennsylvania (2,600). Of the 802 communities, 522 had jukebox license fees. States in which cities had the highest average per-machine taxes were New Jersey ($29), Nevada ($26.50), Georgia ($20) and Illinois ($18). The states with the lowest averages were North Carolina ($5.23), Indiana and Mississippi ($5), and Texas ($2.20). States in which communities polled had the lowest percentage of cities with box fees were Indiana (four of 30 cities polled), Iowa (two of 27), and New York State (10 of 43). Highest percentages were found in California (64 of 68), Florida (25 of 25), North Carolina (22 of 22). Twenty states then had jukebox taxes, averaging $15.[81]

Agitation to end the jukebox copyright exemption was stronger, more intense, and longer lasting than in any previous time period. Representative Hugh Scott Jr. (R) introduced a controversial bill in 1951 that would have had the effect of banning the playing of disks over music machines without payment of royalties to copyright owners. It was identical to Scott's previous measure that failed to get through Congress in 1947 but did draw time and emotion for months during the session, before the House Judiciary Committee. Among the major advocates of Scott's bill, in both 1951 and 1947, were ASCAP and BMI. At the 1947 hearing of the bill one of its most vigorous supporters was Fred Waring. It was reported that ASCAP stood to gain an estimated $9 million a year if the Scott bill passed.[82]

A few months later Senator Estes Kefauver introduced into Congress his own bill to end the box exemption. That bill was figured to be the strongest move in years to bring music machines under copyright provisions since the recent highly publicized Kefauver committee investigations uncovered evidence of criminal infiltration in jukebox firms. Kefauver's bill proposed to amend the Copyright Act by adding a subsection stipulating that "the public reproduction or rendition of a musical composition by or upon a coin-operated machine shall be deemed a public performance for profit by the owner or operator thereof whether or not a fee is charged for admission to the place where such reproduction or rendition occurs." Under the bill the royalty fee to be allowed to play music under copyright was set as follows: "1 cent per use of each copyrighted composition on a disk, per each four minutes or fraction thereof of playing time, per each week or fraction thereof that said disk shall remain in each such coin machine." The bill applied to persons or business entities who owned or operated two or more coin-operated machines. That is, anyone who owned just one box could continue to operate it with no royalty payment involved. Strongly endorsing the bill, ASCAP issued a lengthy statement declaring the juke industry was "the single exception" to the copyright law's requirement for all classes of commercial users to pay compensation to copyright owners for the right to perform their music. ASCAP estimated there were then 500,000 boxes in operation in America generating annual gross receipts in excess of $500 million and producing "tremendous annual profits."[83]

Strongly condemning the ASCAP endorsement, *Billboard* editorialized that it was a "sad and misguided strategy" on the part of the performing rights organization. Part of ASCAP's endorsement statement read: "Convincing evidence that many juke box operating companies have been infiltrated by criminals was uncovered by the Senate's Special Committee to investigate organized crime in interstate commerce, of which Senator Kefauver was chairman." Declaring "This sanctimonious verbiage is neither noble nor true," the editor suggested that ASCAP should stick to performing rights, keep its own house in order, and build good will among its customers, real and potential. It was "bad taste" for ASCAP to issue "questionable" statements.[84]

There were two main differences between the Scott and Kefauver bills. Scott's bill simply proposed to remove the exemption language from the Copyright Act. Under that bill the copyright owner could move against either the owner of the location, the owner of the box, or both. There was also no ceiling on the amount of copyright royalty that could be claimed. Kefauver's bill limited royalty payments to those who owned two or more machines. It also put a ceiling on the royalty amount and specified that amount at one cent per record side per week. Scott's bill quickly disappeared.[85]

Later in 1951 record label opposition to ending the box exemption was voiced by Kenneth Raine of Columbia Records at the House Judiciary Subcommittee's hearings on the Bryson bill. Chair of that subcommittee was Senator Joseph R. Bryson (who had introduced a bill of his own to end the exemption). Raine spoke for RCA Victor, Decca Records, MGM Records, Capitol, and Columbia. His testimony was a significant departure from four years earlier when the labels took a neutral position at congressional hearings on Scott's 1947 proposal. Those five major labels opposed the Bryson bill, said Raine, because 1) coin machines were important and substantial users of popular records, 2) recording artists and composers were paid on the basis of record sales, 3) labels and their employees would suffer directly from reduced sales to coin machines, and 4) the jukebox "is a real source of wholesome entertainment." He added that the popularity of music was attributable as much to use in music machines as by any other means and that the promotion of popular records would be sharply hurt by the impact of the bill. Raine said further: "Naturally we are concerned on our account over the reduction of a large market. A significant quantity of popular records is sold for use in these machines; and unless compelling reasons are advanced for a new burden on sales, we intend to oppose such a burden."[86]

Kefauver also testified at the hearings and argued that only jukes were exempt from carrying their royalty load. He pointed out that "radio, television, restaurants, dance halls, hotels and every public place of entertainment but one that plays music for profit" was obliged to pay the amount required by the Copyright Act. Drawing upon his experience on the Crime Investigating Committee, Kefauver charged that many large box operating firms were controlled by "some of the country's most vicious criminal elements" and that many examples of "strong arm" tactics were uncovered. Still, he emphasized the box industry was a legitimate one. Hammond Chaffetz, lawyer for four of the five box manufacturers, cited operators as buying 50 million records yearly, 15 percent of all disks pressed. He insisted composers were well paid and added that the popularization of tunes by way of jukes had been materially responsible for the robust sales of records. Noting that a one-cent-per-side royalty might seem small, Chaffetz argued the total was substantial and that an operator of 50 machines would be required to pay a minimum of $1,560 annually in royalties. A firm of accountants based in D.C. prepared statistics on jukebox incomes, compiled from 1,598 responses to an industry poll. Of $63 million collected by the 98,375 boxes represented in the study, the owner operator received $322 yearly per machine as his 50 percent cut of the gross receipts.[87]

In response to those numbers, ASCAP attorney Oscar Cox said the Price, Waterhouse & Company survey of juke operators' income could not be taken seriously because the firm had not examined income tax returns of the operators. Citing the Kefauver crime committee's report, which, said Cox, implied that gangsterism had infiltrated the juke industry, he added that "consequently we can't take their statements at face value."[88]

At the request of all the major disk labels, Mitch Miller, Columbia Records artists and repertory chief, submitted a written statement to the House Judiciary subcommittee opposing the proposed bill. He contended that only the labels and the coin machines were responsible for making the pop hits.[89]

David C. Rockola, president of Rock-Ola, told the subcommittee, "I think you will agree with me that he (John Q. Public) is not likely to look with any favor upon any law which will now tax his enjoyment of the 'poor man's opera.'" Hotels, taverns, and restaurants united through their various associations to oppose the Bryson bill. They asked the subcommittee to amend the bill to make it illegal for any juke operator to pass along any added royalty costs to proprietors. They worried, as the bill read, that hotel proprietors would be liable for royalties if they were not paid by the owner of the machine.[90]

Early in 1952 a parade of box operators and record distributors from all over America told the subcommittee the Bryson bill was unworkable, discriminated against small business, and would not only drive many operators out of business but also cut down profits of composers and publishers. Many operators predicted that the monthly royalty reports required under the bill would cost them as much to prepare as the cost of royalty payments themselves. One witness predicted the bill would leave him only 80 cents per man hour worked. H. K. Kyde, Sherman, Texas, box operator said, "We, the operators, feel that it is unconstitutional for [ASCAP] to ask our federal government to pass a law whereby we, as independent businessmen, will be made to open our records and cash registers to further their own welfare and prosperity." The Bryson bill was later shelved.[91]

About a year later the next assault began when Senator Pat McCarran (D., Nev.) introduced a bill to eliminate the exemption. Almost immediately

Teens gather around a juke in Vancouver, BC, circa 1958–1960. *Vancouver Public Library, photo #65189.*

the industry responded by establishing a fund to fight the proposal. With an assessment of 50 cents per box on every operator in the country, the industry hoped to raise $250,000 or more.[92]

Once again hearings were held before the Senate Judiciary Subcommittee, this time on the McCarran bill cosponsored by Senator Everett Dirksen (R., Ill.). A delegation of songwriters turned out to support the bill. One, Robert MacGinsey, said jukes were taking their tunes so fast the public was tired of them before they got around to buying the sheet music.[93]

Census Bureau statistics presented to the hearings showed the juke industry grossed between $250 million and $300 million annually, with an average take of about $650 yearly for each machine. The McCarran bill received widespread support from all segments of the music business such as ASCAP, BMI, the Songwriters Protective Association, and the Music Publishers Protective Association. Sole opposition to the bill came from the juke operators since the record labels, who supported the box industry at the hearings a year earlier, this time maintained a "hands off" attitude.[94]

John W. Griffin, executive secretary of the Recording Industry Association of America, made a statement at the hearings in support of the juke industry. However, he made his statement as an individual, not in his capacity as an RIAA executive. Griffin declared the record industry opposed the McCarran bill because it would have created an effect exactly opposite to the one its proponents intended. That is, if juke operators had to pay royalties, then total disk sales would drop and earnings of composers would be reduced rather than increased.[95]

Hammond Chaffetz testified again, as lawyer for the big four makers— Wurlitzer, Seeburg, AMI, and Rock-Ola. He described ASCAP as a "monster monopoly" that would "strangle" the small box operators, who would be "helpless" before it under the provisions of the bill. Chaffetz added that he was "thoroughly satisfied the operators would die like flies" if the bill became law. Arthur Fisher, the registrar of copyrights, declared he had made a long study of the problem and had conferred with bar associations and copyright associations. "They were in substantially unanimous agreement that the juke box exception is an anomaly and should be corrected. It is an anomaly to our law and the laws of the civilized world." The juke industry argued that 1) boxes paid their way with the two-cent royalty (this was folded into the price of a record and paid by everyone) and helped popularize songs, and thereby sold more records, 2) the McCarran proposal would subject operators and locations to "harassment" by ASCAP and other performing rights groups, 3) if there had to be an increase, then increase the statutory rate from two cents per side (set in the Copyright Act of 1909) to three or four cents, 4) composers were well enough paid, 5) box operators were small business people who averaged only a little over $3,000 a year each, 6) it was not true that there were no coin machines with volume horns, in 1909, as ASCAP contended, and 7) songwriters owed a debt of gratitude to boxes for bringing back the record business after radio nearly killed it off in the early 1930s. None of those arguments carried much weight.[96]

Variety editor Abel Green came out in favor of ending the juke exemption in an editorial. Calling the Copyright Act of 1909 "as obsolete as the tandem bike," he said: "The jukes should pay part of the freight. It's a reasonable request by the music men, and an ethical obligation on the part of the jukes." Green added that "A modest royalty to the music performing rights societies ... is an equitable demand." Like all preceding bills, the

McCarran proposal disappeared, leaving the industry unscathed once again.[97]

Reporter Ben Atlas reviewed the copyright situation and revealed that legislation to wipe out the exemption mandated by the Copyright Act of 1909 had been introduced in nearly every Congress since 1926. There were eight different hearings before congressional committees, most of them running to considerable length. Proposed legislation reached the floor twice; it was debated on the House floor in 1930 and on the Senate floor in 1935. Since 1936, legislation on the subject failed to emerge from committee. Hearings were held during the 69th Congress, 2nd Session (1926–1927), but the bills died. In the 70th Congress (1927–1929), legislation was introduced but died. During the 71st Congress (1929–1931), legislation was introduced and hearings were held by the House Rules Committee. A House floor debate took place in 1930, but the House defeated an amendment to a bill that would have removed the exemption. Hearings were held by the House Subcommittee on Copyrights, Patents and Trademarks in 1932, during the 72nd Congress (1931–1933). During the 74th Congress (1935–1936), two bills were introduced in the Senate and two in the House. Hearings were held before the Senate Subcommittee on Copyrights, Patents and Trademarks in 1935 and before the House Subcommittee on Copyrights, Patents and Trademarks in 1936. From the 75th Congress through the 78th Congress (1937–1944), bills were introduced almost every year but no hearings were held.[98]

Two bills were introduced during the 79th Congress with lengthy hearings staged by the House Subcommittee on Copyrights, Patents and Trademarks. The battle centered on two bills in the 80th Congress (1947–1948), one sponsored by Hugh Scott. In the 82nd Congress (1951–1952), Scott introduced his bill again. Soon thereafter, Kefauver followed with his bill. Four months later a modified version of Kefauver's bill was introduced by Bryson. During the 83rd Congress (1953–1954), McCarran's bill was introduced. Then Everett Dirksen sponsored an identical bill to the old Scott proposal, but Dirksen made it known that he did not want to press his bill. Both proposals faded away. Meanwhile, efforts to get a jukebox royalty exemption clause in the model global copyright treaty failed at Geneva. However, its proponents managed to insert a clause authorizing the creation of an international commission to study the question at any time.[99]

In March 1955, Representative J. Philbin (D., Mass.) rose in Congress to demand justice for America's songwriters from exploitation by juke operators and those who controlled the music business. Unless the operators were willing to negotiate payment to composers for the use of records, he argued, it was the duty of Congress to pass a law putting the jukes under the copyright statute. "If a public restaurant, ice cream parlor, or tavern uses an ordinary phonograph played without inserting a coin, this is considered a public performance for profit. The composers may share in it," he explained. "But if anyone in the same establishment puts a coin in a jukebox, this is not considered a public performance for profit and the composers are excluded from sharing in such receipts." Such conditions, Philbin continued, constituted "gross discrimination against composers, authors and publishers."[100]

Later that year two bills to place boxes under the Copyright Act were introduced in the House. The one sponsored by Philbin would simply have removed the exemption from the act while the one introduced by James C. Murray (D., Ill.) would have required a flat sum, per machine, to be paid as a royalty. Nothing came of either proposal.[101]

The juke industry stood firm throughout all these battles. The 6th annual convention of the Music Operators of America (MOA) opened in Chicago in 1956 to a battle cry of "beat ASCAP." MOA's determination to oppose, without compromise, any attempt to change existing copyright laws was constantly reiterated by group president George A. Miller and MOA general counsel Sidney H. Levine in their reports to the delegates.[102]

And still, the assaults continued. Senator Joseph O'Mahoney, chairman of the Senate Subcommittee on Copyrights, Patents and Trademarks, sponsored a bill to end the exemption. First though, he suggested to both ASCAP and the juke industry that they compromise their differences. To that end, ASCAP invited MOA leaders to a discussion conference. However, that move by ASCAP ran into a stone wall, with MOA flatly turning down the proposal to hold any bargaining talks. MOA president George A. Miller notified O'Mahoney that he did not "contemplate industry suicide" by agreeing in any way to the payment of licensing fees to ASCAP or other performing rights societies. Miller added that efforts to amend the Copyright Act to the coin-machine industry's detriment had been going on for the past 30 years, but Congress "time after time refused to do so much as change a word in this portion of the statute after numerous hearings."[103]

International music groups joined with American organizations in supporting the O'Mahoney proposal. The French performing rights society, the Societe des Auteurs, Compositeurs et editeurs de musique (SACEM), made representations before the U.S. State Department on behalf of the bill on the ground of international reciprocity. It was an argument seconded by virtually every other performing rights society in the world. Those foreign licensing groups pointed out that while American songwriters and publishers collected from performances in overseas boxes, there were no reciprocal collections made from the same source in America. Opposing the bill was MOA and the disk industry through the RIAA. O'Mahoney's proposal soon joined its predecessors in limbo.[104]

Next to introduce a bill was Representative Emanuel Cellar (D., New York), in 1959. In testimony before the House Copyright Subcommittee, Cellar said he was opposed to any general rise in mechanical royalty rates since everybody, including the general public, would pay any such increase. He wanted the box industry stripped of its exemption and for it to pay performing rights societies. Reportedly, ASCAP was then leaning toward having an annual fee in the range of $15 to $25 assessed as a box fee. Cellar accused the juke industry of raising "false and extraneous" issues. Among tactics employed by the industry, he explained, was to label his proposal the "ASCAP bill" and to "do its best to blacken the reputation of ASCAP." He added, "Such partisan attacks on the performing rights societies ... shed no light on the problem and only reveal the dog-in-the-manger attitude of the jukebox industry." Cellar's proposal also faded away.[105]

While the industry once again escaped untouched from the copyright battles, other problems arrived on the scene. The jukes were not always so lucky as to escape cleanly. In March 1956, a federal grand jury in Chicago returned an antitrust indictment against the J. P. Seeburg Corporation of Chicago. At the same time, the U.S. Department of Justice filed a civil antitrust suit against the firm and 31 distributors throughout the country. Contended in the suit was that the company's agreements with the distributors were in restraint of trade and asked for relief in the form of an injunction that would require the company and the distributors to sell machines to anyone. The indictment voted by the grand jury alleged the Seeburg agreements with its distributors bound the latter not to compete with each other and that the distributors, in fact, had refused to sell Seeburg products outside their assigned territories. Also contended was that the distributors refused to sell, or permit the resale of, Seeburg machines to restaurant and tavern owners, thereby compelling the proprietors to lease or rent the machines from operators. Sales practices of the company from 1946 onward were covered in the indictment. Seeburg denied any wrongdoing. Nevertheless, Seeburg took the challenged provisions out of its distributors' contracts a year earlier, when it learned of the Justice Department's attitude toward such provisions in the auto and radio/television industries.[106]

In an editorial response, *Billboard* declared the charges hit at exclusivity and direct location sales. Since Seeburg had already taken out the challenged portions of distributors' contracts, the editor thought the case boiled down to direct location sales. Admitting it was obvious that a location owner or anyone else should have a right to own and operate a juke, he asserted, "it is essential to point out to such people that the whole structure of three established industries—juke boxes, vending machines and amusement games—rests squarely on the economic necessity of the operator." Denying a sale to somebody with ready cash was "therefore to the credit of the distributor, that as an honest businessman not interested in the fast buck of the unscrupulous promoter, but rather in the sound, stable condition of an industry, he points out to such persons the many pitfalls of location ownership and the economic hazards of such buying."[107]

In January 1957, Seeburg was fined $2,000 on the criminal charge of an antitrust violation after the firm changed its original plea of not guilty to one of no contest.[108]

One month later the civil action was settled by the issuance of a consent decree. It prohibited Seeburg and its 31 distributor codefendants from entering into any agreements that would restrain trade in the juke industry. Specifically Seeburg was prohibited from entering into any contracts with its distributors that limited or restricted the territory in which each distributor could sell boxes. The judgement also restrained the defendants individually from any of several practices that could perpetuate the effects of the conspiracy, such as refusing to sell to a person because he resold to someone outside a particular territory or to a location owner. The charges revealed that in 1955 Seeburg produced 40 percent of the boxes manufactured in America that year with a retail value of $2 million.[109]

In April 1958, the Department of Justice announced the issuance of a consent decree prohibiting Wurlitzer from putting restraints on the distribution of its boxes. That judgment ended a civil antitrust proceeding started early in 1957 when the federal government had alleged that Wurlitzer had illegally allocated territories and customers for its music machines.[110]

Articles linking the industry with organized crime had appeared off and on over the decades. Usually, though, attention was brief and limited in area. However, in the 1950s, that area trickle turned into a national flood as the industry came under protracted and national media scrutiny. A confidential report that was the result of a 10-year study by Virgil W. Peterson, operating director of the Chicago Crime Commission, used by the U.S. Department of Justice in 1955 in its probe of a suspected juke monopoly, detailed mobster control of "almost every level of the jukebox industry." The report also stated that virtually every phase of the juke industry was "permeated with hoodlums and the gangster element" and had become a huge racket. In Chicago, according to the study, elements of the Al Capone gang had been in "the driver's seat since 1938" among operators. The conclusion was "inescapable," declared Peterson, "that many principal jukebox manufacturing companies and their officers are very closely connected with various phases of the gambling business and with the slot machine racket in particular. The relationship of the gambling racket and the jukebox business is much closer at the distributing and operating levels of the jukebox industry."[111]

One of the most widely read, and commented upon, articles was the damning account written by Lester Velie that appeared as "Racket in the Juke Box" in the November 1955 issue of *Reader's Digest*. He declared that in many cities boxes were largely the preserve of the underworld, with mobsters dictating who got one, how the take was split and, often, which artists' works appeared on the boxes. After giving a brief outline of how the industry was structured — with phonographs installed on a commission basis and service provided by a union mechanic or electrician — Velie went on to describe how the racket worked. Operators formed a trade association, which was actually a monopoly that apportioned the juke routes among the insiders. Distributors helped the racket along by selling only to association operators. To maintain their monopoly the racketeers used labor unions, usually locals of one of the biggest, the International Brotherhood of Teamsters (AFL). Enforcement was simple. Unless you had the insider's okay to operate a coin phonograph, it would not get a union label. That meant union men — mechanics who belonged to the box local — would not service the machine. Cleveland tavern keeper George Loving told a congressional committee that he tried to buy a juke of his own because he was dissatisfied with the one installed by an operator. He tried five distributors but none would sell to him. One independent operator, barred from the local box association, tried to compete on his own. His customers' windows were smashed. Another Cleveland tavern proprietor testified he managed to buy a machine from a distributor by pretending he was an out-of-town buyer. Soon after, the distributor who sold that unit had his premises bombed.[112]

According to Velie, tavern keepers were so terrorized when they tried to change their jukeboxes that they told investigators they would rather go to jail than testify in open hearings. A year earlier at Cleveland, a congressional committee determined that the "czar" of jukes was William Presser, head of all the Teamsters in Ohio. Only 25 percent of union members in the juke local were mechanics, the rest were operators. You couldn't tell where the union began or where the local association ended. When two reporters with the Cleveland *News* tried to buy a phonograph, they were refused and told, "Get a letter of clearance from Bill Presser." Tavern owners who wanted a juke had to take the split of the receipts dictated by the union/association. The first $20 went to the operator with the remainder divided 60/40 in his favor. It meant that on a week's receipts of $50, only $12 went to the location owner.[113]

Both *Variety* and *Billboard* commented on the Velie piece. *Variety* adopted an almost neutral stance, summarizing some of the negative points. It offered no justification nor any defense of the box industry.[114]

On the other hand, *Billboard*'s response went over and above that of an editorial. It took the form of a page one open letter from *Billboard* publisher W. D. Littleford to *Reader's Digest* editor DeWitt Wallace, in which the Velie article was condemned as a "grave injustice" to the industry. Littleford argued that the article misled readers on two counts. One was that it took a "handful" of facts from three Midwestern cities and concluded that those facts were typical of the industry. Second, the article proceeded to group coin-operated vendors with music machines, and, by innuendo, implied the hoodlums were "fencing off" the sale through vendors of items such as cigarettes, coffee, and cold drinks. What upset Littleford was his perception that Velie moved effortlessly back and forth between jukes and vendors, grouping all types of equipment into what the article called the "coin-vending business." Admitting the juke industry was extremely vulnerable to public attack, Littleford harked back to the late 1920s and early 1930s "when music machines were installed by slot machine operators in the same locations where their gambling equipment was situated. The fact that the juke box was once used as a front — however innocent the juke was and is — established an atmosphere in which all sorts of allegations became credible." *Billboard* had long noted the tie-in between juke operation and the running of other equipment. That is, operators of jukes regularly had both amusement games and vendors on their routes.[115]

In sworn testimony before a Senate committee investigating labor/management rackets in 1957, Sam Getlan, a self-styled former henchman of mob boss Frank Costello, told the senators how he entered into the union business for himself in 1950 and moved the union into a business that then paid him $30,000 a year. The money came from coin-machine operators — of jukes, amusement games, and cigarette machines — mostly for protection. Getlan was secretary/treasurer of Local 26 of the International Jewelry Workers Union, Mount Vernon, New York. In fact, the union had nothing to do with jewelry workers. Members of the union were coin-machine operators who ran 4,000 machines in Westchester, Orange, and Sullivan Counties north of New York City. Each of the 100 union members paid monthly dues of $5, plus 50 cents per month for each machine on location. In return, Getlan promised them one thing — to leave them alone. According to Getlan, he went to work for Costello in 1928–1929, and in the 1930s he was making $7,000 a week running slot machines in Miami.[116]

Billboard's editor decried the influence of such phony unions and their having chosen the coin-machine industry as one of their prime targets. Before any operator signed with any union, advised the editor, he should determine whether he is dealing with an "extortionist or a legitimate segment of the labor movement." Operators were urged to fight any approaches by phony unionists or racketeers.[117]

That committee, the Senate Select Committee on Improper Activities in the Labor Management Field, turned its attention to the juke and vending machine business in the spring of 1959. It was then that the industry picked up the greatest amount of negative publicity with the testimony covered by all the major media. The owner of a small confectionary shop told of a man entering the outlet and telling the owner he was going to install a music machine. "How much do I get?" asked the owner. "If you're lucky, you'll keep your health," was the reply. A man told the manager of a small café in Los Angeles that it was time to throw out her old box and install one of his— the "service charge" on the new one was $18 a week. She protested and went to the police. Soon thereafter, truckers stopped delivering her supplies. Her café went out of business. *Newsweek* estimated there were 550,000 phonographs on location with an annual take of $1 billion. Racketeers were said to be entering every branch of the $2 billion-a-year vending machine business, susceptible because it was a cash business with little in the way of record keeping, making it ideal for money laundering and any coin machine was easy to damage, so the people who had them needed protection. A man bought a tavern in the Midwest, with fixtures and a juke. Even before he reopened, a man told the new owner he couldn't have the old box. The owner ordered the man out. But a few days later a couple of pickets appeared on the sidewalk outside. That "picket line" stopped the Teamsters who delivered ice, beer, whiskey, and food, and who took away the garbage. As his supplies ran out the owner gave in. A new box bearing the sticker "union label" was delivered by the stranger and the owner had no more trouble. Increasingly, the Senate rackets committee found those local unions were becoming affiliated with the Teamsters, who wielded great power over any establishment that had to rely on trucks for supplies.[118]

One who testified was Milton Hammergren. He was retired when he gave his declaration but had been a Wurlitzer vice president. Hammergren stated he sold 550 boxes to Chicago gangsters, an initial order that grew later to 2,700 machines. "We didn't like it, but we had to sell juke boxes," he explained.[119]

Also revealed at the hearings was that Chicago's juke operators paid three organizations around $100,000 annually "for peace." About $74,000 of that went to a firm called the Commercial Phonograph Survey & Service Company owned by Michael Dale of Chicago. It was said to be an organization heavily staffed with former convicts that performed no visible service. Commercial Phonograph collected 90 cents a month from each box in Chicago. In return, it had one retired police sergeant whose duty it was to check the music machines periodically to insure that their licenses were up to date. Three other employees had criminal records but appeared to do no work for the firm.[120]

Albert Denver, president of the Music Operators of New York, testified that his association of 160 juke operators was gradually being driven out of business. In the prior two years his organization had lost 1,631 "cream" locations to the rival Associated Amusement Machine Operators of New York, whose Teamster bosses, declared Senate committee counsel Robert F. Kennedy, were "successors to Murder Inc."[121]

Lorimar Distributing Company of Chicago testified that it forced operators to buy their records from itself. Additionally, operators were forced to pay the firm $3.60 per box per year in protection money. It was estimated the total shakedown cost to Chicago's operators was about $100,000 annually.[122]

As usual, the industry was highly protective of box statistics. However, some material did find its way into the public domain. At the MOA 1951 convention, organization head George Miller said that some 4,000 operating firms in America ran 300,000 to 400,000 machines and that the national average of gross receipts from phonographs was $6.36 a week. When that was split 50/50 with the location, the operator was left with barely enough money to cover expenses, complained Miller. Operators were then paying 59 cents per record.[123]

A decline in the phonograph business could already be seen in the declining number of operators who handled nothing but music machines. That was a common situation in the 1930s and 1940s, but becoming rarer as time passed. In 1953, 84.5 percent of juke operators also ran other equipment; 87.6 percent ran other equipment in 1954. The percentage of box operators who handled amusement games in those two years were, respectively, 80 percent and 83.5 percent; who ran cigarette vendors, 25.6 percent and 26 percent; who operated vendors other than cigarettes, 9.1 percent and 15 percent; who operated kiddie rides, 7.3 percent and 13 percent.[124]

When Theodore Herz, of the firm Price, Waterhouse & Company, presented his firm's juke income survey to the House hearings on the Bryson bill, he characterized the industry as mostly "small business" with relatively small profits and heavy operating costs. His firm tabulated 1,598 replies from operators, of whom 1,024 (64 percent) ran 50 boxes or less. Under 2 percent owned over 300 units each; 2.5 percent owned 200 to 300 machines; 8.4 percent owned 100 to 200, 8.9 percent owned 75 to 100; and 14.8 percent owned 50 to 75 units,. Those 1,598 survey responses represented a total of 98,375 phonographs that produced a total 1950 revenue of $31,639,742 for the operators. With revenue to locations understood to be equal, it meant that the total deposited in those music machines was a little over $63 million, about $644 for each machine and $322 to the operator. Total expenses reported by those operators in 1950 were $23,914,315 — all chargeable to the operators, none to the locations. Specified by the questionnaire was that salary and income taxes of the owner/operator be excluded from the amount of expenses reported. Revenue left after deducting expenses came to $7,725,427 in the aggregate. That was an average margin of $4,835 for each of the 1,598 operators, an average of $402.92 per month (more for large operators, less for smaller ones). That profit margin worked out to 24.4 percent of the operators' revenue, or 12.2 percent of the amount deposited by customers. With those 1,598 operators reporting an aggregate investment of $54,661,560 — $34,206 each on average — the return on investment was 14.2 percent. About 122 records per machine were purchased in 1950 at a cost of $6,021,575 (at 50 cents per disk) for 12,043,151 records. With regard to the Bryson bill it was argued that each machine held 30 disks on average, and at two cents per record per week for copyright an operator of 50 machines would be liable for an annual payment of $1,560. Since the average operator bought 10 new records a month per machine, a 50-unit operator would buy 6,000 a year, at a cost of $3,000. Thus, the proposed copyright payment of $1,560 would mean an increase of more than 50 percent in the cost of his records. One of the weaknesses in such surveys was that they neglected the firm's other business aspects. Characterizing the juke industry as small business ignored the fact that something over 85 percent of box operators ran other equipment. It also made it easier for expenses to become confused and to assign a greater portion of them to music machines than was warranted.[125]

When *Billboard* conducted its sixth annual box operator poll in 1953, it found that when operators installed brand-new machines, 49.1 percent did so on a flat percentage basis, 20 percent on a guarantee (front money) plus percentage, and 21.8 percent on a first money plus percentage basis. Over the previous 12 months, operator share of the gross receipts per machine had been $10.43 a week in 1952 ($9.78 in 1951). Some 52.6 percent of all jukes represented by the survey were located in taverns, as compared to a reported 70 to 75 percent found in taverns at the close of World War II. Taverns were also the most profitable locations. The average operator ran 77.1 boxes in his route. Survey results were projected to estimate the juke industry purchased 64 million records per year.[126]

Another operator poll by *Billboard* showed that 61.4 percent of all phonograph operators ran fewer than 50 machines and that 88.3 percent (in 1956) of the operators also handled other types of coin machines. The average number of boxes per operator was 53.4 in 1956 and 47.8 in 1955. Operators' share of the average weekly gross per box was $13.77 in 1956, $12.38 in 1955, and $9.89 in 1954. Although 45.3 percent of phonographs were located in taverns, they accounted for 43.4 percent of gross receipts; 32.4 percent were in restaurants, accounting for 36.4 percent of collections; 10.2 percent in drugstores, accounting for 9.7 percent of collections and 12.1 percent of boxes were in other locations, yielding 10.5 percent of receipts.[127]

In an effort to determine if there was room in America for more jukeboxes, *Billboard* did one of the more intriguing pieces of data collection. Starting with a pilot study of 49 cities, later expanded to include hundreds, the publication found a correlation between the number of music machines per 1,000 people and the number of eating and drinking places (restaurants and taverns) per 1,000 people. Results revealed the ratio of eating and drinking places per 1,000 people was 2.25, but the box ratio was just 1.93. That led to the conclusion there appeared to be a great deal of room for growth in cities where the juke ratio was less than the other yardstick.[128]

According to figures released by the U.S. Department of Commerce Census Bureau in 1954, the nation's coin-machine operators had average receipts of $629 per phonograph and $722 per amusement game. Issued as part of the department's 1954 census of business, the report was based on a survey of 6,045 operating firms "primarily engaged" in the coin-machine business. Total receipts for the amusement game and box operating industry totaled $212 million. Approximately 88 percent of that figure was accounted for by 3,301 establishments, all of which had some payroll during the year. Coin-machine businesses without payroll—mainly one-person operations—numbered 2,744, with receipts totaling $26 million. Of establishments with payroll, 89 percent listed receipts showing 45.8 percent of income from jukes, 48.6 percent from amusement machines, and 5.6 percent from miscellaneous. Those same establishments reported operation of 136,792 boxes and 123,802 other amusement machines as of December 31, 1954. Music machines located in Nevada and D.C. had the highest receipts per machine, $1,361 and $1,096, respectively. Amusement machines in Washington and Maryland had the highest receipts per machine at $1,304 and $1,245, respectively.[129]

Another *Billboard* operator survey found the operators' share of receipts to be $11.99 per machine per week in 1957 ($13.77 in 1956, $12.38 in 1955, $9.89 in 1954). The average weekly share from the best locations was $32.40; average weekly share per box from the poorest locations was $4.58. Taverns contained 48.8 percent of the phonographs in 1957 (49.3 percent of receipts); restaurants 40.2 percent (41.4 percent); drugstores 4.9 percent (4.8 percent); other 6.1 percent (4.8 percent). Some 56 percent of all units were placed on a flat percentage basis. Total record purchases by the industry in 1957 were reported to be 47.34 million disks.[130]

Journalist Bob Dietmeier drew a picture of the average operator, declaring he was in the $10,000-a-year income bracket, owned his own home, was in his early 40s, was a high school graduate, had two children, and had operated in the same area for 12 years. That average operator made $10,653 (personal income) in 1956 and $9,570 in 1957. Half of the operators made $7,500 a year or less from operating; one in four less than $5,000; and two of three made $10,000 or less. The average was pulled up by a small group of operators who made more than $15,000 a year from operating, 13 percent of the operators in 1957.[131]

In 1959 *Billboard* estimated there were 450,000 boxes operating in America. It was a figure the publication acknowledged it had been using for years, but it still considered the number to be the best estimate. Wavering somewhat, it declared, "In short, study figures support the 450,000 figure in general, but are not sufficiently reliable from a statistical point of view to strongly support that figure." In its expanded look at juke ratios in cities, the publication found the average city had 2.67 eating and drinking places per 1,000 people and 2.4 jukes (based on licenses) per 1,000 people. Great variation was found. For example, in California, Burbank had 0.54 jukes per thousand people while Santa Barbara had 8.8 machines.[132]

Price Waterhouse provided another juke operator income profile at the hearings on the proposed Cellar copyright bill in 1959. This survey was based on 1,285 usable responses from operators and showed that 62 percent of them ran 50 machines or less. Those operators represented 75,756 boxes, which produced total revenue of $33,404,202 in 1958 as the operators' share. Assuming a 50/50 split with locations, it meant $67 million was deposited in those jukes. Individual receipts were $440 a year per box to the operator (out of $880). Total expenses of those surveyed was $25,859,525, leaving revenue after expenses of $7,544,677, or an average margin of $5,871 for each operator ($489 per month). For smaller operators (the 62 percent) the margin averaged $3,596 yearly ($300 per month). That average margin worked out to be about 22.6 percent of the operator's revenue (11.3 percent on the amount deposited). With an average investment of $43,652, the return on investment was 13.45 percent. The average cost of a record to the industry was then estimated at 64 cents. An average of 114 records were bought each year per machine. Price Waterhouse computed the increase in cost to operators of a $25 annual performance royalty per machine at $1,477 per year (based on 59.1 machines per operator). That fee would mean a reduction of 25 percent on the average margin — lowering it from $5,871 to $4,394. For small operators handling 50 machine or less (26 units on average), the impact would reduce the margin 18 percent, or $650, from $3,596 to $2,946.[133]

It was a decade of apparent promise for jukeboxes. The downturn of 1948–1949 had been stemmed, raising hopes. But they never materialized. Largely it was a stagnant decade, although slippage could be seen, as in a decreasing number of records bought by the industry. The move to 45 rpm disks and to dime play later in the decade helped the industry. But those items could not halt a slow erosion due to television and changing living patterns, changes that started to a small extent in the 1940s. No longer did one come across articles about the great future of the industry. Throughout the 1950s the industry wavered, down from its glory years (lasting from around 1934 to 1948), but showed no strong indication of going one way or another.

7

Slow Fade to Obscurity,
1960–2000

"If we must have jukeboxes why can't they be supplied with good Communist music?" Bulgarian Ministry of Culture & Education, 1961.

"Jukebox operators are the only users of music for profit who are not obliged to pay royalties, and there is no special reason for their exemption." Stanley Green, Atlantic Monthly, 1962.

"Overall in the last five years the marketplace [for jukes] has actually declined because of the fast food chains." Wayne Hesch, Chicago operator, 1980.

"[The juke business] is slowly but inexorably dying." Ken Terry, Variety, 1981.

At the start of this period, journalist Aaron Sternfield commented on box programming by noting that juke patrons bought the familiar. While a Bing Crosby, Elvis Presley, or Connie Francis on the title strip was not necessarily a guarantee of success, a familiar name reduced the odds of failure considerably. The same was true for the song itself. Most phonographs were in taverns, and most box patrons were adults. And when those adults were relaxing in their favorite bars, they wanted to hear an old friend sing a familiar song. Thus, reasoned Sternfield, the practice of lifting singles from motion picture soundtracks or from Broadway shows would probably continue. Box operators usually pointed out that their biggest earners were generally established songs with name artists. The motion picture and the Broadway show cloaked the song with enough familiarity so that the juke patron gave it a play "without too much thought." Chances were that the original artist was an established jukebox name. "If he isn't, the record company will get an established jukebox performer and come up with its own version." While Sternfield's analysis may have been right, it indirectly highlighted a problem. The record industry had changed dramatically in the previous half a dozen or so years. Rock and roll dominated. Labels produced a lesser and lesser percentage of numbers that would appeal to Sternfield's idea of patron preferences. Many of the biggest fans of rock, and biggest buyers of disks, were too young to go into those taverns, which did indeed contain about half of all the music machines. Also not helping box business was the spread in the late 1950s, and onward, of the transistor radio, a portable, mobile hit with young people in particular.[1]

Noise from boxes still presented an occasional problem. Music machines in Italy were criticized as a noise-making nuisance in some spots as well as being condemned for importing the stridency and pressure of American life. In response an organization of Italian operators initiated a 1960 "keep it soft" campaign of moderating juke volume. That campaign was conducted primarily by means of large wall posters, placed near the boxes, urging location proprietors to keep the volume of the phonograph turned down.[2]

Even the issue of smut records returned briefly to the spotlight, in 1967. *Billboard* argued that for the previous 30 years there had been three points of view with regard to off-color disks: 1) Keep off-color records off the boxes as we have enough public relations problems already, 2) We should not act as censors so give the public what they want, and 3) I don't like racy records but if my competitor programs them, I have to also. "There is evidence to indicate that the expedient third view has often prevailed in business practice." Problem disks of that time included "Sock It to Me — Baby" by Mitch Ryder and the Detroit Wheels and "Let's Spend the Night Together" by the Rolling Stones. Al Denver, president of the Music Operators of New York, declared, "The association will not tolerate the use of offensive records in New York and will make every effort to ensure that no record is played in a coin-operated phonograph that could not properly be played at home."[3]

A survey taken of the Southern California market at the same time indicated that the use of smut records was "at an all-time low." Cliff Jones, owner of Jones Music in Long Beach, stated: "There is absolutely no call for dirty music. A few years ago several artists made use of double-meaning lyrics to increase record sales. But today dirty music is out." David Solish, an executive with Los Angeles-based operating firm Coin-A-Tune, declared: "Operators are keeping an arm's length away from 'dirty' music. We're legitimate businessmen and programming offensive music only can tarnish the operator and the industry. Purple programming, even for the quick buck, is not worth risking your reputation."[4]

After a long battle over moving to dime play, further increases in the cost of a juke play almost passed unnoticed. In 1966 AMI became the first of the makers to equip its boxes with a dollar-bill acceptor. Two for a quarter play was growing on a regional basis in 1968. With its dollar-accepting unit AMI hoped to help promote that trend. It expected the new pricing to spread to all areas of the country. Rowe Manufacturing was organized in 1926 in Los Angeles. Rowe and AMI merged in 1958. All jukes produced by the company were labeled Rowe AMI, while Rowe's vending products continued to be identified by the Rowe name. By the end of the 1970s juke pricing was moving rapidly to a standard of 25 cents for a single play.[5]

Reflecting the state of the juke industry were the fortunes of MOA (Music Operators of America), the main trade organization. No national juke operator organization existed until MOA formed in 1948. Although vending-machine operators were successful in establishing their own group in 1934, music operators did not achieve unity until 68 officers of various state groups met in 1948. The catalyst that brought MOA into existence was the threat of music copyright legislation aimed at ending the juke exemption, especially worrisome at that time. As MOA fought successfully to help defeat copyright bills its function as a national organization took on more importance.[6]

MOA held its 1961 convention in Miami Beach, Florida. It was the first time in its history that the convention was held outside of Chicago, where most of the coin-machine industry firms were based. Total attendance was about 1,600, down some 50 percent from 1960, and down an even greater amount from earlier years. Total exhibitors numbered 44, compared with 60 in 1960. Generally, over the previous decade exhibitors had numbered in the area of 58 to 60. However, over the previous several years the number of record labels exhibiting at the MOA convention had diminished, with only six showing up at Miami Beach. Even more telling was that three of the five box makers at the time — Seeburg, Rock-Ola, and Wurlitzer — had not exhibited at a MOA convention for the prior two years. The convention for 1962 returned to Chicago. But problems remained. Attendance dropped to 600; there were only 40 exhibitors. Wurlitzer, Seeburg, and Rock-Ola continued to stay away. It led to a complete change in the group's executives.[7]

By around 1964 the association was broke and carrying $5,000 in debt. Things picked up a little and MOA was in better financial shape by the beginning of the 1970s. It tried to respond to issues of the day by scheduling seminars on problems such as the length of single records. (Operators had always disliked any single that went over a maximum of 2½ minutes or so. They hated anything over three minutes. One musical trend of the 1960s was, in fact, records longer than any in the past. Another problem to be tackled was that many album cuts were being played by radio stations causing box programmers to get requests for songs that were not available as a single.) MOA was then starting programs and courses designed to help its members become better businessmen. MOA published a brochure, the "Jukebox Story," as part of a restructuring of its public relations program. In 1971 all five juke manufacturers exhibited at the convention but only four labels participated. One record label, RCA, had not exhibited at MOA for many years. Jukes were promoted and publicized more heavily by MOA in 1973, marking its own 25th anniversary celebration. Material distributed included radio/television scripts and print media kits.[8]

In 1974, MOA changed its name to Amusement and Music Operators Association (AMOA) to reflect the shift of the coin-operated industry from jukes toward pin games, pool tables, and video games. According to a 1981 AMOA survey of operators, the average jukebox made a profit of only $49.95 in 1980.[9]

Writing in 1976, reporter Earl Paige said the juke industry had become in essence a games industry. Actually, he declared, the box as a vehicle for popularizing songs faded in the middle of this century and continued to fade in the 1960s when fewer and fewer record companies exhibited at MOA. In recent years only two or three labels had bothered to exhibit because the feeling in the record industry was that the jukebox was only an after-market. That is, operators bought only hits; they did not break records.[10]

A list was compiled by AMOA for National Jukebox Month, November 1988, and also to observe the juke's 100th anniversary in 1989. Note that the year of inception was by then moved forward from 1888 (which was the start date for the heavily publicized 65th anniversary celebrated in 1953) to 1889. The list was the top 40 jukebox singles of all time. Elvis Presley had three singles, the most of any artist. Nineteen titles came from the 1960s, twelve from the 1950s, and five from the 1970s. The oldest single on the list was Glenn Miller's "In the Mood" (1939); most recent number was George Thorogood's 1982 release "Bad to the Bone." That survey was mailed to the group's 1,200 members who serviced around 115,000 of the nation's estimated 225,000 music machines. Only 180 responded, leaving the list less than truly representative. Number one on the list was Presley's "Hound Dog/Don't Be Cruel" (1956); number two was Patsy Cline's "Crazy" (1961); number three was "Rock Around the Clock" (1955) by Bill Haley and his Comets.[11]

As the popularity of boxes declined, the problem of locations owning their own machines also decreased in importance. A 1961 account from Milwaukee had one operator declaring that 25 percent of metro Milwaukee locations had shifted to direct ownership. However, others disputed that figure and put the number at 10 to 15 percent. Leo Dinon, executive with H&G Amusement Company, argued that many locations were continually after his company to step in and take over a box — after the location had owned it for a couple of years. According to some operators, locations soon learned that operating just one box could be costly and time consuming. Very few locations had the time or expertise for record purchasing. Also, repairs and regular maintenance costs could be higher than expected and the biggest shock came when the location proprietor tried to trade in the unit for a new one only to find his box may have depreciated as much as $1,000 over the course of three years.[12]

Declining popularity or not, as was to be expected, the idea of advertising on the phonographs again resurfaced in 1961. Developing this venture was Audio Advertising Corporation (AAC), which declared its idea might soon be operational. The plan was to have the operator relinquish two selections (one record) on his machine, with the approximately 60 second commercial recorded on the disk. A small clock mechanism was installed in the box causing the ad to be played automatically every 30 minutes or so. If another record was being played at that time, the ad was delayed until the song finished. AAC was organized by Leonard Baitler, who was also managing director of the Miami Automatic Music Operators Association. Under the plan, an advertiser paid AAC $350 per machine per month with a minimum of 100 units in any single market. For his money the advertiser received a specified number of messages in each location at specified time intervals. In exchange for giving up space on his box, AAC would pay the operator a fixed sum per week per location. Ads could be changed every 13 weeks. As was the case in the past, nothing came of this idea.[13]

As already noted, long established maker AMI had run into trouble and merged with Rowe. It was not alone. In March 1973, business magazine *Forbes* ran a brief profile of Wurlitzer, stating it had about 25 percent of the U.S. box market. It was a short article about how Wurlitzer had survived, remained profitable, and provided a good 3,000 jobs. The tone of the piece was rather optimistic. Back in 1962, in one of its trade ads, Wurlitzer stated that it had produced on average over 20,000 phonographs a year for 28 years, exclusive of the war years.[14]

Just one year after the *Forbes* article Wurlitzer apparently decided that jukes were on the way out. In March 1974, the company announced that it would stop manufacturing jukeboxes and laid off 400 of its 700 employees at its North Tonawanda, New York, plant. Remaining employees were to produce organs. Once the king of the box industry, Wurlitzer used to sell 60,000 units annually, representing almost 80 percent of its revenues. In 1973 the firm sold 13,000 units (priced from $1,400 to $2,200 each), amounting to 15 percent of total revenue. Victor Zast, Wurlitzer public relations spokesman, said: "Now instead of going to Archie bars and listening to

Rock-Ola Tempo II, 1960.

jukeboxes, people stay at home to watch television and drink beer or go to sumptuous steak houses in the suburbs. Jukeboxes no longer have a place." By ending juke production Wurlitzer left the market to Rock-Ola, Seeburg, and Rowe AMI. All three specialized in coin-operated machines, unlike Wurlitzer which specialized in pianos and electric organs.[15]

Commenting on the Wurlitzer move, David C. Rockola said the whole industry was then making more money than at any other time. With regard to the demise, he added that "the statements that were contained in [Wurlitzer's] official releases are the furthest thing from the facts. They just couldn't compete." Not long after that, Seeburg ran into financial difficulties and was purchased by Stern Electronics, which marketed boxes under the Seeburg name. In the early 1970s the four U.S. makers reportedly produced 70,000 boxes a year. By the early 1980s production was down to 25,000 per .year.[16]

Reporter Paul Ackerman put a brave face on the situation when he discussed relations between the box and record industries in 1961. He argued that three major labels and one independent almost simultaneously disclosed that they were gearing a substantial part of their singles output for the juke market. There was supposedly an increasing awareness on the part of record companies toward juke operators. "The nation's 500,000 automatic phonographs account for nearly 45 per cent of the singles market." Labels involved were Columbia, Decca Coral, United Artists, and Vassar. Their concept was that special programming was required for juke locations and their execution was the release of special packages for the operator. Music men had complained — with some justification, said Ackerman — that singles were released with store sales in mind and with the operators as an afterthought. Also, they felt the record companies had taken them for granted, reasoning that once a single became a hit on the retail market, the operator had to buy the product. As teens bought most singles sold in retail outlets, a high percentage of new singles product was rock, suitable for soda shop locations, but hardly appropriate for taverns, where the patrons were adults. One result was that juke collections had been way off, observed Ackerman, with 58 percent of American boxes grossing less than $15 per week. To counter that trend the labels were releasing those special packages. For example, United Artists was releasing a silver spotlight series— one coupling was "Never on Sunday" by Don Costa and "Exodus" by Ferrante and Teicher while another disk paired "Theme from the Apartment" by Ferrante and Teicher with "The Magnificent Seven" by Al Caiola. Steve Laurence and Edie Gorme sang on four disks. Decca was releasing a package of 10 Decca Coral singles by artists with considerable adult appeal, including Guy Lombardo, Sammy Kaye, Mills Brothers, McGuire Sisters, and so on. In record stores, teens bought singles while adults bought LP albums.[17]

Different figures told a different story. In 1957 a total of 205 million single disks were sold: 25 million from record stores, 120 million from racks, and 60 million to jukes. Four years later, in 1961, unit sales of singles were 182 million: 92 million from stores, 40 million from racks, and 50 million to jukes. Unit sales of LP albums were 173 million in 1961 and 52 million in

1957. All those LPs, in both years, were sold through racks, stores, and clubs—none were sold to box operators. Dollar sales of all records in 1961 equaled $587 million; retail stores accounted for $305 million (52 percent), racks equaled $147 million (25 percent), clubs totaled $100 million (17 percent), jukeboxes accounted for $35 million (just 6 percent of the total).[18]

Two other incidents marked the decline of the phonographs. In 1983 sales of music cassettes first surpassed vinyl LP sales and in 1991 music compact disk sales surpassed those of cassette tapes.[19]

As the decline set in, and persisted and worsened, many innovations were tried. Myron Kandel reported in 1962 that the "gaudy" box had been given a new look. Seeburg, then the number one maker, was in the process of unveiling a completely new unit with a "dignified" walnut finish, clean console lines, and a "well-modulated stereophonic voice." And instead of playing single disks these new boxes were to concentrate on albums of show tunes, jazz, classical music, and popular standards. By placing the new box in resorts, cocktail lounges, motels, country clubs, cruise ships, and "other places that heretofore have shunned jukeboxes," Seeburg hoped to "open up an entire new market for its instruments." Kandel estimated American box production in 1961 at 50,000 units with Seeburg accounting for half of that number.[20]

Ten years later an account declared there was then more emphasis on less showy boxes, there were more wood-veneer console boxes and less glitter and psychedelic effects. It was all an effort to break into new locations. Edward Morris, Rock-Ola vice president, estimated these new, more dignified units could open up an additional 250,000 locations.[21]

In the mid–1960s when discotheques were all the rage, the nation's four box makers were providing packaged discos for turn-key operation to taverns, at little cost to the innkeeper. In December 1964, Seeburg introduced the first instant disco. Seeburg's package included a multi-channel jukebox with floor-level speakers, prefabricated hardwood dance floor, table displays, and napkins, phosphorescent five- by eight-foot wall panels, featuring wiggly dancers and musicians; specially programmed records; banners and signs; and advertising and publicity materials. Within a few months the other three manufacturers all had their own packages, but none quite as elaborate as the Seeburg package. Thomas L. Herrick, Seeburg vice president for marketing, said, "We're betting it's not a fad." Seeburg sold disco packages for $3,000 to $3,500 to its distributors, who sold them to operators, who then placed the units on location and split the receipts with the location owners. However, the location owner had to guarantee the operators at least $50 a week front money and sign a contract for a term ranging from one to three years. Dancers deposited 50 cents into the juke for a three-song record. Herrick believed that 25 percent of the supposed

500,000 boxes on location in America were suitable for disco operations. He added that his company then had from 700 to 1,000 disco packages operating in 400 cities. Rowe AMI had 25 to 30 sets out with plans to have 800 to 1,000 in operation by the end of 1965. Wurlitzer then had 20 units in place with plans for 500 by year's end. Rock-Ola only had a few packages on location and had not decided whether or not to launch a major nationwide push. Most enthusiastic of the makers, over disco units, were Seeburg and AMI. J. Cameron Gordon, Seeburg president, called the development of the discotheque "the greatest thing to happen to bars since Repeal." Rowe AMI marketing vice president Fred Pollak declared, "It's the urban renewal of the juke joints." Wurlitzer promotion manager A. D. Palmer commented, "I haven't seen any other dance craze that has stayed on top." He felt only 5 percent of juke locations were suitable for discos, adding, "We are involved ourselves to the extent that is required." Rock-Ola advertising manager George Hinker said only, "We're not as excited as Seeburg."[22]

Soundies tried to join music and video in a jukebox format in the 1940s and failed. That concept was revived in the early 1960s, in two different versions, both developed in Europe. One was called Cinebox, an Italian-made cinema box that was receiving its first American location test in 1963 in Philadelphia. Local Rowe AMI distributor David Rosen had two machines out — one in a luncheonette, the other in a café. The 40-selection fare in each unit consisted primarily of Italian and British films, with singers doing their hits against Continental backgrounds, and with some of the numbers depicting simple plots. A three-minute color film cost 25 cents. U.S. product, featuring American recording artists, was said to be on the way. During its first week of operation at the luncheonette, the machine grossed $183. Even here the concept of advertising surfaced. Rosen was selling ads to local sponsors at $5 a week each. Advertising messages were projected in color stills, with the stills appearing automatically when the machine was not in play. While Cinebox was new in the United States, these video jukeboxes were said to be firmly established in Europe. Both Cinebox and the French rival Scopitone were reported to be doing well in the UK and on the continent. Remembering the way Soundies fell flat, U.S. coin men were somewhat reluctant to take another look at the concept. That first test location, the Penn Center, was a 7-day-a-week luncheonette with a juke on site. Rosen placed the machine on a $100-a-week front money guarantee with any receipts over that amount split 50/50 between the operator and the location. Thus, of the $183 take in the first week, $141.50 went to Rosen and $41.50 went to the Penn Center. The regular jukebox there grossed $101 the week before Cinebox was sited (higher than the average week). With Cinebox taking $183, the juke receipts dropped to $61. However, argued Rosen, the juke averaged $89 a week for the long term, which meant Cinebox cut into the box take to the extent of $28. At the second test location, the Spearmint Lounge, Rosen had the same $100-a-week guarantee with a 50/50 split of receipts over that amount. On the first two days at the Spearmint, the Cinebox grossed $23 and $19.75.[23]

Two years later, in 1960, Cinebox went bankrupt. It was then reorganized as Intersphere Development Corporation and changed the name of the product from Cinebox to Colorama. Company officials said, in 1965, that 470 of its $3,700 units were on site in America. The

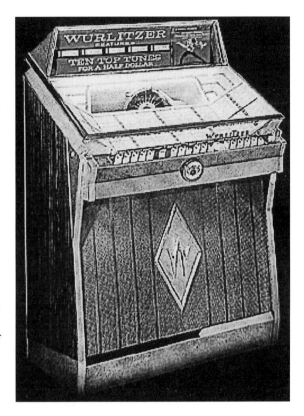

Wurlitzer 2600, 1962.

first U.S.-based manufacture of the product was said to be expected before the end of that year. Intersphere had no plans to use name talent for its short musical features. Rather, it had started in Chicago to film subjects such as the Go-Go Girls at that city's Whiskey A-Go-Go. Colorama was distributed by independent agents with one said to have placed 20 units in Chicago locations on an 80/20 split of receipts, in favor of the operator. No more was heard of Cinebox/Colorama.[24]

French-made rival system, Scopitone, was developed in France around 1961 and was first tested in America in Florida early in 1964, where it was installed mainly in restaurants and bars. Scopitone planned to manufacture 5,000 machines in 1965, double that in 1966, and hold to the figure of 10,000 units annually for some years after that. The U.S. maker was to be a Chicago firm called Tel-A-Sign that manufactured large illuminated plastic signs for gas stations, supermarkets, and so on. Base price of the machine was $3,500 plus $720 for leasing the first film library of 36 selections. A change of film was made weekly or as indicated according to popularity.

After that first leasing charge, the fee was $60 a month for film rentals. Play cost was 25 cents per selection with locations keeping all the revenue. Operators did not buy the units and expressed little interest in doing so. They were sold directly to location proprietors.[25]

In the summer of 1964 an enthusiastic article in the *New Yorker* spoke about a "sort of cinematic jukebox" called Scopitone in a Manhattan bar. The piece advanced the idea that they had become "practically standard barroom equipment." It was said to look much like any other juke, except on top of the unit was a 21-inch screen on which, at the drop of a quarter, a three-minute French musical film was shown. A system of mirrors provided a view of the film from almost any seat in the house. The pub changed the 36-selection film about once a month — "as often as we can get them from France."[26]

Around the same period, *Time* reported there were 500 Scopitone units scattered throughout the United States. One selection available on the machines was "El Gato Montes," which was said to capture the flavor of the annual Pamplona fiesta in Spain with trumpet playing, flamenco dancing, and the shrieks of small boys being gored by rampaging bulls in the streets. Scopitone weekly grosses were said to run from $75 to $375 in metro Miami and New York.[27]

A year later, in the summer of 1965, reporter Ray Brack said there were some 1,200 music-film devices on location in America. In policy and practice, he added, importers of those machines had avoided clashing with the juke industry. However, Brack also observed that those devices "go great guns while a novelty but collections soon begin to lag, much of the equipment is full of mechanical bugs—film product for units is not available in satisfactory quality or sufficient quantity." About 800 of those 1,200 machines were Scopitone units. That firm was then releasing four new films per month featuring such American artists as Barbara McNair, Della Reese, Jane Morgan, Debbie Reynolds, Kay Starr, and Frankie Avalon. By the end of 1965 the balance of those musical films was expected to have shifted from French to English. A new addition to the unit was a device called a "stimulator," which consisted of a timer that automatically switched on the machine to play the preceding selection after the machine had been silent for a specified number of minutes. Brack reported there were three stages for a machine. First was a short high-revenue period due to the novelty factor. Next came familiarization, which led to a leveling off with units frequently removed from locations in this stage. Third and last was a steady-income stage, a stage that Brack admitted had not yet been reached in any American location. Scopitone continued to sell direct to locations, stating in its placement policy that it "is not a competitor of the jukebox. It is most effective in prime locations such as luxury spots, diners, bowling alleys, restaurants." The company then had 20 distributors who had exclusive territory rights and a quota. None of them dealt in other coin-operated equipment. No more was heard of Scopitone.[28]

And then there was the video disc jukebox, marketed by several firms, which received a brief flurry of attention in the first half of the 1980s. The first video juke was shown at the Amusement and Music Operators Association Expo in Chicago at the end of 1979. Tentatively, the cost of the 25-inch video screen coin-operated unit was announced as $6,000, with software at $8 per disc. It was introduced by Show-Time Systems International Inc. of Sandusky, Ohio. High cost was one of the causes of earlier failures such as Scopitone. The price of this device was about triple the cost of a conventional box. Play price was envisioned as a minimum of 50 cents for a single selection.[29]

Nothing much happened until 1982 when Los Angeles-based Video Music International (VMI) introduced its new video tape jukebox. Looking at a 500,000-unit market in the coming three years, VMI planned to offer eight or nine different models, ranging in price from $7,000 to $15,000. Intended locations were restaurants, bars, clubs, military installations, zoos, summer parks, day camps, ocean oil rigs, and so forth. Tapes were to each contain 48 three-minute selections, consisting of record company promotional clips. VMI also planned to solicit advertisers such as liquor and tobacco manufacturers to have continually running ads when a music selection was not being played. Software sales to location owners were expected to be 12 times a year at the rate of $100 per tape per month.[30]

Three months later VMI came out with some firmer figures when it announced software costs to machine owners would be $200 a month. Each tape was to be 2.5 hours long and contain a minimum of 40 selections. Play price was 50 cents per selection. Rates for advertisers were set at $35 a month per location for each 30-second spot. Three different models were to be produced at a cost of $10,000 to $18,500. Three to seven different tapes were to be available each month with programming to also include old concert footage and television specials.[31]

Almost a year after that, in March 1983, VMI projected that 1,800 of its units would be in operation by the end of that year while admitting it then had only 26 machines on location. The company had launched a drive to license record company promotional clips but said its minimal market penetration hindered interest in supplying VMI with product.[32]

Another company entered the industry when New York–based Video Jukebox Inc. unveiled a box with a large screen projection television and laser videodisc technology. Prices for a unit started at $18,000. Lease price was $600 per month with the company estimating income of $1,400 from the 50-cents-per-play unit, plus increased bar trade. Up to 96 selections could be held on each disc, although no deals had been struck with any record labels at the time of the unveiling. The projection screens ranged in width from 6 to 24 feet.[33]

In May 1984, reporter Ken Terry estimated there were only about 1,000 video jukes in commercial operation in America. Rowe International sold 200, VMI sold 125 units, and U.S. Billiards' Video Sound sold about 100. A major stumbling block to the placement of video units was the high price. The retail price of Rowe units was $8,300 (wholesaling for $6,300), VMI $10,000, and U.S. Billiards $6,995. A top-of-the-line audio juke then sold for around $2,000. Rowe then had access to around 2,500 videos from the record labels while VMI had only 240 videos. VMI was turning out a 40-title videocassette every four to six weeks with owners paying $150 for the tape for the first month of use and $75 for each succeeding month. U.S. Billiards supplied tapes with 44 to 50 selections every six to eight weeks for a monthly charge of $135; Rowe charged $157 a month for 40 selections on tape. Most of these units charged customers 50 cents per play. Locations were mostly bars, game arcades, pizza parlors, and restaurants. While some of these makers sold or leased directly to locations, most had reverted to the traditional juke distributor/operator system. Rowe sold its units to operators for $7,000 with a monthly tape rental of $160. It suggested that if the operator charged locations a minimum of $150 per week in front or guarantee money, and split all receipts over that amount 50/50, then the operator could make his investment back in a year. Houston operator Franz & Company leased a video box to an arcade in that city. They charged $200 a week minimum plus 50 percent of any surplus. Franz said the receipts to that point had been running at $230 to $250 per week. And that was about all as the concept of joining audio and video disappeared once again. Not that it was a bad idea. MTV made out very well with the same concept. Today, of course, a bar needs only to have a television connected to cable on site tuned to MTV to get all the video music it wants for free for its customers.[34]

And then came the compact disk (CD) jukebox. At the end of 1985, business journalist Kathleen Deveny estimated there were then 300,000 boxes in operation, compared to a high of 550,000 in the past. When jukes were forced to compete with video games, the business took a dive. Seeburg was for a time the leading maker, but by the time Deveny's piece appeared, Seeburg had been sold several times, declared bankrupt twice, and was finally dissolved by Stern Electronics in 1982. In 1984 two former Seeburg managers paid Stern $2 million for the rights to the Seeburg name and its assets. This newly revitalized Seeburg was putting its hopes on a new machine, a CD juke, which it planned to start shipping in the spring of 1986. That new CD box was to hold 60 CDs, each containing 10 or more tunes that could be played individually. Thus, the new unit offered 600 selections, triple the number available on a conventional box. Selling price for the CD box was set at $3,000, 20 percent higher than the cost of a regular juke. Obstacles to success included the high cost and that restaurant chains popular with the yuppie crowd expressed little interest. Furthermore, the music piped into those singles' spots was carefully planned, and the owners did not want it subject to the "whims of customers." Play price on the CD juke was to be three plays for $1. Illustrating the problem facing operators of conventional jukeboxes was the release of 45 rpm singles late, after the release of the album. For example, Seeburg could not get Michael Jackson's hit song "Thriller" until 18 months after release of the album containing that number.[35]

Rowe International, subsidiary of Central Jersey Industries of Whippany, New Jersey, was then the leader in what remained of the box market. While Seeburg moved to a CD box, Rowe decided not to pursue the CD option but to continue with its video music system joining 45 rpm records and video (beta-format tapes). Each of these machines held 80 records (160 selections) plus 40 video selections that were displayed on a 25-inch monitor. Rowe felt the future was in video, citing the popularity of MTV, the music video channel. Apparently they forgot the distinction between costly and free. A second major error was in choosing beta tape, for beta tape lost out to the still prevailing VHS tape in the format wars of the middle 1980s.[36]

AMOA estimated that up to 20,000 new CD boxes appeared in the American marketplace in 1991, with CD jukes accounting for more than 50,000 of the 250,000 total boxes on site in the United States. An average CD juke cost $5,000, compared to $3,000 for a regular box. Generally, a CD box held up to 100 disks, at an average cost to an operator of $12 to $15 each. Location owners who replaced 45 models with CD boxes claimed the new machines generated about twice the gross income. Average CD play price was 50 cents for a selection, three for $1; average play price on a regular box was 25 cents per number, five selections for $1. By then Rowe had seen the light with CD boxes making up nearly half of its business.[37]

Neil Strauss reported in 1995 that the number of jukeboxes in America then stood at 250,000; 100,000 (40 percent) were CD jukes while 150,000 (60 percent) were conventional units that played 45 rpm single vinyl records. Strauss's piece was mainly one of nostalgia about the old boxes. For Manhattan he gave a list of bars, with name and address, of those that had remained "true to vinyl." CD jukeboxes did indeed gain a permanent place in the jukebox industry. But it was in a market that was in steep decline overall. The change from 45 vinyl disks to CDs was not much different from the earlier change when 45s replaced the old 78 rpm shellac records.[38]

Box exports remained fairly strong, at least through the 1960s. After that the general decline of the overall industry added to foreign saturation and foreign competition put an end to that market. For 1959, 30,099 amusement game machines were exported (worth $5.6 million); in 1960, 46,259 units ($7.8 million). In 1959, 5,790 used jukes were exported ($2.1 million) while 15,940 new boxes were shipped abroad ($11 million). For the following year the figures were, respectively, 6,396 ($2 million) and 16,133 ($10.3 million). The best customer in 1960 was West Germany taking $4 million worth (out of the combined $12.3 million exported in total). Next was Belgium at $3 million; then came the UK at $.75 million. Those respective figures for 1962 were 8,122 ($2.6 million) and 13,718 ($9.8 million). For 1963 the numbers were 9,117 ($2.6 million) and 19,332 ($13.8 million).[39]

The dollar volume of exports of vending machines for 1965 to 1967 were, respectively, $10.5 million, $12.7 million, and $11.6 million. Export of game machines were, respectively, $24.1 million, $29.4 million, and $20.4 million (through July 1967). Jukeboxes exported in 1965 were valued at $14 million (new and used), $12 million in 1966, and $12.4 million in 1967.[40]

When he assessed the jukebox situation in the UK in 1960, reporter Aaron Sternfield estimated some 20,000 boxes were then in operation, and some observers felt the market had a potential of 100,000 units. A lot of those units played only 78 rpm records and were 16-selection models. Sternfield observed: "The big problem has been to give the jukebox an aura of respectability. The British for some obscure reason, have always tended to wrinkle their noses at the mention of the jukebox." One factor helping to overcome that was the popular television show "Jukebox Jury," seen weekly by 12 million viewers. Another method in overcoming objections to the juke was the hideaway unit. It was a demonstration that the machine itself would not be seen but the music would be heard. Jukebox history in the UK began shortly after World War II, wrote Sternfield, when the Armed Forces personnel brought in automatic phonographs for their clubs. The first British maker was J. Norman Ditchburn, who made the 16-selection Music Maker, a 78 rpm machine, in 1947. In 1954 the Bel-AMI was introduced with 80 selections and 45 rpm disks. Play cost in the UK was either 3-penny or 6-penny per selection, with a penny worth slightly more than an American cent. Average weekly gross receipts were about $20 and the operator kept from $10 to $15 of that amount. Locations were usually on a 50/50 commission split, after a fixed sum of front money was taken.[41]

West Germany reportedly had 50,000 jukeboxes on location at the end of 1960. Of that number, some 45,000 were controlled by operators and the remainder run by location owners.[42]

Even inside the then East Bloc nations the box got attention. Machines located in East Germany programmed a high number of jazz selections. The newspaper of the Free German Youth credited the box with brightening the lives of proletarians as well as capitalists, concluding their cafés should be small clubs for people with common interests. "Preferably with small tables around the walls and a sunken floor in the center for dancing, with the music to be supplied either by a band or by an automatic music box." Around the same time, in Hungary, the play price was the equivalent of five cents. However, considering the local wage scale, that was equivalent to 25 cents in America. Nevertheless, boxes were said to be in continuous play. Communist box owners reportedly paid no performing rights royalties— on either side of the Iron Curtain.[43]

Less comfortable at that time with jukes was Bulgaria. It banned the playing of jazz records, attacking jazz as "corruptive and corrosive, a decadent Western influence which has no place in pure Communist life." After a government investigation, the Bulgarian Ministry of Culture and Education said, through its journal *Narodna Kultura*, that the playing of jazz in boxes had gotten way out of hand. The publication complained that jukeboxes blaring Western jazz "are undermining the cultural efforts of the government party among Bulgarian youth." Concluded the journal, "If we must have jukeboxes why can't they be supplied with good Communist music?" This attack was much more on a specific type of music than it was upon the music machines in general.[44]

More drastic action was taken in 1961 in Thailand when Premier Sarit Thanarat announced that jukeboxes were banned in Bangkok. He believed students had been wasting their time listening to jukebox music, which "tends to destroy the culture and traditions of the Thai people."[45]

An article on the situation in Europe in 1968 estimated 40,000 boxes in the UK and 33,000 in Belgium —1 box for every 279 inhabitants. Most jukes there were owned by the location and the proprietor's profit averaged out to between $20 and $40 a month in 1966. The Netherlands had 13,000 machines, of which 80 percent were owned by the location and 20 percent handled by operators. Austria had 7,300 units, of which 70 percent were owned by the location, and France had 30,000 boxes, of which 66 percent were location owned. Ireland had only 550 machines, while Norway had 2,500 (60 percent owned by locations). Denmark had 3,500; Sweden 5,000; Finland 2,700; and Italy 31,300 units, of which 26,000 were owned by coin-machine operators. The article pointed out that the European market had by this time reached the saturation point for boxes in many nations.[46]

That was not good news for American jukebox exporters because in 1967 those European nations took two-thirds of all boxes exported (dollar volume). J. Cameron Gordon, of Automatic Coin Equipment, Cardiff, Wales, estimated in 1969 there were a total of 263,000 boxes in West Germany, France, Italy, the UK, the Benelux nations, and the remainder of Western

Europe — with the Benelux countries having the highest per capita number of jukes in the world. Gordon noted that while U.S. makers had dominated the market during the past 20 years, within the previous three years
there had been a change. There were then four major makers in the UK and
on the continent: Jupiter (France), NSM (Germany), Harting (Germany),
and ACE Group (UK). Gordon thought there were only 10,000 to 12,000
jukes in the UK as late as 1960.[47]

West Germany's box total had reached about 60,000 at the start of
1971, with most of those found in inns and arcades. Within the previous
year there had been attempts to increase the cost of a juke play from five
cents to eight cents, but with no general success. Most boxes in that country operated on five cents per play, three for 13 cents, six for 25 cents. Belgium, still with an estimated 33,000 machines, continued to rank number
one in the world with an average of one box for every 290 citizens. Play
price there was no higher than 10 cents for two plays. Spain then had 4,500
jukes with a price of three cents per play.[48]

Finland had around 3,100 music machines in the fall of 1972, all but
1,000 of them were owned and installed by a government agency. Greece
then had more than 10,000 boxes, with a cost ranging from $833 to $2,800.
Most cafés, clubs, and restaurants took them on a commission basis from
operators with a 55/45 split in favor of the operator. Cost of a play was a
little over 3 cents; six plays cost a bit less than 17 cents.[49]

Continuing on in this period was the battle to bring jukeboxes under
the provisions of the Copyright Act. An editorial for the American Federation of Musicians (AFM) in the publication *International Musician* in September 1961 exaggerated the situation by saying that some 600,000 boxes
were grossing between half a billion and a billion dollars a year. With bills
having been presented almost annually to Congress for decades and with
boxes still allowed to operate with no payment to the creators of the music,
the musicians did not understand "the government's attitude in favoring
jukebox interests over musical ones." When copyrighted music was used
on radio and television, royalties were paid to the composers because the
1909 copyright law also provided that the payment of a royalty of two cents
a record (paid by all purchasers) should not free the record from contribution to copyright in the case of public performance for profit. Those prin-
ciples were accepted, if reluctantly, by radio and television. However, the
juke industry continued to refuse to pay royalties. Back in the gaslight era,
the editorial continued: "a tiny industry had sprung up, centered around
player pianos and hand-cranked, spring-operated phonographs. Machines
capable of mechanically reproducing the sounds of these gadgets were
installed in penny arcades. The novelty-seeker clapped on earphones, etc.—
to hear a tinny sound." Feeling that this gadget was little more than a toy

and one "certainly incapable of 'public' performance, the lawmakers put a clause in the Act exempting coin-operated machines from royalty payments. On this sole fact — the coin-slot clause — the jukebox industry bases its immunity." If a phonograph in a public place had no coin-slot the composer had a right to collect royalties; if it had a coin-slot, which played the record, the composer had no right to receive any compensation. Describing the situation as "ludicrous," the editorial urged its readers to "Write your Congressman about this."[50]

A few months later Sigmund Spaeth wrote an editorial on the same topic in the February 1962 issue of the *Music Journal*. Pointing out many of the same things as the AFM piece, Spaeth railed against the situation and concluded, "It is to be hoped that ways may soon be found of correcting this serious injustice to the creators of America's music and lyrics."[51]

Two months after that, well-known musicologist Stanley Green authored a piece slamming the exemption in an article in *The Atlantic Monthly*. Green observed that the two-cent royalty, still the same amount over half a century after it became law, was divided 50/50 between the songwriters and their publisher and that the juke operator paid the same to buy a record as a member of the general public. However, that record could be played 5,000 times on one juke, grossing $500. If a tavern owner used a radio to entertain his customers, he, too, was subject to a licensing fee. But if he replaced the radio with a juke he didn't have to pay. Every radio and television network, film studio, restaurant, bowling alley, skating rink, or dance hall, said Green, that used music to contribute to its revenue had to obtain a license to play copyrighted works. Alarmed by the injustice to composers and lyricists, a group of citizens headed by Carl Sandberg had formed the Creative Arts Committee for Better Copyright Laws. The chief purpose of the group was to spread the word about the unfairness of the current law, particularly regarding the juke exemption. One of its most powerful arguments was the report of the Register of Copyrights, which stated unequivocally, "Jukebox operators are the only users of music for profit who are not obliged to pay royalties, and there is no special reason for their exemption." Others backing the repeal of the exemption were the Librarian of Congress, the State Department, the American Bar Association, the General Federation of Womens Clubs, the American Patent Law Association, as well as the performing rights groups ASCAP, BMI, and SESAC.[52]

As might be expected, Green's article drew a strong reaction from operators. Joe Robbins, vice president of the Empire Coin Machine Exchange in Chicago, addressed a piece to the *Atlantic* editorial staff in which he said, "it is a well established fact that jukeboxes are instrumental in making hits of many records, and also, are a great factor in establishing unknown recording artists as stars." Actually, that was not true, certainly not in the 1960s.

Robbins went on to say that allowing an article such as Green's to "despoil" the pages of *Atlantic* was something he found "shocking." He concluded: "I am surprised, indeed, that your editorial staff does not more closely ver- ify the authenticity of articles such as this which serve no useful purpose and are simply slanderous and bigoted. An article of this type has no place in a magazine such as yours."[53]

Equally incensed was E. R. Ratajack, an executive with the Music Oper- ators of America (MOA). In a letter published in *Atlantic*, he attacked Green for his exaggeration that a record could or would be played 5,000 times in a box. Then Ratajack exaggerated himself when he said "the jukebox indus- try purchases over 200 million records per year."[54]

Writing in *Billboard* in May 1963, journalist Mildred Hall reported that it was beginning to seem "inevitable" that some sort of legislation to repeal the box exemption would come from the House Judiciary Subcommittee on Patents, Royalties and Copyrights. Recent hearings on the Emanuel Cel- lar anti-exemption bill had made that conclusion seem inevitable to Hall. The Cellar bill proposed establishing a Performing Rights Administration in the Copyright Office, which would license jukes at $5 per box annually as a performance royalty on coin-operated music. At the hearings the major performing rights groups reluctantly agreed to the $5 ceiling, but only as an experimental, interim proposition. Juke interests argued in favor of pay- ing songwriters additional money by increasing the statutory rate from two to four cents per record. ASCAP counsel Herman Finkelstein compared the proposed $5 rate with that in Brazil ($90), France ($65), England ($36), and Germany ($25). He also compared music fee rates for other users; 3.5 per- cent of radio time sales; 3.0 percent of television time sales; 5.5 percent of gross sales of background music, with a minimum of $20 to $30 per year. In contrast, noted Finkelstein, the $5 juke fee amounted to less than two- tenths of 1 percent of revenue.[55]

The House Copyright Committee unexpectedly voted eight to one in June 1963 to repeal the juke copyright exemption, an Emanuel Cellar ini- tiative. However, the $5 annual license fee proposal was dropped on the ground that it was too expensive to administer. Repeal, if it passed all the hurdles, would thus leave box operators to negotiate a royalty fee with the performing rights groups. Next, the measure went to the full House Judi- ciary Committee, one of the furthest advances such legislation had ever made in the House.[56]

Just three months later, the repeal measure, H.R. 7194, had been approved by the Judiciary Committee and was on its way to being brought to a vote in the House of Representatives. The Authors League of America urged all those who lived by writing and royalties to support that pending bill.[57]

An editorial in the *New York Times* called for better copyright law. The move to end the box exemption was part of a larger overhaul of the full copyright system. In speaking about the box aspect of copyright revision, the editorial declared, "The exemption for jukeboxes ought to be removed."[58]

Essentially the two sides were left to negotiate with each other. Time passed. ASCAP's Finkelstein said that in October 1966, MOA broke off negotiations at the point where the music licensing organizations were asking for a fee of $20 per machine per year and the operators were offering $15. A copyright revision proposal before the government would have set the yearly payment at $19.20. Senator John McClellan (D., Ark.), chair of the Senate Judiciary Committee, warned, in March 1967, that if the two groups could not agree Congress might have to pass a law that neither side could live with just to force negotiations.[59]

Section 116 of the Senate revision bill (S. 597), which set up a compulsory licensing procedure and royalty rates for operators who wanted to avoid open-end negotiations with ASCAP, BMI, and SESAC (a very small organization), was indeed a proposal nobody could live with. That bill required registration of each machine with the Copyright Office, re-registration each time it was moved, and a total re-registration of all boxes in January of each year together with a complete list of all selections available on the box during the year. MOA Secretary William Cannon filed a three-foot-high stack of paper representing the amount of paperwork necessary to comply with the proposed law. He said the minimum cost of Section 116 requirements would be $6,088 to report and pay the estimated $1,360 in royalties due annually. James Tolisano, MOA president, argued the average weekly gross per box was $18.50, with the operator keeping half, or $9.25 weekly. Of course, that proposal was never designed to become law. Rather, its purpose was to force the two sides to reach an agreement on their own.[60]

Further negotiations led to a reduction in the annual box royalty fee from $19 to $8. The juke industry's political power to lower the fee and to resist payment altogether for so long baffled some observers in the music field. One reason advanced was a lack of a united front by the music industry; that ASCAP and BMI had not formed a fully united common front because of their own historical disputes. Another factor was said to be a fear that a stiff fight to retain the $19 fee would rock the boat and scare Congress from passing any bill. Unlike the music interests, the jukebox industry was well organized into a national body. Those interests were said to also pack plenty of political power via their grassroots support with the tavern keepers and restaurant owners in cities, towns, and villages.[61]

In 1967 the U.S. House of Representatives passed the Copyright Revision Bill, containing the juke industry-backed Section 116 with an annual

$8 box fee, simplified reporting, and no direct dealings with music licensing groups. It still had to be passed by the U.S. Senate. MOA's Washington counsel, Nick Allen, laid the whole blame for the juke royalty problem on the performing rights organizations and their "insatiable demands for more and bigger royalties under the copyright law." Asked if there had been any large movement to try to hold onto the old 1909 copyright exemption, Allen said only a few individuals had raised that issue — the majority in the industry would go along with the $8 fee. It became clear in 1963, to those close to the legislative scene, that the old exemption could not survive. That year, for the first time in American copyright history, a House subcommittee approved a bill to make boxes liable to performance fees, and the full Judiciary Committee agreed. It became clearer as the major copyright revision action got underway that the total exemption enjoyed by the industry would not be upheld in Congress.[62]

And still more time passed. Seven years later, in 1974, the Senate was still considering the matter. Music interests were then pointing out that in Europe the average box royalty fee was around $50 annually, going as high as $8 a month in some of those nations. Senator John McClellan suggested raising the $8 annual fee in the next Senate revision bill to over $20 if the juke rate remained frozen in the 1975 version (finally passed) of the Senate bill. He said the higher rate would be called for since the Senate, in passing the revision bill, voted to exempt the jukebox rate from any review or adjustment by the Copyright Royalty Tribunal set up in the bill to oversee statutory rates in U.S. copyright law. Only an act of Congress could change the jukebox rate; no other royalty rate was exempted from adjustment by the Tribunal. All the music licensing groups preferred periodic review, and adjustment if needed, by the Tribunal.[63]

Royalties were finally imposed on jukeboxes as of January 1, 1978. Still, music licensing groups would have to do their own policing of boxes in bars, restaurants, and so on by physically checking the certificate on the box. The Copyright Office was not expected to require and maintain updated lists of box locations from operators. That warning came from Copyright Office Registrar Barbara Ringer in late 1977 during a hearing on proposed regulations for compulsory licensing of boxes. Those rules would determine what information was required on operator applications for the annual fee of $8, and on the certificate of registry to be placed on the jukes. The burning issue at the hearing was the performing rights groups' drive to have operators required by rule to identify locations of their boxes and include that data on both the application and certificate. They pointed out that would save their field representatives from having to physically inspect every jukebox in America. Spokesmen for ASCAP, BMI, and SESAC argued that such a central listing of locations was "vital and absolutely essential."

Ringer agreed the Tribunal probably had that right but she doubted they wanted it because it was too much work. AMOA counsel Nicholas Allen told the panel that they had met with music licensors and at one time tentatively agreed that operators might provide lists of their locations "informally" to accommodate licensor field representatives but not as part of the official rules. Later they withdrew that offer completely because operators sharply opposed any location listing as being an "invasion of privacy." Also, it would mean an intolerable burden of paperwork since 60 percent of the boxes were moved around to different locations by operators during a year, said Allen.[64]

Rules for box licensing were finalized at the end of 1977 and those rules did not require operators to provide location listings to music licensors. However, the Copyright Office noted that the Copyright Royalty Tribunal might act further on the issue.[65]

By the end of July 1978, the Copyright Office reported that only about 130,000 boxes had been registered to that date. By then ASCAP had filed its first lawsuit, against a New York operator, for failure to comply. It said it had patiently delayed suing for five months in order to afford all operators ample time to comply with the law. ASCAP promised it would now be vigorous in suing operators who continued "to show contempt for the law of the land and the rights of creators by failing to comply with the Copyright Act." That suit was settled out of court with the operator agreeing to comply with the law — that is, to register and pay the $8 fee — and pay an undisclosed sum to ASCAP "in four figures" to settle infringement claims and reimburse its legal expenses.[66]

Ringer reported that only about 50,000 boxes had been registered by the actual statutory deadline. She commented, "Maybe they are waiting for someone to put the arm on them before they'll comply." With around 130,000 phonographs registered it meant that a little over $1 million in fees had been collected. Box operators worried the rates would eventually go up during one of the Copyright Royalty Tribunal rate reviews that would come at 10-year intervals, beginning in 1990 for jukes after an initial review in 1980. Music interests had prevailed in the end in having jukebox rates subjected to periodic review, as was the case for all other statutory copyright fees.[67]

During 1978, 139,547 jukes were registered, which generated a royalty total of $1,116,376. That royalty sum was divided as follows: ASCAP got 47.5 percent, BMI received 47.5 percent, and SESAC got 5 percent. Those percentages could vary from year to year, depending on the position of each group within the music industry. It meant that ASCAP received $530,000 as its share of jukebox licensing fees in that first year. Putting that in perspective was the fact that ASCAP's receipts in 1978, from domestic licensees, were $95,033,000.[68]

Late in December 1980, as a result of that initial rate review, the Copyright Royalty Tribunal ruled that the annual compulsory license fee for jukes would jump to $25 on January 1, 1982, and to $50 on January 1, 1984. Those amounts were less than was wanted by both ASCAP and SESAC, which sought a $70 fee. BMI wanted a $30 fee plus automatic cost-of-living increases. Under the new ruling the Tribunal planned to adjust the $50 on January 1, 1987, for inflation, using the Consumer Price Index computed from February 1, 1981. Operators opposed any increase and made "strident arguments of economic doom" if any should be implemented. Nevertheless, operators were unwilling to bolster their case with financial statistics from AMOA member firms and were reluctant to permit the government to pry into their business affairs. The Tribunal's lack of subpoena power, a Congressional oversight in the 1976 Copyright Act, proved to be a complicating factor in that body's attempts to reach what it felt was a fair revision of the $8 fee.[69]

In explaining its reason for the $50 fee the Tribunal noted it was entirely reasonable "since in our view the jukebox industry has never previously paid reasonable compensation for the use of copyrighted music." It said it simply could not accept claims from the box industry that the new royalty schedule would have a disruptive influence on the industry. The Tribunal felt that way because the case presented by AMOA "has failed to provide reliable data concerning the operating expenses, revenues, or return on investment of jukebox operators."[70]

Incensed by the Tribunal ruling, the juke industry fought back and succeeded in getting a bill introduced in both houses of Congress in which the $50 annual fee would be scrapped and replaced with a one-time fee of say, $50, or less, instead of yearly. That proposal did not pass but for a time it looked like it might have a chance. Then, in May 1985, both sides announced a compromise agreement had been reached, as a result of 14 months of "arduous negotiations" between music licensor groups and AMOA. The rift between the two sides grew as the fee moved first to $25 then to $50. It was slated to increase again in 1987, based on cost-of-living changes. Under the compromise $10 rebates would be sent to box owners in 1985 and 1986. For 1987, rebates would be sent equal to the amount the cost-of-living adjustments forced the licensing fee over $60, provided at least 110,000 jukes were registered in that year. Rebates would be the same in 1988, provided 115,000 boxes registered that year. No rebates were scheduled to be delivered in 1989, although the two sides were to begin negotiations in that year on fees in the 1990s. Both sides stressed the agreement required AMOA to encourage box owners to comply with compulsory licensing. Only 107,000 phonographs were then registered. AMOA claimed that was 50 percent of the total; music licensors declared it was closer to 25 percent.[71]

As 1987 approached it was announced that the fee in effect from January that year would be $63. AMOA and the licensors announced another joint agreement wherein they would set up a tipster program. Possible infringers would receive an application form and a letter from the licensing division of the Copyright Office informing them that if they did not comply, their names would be turned over to the performing rights groups for legal action. All members of AMOA were urged to cooperate.[72]

Nonetheless, nothing seemed to make any difference. According to the Copyright Office, 104,391 machines were registered in 1984; 96,204 in 1987. Juke royalty totals did rise, but due only to an increased fee. Box royalties for the years 1982 to 1984 were, respectively, $3.3 million, $3.2 million, and $5.8 million.[73]

Still another new agreement was reached between AMOA and the licensors in 1990. It transferred the responsibility of administering licenses from the Copyright Royalty Tribunal to a newly formed entity, the Jukebox License Office (JLO). The 10-year pact, retroactive to January 1, 1990, included several aspects, among them amnesty for operators who had not paid their proper fees in the past and financial commitments from the licensors to promote the juke industry. The pact came about in accordance with the 1988 congressional amendment to the Copyright Act that permitted juke operators to negotiate royalty rates. AMOA was then saying that about 90,000 phonographs, out of 225,000 units, were licensed. For 1990, the fee for the 1st box was $275; for the 2nd through 10th boxes, $55 more in total; and for the 11th machine on up, a total of $48 more. For 1991 the base rate for 11 or more boxes would not exceed $47, and in 1992 it would not exceed $45. Clearly this was an agreement designed to hurt the location proprietor who owned a single box ($275 fee) compared to the operator with 10 boxes ($330 total, $33 per box) or especially to the operator with 50 boxes ($378 total, $7.56 each). An operator with 100 boxes, or 300, also paid a total of $378. Performing rights organizations were contractually obliged to earmark some of their juke royalties to promote the performance of music on boxes. For 1990 and 1991 the licensors agreed to set aside $75,000 each year for that purpose; $65,000 in 1992 and $50,000 in 1993. It had taken almost 70 years for the juke exemption to be removed from the Copyright Act. Ironically, by the time the music licensors were in a position to start to collect, the box industry was only a shadow of its former self and in a steep and irreversible decline. Licensors groups were undoubtedly very disappointed by what materialized after struggling so hard and for so long to have the industry subjected to the copyright regulation.[74]

Survey data on operators was reported for the first few years of the 1960s and then disappeared as the industry slowly slid away. In 1960 a typical operator had 66 locations: 30 in taverns or bars, 19 in restaurants, 10 in soda shops, 5 in diners, and 2 machines in other spots. He bought 93 records over the course of the year for each phonograph and employed the equivalent of three full-time people. Each box took in $14 per week, $7 to the location and $7 to the operator. Some 71 percent of machines were placed on location on a straight commission basis, only 14 percent were on first or front money contracts. Records purchased by the juke industry in 1960 were estimated at 49 million disks. Some 21 percent of the jukes grossed less than $10 per week (owner and location total); 37 percent grossed between $10 and $15; 22 percent were in the $16 to $20 range; 11 percent grossed from $21 to $25; and 9 percent of the boxes grossed $26 and over. Net income for all operators (from juke operations only — 92 percent of them handled at least one other type of coin machine); less than $5,000, 50 percent of the operators; $5,001 to $10,000, 30 percent; $10,001 to $15,000, 10 percent; over $15,000, 10 percent.[75]

For 1961 the average income from juke collections, per operator, was $11,059 (mean). The median income figure was $5,000. About 22 percent of the operators netted between $5,000 and $10,000; 10 percent were in the $10,000 to $15,000 range; and 13 percent had net incomes over $15,000. The number of jukeboxes per operator declined from 66 to 56, but the total number of coin machines the operator had on location rose sharply because juke operators were diversifying more and were going heavily into cigarette machines and other merchandise vendors. Each of the 93 percent who handled game machines on his route had an average of 56 units of games; 40 percent of them handled cigarette machines with a mean average of 84 units (median was 38). Slightly more than 10 percent of the operators handled food and drink machines (on average 10 units). Nearly 15 percent of box operators handled children's rides, with the average route consisting of 29 units. Average weekly juke receipts were $15 a week before the split. Twenty percent of the phonographs grossed less than $10 a week; 40 percent took in from $10 to $15. Another 20 percent averaged $16 to $20 with locations averaging over $20 a week accounting for the remaining 20 percent. Taverns remained the prime location with the average 56-unit route containing 30 tavern stops (53 percent); 21 locations were restaurants (38 percent). Teen hangouts and soda shops made up most of the balance.[76]

Articles dealing with the erosion of the industry occurred frequently in this period. *Variety* noted back in 1973 that problems included defective disks from labels, records that played too long, threatened federal copyright changes, increased competition from home entertainment and television, and increased vandalism and use of slugs. Operators claimed they had to overstock to allow for defective disks. Television was inflicting more pain because of new developments in programming such as Monday night sports telecasts as well as Tuesday to Thursday night movies. Developments in home-oriented amusement machines such as dart boards, pool tables, and shuffleboards were also making their presence known.[77]

In a 1980 account, reporter Alan Penchansky gave a litany of problems facing the industry. Operators faced rising costs and a decline in the number of possible locations. Urban renewal and declining numbers of mom and pop type taverns and restaurants were frequently cited by operators. Wayne Hesch, a Chicago area operator, remarked, "Overall in the last five years the marketplace has actually declined because of the fast food chains." It was then almost impossible for an operator to survive financially strictly on running boxes, as many did in the past. Video-game routes were then doing well. Fast-food outlets did not encourage lingering; jukeboxes did.[78]

Penchansky returned a few months later to report that another reason for the decline included the increased use of piped-in background music and television by locations. Other factors were the high box purchase price and superior profitability of other types of coin-operated machines as a business alternative. Estimates were that in 1978 U.S. box production had fallen to 19,000 units. Research by AMOA put the American jukebox population at 251,000 to 388,000.[79]

Vance Muse wrote a 1981 article for *Rolling Stone* in which he detailed the decline of the box. David Rockola was quoted as saying: "We had our heyday after Prohibition, when bars reopened and push-button entertainment was novel. Most people didn't have radios and record players at home, and certainly not in their cars, so everyone got together at jukeboxes." Rockola added: "Now there's competition everywhere, even between our own games and music divisions. Kids have just so much to spend on goofing off, and they have to choose between a jukebox and a game. To some of them, the ones blasted by music all day, jukeboxes must seem awfully square." Illustrating the lack of accurate numbers on the industry was the fact that Muse estimated there were 500,000 boxes in operation grossing $250 million a year, and that the industry would ship 31,000 new boxes in 1981. Muse's numbers meant a box averaged $10 a week in receipts. His total number estimate was too high by a considerable margin.[80]

Later in 1981 reporter Ken Terry concluded, based on a cross-section of juke operators, that the business "is slowly but inexorably dying." Don Van Brackel was a 25-year industry veteran who ran 440 boxes out of Defiance, Ohio. Five years earlier, he said, he was operating 485 jukes and was receiving half of his total income from them. Yet in 1981, only about 30 percent of his revenue would come from boxes, the rest would be supplied by background music and pinball and video games. That 30/70 ratio of juke to other revenue corresponded exactly with the national average for box operators, according to MOA. Its own estimates were that there were 251,000 to 388,000 phonographs in America, run by 3,000 to 5,000 operators in

1980; in 1973 there were 400,000 to 500,000 units and 7,500 operators. The juke industry bought 75 million single records in 1973 and 45 million in 1980.[81]

Peter McDermott, president of the record selling firm Peter's One-Stop, in Dedham, Massachusetts, blamed the record labels. Like all "one-stop" locations, he wholesaled records from many labels to operators, who could theoretically fill all their disk requirements at one stop. Specifically he argued that RCA Records, a pioneer in the creation of 45s, was leading the way to its demise. Totally eliminated from RCA's current, 1981, 45 catalog were such greats as Duke Ellington, Fats Waller, Hugo Winterhalter, Mario Lanza, and many others. RCA also announced an increase in its 45 list price to $1.99. The one-stop price had risen 15 cents since June 1980, and a further 14 cent rise late in 1981. But the most discouraging aspect, thought McDermott, was the lack of material available for the operator to program locations properly. He suggested asking any one-stop location how many sales were lost because "Turn the Page" (Bob Segar) was not available on a 45. As a result box operators changed records less frequently. The problem grew more serious when one-stops could not fill requests due to the reluctance of record labels to release on 45s the frequently requested selections. Artists such as Led Zeppelin, Van Morrison, Carole King, and Bad Company were "not represented on 45s at all."[82]

When AMOA surveyed operators in 1982, results showed "a rapid move away from jukeboxes and toward video games as the primary source of income for operators." More than 25 percent of those queried reported a loss from box operations during the fiscal year, and 46 percent said they had no locations with only jukes in place, up from 28 percent a year earlier. In neither year did any of the operators deal exclusively in jukeboxes. The average video game revenue per operator in 1982 was $1,608 (with a profit of $270.30 per unit) compared to average box revenue of $968 ($130.86).[83]

Another sure sign of the industry's rapid decline was the nostalgia pieces that began to appear in the media. One article in 1978 was about how box collectors hunted for old jukes, especially those with Art Deco cabinets from the 1930s and 1940s. Included were a listing of a handful of firms in the New York area that sold vintage units; some rented them for parties. Vance Muse's article, which detailed industry problems, also included a nostalgia section about where and how to find jukes to buy for the home. For example, readers were told to travel the backroads and look for old bars, and so on, which might have an old phonograph in storage.[84]

Charles Cross wrote a 1982 piece in *Esquire* in praise of the luxury light-up era machines, and the trend to collect and restore them for home use. In 1983 Robert Palmer remarked that cassettes had been more popular than disks for more than a year and that it had been "awhile" since 45 rpm singles were as popular as albums. Home stereo tape systems, he thought, had grown so sophisticated that to many ears a juke sounded "crude and tinny." Palmer's piece was mainly a guide to bars and other establishments (with names and addresses) that still had jukes on location. James Barron produced a 1989 article about the nostalgia craze, about collecting, about prices, and so on. And there were others.[85]

Back in the glory years of 1934 to 1948, the jukebox was one of the few methods of receiving popular music. By 2000 it was just one of many. With music reception more mobile and personal than ever before, the box choice was nowhere near the first. Also, competition from a host of other sources all caused a decline in juke business. And the box faded away. Its demise was not spectacular; it was not linked to one specific event. Rather, it slowly became irrelevant and slowly went into oblivion. It was obscured for a thousand reasons.

8

Conclusion

While Edison's invention did not catch on in the way its inventor intended, as a business machine, it did lay the groundwork for the modern jukebox. The first 20 years were an experimental time during which Edison's machine became an entertainment device, had a coin chute attached, and enjoyed brief periods of minor popularity as a novelty item. Its low technical quality, and limitations, diminished its appeal. Although it pioneered the phonograph arcade — later the penny arcade — it even lost its position there as the public turned more to the various amusement games that soon appeared in those same arcades. At the same time another type of jukebox made a brief appearance and also failed to take hold. Changes in recording formats also made life difficult for the fledgling box industry as tinfoil cylinders gave way to wax cylinders, then to steel disks, and finally to the shellac records. By 1907 to 1908 the box had faded away. However, the format of the recording industry had finally stabilized. Helping the jukes on the road to oblivion were the coin-operated player pianos, and larger, more elaborate orchestrions, which offered many advantages over the jukes. Perhaps most important of those advantages was that they had plenty of volume. One of the good things that did happen to the box industry was the enacting of the Copyright Act of 1909, which gave the jukes an exemption from royalty payments that would stay in effect for a much longer period of time than probably anyone anticipated. In later years when the juke industry argued to retain the exemption, it often claimed that the legislators of 1909 did it for valid reasons at a time when there were plenty of coin-operated music machines around. In reality there were very few then on location. Player pianos were just starting to take hold while the boxes themselves had all but disappeared. Of the relatively few that remained, many still required the customer to wear earphones — taking the event out of the realm of public performance. Likely the exemption was thrown in as a last minute afterthought to deal with a very minor aspect of the music business, which likely seemed then to have little or no future.

Over the next 25 years the box remained in oblivion as the player piano was the coin-operated music machine of choice. When Prohibition was enacted it meant the end for the expensive orchestrions while also limiting business for the player piano. While the piano ruled it did so in a limited way; most locations provided no music machine at all. Their customers were treated to live music or nothing at all. Radio arrived on the scene and fairly quickly found its way into most American homes. It provided technical advantages the box industry would soon make good use of — mainly electric amplification. Radio helped to generate a large following for individual songs, band leaders, and vocalists with a speed and pervasiveness that was previously unknown. Having people with the names of specific artists and titles on their lips was something jukes would take full advantage of. The companies that would come to be the dominant box makers were then all in business; most of them had been so for many, many years. They produced those player pianos and other amusement devices, including pins and slots. With the piano market gone and with pins and slots under community attack, they were looking for other product lines. Starting in the 1926 to 1927 period, the new and improved jukebox began to appear. Still, little happened for six or seven years as the last piece was not in place. That came at the end of 1933 with the nationwide repeal of Prohibition. Over the next few years an untold number of bars opened throughout America. Suddenly the box industry was faced with a seemingly endless number of new, potential locations.

Few industries grew as rapidly as the juke industry. Toward the end of 1933 there were perhaps 25,000 jukes on location in America. By the end of 1939 that number was around 300,000 (estimates vary widely). Even more impressive was that all this took place during an economic depression that had brought most industries to their knees. Anyone unemployed who had enough capital to become an operator was almost guaranteed a good living. Something like 30 to 40 percent of all coin-machine operators in the 1930s and into the 1940s handled jukes only — a percentage level that would never again be approached. Established operators (of amusement games and vendors) who had long shunned the juke as unworthy suddenly became converts. Manufacturers sold units as fast as they could produce them. Record sales increased dramatically, partly due to the buying by the music-machine operators. Box makers quickly moved away from the plain wooden cabinet into ornate plastic and neon machines, designed to be themselves a focal point in neighborhood taverns and in mom and pop diners. People had music at home on their radios but were limited in other ways. With the Depression in full swing the cost of a record was something to think twice about. As was the cost of buying a home record player. Those items were not staples in every American home in the 1930s; they were still luxury items. Not every family owned a car either. Those who owned an automobile did not usually have a radio in it. Splurging a nickel in a bar to hear a favorite tune was the sort of indulgence most people could make.

The industry became more than a little caught up in its own importance, claiming to be more important than anything else in creating hit songs and artists. In reality jukebox popularity followed on the heels of a popularity created through other media, such as by way of radio or concert tours. Jukeboxes could and did increase the sales of certain records, often dramatically, but they almost never created hits on their own. When people selected a song on a jukebox they picked one they knew. The industry did help music outside the mainstream, such as that created by Black artists and country singers, when those records were programmed locally. That type of music had few, if any, outlets nationwide such as on the radio. Compared to today, mainstream American music was limited to relatively few performers and designed to appeal to everyone. It meant the same few names were remembered by most people in most parts of America. That made programming easier for operators. The jukes enjoyed their greatest popularity in the period 1934 to 1948, at a time when the number of selections offered by each box was at its lowest — 12 to 24 numbers for the most part. Nagging fears that a saturation point had been reached around 1938 or 1939 were quickly forgotten as a war-preparing economy picked up with many new potential locations opening up to service a busier, more fully-employed America. It was partly to counter that saturation fear that the "luxury light-up" era had been introduced. When saturation was reached an industry was reduced to making sales only on a replacement basis. In that situation sales could be increased only by raising the rate at which replacement were made. One way to do that was to introduce yearly (or more frequent) model changes. Wurlitzer organized huge, elaborate coast-to-coast tours wherein its executives wined and dined operators and distributors throughout America. Never again would the industry be so awash in money. As 1940 ended and United States official involvement in World War II loomed, the box industry had no problems to speak of. It believed its best days were to come.

During the World War II years the industry did well financially even though new box production was curtailed. It probably helped operators since the pressure to buy constantly changing new models was removed. Boxes did their part in presenting their patriotic face. As well, the industry was a leader in setting up youth clubs, centered, of course, around a juke. It succeeded to a large extent, with some help, in presenting the jukebox as an important factor in preventing teens' delinquency. As the war ended, the industry looked forward to what it felt would be a great future. It was thinking about all those foreign markets which would reopen; it was also thinking about all those boxes in America that would be five years old or older when new box production again resumed. They would need to be replaced.

Those glory years were limited to about two. Prospects had lured several new makers into the industry but they all quickly expired. Operators faced increased costs and decreased income. That meant they bought fewer new machines than predicted, resulting in overproduction in the industry. All operator costs (new jukes, records, salaries, and so forth) rose sharply. Television arrived on the scene and it quickly caused box receipts to decline. By all evidence jukes badly needed a play price increase to a dime. But it didn't happen for a long time because operators were disorganized. Operators mostly favored dime play but only if all others in the area imposed the same increase. However, every area seemed to have operators all too ready to try to poach a location with the promise of nickel play — if the other operator put the price up. Copyright battles continued. Everybody made less money and that caused the excessively gaudy luxury light-up era to come to an end. Bright spots included a dramatic increase in box exports abroad, and the arrival of the 45 rpm record, replacing the old 78 rpm disks. It was a cost-saving benefit for operators. When the worst of the hard times seemed to have bottomed out in 1949 or 1950, the box industry adopted a renewed optimism. But the very best years, lasting from 1934 to 1948, were over for good.

After that sharp decline, the industry recovered somewhat and more or less stabilized during the 1950s. A healthy export trade helped to mask domestic difficulties to some extent. Income from boxes decreased with operators turning more and more to operating other types of coin machines for additional revenue. Pressure to end the copyright exemption was never so intense. The saturation point had been reached. A trend to fast-food chains — at the expense of mom-and-pop cafés — was hard on the jukes. Those fast-food places did not take boxes. Television continued to be a drag on business. People stayed home more to watch it and when they went out to taverns the video set often held sway. Transistor radios made their debut as music delivery became more personal and more mobile. Changes in the record industry continued as albums began to overtake the single disk. Many more changes would come. As the 1950s ended there were no articles pointing out the bright future in store for the box. Instead, there were an increasing number of pieces on the escalating number of problems facing the industry. Few offered solutions.

Saturation had hit the domestic market during the 1950s. It hit the export market the following decade. From that point on the industry went into a steady decline and became increasingly marginalized and irrelevant.

Most of the famous old names remained in the business to some extent, even resurrected Wurlitzer. But all those firms had been sold, resurrected, and relocated so many times they could hardly be called the original companies. All of them did most of their business in other lines.

Back in the glory years of 1934 to 1948 the box was important as one of the few ways to disseminate popular music. In neighborhood taverns there was nothing to compete against the box. The ultra-gaudy jukes of the luxury light-up era did not popularize the music machines. Rather, the popularity of the box generated so much income for the machines the industry went to financial extremes.

Rapid changes in the recording industry all took their toll on juke business. Single records became less important as albums took over leadership; radio stations increasingly concentrated on album cuts not always available on singles; and vinyl records were supplanted by cassettes, which later gave way to CDs. Jukes never were able to crack the high-end market of up-scale hotels, restaurants, and nightspots. More and more the independently owned down-scale neighborhood diners were replaced by the fast-food chains. Television took over taverns. Boxes never created hits. They did increase the sales of hit records made hits through other media. As well, they often spurred the sale of such hits for the home record player. Juke business was important to the recording industry from the 1930s through the 1950s. However, after that it became rapidly irrelevant, a tiny after-market.

Every attempt the juke made to reinvent itself failed. Today, operators sometimes handle boxes as a courtesy or enticement for locations to enable them to place their other equipment on site. That is, they continued to handle boxes and accept a less than satisfactory profit because it was good for their business overall. No operator handles just boxes; there has not been one for decades. With regard to the total number of boxes the numbers have always been vague, and contradictory. At most there were perhaps 400,000 to 450,000 boxes, back in the late 1940s, or into the 1950s. Today that number is under 200,000, perhaps well under. Whatever the number, day by day they continue to disappear.

Appendix A

City Jukebox Taxes and Ratios of Jukes and Locations to Population (1958)

KEY TO TABLE HEADINGS

A Number of Licensed Boxes D Eating and Drinking Places
B Per License Tax or Fee   E # of Licensed Boxes per 1,000 Pop
C Population (000)   F # of E&D Places per 1,000 Pop

	A	B	C	D	E	F
			ALABAMA			
Birmingham	639	$10	361.6	482	1.77	1.33
Decatur	50	$10.50	25.3	39	1.98	1.54
Dothan	na	$ 5	29.1	45		1.55
Gadsden	105	$10	67.2	73	1.56	1.09
Huntsville	na	$25	57.1	66		1.16
Mobile	314	$25	175.6	276	1.79	1.57
Montgomery	372	$15.50	129.1	159	2.88	1.23
Opelika	21	$17.50	12.3	27	1.71	2.20
Selma	121	$10.50	28.3	60	4.28	2.12
Troy	na	$10	8.6	21		2.44
Tuscaloosa	50	$10	57.1	57	0.88	1.00
			ARIZONA			
Flagstaff	100	$ 5	7.7	37	12.99	4.81
Mesa	none	no fee	27	50		1.85
Phoenix	441	$10	186.5	521	2.36	2.79
Tempe	26	$20	7.7	36	3.38	4.68
Tucson	na	$10	104.9	246		2.35
Yuma	600	$10	9.1	81	65.93	8.90

KEY TO TABLE HEADINGS

A Number of Licensed Boxes   D Eating and Drinking Places
B Per License Tax or Fee   E # of Licensed Boxes per 1,000 Pop
C Population (000)   F # of E&D Places per 1,000 Pop

	A	B	C	D	E	F
			ARKANSAS			
Camden	70	$ 5	17.6	34	3.98	1.93
De Queen	10	$ 5	3.0	7	3.33	2.33
Forest City	22	$ 5	7.6	23	2.89	3.03
Jonesboro	33	$ 5	20.1	30	1.64	1.49
Paragould	38	$ 5	9.7	43	3.92	4.43
Pine Bluff	100	$ 5	41.5	96	2.41	2.31
Springdale	na	$ 5	7.3	23		3.15
West Memphis	2	$20	17.8	22	0.11	1.24
			CALIFORNIA			
Alameda	40	$10	71.8	84	0.56	1.17
Alhambra	na	$15	56.3	87		1.55
Anaheim	30	$12	62.3	37	0.48	0.59
Berkeley	na	$ 2	119.5	163		1.36
Brawley	40	$40	15.0	54	2.67	3.60
Burbank	50	$12	92.9	171	0.54	1.84
Chico	26	$ 7	14.5	54	1.79	3.72
Colton	20	$30	17.3	33	1.16	1.91
Colusa	14	$20	3.3	19	4.24	5.76
Concord	21	$20	28.7	34	0.73	1.18
Corning	8	$12	2.5	13	3.20	5.20
Culver	29	$ 8	35.0	85	0.83	2.43
El Centro	80	$25	18.3	45	4.37	2.46
Escondido	na	$10	10.1	28		2.77
Eureka	55	$ 6	28.9	88	1.90	3.04
Fresno	none	no fee	119.9	353		2.94
Fullerton	3	$12	49.3	41	0.06	0.83
Gilroy	27	$20	6.0	36	4.50	6.00
Glendale	30	$ 3	119.9	161	0.25	1.34
Hollister	20	$15	5.8	22	3.45	3.79
Huntington	40	$10	33.0	123	1.21	3.73
Inglewood	57	$10	60.3	142	0.95	2.35
Lodi	na	$15	16.6	73		4.40
Long Beach	na	$10	326.9	697		2.13
Los Angeles	3896	$ 7.50	2356.4	4448	1.65	1.89
Los Gatos	na	$ 5	4.9	25		5.10
Madera	25	$10	12.7	44	1.97	3.46
Merced	50	$10	20.5	76	2.44	3.71
Modesto	na	$10	37.1	136		3.67
Monrovia	15	$15	27.1	41	0.55	1.51
Napa	26	$12	15.3	58	1.70	3.79

Oakland	813	$ 5	412.0	1044	1.97	2.53
Oceanside	68	$ 4	22.4	57	3.04	2.54
Orange	none	no fee	16.7	23		1.38
Oxnard	75	$ 5	31.9	81	2.35	2.54
Palm Springs	na	$500	12.2	43		3.52
Palo Alto	none	no fee	45.8	59		1.29
Paso Robles	30	$ 20	6.2	33	4.84	5.32
Petaluma	65	$ 15	10.3	43	6.31	4.17
Pomona	na	$ 50	60.1	102		1.70
Porterville	none	no fee	7.8	47		6.03
Redding	na	$ 4	11.9	63		5.29
Redlands	14	$ 36	22.7	29	0.62	1.28
Redondo Beach	55	$ 10	42.9	55	1.28	1.28
Redwood City	33	$ 12	46.0	79	0.72	1.72
Richmond	82	$ 18	77.8	149	1.05	1.92
Sacramento	351	$ 7	166.2	618	2.11	3.72
San Bernardino	114	$ 10	89.4	196	1.28	2.19
San Diego	800	$ 5	505.9	832	1.58	1.64
San Francisco	396	$ 12	814.4	2602	0.49	3.19
Riverside	71	$ 50	76.3	121	0.93	1.59
Roseville	30	$ 5	10.3	32	2.91	3.11
San Leandro	75	$ 10	51.5	100	1.46	1.94
San Luis Obispo	na	$ 4	17.2	45		2.62
San Jose	204	$ 8	133.0	321	1.53	2.41
San Mateo	50	$ 15	66.6	100	0.75	1.50
San Rafael	39	$ 6	16.5	65	2.36	3.94
Santa Ana	65	$ 15	71.9	136	0.90	1.89
Santa Barbara	500	$ 7.50	56.9	131	8.79	2.30
Santa Cruz	102	$ 20	23.3	119	4.38	5.11
Santa Monica	na	$ 10	82.1	208		2.53
Santa Paula	30	$ 24	12.2	29	2.46	2.38
Santa Rosa	89	$ 25	34.3	87	2.59	2.54
Stockton	256	$ 15	85.5	341	2.99	3.99
Vallejo	none	no fee	44.1	115		2.61
Ventura	40	$ 5	26.8	62	1.49	2.31
Watsonville	53	$ 12	11.6	64	4.57	5.52
Whittier	5	$ 30	35.0	77	0.14	2.20

COLORADO

Alamosa	na	$ 25	5.4	16		2.96
Colorado Springs	84	$ 15	65.0	138	1.29	2.12
Denver	518	$ 12.50	514.9	802	1.01	1.56
Durango	30	$ 65	9.5	24	3.16	2.53
Fort Collins	none	no fee	14.9	37		2.48
Grand Junction	30	$ 15	14.5	32	2.07	2.21
Greeley	none	no fee	27.5	44		1.60
La Junta	24	$ 12.50	7.7	27	3.12	3.51
Lamar	20	$ 5	6.8	25	2.94	3.68
Loveland	none	no fee	6.8	27		3.97
Montrose	10	$ 10	5.0	14	2.00	2.80
Pueblo	162	$ 15	98.0	181	1.65	1.85

KEY TO TABLE HEADINGS

A Number of Licensed Boxes   D Eating and Drinking Places
B Per License Tax or Fee   E # of Licensed Boxes per 1,000 Pop
C Population (000)   F # of E&D Places per 1,000 Pop

	A	*B*	*C*	*D*	*E*	*F*
Rocky Ford	16	$ 5	4.1	16	3.90	3.90
Salida	17	$10	4.6	20	3.70	4.35
Sterling	none	no fee	7.5	27		3.60
Trinidad	na	$12	12.2	50		4.10
Walsenburg	22	$ 5	5.6	26	3.93	4.64

CONNECTICUT

Bridgeport	none	no fee	170.0	391		2.30
Bristol	none	no fee	43.4	79		1.82
Hartford	1000	$ 6	186.8	439	5.35	2.35
Meriden	none	no fee	48.3	120		2.48
Naugatuck	none	no fee	20.5	52		2.54
New Britain	71	$10	85.9	153	0.83	1.78
New London	20	$ 5	31.1	109	0.64	3.50
Norwich	none	no fee	40.8	65		1.59
Stamford	none	no fee	85.6	181		2.11
Torrington	none	no fee	28.9	65		2.25

DELAWARE

Dover	na	$ 5	7.6	19		2.50

FLORIDA

Bradenton	48	$25	22.7	46	2.11	2.03
Daytona Beach	81	$12	49.4	143	1.64	2.89
De Land	9	$20	8.7	28	1.03	3.22
Fort Lauderdale	332	$15	76.1	214	4.36	2.81
Fort Myers	na	$35	13.2	51		3.86
Fort Pierce	81	$10	23.9	53	3.39	2.22
Gainesville	47	$ 5	36.9	47	1.27	1.27
Jacksonville	300	$ 2.50	238.1	430	1.26	1.81
Key West	75	$15	40.2	98	1.87	2.44
Lake Wales	12	$25	6.8	17	1.76	2.50
Leesburg	30	$10	7.4	24	4.05	3.24
Marianna	19	$12.50	5.8	22	3.28	3.79
Melbourne	na	$10	4.2	39		9.29
Miami	na	$18.75	272.4	1140		4.19
Miami Beach	162	$30.00	54.1	268	2.99	4.95
Orlando	na	$12.50	80.8	208		2.57
Palatka	120	$40.00	9.2	35	13.04	3.80
Panama	60	$25	33.1	75	1.81	2.27
Pensacola	na	$10	52.8	139		2.63
St Augustine	100	$ 7.50	13.6	81	7.35	5.96

Sanford	50	$25	11.9	28	4.20	2.35
Sarasota	na	$10	35.4	66		1.86
Tallahassee	165	$20	46.1	66	3.58	1.43
Tampa	600	$15	259.9	550	2.31	2.12
West Palm Beach	129	$12.50	62.8	173	2.05	2.75

GEORGIA

Albany	na	$10	42.6	55		1.29
Americus	40	$20	11.4	15	3.51	1.32
Athens	45	$13	34.5	45	1.30	1.30
Atlanta	na	$30	509.2	731		1.44
Augusta	na	$25	109.1	174		1.59
Cartersville	13	$15	7.3	15	1.78	2.05
Cedartown	15	$25	9.5	11	1.58	1.16
Columbus	224	$25	97.0	183	2.31	1.89
Dublin	44	$33	10.2	25	4.31	2.45
Gainesville	na	$10	11.9	22		1.85
Griffin	43	$20	14.0	39	3.07	2.79
Macon	81	$25	85.2	139	0.95	1.63
Moultrie	20	$20	11.6	23	1.72	1.98
Rome	125	$10	35.6	77	3.51	2.16
Savannah	na	$25	137.1	193		1.41
Thomasville	50	$27.50	22.4	22	2.23	0.98
Tifton	18	$20	6.3	17	2.86	2.70
West Point	10	$10	4.1	7	2.44	1.71

IDAHO

Boise	none	no fee	35.1	111		3.16
Caldwell	none	no fee	12.2	29		2.38
Idaho Falls	none	no fee	26.8	58		2.16
Lewiston	none	no fee	13.0	66		5.08
Nampa	none	no fee	20.2	43		2.13
Pocatello	44	$10	27.9	74	1.58	2.65
Twin Falls	none	no fee	23.5	58		2.47

ILLINOIS

Alton	na	$15	35.6	106		2.98
Aurora	92	$10	57.8	122	1.59	2.11
Beardstown	none	no fee	6.1	23		3.77
Belleville	none	no fee	36.6	120		3.28
Benton	12	$25	7.8	17	1.54	2.18
Canton	none	no fee	11.9	37		3.11
Casey	none	no fee	2.7	17		6.30
Centralia	55	$20	13.9	51	3.96	3.67
Charleston	9	$25	9.2	23	0.98	2.50
Chicago	8513	$25	3820.4	9044	2.23	2.37
Clinton	21	$20	5.9	20	3.56	3.39
Decatur	143	$30	74.1	176	1.93	2.38
Dixon	none	no fee	18.9	32		1.69
Edwardsville	5	$10	8.8	32	0.57	3.64
Elgin	55	$10	49.9	90	1.10	1.80

KEY TO TABLE HEADINGS

A Number of Licensed Boxes	D Eating and Drinking Places
B Per License Tax or Fee	E # of Licensed Boxes per 1,000 Pop
C Population (000)	F # of E&D Places per 1,000 Pop

	A	*B*	*C*	*D*	*E*	*F*
Flora	20	$25	5.3	15	3.77	2.83
Galesburg	none	no fee	36.1	79		2.19
Hoopeston	14	$25	6.0	17	2.33	2.83
Jacksonville	none	no fee	25.8	56		2.17
Joliet	none	no fee	64.5	236		3.66
Kewanee	45	$15	16.8	55	2.68	3.27
Lincoln	none	no fee	16.4	35		2.13
Macomb	none	no fee	10.5	28		2.67
Mattoon	42	$12	20.1	46	2.09	2.29
Monmouth	20	$20	10.2	25	1.96	2.45
Murphysboro	22	$15	9.2	34	2.39	3.70
Olney	12	$15	8.6	23	1.40	2.67
Ottawa	41	$15	17.0	85	2.41	5.00
Paris	26	$25	9.8	36	2.65	3.67
Pekin	25	$15	25.9	53	0.97	2.05
Peoria	303	$12	119.3	340	2.54	2.85
Pontiac	none	no fee	9.0	25		2.78
Quincy	223	$15	43.4	157	5.14	3.62
Rock Falls	na	$20	10.2	23		2.25
Rockford	none	no fee	123.3	273		2.21
Rock Island	124	$25	52.0	157	2.38	3.02
Springfield	174	$35	90.3	348	1.93	3.85
Taylorville	20	$25	9.2	45	2.17	4.89
Waukegan	105	$25	50.1	148	2.10	2.95

INDIANA

Alexandria	none	no fee	5.1	17		3.33
Attica	none	no fee	3.9	13		3.33
Bicknell	7	$ 4	4.8	18	1.46	3.75
Columbia City	none	no fee	4.7	15		3.19
Connersville	none	no fee	15.6	31		1.99
Elwood	none	no fee	11.4	23		2.02
Evansville	200	$ 3	142.5	351	1.40	2.46
Fort Wayne	none	no fee	148.2	298		2.01
Frankfort	none	no fee	15.0	34		2.27
Hammond	none	no fee	107.9	178		1.65
Huntington	none	no fee	15.1	38		2.52
Indianapolis	na	$ 1	463.2	933		2.01
Jasper	none	no fee	5.2	16		3.08
Lafayette	none	no fee	42.6	88		2.07
La Porte	none	no fee	21.9	49		2.24
Linton	none	no fee	6.0	24		4.00

Martinsville	none	no fee	6.0	13		2.17
Michigan City	50	$ 5	32.4	84	1.54	2.59
New Castle	none	no fee	22.3	35		1.57
Plymouth	na	na	7.3	18		2.47
Portland	none	no fee	7.1	25		3.52
Rensselaer	none	no fee	4.1	10		2.44
Richmond	none	no fee	46.4	94		2.03
Rochester	none	no fee	4.7	13		2.77
Spencer	8	$12	2.4	na	3.33	
Terre Haute	none	no fee	80.9	212		2.62
Tipton	none	no fee	5.6	16		2.86
Valparaiso	none	no fee	13.4	31		2.31
Vincenness	none	no fee	21.5	49		2.28
Warsaw	none	no fee	6.6	23		3.48

IOWA

Ames	none	no fee	26.5	47		1.77
Atlantic	11	$10	6.5	23	1.69	3.54
Burlington	none	no fee	32.5	82		2.52
Carroll	none	no fee	6.2	31		5.00
Cedar Falls	none	no fee	14.3	32		2.24
Cedar Rapids	none	no fee	85.7	165		1.93
Carterville	none	no fee	7.6	22		2.89
Charles City	none	no fee	10.3	25		2.43
Cherokee	none	no fee	7.7	21		2.73
Clinton	none	no fee	35.3	80		2.27
Creston	none	no fee	8.3	31		3.73
Davenport	125	$25	85.9	214	1.46	2.49
Des Moines	none	no fee	209.1	475		2.27
Estherville	none	no fee	6.7	17		2.54
Fairfield	none	no fee	7.3	21		2.88
Fort Madison	none	no fee	15.0	33		2.20
Iowa City	none	no fee	34.7	59		1.70
Marshalltown	none	no fee	21.7	55		2.53
Mount Pleasant	none	no fee	5.8	26		4.48
Newton	none	no fee	13.6	32		2.35
Oskaloosa	none	no fee	11.1	40		3.60
Perry	none	no fee	6.2	15		2.42
Spencer	none	no fee	7.4	20		2.70
Vinton	none	no fee	4.3	17		3.95
Washington	none	no fee	5.9	23		3.90
Waterloo	none	no fee	76.1	164		2.16

KANSAS

Abilene	10	$12	5.8	24	1.72	4.14
Arkansas City	none	no fee	12.9	41		3.18
Atchison	28	$10	12.8	40	2.19	3.13
Burlington	10	$ 5	2.3	na	4.35	
Cherryvale	none	no fee	3.0	8		2.67
Clay Center	18	$10	4.5	20	4.00	4.44
Coffeyville	none	no fee	18.0	49		2.72

KEY TO TABLE HEADINGS

A Number of Licensed Boxes   D Eating and Drinking Places
B Per License Tax or Fee   E # of Licensed Boxes per 1,000 Pop
C Population (000)   F # of E&D Places per 1,000 Pop

	A	*B*	*C*	*D*	*E*	*F*
Concordia	20	$15	7.0	21	2.86	3.00
Council Grove	7	$10	2.8	11	2.50	3.93
Dodge City	20	$ 5	11.4	43	1.75	3.77
El Dorado	18	$25	12.3	31	1.46	2.52
Emporia	na	$ 5	14.7	36		2.45
Fredonia	22	$16	3.3	8	6.67	2.42
Garden City	26	$ 5	10.8	30	2.41	2.78
Goodland	na	$25	4.5	9		2.00
Hays	24	$20	9.5	26	2.53	2.74
Hutchinson	69	$15	43.2	124	1.60	2.87
Independence	na	$10	11.8	27		2.29
Iola	na	$12	6.8	20		2.94
Junction City	45	$30	14.0	40	3.21	2.86
Kansas City	none	no fee	137.4	294		2.14
Lawrence	none	no fee	24.0	59		2.46
Leavenworth	77	$10	22.0	76	3.50	3.45
Liberall	20	$20	8.3	24	2.41	2.89
Manhattan	38	$15	21.6	49	1.76	2.27
McPherson	13	$ 5	8.6	13	1.51	1.51
Neodesha	none	no fee	4.1	13		3.17
Newton	25	$15	12.5	26	2.00	2.08
Ottawa	none	no fee	10.3	21		2.04
Parsons	none	no fee	15.5	30		1.94
Pittsburg	97	$ 5	24.1	63	4.02	2.61
Pratt	none	no fee	8.3	21		2.53
Salina	50	$15	33.1	104	1.51	3.14
Topeka	160	$ 7.50	100.7	212	1.59	2.11
Wellington	none	no fee	9.0	22		2.44

KENTUCKY

	A	*B*	*C*	*D*	*E*	*F*
Ashland	31	$10	33.6	41	0.92	1.22
Frankfort	40	$10	26.2	34	1.53	1.30
Fulton	12	$10	3.2	11	3.75	3.44
Glasgow	15	$10	7.0	15	2.14	2.14
Henderson	50	$10	16.0	43	3.13	2.69
Lexington	500	$10	59.2	184	8.45	3.11
Louisville	957	$15	618.4	940	1.55	1.52
Madisonville	none	no fee	11.1	23		2.07
Mayfield	25	$10	9.0	22	2.78	2.44
Paducah	200	$10	50.1	121	3.99	2.42
Paris	30	$10	6.9	21	4.35	3.04
Richmond	na	$10	10.3	29		2.82

LOUISIANA

Alexandria	94	$ 10	43.5	110	2.16	2.53
Baton Rouge	350	$ 10	159.1	222	2.20	1.40
Crowley	32	$ 10	12.8	39	2.50	3.05
Jennings	none	no fee	10.7	13		1.21
Lafayette	na	$ 10	48.8	95		1.95
Opelousas	59	$ 10	11.7	45	5.04	3.85
Shreveport	na	$ 10	158.9	247		1.55

MAINE

Bath	none	no fee	10.6	19		1.79
Portland	none	no fee	80.6	138		1.71
Waterville	none	no fee	19.4	49		2.53

MARYLAND

Baltimore	2550	$ 25	1001.9	2516	2.55	2.51
Cumberland	none	no fee	39.4	112		2.84
Frederick	none	no fee	20.9	66		3.16
Hagerstown	none	no fee	40.1	120		2.99
Salisbury	none	no fee	15.1	40		2.65

MASSACHUSETTS

Boston	950	$100	714.1	1703	1.33	2.38
Fall River	none	no fee	110.1	208		1.89
Fitchburg	67	$ 5	43.5	82	1.54	1.89
Framingham	37	$ 5	31.6	na	1.17	
Gardner	5	$ 50	20.1	33	0.25	1.64
Gloucester	27	$ 5	26.2	52	1.03	1.98
Haverhill	none	no fee	47.6	86		1.81
Holyoke	none	no fee	55.5	117		2.11
Lowell	none	no fee	94.6	180		1.90
Lynn	none	no fee	102.2	194		1.90
Malden	none	no fee	61.2	68		1.11
New Beford	238	$ 5	108.9	239	2.19	2.19
Newbury	15	$ 2	14.1	36	1.06	2.55
North Adams	na	$ 5	21.5	39		1.81
Worchester	200	$ 50	204.8	371	0.98	1.81

MICHIGAN

Adrian	na	$ 10	23.5	39		1.66
Albion	18	$ 10	10.4	31	1.73	2.98
Ann Arbor	none	no fee	64.1	85		1.33
Bay City	143	$ 5	61.0	142	2.34	2.33
Benton Harbor	49	$ 15	20.6	63	2.38	3.06
Big Rapids	25	$ 12	6.7	19	3.73	2.84
Cadillac	14	$ 5	10.4	14	1.35	1.35
Cheboygan	none	no fee	5.7	22		3.86
Detroit	4170	$ 25	1930.1	4206	2.16	2.18
Dowagiac	na	$ 10	6.5	14		2.15
Escanaba	none	no fee	15.2	54		3.55

KEY TO TABLE HEADINGS

A Number of Licensed Boxes   D Eating and Drinking Places
B Per License Tax or Fee   E # of Licensed Boxes per 1,000 Pop
C Population (000)   F # of E&D Places per 1,000 Pop

	A	*B*	*C*	*D*	*E*	*F*
Flint	na	$10	100.5	421		4.19
Grand Rapids	240	$15	196.2	364	1.22	1.86
Greenville	na	$ 7.50	6.7	13		1.94
Hillsdale	none	no fee	7.3	18		2.47
Ludington	none	no fee	9.5	26		2.74
Marshall	16	$10	5.8	19	2.76	3.28
Menminee	none	no fee	11.2	34		3.04
Mount Pleasant	20	$ 5	11.4	35	1.75	3.07
Niles	21	$25	13.1	41	1.60	3.13
Royal Oak	none	no fee	76.9	72		0.94
Saginaw	na	$10	105.0	195		1.86
Sault Sainte Marie	na	$ 2	20.3	41		2.02
Traverse City	none	no fee	17.0	39		2.29
Ypsilanti	none	no fee	21.9	41		1.87

MINNESOTA

	A	*B*	*C*	*D*	*E*	*F*
Austin	none	no fee	29.0	68		2.34
Bemidji	na	na	10.0	28		2.80
Brainerd	36	$10	12.6	35	2.86	2.78
Crookston	none	no fee	7.4	18		2.43
Duluth	87	$20.25	113.7	215	0.77	1.89
Fergus Falls	na	$ 7.50	12.9	29		2.25
Little Falls	none	no fee	6.7	22		3.28
Marshall	none	no fee	5.9	14		2.37
Minneapolis	769	$14	561.7	1120	1.37	1.99
Moorhead	21	$12	14.9	23	1.41	1.54
New Ulm	31	$12	9.3	41	3.33	4.41
Red Wing	none	no fee	10.6	32		3.02
Rochester	none	no fee	34.9	91		2.61
St Cloud	none	no fee	33.6	69		2.05
St Paul	459	$10	347.2	618	1.32	1.78
Stillwater	18	$10	7.7	19	2.34	2.47
Willmar	na	na	9.4	26		2.77
Winona	none	no fee	28.5	81		2.84

MISSISSIPPI

	A	*B*	*C*	*D*	*E*	*F*
Clarksdale	35	$ 5	16.5	36	2.12	2.18
Greenville	450	$ 5	36.7	49	12.26	1.34
Greenport	35	$ 5	21.1	32	1.66	1.52
Gulfport	80	$ 5	31.4	59	2.55	1.88
Jackson	275	$ 5	124.1	181	2.22	1.46
Laurel	100	$ 5	29.1	45	3.44	1.55

McComb	na	$ 5	10.4	23		2.21
Meridian	125	$ 5	48.1	71	2.60	1.48
Vicksburg	157	$ 5	32.3	52	4.86	1.61

MISSOURI

Carthage	12	$10	11.2	26	1.07	2.32
Excelsior Springs	none	no fee	5.9	23		3.90
Festus	none	no fee	5.2	16		3.08
Independence	na	$15	54.9	68		1.24
Jefferson City	na	$ 5	33.8	55		1.63
Joplin	63	$ 5	41.9	141	1.50	3.37
Lamar	none	no fee	3.2	13		4.06
Lexington	none	no fee	5.1	20		3.92
Macon	na	$25	4.2	10		2.38
Marshall	none	no fee	8.9	27		3.03
Mexico	none	no fee	11.6	24		2.07
Moberly	none	no fee	13.1	32		2.44
Neosho	na	$10	5.8	20		3.45
Nevada	none	no fee	8.0	27		3.38
Poplar Bluff	none	no fee	15.1	49		3.25
Rolla	none	no fee	9.4	24		2.55
St Charles	8	$10	14.3	48	0.56	3.36
St Joseph	na	$10	83.1	226		2.72
St Louis	na	$ 1	852.7	2682		3.15
Sedalia	none	no fee	28.8	56		1.94
Springfield	100	$ 5	96.9	189	1.03	1.95
Trenton	none	no fee	6.2	26		4.19

MONTANA

Billings	65	$25	47.1	91	1.38	1.93
Glendive	none	no fee	5.3	19		3.58
Great Falls	none	no fee	50.9	100		1.96
Havre	none	no fee	8.1	32		3.95
Helena	none	no fee	22.3	55		2.47
Kalispell	none	no fee	9.7	35		3.61
Miles City	none	no fee	9.2	28		3.04

NEBRASKA

Beatrice	none	no fee	11.8	31		2.63
Columbus	none	no fee	8.9	39		4.38
Fairbury	none	no fee	6.4	14		2.19
Falls City	none	no fee	6.2	24		3.87
Fremont	none	no fee	20.1	46		2.29
Holdrege	na	na	4.4	14		3.18
Kearney	18	$10	14.4	36	1.25	2.50
Lincoln	77	$10	124.9	202	0.62	1.62
Nebraska City	none	no fee	6.9	31		4.49
Norfolk	none	no fee	11.3	43		3.81
North Platte	37	$ 5	15.4	53	2.40	3.44
Omaha	389	$10	297.4	619	1.31	2.08
York	na	na	6.2	19		3.06

KEY TO TABLE HEADINGS

A Number of Licensed Boxes   D Eating and Drinking Places
B Per License Tax or Fee   E # of Licensed Boxes per 1,000 Pop
C Population (000)   F # of E&D Places per 1,000 Pop

	A	*B*	*C*	*D*	*E*	*F*
			NEVADA			
Carson City	na	$20	4.7	26		5.53
Elko	none	no fee	5.4	33		6.11
Ely	25	$20	3.6	17	6.94	4.72
Las Vegas	115	$40	51.4	121	2.24	2.35
Reno	99	$26	51.1	161	1.94	3.15
			NEW HAMPSHIRE			
Manchester	19	$10	86.8	148	0.22	1.71
Nashua	none	no fee	37.5	68		1.81
Portsmouth	none	no fee	20.8	54		2.60
			NEW JERSEY			
Atlantic City	243	$30	60.1	492	4.04	8.19
Camden	253	$25	140.4	346	1.80	2.46
Morristown	none	no fee	21.4	42		1.96
Newark	none	no fee	476.3	1447		3.04
Paterson	none	no fee	147.4	459		3.11
Perth Amboy	81	$25	45.5	143	1.78	3.14
Trenton	250	$15	137.5	519	1.82	3.77
Vineland	none	no fee	42.2	66		1.56
Woodbury	8	$50	10.9	16	0.73	1.47
			NEW MEXICO			
Alamogordo	50	$20	6.8	23	7.35	3.38
Albuquerque	na	$ 6	181.9	342		1.88
Artesia	na	na	8.2	18		2.20
Clovis	150	$ 5	24.9	34	6.02	1.37
Farmington	9	$40	18.4	31	0.49	1.68
Gallup	464	$15	9.1	60	50.99	6.59
Hobbs	80	$10	29.8	41	2.68	1.38
Las Cruces	na	na	12.3	42		3.41
Las Vegas	30	$12	7.2	17	4.17	2.36
Raton	35	$20	8.2	36	4.27	4.39
Roswell	none	no fee	34.7	66		1.90
Santa Fe	250	$10	34.3	88	7.29	2.57
Silver City	24	$ 2.50	7.0	23	3.43	3.29
			NEW YORK			
Amsterdam	none	no fee	31.3	123		3.93
Batavia	none	no fee	17.8	57		3.20
Binghampton	none	no fee	80.8	254		3.14

Buffalo	1475	$20	581.3	1642	2.54	2.82
Corning	none	no fee	19.6	52		2.65
Cortland	na	$25	20.1	69		3.43
Dunkirk	none	no fee	18.0	69		3.83
Elmira	none	no fee	51.7	158		3.06
Endicott	na	na	22.8	85		3.73
Geneva	12	$15	17.1	61	0.70	3.57
Glens Falls	none	no fee	20.4	68		3.33
Gloversville	none	no fee	24.2	67		2.77
Hudson	none	no fee	11.6	52		4.48
Ithaca	none	no fee	31.5	74		2.35
Jamestown	82	$10	42.9	115	1.91	2.68
Kingston	none	no fee	30.8	117		3.80
Lockport	none	no fee	26.4	85		3.22
Medina	none	no fee	6.2	16		2.58
Middletown	none	no fee	23.7	90		3.80
Mount Vernon	none	no fee	76.4	143		1.87
Newburgh	none	no fee	32.6	150		4.60
New Rochelle	none	no fee	74.9	123		1.64
New York	na	$ 1	7838.0	7088		0.90
Niagara Falls	none	no fee	102.3	348		3.40
North Tonawanda	none	no fee	31.6	70		2.22
Norwich	none	no fee	8.8	37		4.20
Ogdensburg	none	no fee	16.2	35		2.16
Olean	none	no fee	24.2	59		2.44
Oneida	36	$ 5	11.3	29	3.19	2.57
Oneonta	56	$25	13.6	52	4.12	3.82
Ossining	none	no fee	16.1	41		2.55
Oswego	none	no fee	23.3	81		3.48
Peekskill	none	no fee	17.7	79		4.46
Plattsburgh	62	$27.50	18.9	56	3.28	2.96
Port Jervis	none	no fee	9.4	47		5.00
Poughkeepsie	none	no fee	44.8	155		3.46
Salamanca	none	no fee	8.9	28		3.15
Saranac Lake	none	no fee	6.9	29		4.20
Sarasota Springs	na	na	15.5	92		5.94
Saugerties	none	no fee	3.9	35		8.97
Syracuse	434	$15	215.6	547	2.01	2.54
Watertown	100	$25	35.9	79	2.79	2.20
White Plains	none	no fee	50.7	144		2.84

NORTH CAROLINA

Asheville	87	$ 5	59.0	126	1.47	2.14
Charlotte	200	$ 5	163.0	285	1.23	1.75
Durham	95	$ 5	77.3	129	1.23	1.67
Elizabeth	35	$ 5	12.7	19	2.76	1.50
Fayettevile	75	$ 5	49.7	104	1.51	2.09
Gastonia	na	$ 5	36.2	57		1.57
Goldsboro	25	$ 5	27.9	27	0.90	0.97
Greensboro	385	$ 5	94.7	152	4.07	1.61
Greenville	12	$ 5	20.6	60	0.58	2.91

KEY TO TABLE HEADINGS

A Number of Licensed Boxes   D Eating and Drinking Places
B Per License Tax or Fee   E # of Licensed Boxes per 1,000 Pop
C Population (000)   F # of E&D Places per 1,000 Pop

	A	B	C	D	E	F
Hickory	na	$ 5	14.8	35		2.36
Lenoir	20	$ 5	10.8	21	1.85	1.94
Lexington	20	$10	13.6	34	1.47	2.50
Lumberton	na	$ 5	14.4	18		1.25
Reidsville	19	$ 5	11.7	25	1.62	2.14
Rocky Mount	43	$ 5	34.1	47	1.26	1.38
Sanford	na	$ 5	10.0	14		1.40
Spencer	5	$ 5	3.2	8	1.56	2.50
Statesville	30	$ 5	20.8	32	1.44	1.54
Washington	18	$ 5	9.7	28	1.86	2.89
Wilmington	85	$ 5	54.6	113	1.56	2.07
Wilson	35	$ 5	26.8	44	1.31	1.64
Winston-Salem	130	$ 5	120.2	176	1.08	1.46

NORTH DAKOTA

	A	B	C	D	E	F
Dickinson	none	no fee	7.5	24		3.20
Grand Forks	none	no fee	33.4	65		1.95
Minot	none	no fee	30.9	51		1.65
Williston	none	no fee	10.9	28		2.57

OHIO

	A	B	C	D	E	F
Akron	none	no fee	305.9	668		2.18
Ashland	none	no fee	14.3	38		2.66
Athens	none	no fee	13.5	41		3.04
Bellevue	none	no fee	6.9	16		2.32
Cambridge	19	$10	14.7	49	1.29	3.33
Canton	225	$15	124.7	356	1.80	2.85
Celina	none	no fee	5.7	14		2.46
Chillicothe	none	no fee	28.1	72		2.56
Cincinnati	none	no fee	549.1	1253		2.28
Cleveland	1580	$ 5	913.1	2377	1.73	2.60
Columbus	657	$10	450.9	932	1.46	2.07
Defiance	na	$ 5	11.3	32		2.83
Delaware	24	$ 1	11.8	31	2.03	2.63
Dover	32	$10	9.9	29	3.23	2.93
Elyria	none	no fee	36.7	75		2.04
Galion	none	no fee	10.0	27		2.70
Ironton	32	$12	16.3	52	1.96	3.19
Lima	none	no fee	59.0	147		2.49
Lorain	175	$15	55.0	147	3.18	2.67
Marion	60	$ 1	38.8	85	1.55	2.19
Massillon	45	$15	36.4	81	1.24	2.23

Middletown	none	no fee	44.1	92		2.09
Mount Vernon	none	no fee	12.2	34		2.79
Painesville	none	no fee	14.4	24		1.67
Portsmouth	130	$ 10	44.3	105	2.93	2.37
Sandusky	none	no fee	31.1	107		3.44
Sidney	none	no fee	11.5	19		1.65
Tiffin	none	no fee	22.9	44		1.92
Toledo	804	$ 25	332.1	879	2.42	2.65
Troy	none	no fee	10.7	19		1.78
Urbana	none	no fee	9.3	22		2.37
Van Wert	none	no fee	10.4	26		2.50
Warren	none	no fee	59.1	156		2.64
Wilmington	none	no fee	7.4	16		2.16
Wooster	none	no fee	14.0	45		3.21
Youngstown	350	$ 5	182.9	411	1.91	2.25
Zanesville	132	$ 10	45.5	132	2.90	2.90

OKLAHOMA

Ada	20	$ 6	16.0	44	1.25	2.75
Chickasha	none	no fee	15.8	31		1.96
Claremore	13	$ 10	5.5	23	2.36	4.18
Clinton	32	$ 5	7.6	23	4.21	3.03
Cushing	none	no fee	8.4	20		2.38
Duncan	none	no fee	15.3	40		2.61
Elk City	none	no fee	8.0	26		3.25
El Reno	25	$ 10	11.0	33	2.27	3.00
Enid	31	$ 20	43.2	93	0.72	2.15
Guthrie	25	$ 10	10.1	28	2.48	2.77
Guymon	none	no fee	4.7	22		4.68
Henryetta	31	$ 10	8.0	34	3.88	4.25
Hugo	na	$ 10	6.0	11		1.83
Muskogee	48	$ 20	39.6	94	1.21	2.37
Nowata	none	no fee	4.0	16		4.00
Okemah	none	no fee	3.5	20		5.71
Oklahoma City	550	$ 5	301.7	665	1.82	2.20
Shawnee	37	$ 20	31.4	54	1.18	1.72
Tulsa	414	$ 10	258.2	496	1.60	1.92

OREGON

Artoria	25	$ 10	12.3	48	2.03	3.90
Baker	17	$200	9.5	29	1.79	3.05
Bend	20	$ 24	11.4	28	1.75	2.46
Coosbay	26	$ 12	6.2	36	4.19	5.81
Corvalis	10	$ 20	21.9	33	0.46	1.51
Eugene	44	$ 12	47.1	103	0.93	2.19
Grants Pass	none	no fee	8.1	41		5.06
Klamath Falls	50	na	15.9	70	3.14	4.40
Medford	25	$ 10	22.9	53	1.09	2.31
Pendleton	28	$ 20	11.8	38	2.37	3.22
Portland	552	$ 25	416.7	1171	1.32	2.81
The Dalles	25	$ 35	9.9	29	2.53	2.93

KEY TO TABLE HEADINGS

A Number of Licensed Boxes   D Eating and Drinking Places
B Per License Tax or Fee   E # of Licensed Boxes per 1,000 Pop
C Population (000)   F # of E&D Places per 1,000 Pop

	A	B	C	D	E	F
			PENNSYLVANIA			
Altoona	100	$30	77.1	134	1.30	1.74
Ambridge	80	$15	16.4	80	4.88	4.88
Ashland	none	no fee	6.2	26		4.19
Bangor	14	$15	6.1	17	2.30	2.79
Beaver	3	$15	6.4	8	0.47	1.25
Beaver Falls	43	$25	17.4	42	2.47	2.41
Bedford	none	no fee	3.5	14		4.00
Bethlehem	none	no fee	74.3	168		2.26
Butler	43	$12	23.4	53	1.84	2.26
Bloomsburg	none	no fee	10.6	43		4.06
Carlisle	27	$15	16.8	42	1.61	2.50
Chambersburg	none	no fee	20.3	49		2.41
Chester	none	no fee	69.1	259		3.75
Coatesville	39	$35	13.8	39	2.83	2.83
Columbia	31	$25	12.0	29	2.58	2.42
Connellsville	35	$50	13.3	41	2.63	3.08
Easton	83	na	38.0	120	2.18	3.16
Erie	245	$25	136.6	350	1.79	2.56
Greensburg	none	no fee	16.9	61		3.61
Hanover	29	$25	14.0	43	2.07	3.07
Harrisburg	222	$ 7.50	93.0	292	2.39	3.14
Hazleton	100	$10	35.4	88	2.82	2.49
Huntingdon	none	no fee	7.3	22		3.01
Jersey Shore	35	$20	5.6	16	6.25	2.86
Johnstown	180	$25	65.1	161	2.76	2.47
Lancaster	159	$15	67.0	170	2.37	2.54
Latrobe	41	$25	11.8	30	3.47	2.54
Lewistown	none	no fee	13.9	47		3.38
Mahanoy	none	no fee	10.9	58		5.32
Meadville	59	$ 7.50	20.3	53	2.91	2.61
Milton	na	$15	8.6	26		3.02
Monessen	25	$25	17.9	48	1.40	2.68
Monongahela	25	$25	8.9	22	2.81	2.47
New Castle	110	$15	51.2	101	2.15	1.97
New Kensington	40	$20	26.6	65	1.50	2.44
Norristown	na	$50	41.3	119		2.88
Philadelphia	5118	$25	2180.2	4852	2.35	2.23
Philipsburg	none	no fee	4.0	16		4.00
Phoenixville	none	no fee	13.0	33		2.54
Pittsburgh	none	no fee	679.8	1457		2.14
Pittston	37	$15	21.2	52	1.75	2.45

Pottstown	50	$15	25.4	59	1.97	2.32
Pottsville	none	no fee	23.4	76		3.25
Punxsutawney	none	no fee	9.0	22		2.44
Reading	358	$20	111.8	319	3.20	2.85
Scranton	200	$10	130.5	332	1.53	2.54
Somerset	24	$25	5.9	16	4.07	2.71
Stroudsburg	none	no fee	6.4	30		4.69
Susquehanna	15	$25	2.6	16	5.77	6.15
Tamaqua	none	no fee	11.5	51		4.43
Tarentum	23	$25	18.9	29	1.22	1.53
Titusville	53	$25	8.9	18	5.96	2.02
Uniontown	na	$50	20.0	113		5.65
Vandergrift	none	no fee	9.5	24		2.53
West Chester	none	no fee	15.2	57		3.75
Wilkes-Barre	500	$ 5	73.3	312	6.82	4.26
York	128	$ 5	63.4	206	2.02	3.25

RHODE ISLAND

Newport	200	$25	43.1	92	4.64	2.13
Pawtucket	none	no fee	85.6	200		2.34
Providence	none	no fee	232.7	653		2.81
West Warwick	none	no fee	21.0	83		3.95

SOUTH CAROLINA

Aiken	18	$ 7.50	11.2	26	1.61	2.32
Florence	45	$12.50	27.2	52	1.65	1.91
Rock Hill	na	$ 7.50	30.1	38		1.26
Union	17	$ 7.50	9.7	17	1.75	1.75

SOUTH DAKOTA

Huron	none	no fee	14.8	39		2.64
Madison	5	$15	5.2	13	0.96	2.50
Pierre	none	no fee	7.2	29		4.03
Watertown	none	no fee	14.7	48		3.27

TENNESSEE

Chattanoga	na	$ 6.50	157.1	328		2.09
Columbia	na	$ 5	10.9	28		2.57
Jackson	125	$ 8.50	36.9	80	3.39	2.17
Johnson City	33	$ 6	28.5	49	1.16	1.72
Memphis	952	$10.25	462.1	702	2.06	1.52
Morristown	35	$10	13.0	19	2.69	1.46
Murfreesboro	na	$ 7.50	13.1	34		2.60
Nashville	350	$ 5	180.9	452	1.93	2.50
Paris	18	$ 5	8.8	29	2.05	3.30
Shelbyville	na	$ 6	9.5	18		1.89
Union City	35	$ 5	7.7	39	4.55	5.06

TEXAS

Abilene	none	no fee	64.4	80		1.24
Alice	60	$ 1.25	21.4	45	2.80	2.10

KEY TO TABLE HEADINGS

A Number of Licensed Boxes		D Eating and Drinking Places	
B Per License Tax or Fee		E # of Licensed Boxes per 1,000 Pop	
C Population (000)		F # of E&D Places per 1,000 Pop	

	A	B	C	D	E	F
Beaumont	760	$ 2.50	116.7	218	6.51	1.87
Borger	37	$ 2.50	25.0	48	1.48	1.92
Bryan	139	$ 2.50	31.0	61	4.48	1.97
Childress	none	no fee	7.6	18		2.37
Cleburne	none	no fee	12.9	26		2.02
Corpus Christi	460	$ 2.50	176.8	362	2.60	2.05
Cuero	30	$ 1.25	7.5	36	4.00	4.80
Dallas	1400	$ 2.50	628.6	1279	2.23	2.03
Edinburg	none	no fee	12.4	43		3.47
El Paso	415	$ 2.50	250.1	355	1.66	1.42
Ennis	none	no fee	7.8	15		1.92
Fort Worth	na	$ 2.50	374.6	699		1.87
Garland	none	no fee	10.3	22		2.14
Greenville	none	no fee	14.7	31		2.11
Harlingen	22	$ 2.50	377.7	61	0.06	0.16
Houston	na	$ 2.50	868.7	1596		1.84
Killeen	69	$ 2.50	7.0	21	9.86	3.00
Levelland	none	no fee	8.3	13		1.57
Marshall	none	no fee	27.7	29		1.05
McKinney	none	no fee	10.5	17		1.62
Midland	none	no fee	52.8	65		1.23
Macogdoches	none	no fee	12.3	19		1.54
Orange	none	no fee	33.4	58		1.74
Pampa	na	$ 2.50	16.6	45		2.71
Palestine	na	na	12.5	19		1.52
Plainview	none	no fee	14.0	31		2.21
San Antonio	1500	$ 2.50	541.3	1209	2.77	2.23
Sherman	none	no fee	28.5	41		1.44
Snyder	none	no fee	12.0	26		2.17
Sulphur Springs	none	no fee	9.0	14		1.56
Taylor	none	no fee	9.1	48		5.27
Temple	na	$ 2.50	34.8	91		2.61
Vernon	none	no fee	12.7	40		3.15
Victoria	100	$ 2.50	23.9	84	4.18	3.51
Waco	233	$ 2.50	108.5	226	2.15	2.08
Weatherford	none	no fee	8.1	18		2.22
Wichita Falls	100	$ 2.50	110.8	165	0.90	1.49

UTAH

Ogden	103	$15	69.1	123	1.49	1.78
Provo	20	$ 5	38.6	38	0.52	0.98
Salt Lake City	253	$15	225.4	373	1.12	1.65

VERMONT

Bennington	none	no fee	12.4	22		1.77
Montpelier	none	no fee	9.2	19		2.07
Rutland	none	no fee	17.7	34		1.92
Saint Johnsbury	none	no fee	7.4	19		2.57

VIRGINIA

Alexandria	na	$ 10	93.5	102		1.09
Arlington	na	$ 5	178.5	99		0.55
Charlottesville	50	$ 5	30.3	59	1.65	1.95
Danville	na	$ 5	52.7	90		1.71
Fredericksburg	44	$ 25	12.2	50	3.61	4.10
Harrisonburg	na	$ 8.63	10.8	21		1.94
Martinsville	na	$ 15	17.3	33		1.91
Newport News	150	$ 6	48.9	142	3.07	2.90
Norfolk	475	$ 10	314.6	458	1.51	1.46
Petersburg	na	$ 5.75	39.4	81		2.06
Richmond	na	$ 10	242.7	461		1.90
Roanoke	250	$ 30	105.9	175	2.36	1.65
Strasburg	3	$ 2.50	2.3	na	1.30	
Suffolk	30	$ 18	12.3	27	2.44	2.20
Waynesboro	50	$ 10.75	12.4	21	4.03	1.69
Winchester	200	$ 5.75	13.8	62	14.49	4.49

WASHINGTON

Aberdeen	85	$180	21.8	75	3.90	3.44
Bellingham	60	$ 12	38.9	92	1.54	2.37
Ellensburg	none	no fee	8.4	25		2.98
Everett	none	no fee	37.0	111		3.00
Mount Vernon	19	$ 20	5.2	36	3.65	6.92
Port Angeles	21	$ 12	11.2	38	1.88	3.39
Seattle	1200	$ 10	581.3	1389	2.06	2.39
Spokane	none	no fee	195.5	369		1.89
Tacoma	255	$ 12	159.6	332	1.60	2.08
Vancouver	none	no fee	43.1	69		1.60
Walla Walla	none	no fee	25.9	59		2.28
Wenatchee	na	$ 10	13.1	39		2.98
Yakima	78	$ 5	45.9	122	1.70	2.66

WEST VIRGINIA

Bluefield	28	$ 25	27.2	52	1.03	1.91
Charleston	300	$ 5.50	82.5	213	3.64	2.58
Clarksburg	na	$ 40	34.9	102		2.92
Fairmont	none	no fee	32.3	83		2.57
Grafton	21	$ 5	7.4	20	2.84	2.70
Logan	na	$ 5	5.1	38		7.45
Martinsburg	na	na	15.6	41		2.63
Morgantown	40	$ 10.50	30.8	73	1.30	2.37
Parkersburg	72	$ 5.50	45.6	110	1.58	2.41
Weirton	75	$ 10	36.4	89	2.06	2.45
Wellsburg	40	$ 5	5.8	34	6.90	5.86

KEY TO TABLE HEADINGS

A Number of Licensed Boxes   D Eating and Drinking Places
B Per License Tax or Fee   E # of Licensed Boxes per 1,000 Pop
C Population (000)   F # of E&D Places per 1,000 Pop

	A	*B*	*C*	*D*	*E*	*F*
Wheeling	245	$10.50	65.1	248	3.76	3.81
Williamson	28	$12.50	8.6	21	3.26	2.44
			WISCONSIN			
Antigo	none	no fee	9.9	63		6.36
Ashland	53	$10	10.6	57	5.00	5.38
Baraboo	none	no fee	7.3	37		5.07
Beaver Dam	none	no fee	11.9	63		5.29
Chippewa Falls	23	$25	11.1	63	2.07	5.68
Eau Claire	75	$25	41.4	105	1.81	2.54
Fond du Lac	none	no fee	33.6	134		3.99
Janesville	none	no fee	31.1	97		3.12
La Crosse	150	$10	52.7	227	2.85	4.31
Madison	193	$10	122.5	268	1.58	2.19
Manitowoc	none	no fee	30.7	135		4.40
Marinette	none	no fee	14.2	72		5.07
Merrill	none	no fee	9.00	66		7.33
Milwaukee	2560	$ 5	770.2	2579	3.32	3.35
Monroe	none	no fee	7.0	33		4.71
Neenah	none	no fee	12.4	49		3.95
Oshkosh	145	$ 5	47.2	158	3.07	3.35

Source:
Billboard, May 5, 1958, pp. 52+

Appendix B

Jukebox Exports

	1939			1940		
	no.	$ value	avg. $	no.	$ value	avg. $
Argentina	11	1,073	98	14	1,798	128
Australia	39	4,383	112	4	373	93
Bahamas					125	
Belgium	5	970	194	5	645	129
Bermuda	6	1,112	185			
Brazil	16	2,917	182	41	8,403	205
British Guiana				1	135	135
British Honduras	2	320	160			
British India				2	113	57
British Malaya				2	610	305
British Poss. Misc.	4	717	179			
British West Indies	6	1,232	205	1	162	162
Canada	1,092	195,262	179	995	190,608	192
Ceylon				3	270	90
Chile				40	6,457	161
China	1	335	335	3	248	83
Colombia	23	5,856	255	109	32,873	302
Costa Rica	7	1,566	224	4	884	221
Cuba	280	62,002	221	100	17,023	170
Dominican Republic	3	330	110	18	839	47
Egypt				2	190	95
Finland	37	8,590	232			
France	15	3,756	250			
Guatemala	13	3,354	258	18	3,761	209
Germany	1	70	70			
Honduras				4	448	112
Hong Kong	2	346	173	18	3,494	194
Ireland				2	656	328
Jamaica	2	312	156	3	892	297
Mexico	1,665	279,482	168	1,676	222,993	133
Mozambique	5	2,149	430			
Netherlands	13	1,954	150	3	551	184

	no.	1939 $ value	avg. $	no.	1940 $ value	avg. $
Netherlands West Indies	6	1,042	174	9	1,627	181
New Zealand	3	307	102			
Panama (Canal Zone)	3	485	162	7	2,675	382
Panama (Republic)	25	5,103	204	121	25,808	213
Peru				8	2,612	327
Philippine Islands	42	6,884	164	80	21,759	272
Portugese Africa				1	65	65
Portugal				1	90	90
Russia				4	1,124	281
Salvador	19	4,715	248	27	4,698	174
South Africa	13	3,833	295	13	1,266	97
Spain				2	310	155
Surinam	2	195	98			
Sweden	28	3,102	111			
Thailand				3	291	97
Trinidad and Tobago				2	495	248
United Kingdom	189	34,711	184	1	113	113
Uruguay				14	1,905	136
Venezuela	11	2,439	222	34	7,602	224
other countries						
Totals	3589	640,904	179	3395	566,991	167

	no.	1945 $ value	avg. $	no.	1946 $ value	avg. $
Algeria	1	165	165			
Argentina					26,264	
Australia					500	
Azores	1	375	375			
Bahamas					125	
Belgium					8,335	
Bermuda					3,434	
Brazil	4	1,519	380		10,613	
British Guiana					1,420	
Canada	333	30,707	92	2,682	949,170	354
Chile					2,810	
China					3,010	
Columbia	121	53,500	442	358	212,410	593
Costa Rica	10	4,206	421		1,910	
Cuba	29	6,727	232	844	148,060	175
Curacao					2,157	
Dominican Republic					90	
Ecuador					2,275	
Guatemala	18	4,002	222		19,086	
Haiti	2	200	100			
Honduras	1	50	50		1,010	
Liberia	1	290	290			
Mexico	799	194,237	243	1,792	616,899	344

		1945			1946	
	no.	*$ value*	*avg. $*	*no.*	*$ value*	*avg. $*
Newfoundland	1	250	250		5,042	
Nicaragua					1,181	
Panama (Canal Zone)	2	750	375			
Panama (Republic)					22,400	
Peru	4	608	152			
Philippine Islands	8	2,200	275		26,774	
Salvador					20,038	
South Africa				154	96,215	625
Sweden	1	700	700		950	
Venezuela	28	8,866	317		47,295	
other countries					3,169	
Totals	1364	309,352	227	6170	2,232,642	362

		1947			1948	
	no.	*$ value*	*avg. $*	*no.*	*$ value*	*avg. $*
Argentina		145,704		77	24,739	321
Australia		4,050		12	4,050	338
Bahamas		658		1	658	658
Belgium		28,854		6	3,336	556
Bermuda		4,617		1	800	800
Brazil		41,477		14	8,384	599
Canada	5,512	1,233,213	224	106	31,203	294
Columbia	540	313,222	580	959	450,803	470
Costa Rica		8,062		44	12,376	281
Cuba	1,128	424,123	376	739	322,426	436
Curacao				54	24,647	456
Dominican Republic		2,283		33	8,344	253
Ecuador		3,140				
Guatemala		109,936		47	33,380	710
Haiti		752		4	2,008	502
Honduras		15,624		43	20,920	487
India		1,806		3	1,973	658
Ireland				4	980	245
Jamaica		793		2	599	300
Japan		1,806		62	24,777	400
Mexico	2,320	824,493	355	175	35,184	201
Netherlands		1,405				
Newfoundland		27,472		64	21,883	342
Nicaragua		4,892		19	3,106	163
Panama (Canal Zone)		675		35	14,852	424
Panama (Republic)		55,487		36	20,586	572
Peru		6,269		1	632	632
Philippine Islands		114,019		240	89,613	373
Portugal		3,815		2	900	450
Saudi Arabia				6	6,530	1088
Salvador		87,103		52	28,868	555
South Africa		189,370		351	149,512	426
Sweden				3	2,146	715

	no.	1947 $ value	avg. $	no.	1948 $ value	avg. $
Switzerland		693		4	3,261	815
United Kingdom		13,920				
Venezuela	391	238,442	610	560	333,511	596
other countries		59,684		135	9,458	70
Totals	12379	3,967,859	321	3894	1,696,445	436

	no.	1949 $ value	avg. $	no.	1950 $ value	avg. $
Australia		500			2,304	
Bahamas		605			1,104	
Belgium		49,373		456	255,491	560
Bermuda					760	
Bolivia					1,935	
Brazil		650				
Canada		1,649		811	264,087	326
Ceylon		571				
Chile					1,460	
Columbia		42,310			62,549	
Costa Rica		2,456			767	
Cuba	496	163,183	329	885	275,628	311
Curacao		1,312				
Dominican Republic		16,891			10,859	
Egypt					3,490	
Finland		8,000				
Guatemala	120	65,427	545		90,840	
Germany					2,697	
Haiti		11,029			5,732	
Honduras		49,054			67,088	
Hong Kong		12,938				
Ireland					2,055	
Japan		24,777			44,423	
Mexico		29,954			21,092	
Netherlands West Indies		22,166				
New Zealand		605				
Newfoundland		17,420				
Nicaragua		1,250			14,265	
Panama (Canal Zone)		933				
Panama (Republic)	88	50,426	573		59,960	
Peru		1,211				
Philippine Islands	146	65,364	448		6,175	
Portugese Africa						
Portugal		3,025			800	
Saudi Arabia		2,663				
Salvador		43,676		214	112,607	526
South Africa		1,362				
Sweden					1,170	
Switzerland		31,387			71,285	
United Kingdom					1,830	

	1949 no.	1949 $ value	1949 avg. $	1950 no.	1950 $ value	1950 avg. $
Uruguay					2,527	
Venezuela	883	402,247	456	826	463,932	562
other countries		136,245			23,820	
Totals	2954	1,260,659	427	4387	1,872,732	427

	1951 no.	1951 $ value	1951 avg. $	1952 no.	1952 $ value	1952 avg. $
Australia					11,410	
Bahamas		8,110			845	
Belgium	660	285,131	432	1,281	491,317	384
Bermuda		2,860				
Bolivia		1,003				
Brazil		3,150				
Canada	2,453	633,307	258	2,329	714,186	307
Chile		6,383			16,694	
Columbia		35,888		179	88,470	494
Costa Rica		1,554			4,898	
Cuba	1,210	505,986	418	1,580	529,942	335
Dominican Republic		28,542			30,280	
Denmark		2,112				
Ecuador		1,000				
Egypt		3,825			345	
Finland						
France				325	60,923	187
Guatemala		132,538			59,724	
Germany		2,072		20	1,210	61
Greece						
Haiti		6,993			2,693	
Honduras		39,446			30,371	
Ireland		15,849			5,410	
Japan		75,961		71	43,782	617
Mexico	1,047	201,117	192	1,967	550,236	280
Netherlands		19,815		312	81,637	262
New Zealand					650	
Nicaragua		14,486		69	36,776	533
Palestine		2,675				
Panama (Canal Zone)					532	
Panama (Republic)		30,858		67	43,098	643
Peru				81	21,239	262
Philippine Islands		19,558		83	25,332	305
Salvador		157,347		147	98,870	673
South Africa					4,929	
Sweden		1,989			972	
Switzerland		46,116		175	84,843	485
United Kingdom		8,955			200	
Uruguay		21,659			24,831	
Venezuela	1,253	714,738	570	1,598	1,080,782	676

| | | *1951* | | | *1952* | |
	no.	*$ value*	*avg. $*	*no.*	*$ value*	*avg. $*
other countries		27,726		617	100,796	163
Totals	8442	3,058,749	362	10,901	4,248,223	390

| | | *1953* | | | *1954* | |
	no.	*$ value*	*avg. $*	*no.*	*$ value*	*avg. $*
Belgium	2,796	880,795		3,272	1,445,691	442
Canada	2,008	811,742		2,206	1,107,814	502
Columbia	1,567	675,712		2,701	1,050,705	389
Cuba	818	331,800		1,152	452,822	393
France	876	381,425		461	277,284	601
Guatemala		110,581				
Germany	348	209,777		3,044	2,120,248	697
Japan	215	102,677		146	160,973	1103
Mexico	1,346	499,100		1,954	871,168	446
Netherlands	628	190,701		2,080	739,007	355
Nicaragua	137	80,189		159	95,725	602
Panama (Republic)	168	123,164		141	93,078	660
Peru	143	72,807		384	170,843	445
Philippine Islands	108	41,655		211	121,037	574
Salvador	254	169,743		296	190,303	643
Switzerland	137	81,289		384	236,370	616
Venezuela	1,838	1,263,096		1,817	1,265,335	696
other countries	802	290,000		1,275	257,101	202
Totals	14,189	6,317,533	445	21,683	10,655,504	491

| | | *1960* | | | *1960* | |
	no. (new)	*$ value*	*avg. $*	*no. (used)*	*$ value*	*avg. $*
Australia	237	144,709	611	343	106,057	309
Austria	13	10,692	822	54	39,589	733
Belgium	3,130	2,002,755	640	3,474	1,035,156	298
Canada	970	681,608	703	211	39,317	186
Denmark	192	134,443	700			
France	118	90,412	766	109	68,162	625
Germany	5,778	3,750,199	649	518	244,083	471
Italy	961	343,761	358	45	16,518	367
Mexico	85	72,894	858	167	49,225	295
Nan Island*	301	220,763	733	52	28,210	543
Netherlands	143	93,916	657	334	97,965	293
Norway	379	254,906	673			
Philippine Islands	125	97,170	777	143	57,969	405
Sweden	104	75,645	727	19	5,572	293
Switzerland	696	487,652	701	13	6,631	510
United Kingdom	3,116	699,989	225	131	47,317	361
Venezuela	478	366,648	767	8	6,360	795
other countries	1,307	865,934	663	775	177,171	229
Totals	18,133	10,394,096	573	6,396	2,025,302	317

	1961			1961		
	no. (new)	*$ value*	*avg. $*	*no. (used)*	*$ value*	*avg. $*
Australia	65	44,511	685	148	37,859	256
Belgium	2,698	1,836,887	681	2,665	823,803	309
Canada	930	931,322	1001	276	47,697	173
Chile	213	160,167	752	4	1,980	495
Ecuador	215	150,590	700	11	5,568	506
France	491	357,834	729	154	79,638	517
Germany	5,778	3,512,264	608	539	178,011	330
Italy	402	287,280	715	143	63,291	443
Jamaica	251	191,176	762	21	7,420	353
Japan	115	71,960	626	458	88,570	193
Mexico	67	62,955	940	199	56,914	286
Nan Island*	585	479,957	820	145	64,810	447
Netherlands	177	130,955	740	334	81,583	244
Nicaragua	164	113,854	694	38	13,452	354
Peru	133	100,844	758	40	23,691	592
Sweden	129	95,166	738	63	35,280	560
Switzerland	781	568,515	728	93	69,283	745
United Kingdom	630	438,151	695	186	80,322	432
Venezuela	446	322,346	723	10	2,122	212
other countries	720	535,256	743	855	255,726	299
Totals	14,990	10,391,990	693	6,382	2,017,020	316

	1963			1963		
	no. (new)	*$ value*	*avg. $*	*no. (used)*	*$ value*	*avg. $*
Australia	63	43,462	690	105	26,849	256
Austria	142	111,038	782			
Belgium	5,326	4,358,561	818	3,479	947,912	272
Canada	1,415	962,767	680	162	36,300	224
Costa Rica	51	40,837	801			
Dominican Republic	102	66,785	655	366	88,787	243
Finland	500	390,437	781			
France	526	451,455	858	64	17,285	270
Germany	5,997	3,677,092	613	334	89,980	269
Greece	47	38,598	821	362	81,852	226
Italy	966	665,626	689	44	27,276	620
Japan	948	671,114	708	1,249	342,388	274
Nan Island*	69	58,866	853	570	202,403	355
Netherlands	177	138,099	780	237	62,080	262
Panama (Republic)	99	67,313	680			
Peru	112	98,612	880	48	14,047	293
Sweden	127	90,562	713			
Switzerland	981	825,683	842	153	111,145	726
United Kingdom	676	496,679	735	602	151,597	252
Venezuela	648	268,488	414			
other countries	360	285,418	793	1,242	352,368	284
Totals	19,332	13,807,492	714	9,017	2,552,269	283

	1965 $ value	1966 $ value	1967 $ value
Argentina	22,608	39,807	26,007
Australia	18,150		69,598
Austria	153,200	143,185	150,831
Bahamas	52,625	34,780	50,195
Belgium	3,404,413	2,213,998	1,737,928
Canada	887,273	601,747	911,053
Costa Rica	103,933	40,455	47,879
Cyprus	22,943		
Denmark	58,549	23,800	37,667
Ecuador	16,992		
Finland	118,165	103,530	
France	538,236	533,290	366,766
Guatemala	16,197	15,428	15,141
Germany	4,800,698	3,569,919	3,235,838
Greece	36,529	31,212	14,660
Honduras	22,518	35,038	51,657
Hong Kong	38,538	336,615	279,504
Israel			31,324
Italy	290,439	425,342	1,002,308
Jamaica	99,784	34,217	48,407
Japan	983,576	1,341,362	2,227,359
Kenya		12,407	
Mexico	48,058	40,273	28,570
Netherlands	276,536	190,075	267,395
Nicaragua	91,577	58,972	29,318
Norway	18,559		13,463
Panama (Republic)	112,219	115,879	188,675
Peru	147,712	238,144	111,440
Salvador	12,607	18,030	
Sweden	87,238	84,769	57,548
Switzerland	427,763	409,298	363,656
Thailand			48,342
Trinidad and Tobago	19,941	12,383	17,096
United Kingdom	691,431	739,393	733,034
Uruguay			
Venezuela	179,712	138,387	63,183
other countries	180,256	348,735	227,630
Totals	13,978,975	11,930,470	12,453,472

* This was the U.S. government's designation of certain Pacific military bases.

Sources:

Billboard, Sept. 27, 1941, sup. p. 10.   *Billboard*, March 6, 1954, p. 52.
Billboard, May 23, 1953, p. 85.   *Billboard*, April 24, 1954, p. 78.
Billboard, March 30, 1946, p. 133.   *Billboard*, April 30, 1955, p. 87.
Billboard, April 2, 1949, p. 141.   *Billboard*, June 12, 1961, p. 44
Billboard, April 14, 1951, p. 79.   *Billboard*, Aug. 4, 1962, sup. p. 160.
Billboard, March 22, 1952, p. 80.   *Billboard*, July 11, 1964, p. 42.
Billboard, June 7, 1952, p. 76.   *Billboard*, July 6, 1968, p. 45.

Appendix C

Jukebox License/Fee/Tax by State

	Tax/Lic (1958)	Annual per Box	Tax/Lic (1965)	Annual per Box
Alabama	yes	$8	yes	$8
Alaska	na		yes	$48
Arizona	no		no	
Arkansas	yes	$5	yes	$250 per operator
California	no		no	
Colorado	no		no	
Connecticut	no		no	
Delaware	yes	$20 — 5-cent play; $40 — 10-cent play	yes	$30 — 5-cent play; $50 — 10-cent play
Dist. of Col.	no		no	
Florida	yes	$7.75	yes	$5
Georgia	no		no	
Hawaii	na		no	
Idaho	yes	$80	no	
Illinois	no		yes	$10
Indiana	no		no	
Iowa	no		no	
Kansas	no		no	
Kentucky	yes	$10	yes	$10
Louisiana	yes	$10	yes	$10
Maine	no		no	
Maryland	yes	$10; $1 for each additional speaker	yes	$10
Massachusetts	yes	$50 — Sunday operation tax	no	
Michigan	no		no	
Minnesota	no		no	
Mississippi	yes	$10 — 5-cent play; $20 — 10-cent play	yes	$10 — 5-cent play; $20 — 10-cent play

	Tax/Lic (1958)	*Annual per Box*	*Tax/Lic* (1965)	*Annual per Box*
Missouri	no		no	
Montana	no		no	
Nebraska	no		no	
Nevada	no		no	
New Hampshire	no		no	
New Jersey	no		no	
New Mexico	no		no	
New York	no		no	
North Carolina	yes	$100 per operator; $10 per machine	yes	$100 per operator; $10 per machine
North Dakota	yes	$15	yes	$15
Ohio	no		. no	
Oklahoma	yes	$40	yes	$40
Oregon	yes	$10; $1 for each additional speaker	yes	$10
Pennsylvania	no		no	
Rhode Island	no		no	
South Carolina	yes	$25	yes	$25
South Dakota	no		no	
Tennessee	yes	$5 — 5-cent play; $10 — 10-cent play	yes	$5 — 5-cent play; $10 — 10-cent play
Texas	yes	$5	yes	$10
Utah	no		no	
Vermont	yes	$25	yes	$25
Virginia	yes	$5	yes	$5
Washington	no	$1 registration fee	no	$1 registration fee
West Virginia	yes	$5.50	yes	5-cent machines, $5 per box ($150 total for 20 or more machines); 10-cent machines, $10 per box ($225 total for 20 or more machines).
Wisconsin	no		no	
Wyoming	no		no	

Sources:

Billboard, May 5, 1958, p.54

Billboard, September, 18, 1965, pp. 66+.

Appendix D

U.S. Exports of Coin-Operated Machines

	Jukeboxes		Vending Machines		Game Machines		Juke % of total
	No.	$ Value	No.	$ Value	No.	$ Value	$ Value
1945	1364	309,352	2037	36,526	3832	188,546	57.89
1946	6170	2,075,936	3156	119,207	5070	459,935	78.19
1947	12379	3,967,859	6785	471,234	7378	681,009	77.50
1948	3894	1,623,978	6437	332,059	3852	353,544	70.31
1950	4387	1,872,732	2540	501,843	7528	701,971	60.87
1954	21683	10,655,504	20014	1,098,058	22485	3,188,087	71.31
1960	24529	12,419,398			46259	7,828,749	
1961	21370	12,409,010			39101	10,187,862	
1963	28349	16,359,761			54645	20,872,438	
1965		13,978,975		10,252,275		17,091,863	33.83
1966		11,930,470		12,644,714		28,888,065	22.32
1967		12,453,472		11,027,492		20,298,502	28.45

Sources:

Billboard, March 30, 1946, p. 133.
Billboard, March 13, 1946, p. 112.
Billboard, April 2, 1949, p. 141.
Billboard, April 14, 1951, p. 79.
Billboard, April 30, 1955, pp. 88-89.
Billboard, June 12, 1961, p. 44.
Billboard, August 4, 1962, sup p. 160
Billboard, July 11, 1964, p. 42.
Billboard, July 6, 1968, p. 45.

Notes

Chapter 1

1. J. Krivine. *Juke Box Saturday Night*. London: New English Library, 1977, p. 9.
2. Ibid., p. 10.
3. Ibid., p. 11; "The juke box's 60th birthday." *Billboard*, January 24, 1948, p. 132.
4. J. Krivine, op. cit., p. 11.
5. "The juke box's 60th birthday," op. cit., p. 132.
6. Ibid.
7. Ibid., p. 134.
8. J. Krivine, op. cit., p. 13.
9. "The juke box's 60th birthday," op. cit., p. 134.
10. Ibid.
11. Ibid., pp. 134, 136; J. Krivine, op. cit., p. 14.
12. J. Krivine, op. cit., p. 13; "The juke box's 60th birthday," op. cit., p. 136.
13. "The juke box's 60th birthday," op. cit., p. 136.
14. Ibid.
15. J. Krivine, op. cit., pp. 13–15.
16. "Selectivity: the magic that built the juke box industry." *Billboard*, May 23, 1953, 81; "The juke box's 60th birthday," op. cit., p. 140.
17. "The juke box's 60th birthday," op. cit., p. 140.
18. Ibid.
19. Ibid.
20. Ibid.; J. Krivine, op. cit., p. 18.
21. "The juke box's 60th birthday," op. cit., p. 140.
22. Ibid., pp. 140–141.
23. Q. David Bowers. *Put Another Nickel In.* Vestral, New York: The Vestral Press, 1966, p. 1; Arthur E. Yohalem. "Traces ancestry of juke box." *Billboard*, July 20, 1946, pp. 116, 121.
24. Arthur E. Yohalem, op. cit.
25. Ibid.
26. Ibid.
27. "The juke box's 60th birthday," op. cit., p. 140.
28. J. Krivine, op. cit., p. 18; Walter Hurd. "America's new industry." *Billboard*, September 28, 1940, sup., p. 4; Louis Nichols, *New York Times Magazine*, October 3, 1941, p. 22; "65 years of juke box growth." *Billboard*, May 23, 1953, p. 59.
29. Herman Finkelstein. "These things are mine." *Variety*, January 5, 1955, p. 225.
30. Mildred Hall. "Cellar asks MOA-ASCAP arbitrate." *Billboard*, June 22, 1959, pp. 130–131.
31. "Why are phonos called jook organs? Florida offers clue." *Billboard*, February 24, 1940, p. 71.
32. "Phono business may find way to capitalize on 'juke box' name." *Billboard*, October 5, 1940, p. 69.
33. Geoffrey Parsons Jr. and Robert Yoder. "A nickel a tune." *Reader's Digest* 38 (February, 1941): 113.
34. Vincent Lynch. *Jukebox: the Golden Age.* New York: Putnam, 1981, p. 10.
35. "'Juke box' going high hat." *New York Times*, December 21, 1946, p. 29.
36. "Jukebox remains same even under different name." *Billboard*, January 9, 1971, pp. 35, 38.
37. *Oxford English Dictionary*, 2nd ed. Oxford: Clarendon House, 1989, vol. 8, p. 303.

Chapter 2

1. Q. David Bowers. *Put Another Nickel In.* Vestal, New York: The Vestal Press, 1966, pp. 3–5.
2. Ibid., p. 14.

3. Arthur H. Sanders. "Yesterday's juke-box." *Hobbies* 56 (August, 1951): 30–32.
4. Q. David Bowers, op. cit., pp. 21, 23.
5. Ibid., p. 28.
6. Ibid., pp. 28–29.
7. Merl Solomon. "Wurlitzer — nearly 300 years in music." *Billboard*, October 12, 1968, pp. MOA10, MOA28.
8. Q. David Bowers, op. cit., pp. 74–75.
9. Ibid., pp. 76–79.
10. Ibid., pp. 93–94.
11. Ibid., p. 96.
12. Ibid.
13. Ibid., p. 99.
14. Ibid., p. 104.
15. Ibid., pp. 108, 114.
16. Ibid., p. 114.
17. Ibid., p. 119.
18. Ibid., pp. 160, 177.
19. Ibid., p. 44.
20. Ibid., pp. 55, 61.
21. Ibid., p. 1.
22. Bernard Cohen. "Seeburg — creative energy and expansive bigness." *Billboard*, October 12, 1968, p. MOA20; "Over 30 years in music." *Billboard*, January 18, 1936, p. 74; Q. David Bowers, op. cit., p. 38.
23. Ray Brack. "Golden age of music merchandising." *Billboard*, October 12, 1968, p. MOA42.
24. Ibid.
25. Ibid.
26. Ibid., p. MOA44.
27. "Picking the right records for the right spot." *Billboard*, September 27, 1941, sup., p. 44.
28. "Phono exec speaks on music policy." *Billboard*, May 14, 1938, p. 84.
29. "Juke box build in 1885 plays rolls, 3 musical instruments." *Billboard*, May 3, 1947, p. 118.
30. Q. David Bowers, op. cit., p. 29.
31. H. F. Reves. "Vending machines in Detroit." *Billboard*, December 25, 1937, pp. 70–71.
32. Walter Hurd. "America's new industry." *Billboard*, September 28, 1940, sup., pp. 3–4.
33. Bill Gersh. "Music machine history." *Billboard*, July 10, 1937, pp. 79–80.
34. James B. Dittman. "Innovation: a trademark of Rowe." *Billboard*, October 12, 1968, p. MOA16.
35. J. Krivine. *Juke Box Saturday Night*. London: New English Library, 1977, p. 34.
36. Bernard Cohen, op. cit., p. MOA20.
37. J. Krivine, op. cit., pp. 28–29.
38. Ibid., p. 36; Vincent Lynch. *Jukebox: The Golden Age*. New York: Putnam, 1981, pp. 13–14.
39. Olin Hoskins. "Rock-Ola: a dedication to dependability." *Billboard*, October 12, 1968,

pp. MOA12, MOA28; J. Krivine, op. cit., p. 54.
40. Ibid.
41. J. Krivine, op. cit., p. 22.
42. Ibid.
43. A. C. Hartmann. "Coin-operated amusement machine industry gives depression a blow." *Billboard*, March 12, 1932, p. 28.
44. "Thousands of 5c music boxes are important market for discs." *Variety*, June 9, 1931, p. 59.
45. Vincent Lynch, op. cit., p. 14.

Chapter 3

1. Vincent Lynch. *Jukebox: The Golden Age*. New York: Putnam, 1981, p. 14; J. Krivine. *Juke Box Saturday Night*. London: New English Library, 1977, p. 38.
2. "U.S. phonograph record sales, 1921–1961." *Billboard*, August 4, 1962, sup., p. 9.
3. "Wall St. Journal recounts history of record industry." *Billboard*, November 29, 1941, p. 90.
4. Ibid., p. 91.
5. Ibid.
6. Ibid.
7. "Weekly music notes." *Billboard*, October 12, 1935, p. 73.
8. Ibid.; "10 best records for the week of Nov. 2." *Billboard*, November 16, 1935, p. 64.
9. "The week's best records." *Billboard*, December 18, 1937, p. 74.
10. "Record Buying Guide." *Billboard*, April 15, 1939, p. 74.
11. "Record Buying Guide." *Billboard*, August 26, 1939, p. 126.
12. "Record Guide chalks up 84 recording artists in 1939." *Billboard*, January 20, 1940, p. 74.
13. "10 Best Sellers on Coin-Machines." *Variety*, December 4, 1940, p. 44.
14. "Modern Vending record praised by Wurlitzer." *Billboard*, November 28, 1936, p. 125; "Keeney busy on 5 games." *Billboard*, February 25, 1939, p. 79.
15. "Modern Vending sets a record." *Billboard*, June 13, 1936, p. 70.
16. Advertisement. *Billboard*, February 25, 1939, p. 69; Advertisement. *Billboard*, May 6, 1939, p. 78.
17. Earl Holland. "Selecting records and programs." *Billboard*, November 16, 1935, p. 64.
18. "What the records are doing for me." *Billboard*, October 22, 1935, p. 65.
19. "Picking the right records for the right spots." *Billboard*, September 27, 1941, sup., p. 44.
20. "Objectionable records seen as a menace

to the industry." *Billboard*, November 7, 1936, pp. 74–75.

21. Ibid.
22. "Music operators again cautioned." *Billboard*, December 26, 1936, p. 124.
23. Ralph G. Neal. "Profit tips for music operators." *Billboard*, December 5, 1936, p. 78.
24. H. F. Reves. "Progress in the music field." *Billboard*, January 16, 1937, p. 85.
25. Arthur C. Hughes. "Are risky records good business." *Billboard*, January 16, 1937, p. 93.
26. "Phono ops hit smutty records." *Billboard*, July 10, 1937, p. 80.
27. "N.J. op crusades against smut disks." *Billboard*, October 30, 1937, p. 76.
28. "Smut records hurt phonos and games." *Billboard*, November 6, 1937, p. 80.
29. James T. Mangan. "Lecherous records." *Billboard*, December 4, 1937, p. 70.
30. S. C. Schulz. "Why jeopardize your biz?" *Billboard*, December 11, 1937, p. 80.
31. M. H. Orodenker. "Hot off the records." *Billboard*, December 18, 1937, p. 72.
32. David C. Rockola. "Music enemy no. 1." *Billboard*, December 25, 1937, p. 68.
33. "Smutty discs plague ops." *Billboard*, February 11, 1939, p. 71.
34. "Record Buying Guide." *Billboard*, April 15, 1939, p. 74; "Record Buying Guide." *Billboard*, August 26, 1939, p. 126.
35. M. G. Hammergren. "An industry grows up. " *Billboard*, January 20, 1940, p. 74.
36. "APMA hits smutty disks." *Billboard*, January 20, 1940, p. 82.
37. "Detroiters hit naughty disks." *Billboard*, August 3, 1940, p. 70.
38. "Phono manufacturers in new move against smut." *Billboard*, December 28, 1940, p. 133.
39. "Successful operator handles music exclusively in nation's capital." *Billboard*, May 11, 1935, p. 61.
40. Ibid.
41. "Music biz goes in town of 800." *Billboard*, May 29, 1937, p. 90.
42. Babe Kaufman. "We doubled the take." *Billboard*, October 15, 1938, pp. 67–68.
43. Ibid.
44. Ibid.
45. Ibid.
46. "Texas music ops select officers at conference." *Billboard*, October 5, 1935, p. 62.
47. R. G. Norman. "Music for long-pull profits." *Billboard*, November 30, 1935, p. 114.
48. Ibid.
49. Ralph J. Mills. "Consider the phonograph." *Billboard*, November 30, 1935, p. 117.
50. Ibid.
51. H. F. Reves. "Progress in the music field." *Billboard*, January 16, 1937, pp. 84–85.

52. Ibid.
53. "Seeburg phonos in restaurant chain." *Billboard*, November 27, 1937, p. 136.
54. "Rock-Ola op tests new style location." *Billboard*, May 7, 1938, p. 84.
55. "Phonos being spotted in swank Philly night clubs." *Billboard*, April 13, 1949, p. 152.
56. Ibid.
57. "More phonos in night clubs as fall season gets going." *Billboard*, October 5, 1940, p. 68.
58. "Wurlitzer reveals Colonial model." *Billboard*, November 16, 1940, p. 70.
59. "Picking the right records for the right spot." *Billboard*, September 28, 1940, p. 6.
60. Ibid.
61. Ibid.
62. Ibid., p. 58.
63. Ibid., p. 59.
64. "Location letter warns of radio." *Billboard*, July 31, 1937, p. 89.
65. "Turnstile slugs circulate widely." *Billboard*, June 29, 1935, p. 106.
66. "Slugs a pinball menace." *Billboard*, June 29, 1935, p. 106; Bill Gersh. "Slugs must go." *Billboard*, June 29, 1935, p. 107.
67. "Mills introduces new phono at convention." *Billboard*, January 18, 1936, p. 72; "Cheaters cheated." *Billboard*, August 8, 1936, p. 70; "Badger over quota in sales drive." *Billboard*, May 6, 1938, p. 78.
68. "Successful operator handles music exclusively in nation's capital." *Billboard*, May 11, 1935, p. 61.
69. E. C. Johnson. "Don't give away your profits." *Billboard*, July 20, 1935, p. 65.
70. Ibid.
71. "Music must make fair commission." *Billboard*, December 21, 1935, p. 61.
72. Ralph G. Neal. "Profit tips for music operators." *Billboard*, December 5, 1936, pp. 78–79.
73. "Detroit music men ban competition one month." *Billboard*, November 5, 1938, p. 69.
74. "Music operators." *Billboard*, May 6, 1939, p. 78.
75. M. G. Hammergren. "An industry grows up. " *Billboard*, January 20, 1940, p. 74.
76. Henry T. Roberts. "The percentage problem." *Billboard*, June 22, 1940, p. 78.
77. "Pinball games used frequently in movies, with results pro and con." *Billboard*, May 11, 1935, p. 63.
78. "Wurlitzer plays for movie stars." *Billboard*, October 30, 1937, p. 76.
79. "Rock-Ola machine aboard Queen Mary." *Billboard*, June 20, 1936, p. 70.
80. "Music machines booming in Detroit." *Billboard*, August 8, 1936, p. 70.
81. John B. Winthrop. "Boosting the phonograph take." *Billboard*, August 2, 1936, p. 76.
82. Grant Shay. "Selling music." *Billboard*, February 8, 1936, p. 68.

83. "Rock-Ola firm features 'idea exchange' for ops." *Billboard*, October 10, 1936, p. 76.
84. "Music operators." *Billboard*, May 6, 1939, p. 78.
85. "CFRB's Clair Wallace puts in plug on automatic phonographs." *Billboard*, November 23, 1940, p. 60.
86. "Milwaukee firm boosts popular records in big promotion plan." *Billboard*, October 28, 1939, p. 74.
87. "Ork leader boosts phonos on stage." *Billboard*, November 16, 1940, p. 70.
88. "Partners in business." *Billboard*, January 18, 1941, p. 100.
89. Ibid., pp. 100–101.
90. "Amusement biz puts music boxes to use in many ways." *Billboard*, August 24, 1940, p. 75.
91. "Music machines and the music industry." *Billboard*, September 27, 1941, sup., p. 14.
92. Ibid., p. 15.
93. "Record plan is growing." *Billboard*, May 14, 1938, p. 84.
94. Tom Murray. "Ops view advertising records." *Billboard*, February 25, 1939, p. 71.
95. "Fortune magazine credits modern phonograph for reviving records." *Billboard*, September 23, 1939, p. 69.
96. "Advertising paper quotes." *Billboard*, September 23, 1939, p. 69.
97. "Man at bar turns into a music critic." *Billboard*, November 11, 1939, p. 69.
98. Ibid.
99. "Rock-Ola runs double shifts." *Billboard*, August 15, 1936, p. 70; "Rock-Ola Imperial reaches new high." *Billboard*, July 31, 1937, p. 88.
100. "Wurlitzer biz over 3 years." *Billboard*, May 29, 1937, p. 90; "Wurlitzer firm at full speed." *Billboard*, August 29, 1936, p. 112.
101. R. G. Norman. "Music for long-pull profits." *Billboard*, November 30, 1935, p. 114.
102. "Tells locations to patronize op. " *Billboard*, July 10, 1937, p. 81.
103. "Wurlitzer in Chicago at end of second week." *Billboard*, July 23, 1938, pp. 76, 86; "First Wurlitzer banquet sets high mark for tour." *Billboard*, July 16, 1938, p. 65.
104. "First Wurlitzer banquet sets high mark for tour." *Billboard*, July 16, 1938, p. 65.
105. Ralph G. Neal. "Music operator analyzes his business." *Billboard*, April 10, 1937, p. 182.
106. "Music operators." *Billboard*, May 6, 1939, p. 78.
107. Roger Rapoport. "Oldies but goodies." *Americana* 9 (November/December, 1981): 25.
108. Walter W. Hurd. "Used phonograph prices." *Billboard*, April 16, 1938, p. 86.
109. Ibid.
110. Wurlitzer ad. *Billboard*, May 11, 1935, p. 63; "Seeburg announces features of new 1937 line of phonographs." *Billboard*, December 26, 1936, p. 124.
111. "Rock-Ola finds 20 records favored." *Billboard*, January 8, 1938, p. 68.
112. "Wurlitzer Co. develops record-counting device." *Billboard*, August 8, 1936, p. 70.
113. "Mills Do-Re-Mi has many novel features." *Billboard*, August 29, 1936, p. 112.
114. Advertisement. *Billboard*, August 27, 1938, p. 109.
115. "Keeney wallbox in distrib's hands." *Billboard*, February 24, 1940, p. 71.
116. "No summer price change." *Billboard*, June 26, 1937, p. 132.
117. "AMI sales policy, equipment revealed." *Billboard*, March 15, 1941, p. 62.
118. "No mid-season models pleases Rock-Ola ops." *Billboard*, June 11, 1938, p. 74.
119. "Phono-Mike tells success at show." *Billboard*, February 10, 1940, p. 66.
120. L. C. Force. "Little Willie's growed up. " *Billboard*, January 18, 1936, p. 74.
121. Walter W. Hurd. "Music." *Billboard*, September 4, 1927, p. 76.
122. "Public informed of phonograph benefits in radio announcement." *Billboard*, June 25, 1938, pp. 114–115.
123. Walter W. Hurd. "The year 1937." *Billboard*, January 1, 1938, p. 126.
124. Ibid.
125. "Phonos must be important, declares Wisconsin paper." *Billboard*, October 26, 1940, p. 67.
126. Herb J. Allen. "Records for operators' needs." *Billboard*, January 18, 1936, p. 72.
127. Ibid.
128. Ibid.
129. "Weekly music notes." *Billboard*, November 6, 1937, p. 80; "U.S. phonograph record sales, 1921–1961." *Billboard*, August 4, 1962, sup., p. 9.
130. Nat Cohn. "Music for sale." *Billboard*, August 6, 1938, p. 66.
131. Tommy Dorsey. "The importance of the music machine operator." *Billboard*, December 30, 1939, p. 146.
132. "Jimmy Dorsey praises music machines in Philly broadcast." *Billboard*, November 9, 1940, p. 68.
133. "Biggest record market is phonos, says A.P. writer." *Billboard*, January 20, 1940, p. 74; "U.S. phonograph record sales ..." op. cit.
134. Irving Mills. "Phonograph records—the new talent medium." *Billboard*, August 27, 1938, p. 109.
135. "Glenn Miller, heralded No. 1 swing king." *Billboard*, December 2, 1939, p. 134.

136. Daniel Richman. "Making records for the operator." *Billboard*, September 23, 1939, p. 3.

137. "Record conscious." *Billboard*, December 9, 1939, p. 64.

138. "Phonographs supplant radio as maker of song hits." *Billboard*, February 10, 1940, p. 66.

139. Eva M. Warner. "Buffalo survey shows interesting facts about phono record trends." *Billboard*, September 28, 1940, pp. 74, 76.

140. Ibid.

141. Daniel Richman. "Music machines prove foremost influence of retail record sales." *Billboard*, September 28, 1940, sup., p. 14.

142. Barry Ulanov. "The jukes take over swing." *American Mercury* 51 (October, 1940): 172–6.

143. Harold Humphrey. "Analyzing the hit records." *Billboard*, September 27, 1941, sup., pp. 30, 94.

144. Ben Katz. "Music machines' influence on home record sales." *Billboard*, September 27, 1941, sup., p. 28.

145. Ibid.

146. "Wall St. Journal recounts history of record industry." *Billboard*, November 29, 1941, p. 91.

147. Helene Palmer. "My two weeks visiting Europe." *Billboard*, June 29, 1935, p. 100.

148. "Obstacles to phono exports." *Billboard*, July 17, 1937, p. 80.

149. Ibid.

150. Hans Ullendorff. "Coin machines in Europe." *Billboard*, March 5, 1938, pp. 80–81.

151. "Phono gets big play in Panama." *Billboard*, April 5, 1939, p. 74.

152. "Phonos in France." *Billboard*, August 5, 1939, p. 66.

153. "Sees bigger use of phonos in Mexico." *Billboard*, May 4, 1940, p. 76.

154. "Mexico enforces warning against phono loudness." *Billboard*, August 3, 1940, p. 70.

155. "$640,974 in music machines exported to 34 lands in '39." *Billboard*, March 2, 1940, p. 72.

156. "Music publishers cast fierce frowns at discs' slot machine methods." *Variety*, January 13, 1937, p. 47.

157. "Coin machines' $175,000,000 U.S. gross." *Variety*, July 12, 1939, p. 39.

158. "Further analysis cues jukebox take nearer $150,000,000 a year." *Variety*, August 21, 1940, p. 49.

159. Ibid., pp. 49, 60.

160. Ibid.

161. "Few industries have so quickly given jobs to so many." *Billboard*, September 28, 1940, sup., p. 4.

162. "Editor gives phono figures." *Billboard*, October 5, 1940, p. 68.

163. "America's jookbox craze." *Newsweek* 15 (June 3, 1940): 48, 50.

164. Walter Hurd. "America's new industry." *Billboard*, September 28, 1940, sup., pp. 3–5.

165. Walter Hurd. "The year 1940." *Billboard*, January 18, 1941, pp. 66+.

166. Geoffrey Parsons Jr. and Robert Yoder. "A nickel a tune." *Reader's Digest* 38 (February, 1941): 114–115.

167. Walter W. Hurd. "A busy year." *Billboard*, September 27, 1941, sup., pp. 84–85.

168. Ibid.

169. Maynard L. Reuter. "Music for millions." *Billboard*, September 27, 1941, sup., pp. 8–9.

170. Ibid.

171. Lewis Nichols. "The ubiquitous juke box." *New York Times Magazine*, October 3, 1941, p. 22.

172. "Texas taxes coin machines." *Billboard*, May 18, 1935, p. 73; "Provisions of new Texas law." *Billboard*, May 25, 1935, p. 83.

173. "Music operators win injunction." *Billboard*, November 16, 1935, p. 64.

174. "Music operators talk problems." *Billboard*, March 20, 1937, p. 76.

175. "Doc Berenson gets action." *Billboard*, December 18, 1937, p. 76.

176. "Phonos avoid Arizona tax." *Billboard*, May 28, 1938, p. 91.

177. "City tax on coin machine attacked." *Variety*, July 26, 1939, p. 41.

178. "Ops win a lower tax." *Billboard*, July 22, 1939, p. 70.

179. "Coin-operated phonograph not Sunday violation." *Variety*, February 8, 1939, p. 39.

180. "Jukeboxes back: forget old law." *Variety*, December 4, 1940, p. 44.

181. "Phonograph tax rulings." *Billboard*, October 18, 1941, p. 62.

182. Walter W. Hurd. "Social Policy." *Billboard*, August 13, 1938, p. 68.

183. Ibid.

184. "Music publishers cast fierce frowns at discs' slot machine methods." *Variety*, January 13, 1937, p. 47.

185. "Attention, phono ops." *Billboard*, September 4, 1937, p. 80.

186. Andrew D. Weinberger. "The law and the music machine." *Billboard*, September 28, 1940, sup., p. 41.

187. "What is AFM?" *Billboard*, August 31, 1940, pp. 109–111.

188. "What is MPPA?" *Billboard*, August 31, 1940, pp. 108, 110.

189. "What is BMI?" *Billboard*, August 31, 1940, pp. 109, 111.

190. "What is ASCAP?" *Billboard*, August 31, 1940, pp. 108, 110.

191. Walter W. Hurd. "Unemployment." *Billboard*, September 11, 1937, p. 74.

192. Ibid.

193. Ben Boldt. "Phonograph industry brings opportunities for musicians." *Billboard*, October 19, 1940, p. 65.
194. "Why the noise." *Billboard*, May 8, 1937, p. 80.
195. Frank W. Wood. "What's wrong with the coin machine industry?" *Billboard*, February 25, 1939, pp. 78–79.
196. "Wurlitzer in Chicago at end of second week." *Billboard*, July 23, 1938, pp. 76, 86.
197. "International phono association head addresses Los Angeles ops." *Billboard*, February 25, 1939, p. 69.
198. "Phonographs fare better." *Billboard*, April 6, 1940, p. 67.
199. George Crook. "How business profits from coin machines." *Billboard*, November 13, 1937, p. 76.
200. J. Krivine. *Juke Box Saturday Night*. London: New English Library, 1977, pp. 42, 66.
201. Ibid., pp. 72, 128.

Chapter 4

1. Walter W. Hurd. "Music cheers." *Billboard*, June 1, 1940, p. 70.
2. Ibid.
3. Homer E. Capehart. "Americanism and music." *Billboard*, July 27, 1940, p. 78.
4. "Use of patriotic records in music boxes increasing." *Billboard*, July 27, 1940, p. 82.
5. "N.Y. Herald Tribune editorial cites automatic phono value in promoting patriotic songs." *Billboard*, February 28, 1942, p. 60.
6. "Michigan phono assn. Supports steps for unifying industry's efforts in defense bond drive." *Billboard*, October 18, 1941, p. 62; "Music guards teen-age morals." *Billboard*, December 18, 1943, p. 62.
7. "Juke boxes limited by priority order." *New York Times*, December 11, 1940, p. 30.
8. "Servicemen prefer jukes." *Billboard*, April 10, 1943, p. 94.
9. Walter Hurd. "No junking of jukes." *Billboard*, September 25, 1943, sup., pp. 26–27.
10. Ibid., pp. 27, 166.
11. "Soldier pushes button, music rolls out Bach as juke box quivers from frightful shock." *New York Times*, September 6, 1944, p. 21.
12. "Picking records—an art or a science?" *Billboard*, January 3, 1942, p. 61.
13. Ibid.
14. Ibid.
15. "Hillbillies owe rise to jukes." *Billboard*, August 28, 1943, pp. 70, 75.
16. "Ex-hillbillies find music they like at Baltimore spots." *Billboard*, August 28, 1943, p. 71.

17. "Minneapolis has 1,100 juke boxes, survey reveals." *Billboard*, August 28, 1943, p. 71.
18. "Hit records boost play." *Billboard*, March 13, 1943, p. 59.
19. "Chi op evolves own system for picking click disks." *Billboard*, July 29, 1944, p. 89.
20. "Newcomers in music choice." *Billboard*, March 13, 1943, p. 59.
21. "Begin the Beguine gets no. 1 spot on Denver phono 6 yrs." *Billboard*, April 21, 1945, p. 65.
22. "No chance for jukes to use classics, reporter discovers." *Billboard*, February 10, 1945, p. 63.
23. "A nickel's worth of silence? An idea by Cleveland mayor." *Billboard*, January 1, 1944, p. 50.
24. "Judge puts juke out of order to have quiet bite." *Billboard*, December 2, 1944, p. 91.
25. "Juke boxes bring fines." *New York Times*, August 28, 1945, p. 22.
26. "Philly music men on record against smutty recordings." *Billboard*, February 28, 1942, pp. 60, 66.
27. "Massachusetts ops plan test against Sunday juke fees." *Billboard*, August 29, 1942, p. 71.
28. J. M. Dalziel. "The jook." *Billboard*, February 22, 1941, p. 73.
29. "Market reports." *Billboard*, November 13, 1943, p. 60.
30. "Another dept. store installs juke box." *Billboard*, May 26, 1945, p. 73.
31. "Industry wins a slug fight." *Billboard*, April 15, 1944, pp. 61, 68.
32. K. C. Kline. "Operator can well spend hours watching patrons play machines." *Billboard*, November 14, 1942, p. 65.
33. "Juke romancers marry as Bing sings 'Gotta Be Free.'" *Billboard*, January 27, 1945, p. 63.
34. "Scientist finds jitterbugs dying; ops dancemen glad." *Billboard*, February 25, 1939, p. 77.
35. "Jivers featured by Mills Novelty." *Billboard*, February 17, 1940, p. 64.
36. "Plan for youth clubs." *Billboard*, May 1, 1943, p. 62.
37. "Teen-age clubs grow." *Billboard*, May 29, 1943, pp. 92, 96.
38. "Centers meet war needs for both young and old." *Billboard*, June 12, 1943, p. 62.
39. "Suggest teenage centers." *Billboard*, August 7, 1943, p. 62.
40. "Ops help set up teen clubs." *Billboard*, August 14, 1943, p. 62.
41. "Music boxes win approval." *Billboard*, October 23, 1943, p. 62.
42. Walter W. Hurd. "Permanent project." *Billboard*, November 6, 1943, p. 58.
43. Ibid.

44. "Juke boxes set stage for teen-age night clubs." *Billboard*, November 6, 1943, p. 62.
45. "Juke boxes prove worth." *Billboard*, November 27, 1943, p. 98.
46. "Assn. pledges juke to each teen-age club." *Billboard*, January 29, 1944, p. 62.
47. Margaret Wells. "Coinmen and teen-age clubs." *Billboard*, March 4, 1944, pp. 66, 76.
48. Ibid.
49. "Juke box tops teen-age club fun; use games." *Billboard*, March 25, 1944, p. 90.
50. "Plan bigger program for teen-age clubs." *Billboard*, December 2, 1944, p. 91.
51. "2,200 teen-age centers in U.S. with jukes, govt. says." *Billboard*, November 17, 1945, p. 78; "FBI urges teen-age help." *Billboard*, December 22, 1945, pp. 76, 79.
52. "Juke boxes and youth." *Billboard*, January 30, 1943, p. 64.
53. "Local committees." *Billboard*, May 8, 1943, p. 58.
54. "Memphis sings new tune." *Billboard*, January 15, 1944, p. 63.
55. "San Fran denies control of phonos to police dept." *Billboard*, March 18, 1944, p. 61.
56. "Minneapolis passes juke box ordinance." *Billboard*, July 8, 1944, p. 64.
57. "See phonographs as prime exploitation outlet for pix." *Billboard*, March 28, 1942, p. 108.
58. "Spike Jones's band starts tour: to court operators." *Billboard*, August 7, 1943, p. 62.
59. "Marian Anderson adds voice to great artists' praise of jukes." *Billboard*, February 10, 1945, p. 65.
60. Tom Murray. "Year's trial proves Panther Novelty's weekly sponsored broadcast big biz booster." *Billboard*, Sept. 5, 1942, p. 65.
61. "Wurlitzer 1st coin firm to air radio show nation-wide." *Billboard*, February 10, 1945, p. 63.
62. "Makes grade!" *Billboard*, December 22, 1945, p. 76.
63. "Location ads boost play of juke boxes." *Billboard*, August 28, 1943, p. 70.
64. "Philly music men on record against smutty recordings." *Billboard*, February 28, 1942, p. 60.
65. "Ads for jukes." *Business Week*, October 27, 1945, pp. 82, 84.
66. "Assn. members pledged to retain juke box control." *Billboard*, January 29, 1944, p. 62.
67. "Wall boxes prove to be 'clinchers' for holding spots." *Billboard*, March 11, 1944, p. 69.
68. "Trade watches 'music in color.'" *Billboard*, June 23, 1945, p. 65.
69. Barry Ulanov. "The jukes take over swing." *American Mercury* 51 (October, 1940): 177.
70. Walter W. Hurd. "The year 1940." *Billboard*, January 18, 1941, p. 70.
71. Geoffrey Parsons Jr. and Robert Yoder. "A nickel a tune." *Reader's Digest* 38 (February, 1941): 115.
72. "Music men meet phone music demand with joint company." *Billboard*, February 28, 1942, p. 60.
73. "Phone music firm opens in Chi." *Billboard*, November 17, 1945, pp. 78, 80.
74. "Tune announcement goes with new wall box music." *Billboard*, May 18, 1946, p. 128.
75. Barry Ulanov, op. cit., p. 177.
76. Walter W. Hurd. "The year 1940." *Billboard*, January 18, 1941, pp. 67, 70.
77. Geoffrey Parsons Jr. and Robert Yoder, op. cit., p. 115.
78. "Newspaper revives Jimmy Roosevelt's coin mach. career." *Billboard*, December 12, 1942, p. 62.
79. "Movie juke boxes ... what about them?" *Billboard*, September 25, 1943, sup., p. 73.
80. Ibid.
81. "Juke box pix biz set for com'l use." *Variety*, December 12, 1945, p. 41.
82. "Jukes helped disk firms recover from sales slump." *Billboard*, November 6, 1943, p. 63.
83. "Juke medium spurs record sales." *Billboard*, February 17, 1945, p. 66.
84. "More folk disks say ops." *Billboard*, May 12, 1945, p. 65.
85. "Big three main op source." *Billboard*, May 26, 1945, p. 73.
86. "U.S. phonograph sales, 1921–1961." *Billboard*, August 4, 1962, sup., p. 9.
87. "Cleveland soldier says no jukes in Sydney, Australia." *Billboard*, June 19, 1943, p. 63; "Australia takes to jukes." *Billboard*, December 1, 1944, pp. 110, 114.
88. "Juke leads Mexico entertainment." *Billboard*, July 28, 1945, pp. 73, 75.
89. "Coin exports at $552,000." *Billboard*, March 30, 1946, p. 133.
90. "The coin machine industry." *Billboard*, February 27, 1943, p. 74.
91. "Music boxes lead field in collections, Baltimorean says." *Billboard*, August 28, 1943, p. 70.
92. "Jukes set musical tastes." *Billboard*, February 10, 1945, p. 63.
93. "Massachusetts ops plan test against Sunday juke fees." *Billboard*, August 29, 1942, p. 71.
94. "Consider ban on juke play." *Billboard*, April 17, 1943, p. 58; "Juke ban discouraged." *Billboard*, April 24, 1943, p. 66.
95. "Ky. Circuit court ruling hurts jukes." *Billboard*, December 23, 1944, p. 65.
96. "Music men accept excise tax without objections." *Billboard*, October 31, 1942, p. 62.
97. "Oklahoma sets up grab plan; doomed to failure." *Billboard*, April 10, 1943, p. 94.

98. "Mass. House debates tax." *Billboard*, June 12, 1943, p. 62.
99. "San Fran denies control of phonos to police dept." *Billboard*, March 18, 1944, p. 61.
100. "Court hits high juke tax." *Billboard*, June 2, 1945, pp. 65–66; "Chicago juke tax annulled." *Billboard*, December 8, 1945, pp. 79, 84.
101. "Lansing juke tax killed." *Billboard*, August 4, 1945, pp. 71–73.
102. "ASCAP's two suits on copyright a test case on jukebox rendition." *Variety*, May 19, 1943, p. 39.
103. "Juke boxes." *The Musician* 50 (January, 1945): 10.
104. "Propose 20 per cent grab." *Billboard*, December 12, 1942, p. 60.
105. "Industry mentions." *Billboard*, December 12, 1942, p. 60.
106. "Press plays up unfortunate news happening in Chi." *Billboard*, November 6, 1943, p. 62.
107. "Lansky-Smith new Wurlitzer N.Y., N.J., Conn. distribs." *Billboard*, March 13, 1943, p. 59.

Chapter 5

1. "Big job ahead for disk makers." *Billboard*, August 12, 1944, p. 65.
2. "Ops see cocktail lounges as top p. -w. locations for juke boxes and photomatics." *Billboard*, January 13, 1945, p. 63.
3. "No glut seen for used phono following V-Day." *Billboard*, April 21, 1945, p. 65.
4. "Juke box bonanza." *Business Week*, February 16, 1946, pp. 37–38.
5. Norman Weiser. "Programming key to better take." *Billboard*, March 4, 1950, sup., p. 22.
6. "3 house tunes build off-season grosses." *Billboard*, November 11, 1950, p. 78.
7. "Police curfew silences Irvington's juke boxes." *New York Times*, July 19, 1947, p. 15.
8. "Survey juke volume problems." *Billboard*, July 26, 1947, pp. 112, 131.
9. "Location owners, Chi juke ops lash out at smut recordings." *Billboard*, May 24, 1947, p. 108.
10. Cam Shedden. "More beer, happy days for ops." *Billboard*, September 7, 1946, pp. 113, 122.
11. Fred Amann. "Survey marginal locations." *Billboard*, August 23, 1947, p. 115.
12. Ibid., pp. 115, 120.
13. Norm Weiser. "Juke box Saturday night." *Billboard*, April 10, 1948, pp. 101, 109, 113.
14. Dick Schreiber. "Operators talk commissions." *Billboard*, June 4, 1949, pp. 113–114.
15. Ibid.
16. "Better PR by ops seen aid to take hike." *Billboard*, July 9, 1949, pp. 149, 152.
17. "Denver ops to ask locations for % changes." *Billboard*, April 1, 1950, p. 110.
18. "Three shot in brawl over juke box tune." *New York Times*, March 2, 1948, p. 28.
19. "Mule train." *Billboard*, December 3, 1949, p. 99.
20. "Anti-delinquency." *Billboard*, July 23, 1949, p. 100.
21. Norman Weiser. "Juke boxes jingle jangle." *Billboard*, February 19, 1949, pp. 98, 102.
22. "Juke rentals—solution?" *Billboard*, May 3, 1947, pp. 114, 116.
23. Ibid., p. 116.
24. Robert Chandler. "Jukers want recognition." *Billboard*, March 8, 1950, p. 43.
25. "Lease idea grows on juke ops." *Billboard*, June 29, 1946, pp. 118, 143.
26. "Hit location-owned jukes." *Billboard*, September 13, 1947, pp. 104, 120.
27. Ibid.
28. "Ops—industry's cornerstone." *Billboard*, September 13, 1947, p. 104.
29. "Tavern men nix juke ownership." *Billboard*, September 20, 1947, pp. 120, 126.
30. "Juke boxes not all gold mines, Nebraskans report." *Billboard*, August 14, 1943, p. 62.
31. "Ten-cent play still up in air." *Billboard*, June 8, 1946, pp. 110, 114.
32. "Open drive for dime juke play." *Billboard*, October 12, 1946, pp. 92, 100.
33. "Trade on juke price hike." *Billboard*, October 19, 1946, pp. 96, 103.
34. "Dime juke play Missouri, Kan. operator trend." *Billboard*, November 2, 1946, p. 100.
35. "Albany liquor group on buyers' strike." *New York Times*, November 23, 1946, p. 26.
36. "Juke box playing now a dime." *New York Times*, November 26, 1946, p. 35.
37. "Manufacturer for 5c play." *Billboard*, December 7, 1946, pp. 94, 102.
38. "75 wall box units on 10c play in K.C." *Billboard*, December 7, 1946, p. 98.
39. "KC paper notes 10c play move in story & column comment." *Billboard*, December 14, 1946, p. 100.
40. "Dime play poll results." *Billboard*, December 14, 1946, p. 100.
41. "The operator must decide." *Billboard*, December 14, 1946, p. 100.
42. "Mobile music operators vote for ten-cent play." *Billboard*, December 14, 1946, p. 100.
43. "Quizees say dime play won't work." *Billboard*, December 28, 1946, p. 93.
44. "Reporter foresees oblivion for dime jukes—but quick!" *Billboard*, December 28, 1946, p. 94.
45. "Worcester ops hike juke box price to dime." *Billboard*, January 4, 1947, p. 51.

46. "Dime juke play top topic." *Billboard*, January 4, 1947, p. 51.
47. "Teen-agers can afford a dime, juke exec says." *Billboard*, January 11, 1947, p. 99.
48. Robert M. Seals. "Dime play … or nickel?" *Billboard*, February 1, 1947, p. 144.
49. "Chicago music ops try play price experiment." *Billboard*, November 1, 1947, p. 102.
50. "L.A.-Chicago op survey shows divided opinion on 6–for-quarter juke play." *Billboard*, March 13, 1948, pp. 100, 107.
51. Norman Weiser. "Ops discuss 10–cent play." *Billboard*, May 22, 1948, pp. 112–113, 119.
52. Norman Weiser. "10–cent play seen doomed." *Billboard*, May 29, 1948, pp. 115, 125.
53. "Anti 10–cent play." *Billboard*, May 29, 1948, p. 125.
54. "Ops gear jukes for dime play." *Variety*, February 14, 1950, p. 40.
55. "Dime play tests still hit-or-miss." *Billboard*, November 11, 1950, pp. 78, 80.
56. "Eastern juke ops dime shy; seek better commission deal." *Billboard*, January 6, 1951, pp. 47, 51.
57. "Iowa ops support 7½-cent coin; air legal problems." *Billboard*, March 19, 1949, p. 113.
58. "Juke operators see tele failing to nip their biz." *Variety*, February 22, 1950, p. 43; "Juke box group to seek new coins." *New York Times*, March 8, 1959, p. 37.
59. "Two Bridgeport ops voice opinion on 7 ½-cent coin." *Billboard*, March 25, 1950, p. 112.
60. "Senate currency group hears 7½c suggestion as jukebox compromise." *Variety*, March 29, 1950, p. 58.
61. "Juke ops on tavern tele." *Billboard*, June 21, 1947, p. 107.
62. Ibid., pp. 107, 136.
63. Ibid., p. 136.
64. "Tavern tele in many Chicago spots music ops' biggest current location headache." *Billboard*, June 28, 1947, p. 113.
65. "Los Angeles juke box ops believe tavern video use only a temporary measure." *Billboard*, October 18, 1947, p. 103.
66. "Ops to meet tele in 40 cities by '49." *Billboard*, May 29, 1948, p. 125.
67. "Video sports give ops headache." *Billboard*, February 5, 1949, pp. 101, 105.
68. "Location tele interest hits skids." *Billboard*, October 8, 1949, p. 116.
69. Ibid.
70. "Most jukebox operators don't fear tele is threat to their industry." *Variety*, March 8, 1950, p. 43.
71. "Videograph gets the jump with coin juke-TV combos." *Billboard*, October 18, 1947, p. 103.

72. "Television in juke box." *New York Times*, June 28, 1949, p. 29.
73. "Juke operators see tele failing to nip their biz." *Variety*, February 22, 1950, p. 43.
74. "Most jukebox operators don't fear tele is threat to their industry." *Variety*, March 8, 1950, p. 43.
75. Samuel L. Abrams. "Public relations success story." *Billboard*, May 18, 1946, pp. 128, 132.
76. "Victor gives with hit disks in ops' Cleveland tie-up." *Billboard*, October 19, 1946, p. 103.
77. "'I Wonder Who's Kissing Her Now' Cleveland's choice." *Billboard*, July 26, 1947, p. 62.
78. Tom McDonough. "Hit tune promotion." *Billboard*, January 24, 1948, p. 130.
79. "Penn ops set hit parties." *Billboard*, May 24, 1947, p. 108.
80. "MAPOA sets delegates to state meet; revive hit tune parties." *Billboard*, June 25, 1949, p. 103.
81. Norman Weiser. "Music ops find keys to increased $." *Billboard*, October 8, 1949, p. 115.
82. "Radio promotion." *Billboard*, February 19, 1949, p. 98.
83. "Iowa ops support 7½-cent coin; air legal problems." *Billboard*, March 19, 1949, p. 113.
84. "Wurlitzer uses TV promotion to fight video competition." *Billboard*, June 24, 1950, p. 3.
85. Fred Amann. "Location promotion pays off." *Billboard*, March 4, 1950, p. 20.
86. Ibid.
87. "Canadian Ace, Century Music to test Sar juke-advertising unit." *Billboard*, February 19, 1949, p. 98.
88. "Neat and very gaudy." *Newsweek* 30 (October 6, 1947): 62, 64.
89. "Celebration for 10,000th Aireon juke box in K.C." *Billboard*, December 7, 1946, p. 94; "Aireon facilities on block." *Billboard*, February 18, 1950, p. 93.
90. Dick Schreiber. "Ops discuss buying preferences." *Billboard*, June 11, 1949, pp. 113–114.
91. Ibid.
92. "Disk makers see juke platter sales hypo as hit tune popularizer." *Billboard*, May 18, 1946, p. 130.
93. "Jukers vote diskery faves." *Billboard*, August 9, 1947, p. 112.
94. "K.C. ops report disk price rise." *Billboard*, September 20, 1947, p. 120.
95. "Diskeries vie for juke box biz with direct sales tack." *Billboard*, April 22, 1950, pp. 3, 24.
96. "U.S. phonograph record sales, 1921–1961." *Billboard*, August 4, 1962, sup., p. 9.

97. Norman Weiser. "New disks not to affect jukes." *Billboard*, April 2, 1949, pp. 133, 136.
98. Ibid.
99. "Wurlitzer debuts new juke." *Billboard*, February 18, 1950, pp. 93, 99.
100. Norman Weiser. "New speed jukes." *Billboard*, May 27, 1950, p. 154.
101. "RCA-Col battle of disk speeds spreads to jukebox industry." *Billboard*, July 5, 1950, p. 35.
102. "1st 45 juke is released by Seeburg." *Billboard*, October 28, 1950, pp. 3, 114.
103. "45s moving into greater prominence on jukes, threatening 78s' position." *Variety*, November 29, 1950, p. 42.
104. "Export problems revealed by juke box manufacturer." *Billboard*, May 10, 1947, p. 116.
105. "Atlas man says juke Mexico's top coin mach." *Billboard*, May 24, 1947, p. 108.
106. "Jukes solid in South Africa." *Billboard*, May 31, 1947, pp. 108, 110.
107. Tom McDonough. "Exports heavy despite embargo." *Billboard*, April 2, 1949, pp. 103, 141.
108. "Jukebox invasion." *Time* 56 (July 24, 1950): 32.
109. "Juke-boxes face uplift." *New York Times*, August 22, 1946, p. 29; "Syracuse juke box fee passes council." *Billboard*, January 12, 1947, p. 99.
110. "Ala. turns down petition for jukes." *Billboard*, December 28, 1946, p. 93.
111. "Open Alabama taverns to jukes." *Billboard*, November 29, 1947, pp. 156, 163.
112. "Alabama governor appoints new ABC board." *Billboard*, February 7, 1948, pp. 106, 108.
113. "Mobile taverns beat juke ban by renting equipment." *Billboard*, May 22, 1948, p. 115.
114. "Youngstown phono tax trimmed." *Billboard*, July 6, 1946, pp. 112, 142.
115. "Settle Chicago juke tax." *Billboard*, November 2, 1946, pp. 95, 100.
116. "Juke-box tax drafter." *New York Times*, April 29, 1947, p. 22.
117. "Court upholds city juke tax." *Billboard*, March 8, 1947, p. 103.
118. "Juke legislative pot boiling." *Billboard*, March 8, 1947, p. 103.
119. "Bloomington passes machine license law." *Billboard*, June 21, 1947, p. 136; "Council Bluffs sets new juke, game licenses." *Billboard*, June 11, 1949, p. 113.
120. "L.A. locations must pay new $7.50 license." *Billboard*, February 18, 1950, p. 93.
121. "Radio, BMI, films back ASCAP in bid for coin machine revenue." *Variety*, January 29, 1947, p. 42.
122. "Juke legislative pot boiling." *Billboard*, March 8, 1947, p. 104.
123. "Ask new law on juke box." *New York Times*, May 24, 1947, p. 10; "Jukes battle tide rising against copyright exemption." *Billboard*, June 21, 1947, pp. 3, 25.
124. "Petrillo nixes plea for bite on juke take." *Billboard*, June 18, 1949, p. 110.
125. "Ass'n offsets bad press." *Billboard*, November 23, 1946, pp. 102, 106.
126. "Writer reports one juke box for every 500 persons of U.S." *Billboard*, May 4, 1946, p. 136; "$232,000,000 in '46 from jukes." *Variety*, January 8, 1947, p. 218.
127. "Census shows 99,000 jukes made in 1947." *Billboard*, June 11, 1949, p. 113.
128. Dick Schreiber. "Ops discuss incomes & expenses." *Billboard*, June 18, 1949, pp. 109–110.
129. "Ops air views on salaries." *Billboard*, June 25, 1949, pp. 94, 103.
130. "Music operator survey." *Billboard*, October 7, 1950, pp. 78+.
131. "Analyze juke box trends." *Billboard*, January 10, 1948, pp. 87, 92.
132. Ibid.
133. Norman Weiser. "How can ops hike income?" *Billboard*, June 12, 1948, pp. 107–111.
134. "The juke box network: the manufacturing story." *Billboard*, January 22, 1949, sup., p. 17.
135. "The juke box network: part 2, the distributor's story." *Billboard*, January 22, 1949, sup., p. 18.
136. "N.E. ops wed jukes, cig. mchs." *Billboard*, November 19, 1949, pp. 93, 95.
137. Dick Schreiber. "1950: a solid market." *Billboard*, March 4, 1950, sup., p. 17.

Chapter 6

1. James L. Lennon. "Coin machine biz grows up. " *Variety*, October 1, 1952, p. 28.
2. Jim Wickman. "Color TV threatens tavern juke boxes." *Billboard*, May 29, 1954, pp. 1, 100.
3. "Keys to profits: care in programming box." *Billboard*, May 23, 1953, p. 60.
4. Jim Wickman. "U.S. finicky about juke boxes' music." *Billboard*, July 23, 1955, pp. 1, 126.
5. "Blank disk urged in jukes so one can buy silence." *New York Times*, January 1, 1953, p. 30.
6. "Silence is golden in Danish juke." *Billboard*, April 23, 1955, p. 30.
7. Hal Reves. "Tailor-made music offers new horizons to juke ops." *Billboard*, July 10, 1954, pp. 69, 72.
8. Ibid.
9. "Juke profits tops: 24-hr. cafes & bars." *Billboard*, March 30, 1957, p. 110.

10. Ibid.
11. "Juke dispute causes tiff in tavern." *Billboard*, February 2, 1957, pp. 80, 89.
12. "Auto. phono rental demand tops supply." *Billboard*, December 29, 1958, pp. 51, 60.
13. Dick Schreiber. "Only 17 per cent of music operators use contracts." *Billboard*, November 15, 1952, pp. 93–94; "40% of nation's music operators use written contracts." *Billboard*, May 28, 1955, pp. 91–92.
14. "Route study hypes nickel-dime fuss." *Billboard*, February 10, 1951, p. 76.
15. "Ops go to dime on country-wide basis." *Billboard*, March 3, 1951, pp. 68, 75.
16. Norman Weiser. "Income vs. cost crisis." *Billboard*, March 17, 1951, p. 72.
17. "Dime jukes take Chicago beating." *Variety*, May 30, 1951, p. 41.
18. "Chi ops push dime play; over 'hump.'" *Billboard*, June 9, 1951, pp. 76, 81.
19. "Public, location promotion top 10-cent play factors." *Billboard*, June 15, 1951, p. 72.
20. "Dime play question remains unanswered." *Billboard*, October 31, 1951, p. 68.
21. "Nickel still tops with juke ops; no plans for upping tab to dime." *Variety*, December 16, 1953, p. 41.
22. "N.Y. juke ops up spins to 10c." *Variety*, March 2, 1955, p. 55; "Sked dime play move in central Fla. in 2 weeks." *Billboard*, March 19, 1955, p. 74; "Ops sked dime push in Boston on May 1." *Billboard*, March 19, 1955, p. 74.
23. "Operator survey panel airs nationwide 10c play." *Billboard*, March 19, 1955, pp. 74, 85.
24. "AMI, Wurlitzer to all-dime output; Rock-Ola mulls move." *Billboard*, April 16, 1955, p. 71.
25. "Juke 10c play hits op snag in Twin Cities." *Billboard*, March 10, 1956, p. 84; "Peoria ops try 10c play again; move is strong." *Billboard*, March 10, 1956, p. 84; "Music goes 'round 25,000,000 times in juke boxes' day." *Billboard*, May 12, 1956, p. 43.
26. "What's holding up dime music play?" *Billboard*, June 2, 1956, p. 67.
27. "Ad campaign helps Denver ops to dime." *Billboard*, July 15, 1957, p. 124.
28. Aaron Sternfield. "5c juke bastions crumbled by dime." *Billboard*, August 26, 1957, p. 1.
29. Nick Biro. "Dime conversion spurred: 53 cities." *Billboard*, July 22, 1957, pp. 104, 112.
30. "Juke box industry to mark 65th anniversary in May." *Billboard*, May 2, 1953, pp. 1, 92.
31. "Operators, manufacturers set anniversary promotion drive." *Billboard*, May 23, 1953, p. 62; "Text of Juke Box Week Detroit proclamation." *Billboard*, May 30, 1953, p. 82.
32. "Celebrates 66th year with good will drive." *Billboard*, June 26, 1954, p. 101.
33. "Ladies, gents! Meet the juke box man." *Billboard*, October 15, 1955, pp. 1, 80.
34. Ibid.; "Weekly MOA radio show gets under way." *Billboard*, October 15, 1955, p. 80.
35. Bob Dietmeier. "New ideas, records pep up a slow juke." *Billboard*, April 6, 1957, p. 84.
36. "Juke assn. Execs adopt plan to mass-advertise via music boxes." *Billboard*, August 7, 1954, p. 14.
37. "MOA ops hear Pantages outline advertising plan." *Billboard*, April 16, 1955, p. 72.
38. "MOA opens in Chi to 'beat ASCAP' theme on jukebox tap." *Variety*, May 9, 1956, p. 43.
39. "Wurlitzer deal ends Capehart juke saga." *Billboard*, September 22, 1951, p. 94.
40. "H.C. Evans & Co. juke box division sold for $200,000." *Billboard*, April 16, 1955, p. 71.
41. "Rock juke scores multi-selection record." *Billboard*, October 11, 1952, p. 88.
42. Dick Schreiber. "Machine output sets a record." *Billboard*, March 6, 1954, p. 48.
43. Bob Dietmeier. "More jumbo jukes spell more disks." *Billboard*, February 2, 1957, pp. 1, 80.
44. "Juke box disk purchases up to 50,000,000 a year." *Billboard*, January 19, 1952, pp. 1, 16.
45. "Juke op trend crimps potential." *Billboard*, May 2, 1953, p. 16.
46. "How juke boxes sustain disks build them into hit category." *Billboard*, May 23, 1953, p. 81.
47. Is Horowitz. "Juke box influence on record business." *Billboard*, May 23, 1953, p. 91.
48. Herm Schoenfeld. "Jukebox: a windfall probe." *Variety*, February 18, 1959, p. 41.
49. "U.S. phonograph record sales, 1921–1961." *Billboard*, August 4, 1962, sup., p. 9.
50. Tom McDonough. "Export mart CM bonanza." *Billboard*, October 13, 1951, p. 67.
51. "Juke exports jump in value, may top $3 million for 1951." *Billboard*, March 22, 1952, pp. 80, 82.
52. "Juke makers find good biz in exports." *Billboard*, April 19, 1952, pp. 84, 96.
53. "Riojas co. history a trade parallel." *Billboard*, September 22, 1951, p. 94.
54. "Venezuela heads top 5 import list." *Billboard*, June 7, 1952, pp. 76, 83.
55. "Jukes score hit in Japan despite prices." *Billboard*, July 12, 1952, p. 78.
56. "Bacon finds European market still untapped." *Billboard*, July 12, 1952, p. 78.
57. "Coin machines hit $7,621,879 export." *Billboard*, April 4, 1953, pp. 1, 76.
58. Steve Schickel. "Venezuela again top juke box importer." *Billboard*, April 4, 1953, p. 79.

59. "How exports grow." *Billboard*, April 4, 1953, p. 76.

60. "A march against juke boxes." *New York Times*, May 3, 1953, p. 27.

61. Robert Dietmeier. "1953 export record; $6,000,000 in jukes." *Billboard*, March 6, 1954, p. 52; "1953 juke exports up 50%; 14,089 units at $6,317,533." *Billboard*, April 24, 1954, p. 78.

62. "Infant German juke box industry booming." *Billboard*, October 2, 1954, p. 85.

63. "Native jukeboxes threat to U.S. biz in West Germany." *Variety*, March 2, 1955, p. 55.

64. "France, once Debussy, now goes for jukes." *Billboard*, March 19, 1955, p. 85.

65. Ken Knauf. "Juke box bonanza: world market boom." *Billboard*, March 26, 1955, p. 52.

66. Ibid.

67. "Juke boxes: big business booms around the world." *Billboard*, April 30, 1955, pp. 86–87.

68. "World game markets import $3 mil in U.S. units in '54." *Billboard*, April 30, 1955, p. 88; "20,000 U.S. venders shipped around the globe in 1954." *Billboard*, April 30, 1955, p. 89.

69. Bob Dietmeier. "Banner year ahead for juke industry." *Billboard*, July 30, 1955, pp. 1, 86; "Bogota curbs juke boxes." *New York Times*, May 2, 1956, p. 26.

70. "Selling the U.S. jukebox abroad." *Business Week*, September 1, 1956, pp. 101–102.

71. "Austria swings to juke box beat." *Variety*, January 9, 1957, pp. 4, 60.

72. "Jukeboxes take big hold in Paris." *Variety*, July 10, 1957, p. 109.

73. Bob Dietmeier. "Juke world boom still on upbeat." *Billboard*, July 22, 1957, pp. 1, 104.

74. "Making an appointment to play a jukebox." *Variety*, July 23, 1958, p. 2.

75. Aaron Sternfield. "Jukes build own niche in Mexico." *Billboard*, August 25, 1958, pp. 1, 4.

76. Omer Anderson. "British juke box boom in offing, as dollar bars ease." *Billboard*, June 22, 1959, p. 126.

77. "Mex music union asks gov't aid vs. jukebox monster." *Variety*, August 5, 1959, p. 62.

78. "Mexican trade hit by curfew on juke boxes." *Billboard*, December 7, 1959, p. 81.

79. Omer Anderson. "Red Europe bows to juke box passion." *Billboard*, December 7, 1958, pp. 1, 81.

80. "Music operators shoulder record taxes in 21 states." *Billboard*, June 2, 1956, pp. 66, 81.

81. "Two of three cities in 800 have annual juke box tax." *Billboard*, May 5, 1958, pp. 52+.

82. "Juke-royalty bill again to the fore." *Billboard*, February 17, 1951, pp. 10, 72; "Cong Miller warns juke operators on drastic fed amusement taxation." *Variety*, March 28, 1951, p. 40.

83. "ASCAP endorses Kefauver plan on juke royalties." *Variety*, May 30, 1951, p. 41.

84. "ASCAP pulls a faux pas." *Billboard*, June 9, 1951, p. 10.

85. "Jukebox copyright act amendment given good chance." *Variety*, October 31, 1951, p. 40.

86. "Record companies oppose juke's royalty payments." *Billboard*, November 3, 1951, pp. 1, 16

87. "Jukebox industry bucks Kefauver in D.C. hearings on royalty bill." *Variety*, February 6, 1952, pp. 43, 50.

88. "Juke royalty battle heated as both sides meet head-on." *Billboard*, February 16, 1952, p. 17.

89. "Major pubs steam at Mitch Miller telling House diskers make the hits." *Variety*, February 13, 1952, p. 51.

90. "Rockola calls jukes 'poor man's opera.'" *Billboard*, February 16, 1952, pp. 17, 80.

91. "Juke box bill is unworkable." *Billboard*, February 16, 1952, pp. 17, 83.

92. "Juke ops' war chest to fight D.C. licensing." *Variety*, March 25, 1953, pp. 53, 58.

93. "Composers sing the blues to reap juke box coins." *New York Times*, July 16, 1953, p. 19.

94. "BMI's Kaye-bomb vs. jukeboxes." *Variety*, July 22, 1953, pp. 43, 45; "Music biz focuses on D.C. hearings over McCarran bill to license jukes." *Billboard*, October 14, 1953, p. 73.

95. "Griffin 'individually' (not for RIAA, it sez here) pro-jukebox ops." *Variety*, October 28, 1953, pp. 39, 42.

96. "Jukes, cleffers get day in court on copyright bill." *Variety*, October 28, 1953, pp. 39, 42.

97. Abel Green. "Time for a change." *Variety*, November 4, 1953, p. 43.

98. Ben Atlas. "Attempts to end copyright exemptions date back to '26." *Billboard*, December 4, 1954, pp. 21, 72.

99. Ibid.

100. "Solon calls for 'justice' to cleffers." *Variety*, March 16, 1955, pp. 1, 18.

101. "Congressmen add two copyright bills aimed at juke exemption." *Billboard*, June 22, 1955, p. 49.

102. "MOA opens in Chi to 'beat ASCAP' theme on jukebox tap." *Variety*, May 9, 1956, pp. 41–46.

103. "Jukes won't talk to ASCAP." *Variety*, December 19, 1956, pp. 51, 60.

104. "Int'l trade groups join Yanks in support

of tax on jukeboxes." *Variety*, February 5, 1958, pp. 53, 58.

105. "Juke ops, performing rights societies in no mood to compromise in House hearings to revamp Copyright Act." *Variety*, June 17, 1959, pp. 39, 48.

106. "Grand jury cites juke box maker." *New York Times*, March 3, 1956, p. 29.

107. "Anti-trust charges." *Billboard*, March 10, 1956, p. 84.

108. "Seeburg is fined $2,000." *New York Times*, January 16, 1957, p. 41.

109. "Seeburg settles antitrust action with consent decree." *Billboard*, February 9, 1957, p. 78.

110. "Juke box suit settled." *New York Times*, April 16, 1958, p. 52.

111. "Chi commission fingers mobster control of jukes." *Variety*, April 27, 1955, pp. 1, 8.

112. Lester Velie. "Racket in the juke box." *Reader's Digest* 67 (November, 1955): 65–71.

113. Ibid.

114. "Reader's Digest on 'Racket in the juke box.'" *Variety*, October 19, 1955, pp. 61, 63.

115. W. D. Littleford. "To the Reader's Digest." *Billboard*, October 29, 1955, pp. 1, 74.

116. Aaron Sternfield. "Union racketeer tells how he organized 100 operators." *Billboard*, August 12, 1957, pp. 121, 133.

117. "It's cheaper to fight." *Billboard*, August 12, 1957, p. 121.

118. "The great jukebox shakedown." *Newsweek* 53 (February 9, 1959): 27–28.

119. Joseph A. Loftus. "Juke box inquiry hears of gangster infiltration." *New York Times*, February 11, 1959, pp. 1, 34.

120. Russell Baker. "Pushing of disks bared at inquiry." *New York Times*, February 21, 1959, p. 10.

121. "The hit parade." *Time* 73 (February 23, 1959): 20.

122. "The jukebox tune." *Time* 73 (March 2, 1959): 15.

123. "Juke box men singing those red ink blues." *New York Times*, March 20, 1951, p. 30; "Cong. Miller warns juke operators on drastic fed amusement taxation." *Variety*, March 28, 1951, p. 37.

124. "Reduced metal quotas cut juke boxes; manufacture." *New York Times*, November 9, 1951, p. 42; "Juke box trends." *Billboard*, March 24, 1956, p. 80.

125. "Juke biz costly operation with small-profit returns." *Billboard*, February 9, 1952, p. 78.

126. "6th annual operator poll." *Billboard*, May 23, 1953, pp. 104+.

127. "Operator poll, part I." *Billboard*, May 20, 1957, p. 50+.

128. Bob Dietmeier. "How many jukes are there and is there room for more?" *Billboard*, May 20, 1957, p. 86.

129. "U.S. releases 1954 juke, game totals." *Billboard*, July 15, 1957, pp. 124, 136.

130. "1958 juke box operator poll." *Billboard*, May 5, 1958, pp. 32–37.

131. Bob Dietmeier. "How much do juke operators make?" *Billboard*, July 14, 1958, pp. 1, 72.

132. "How many jukes? 450,000 good bet." *Billboard*, April 6, 1959, pp. 32+.

133. "House group mulls survey figures on juke operations." *Billboard*, June 22, 1959, p. 127.

Chapter 7

1. Aaron Sternfield. "Operators look to movies, shows as greatest source of juke plays." *Billboard*, March 24, 1962, p. 12.

2. "Soft phono volume soothes public gripes, Italians find." *Billboard*, October 10, 1960, p. 76.

3. "Risque records." *Billboard*, April 1, 1967, p. 69.

4. "Image-conscious operators shun double-entendre disks." *Billboard*, April 1, 1967, p. 69.

5. James B. Dittman. "Innovation: a trademark of Rowe." *Billboard*, October 12, 1968, p. MOA16; Alan Penchansky. "Operators hail video jukebox future." *Billboard*, November 24, 1979, p. 46.

6. "MOA: hope, heritage of jukebox operators." *Billboard*, December 27, 1969, p. 72.

7. Nick Biro. "Miller, Ratajack, pinpoint MOA problems." *Billboard*, May 29, 1961, p. 35; "MOA: hope, heritage of jukebox operators." *Billboard*, December 27, 1969, p. 72.

8. Earl Paige. "MOA's programs designed to assist members and instill new public image." *Billboard*, October 16, 1971, p. MOA1; "Business assn set for largest show." *Billboard*, September 16, 1972, pp. 27–28.

9. "The jukebox, it seems, is a hit of the past." *New York Times*, July 21, 1982, p. C12.

10. Earl Paige. "The jukebox story." *Billboard*, July 4, 1976, pp. MR150, MR152.

11. Moira McCormick. "Elvis tops list of jukebox hits." *Billboard*, August 20, 1988, pp. 6, 77.

12. "Ops pooh-pooh owned locations." *Billboard*, August 14, 1961, p. 62.

13. Aaron Sternfield. "Juke box commercials may bring in extra operator loot." *Billboard*, April 17, 1961, pp. 1, 49.

14. "In tune again?" *Forbes* 111 (March 1, 1973): 64; "500,000 Wurlitzer phonographs." *Billboard*, August 4, 1962, p. 3.

15. Steven Greenhouse. "Swan Song." *New York Times*, March 10, 1974, sec. 3, p. 15.

16. "Rock-Ola take biggest in 40 years as rival folds." *Billboard*, March 23, 1974, p. 38; "The jukebox it seems, is a hit of the past." *New York Times*, July 21, 1982, p. C12.

17. Paul Ackerman. "Juke box altering singles A&R." *Billboard*, July 21, 1961, pp. 1, 66.

18. "U.S. record sales." *Billboard*, August 4, 1962, sup., p. 8.

19. Jack Desrocher. "Database." *U.S. News & World Report* 112 (February 17, 1992): 10.

20. Myron Kandel. "Face-lifting set for jukeboxes." *New York Times*, September 17, 1962, p. 47.

21. "Jukeboxes try more elegant image in bid to expand number of locations." *Variety*, April 26, 1972, p. 57.

22. "Instant discotheque: just add dancers." *Business Week*, February 27, 1965, pp. 108–110.

23. Aaron Sternfield. "Cinebox tests warm in Philly." *Billboard*, May 11, 1963, pp. 1, 53.

24. Ray Brack. "Cinema juke box: just a novelty?" *Billboard*, July 10, 1965, p. 48.

25. William M. Freeman. "A new 'juke box' finds popularity." *New York Times*, November 8, 1964, sec. 3, p. 5.

26. "Yippee!" *New Yorker* 40 (July 11, 1964): 21–22.

27. "Scooby-Ooby Scopitone." *Time* 84 (August 21, 1964): 49.

28. Ray Brack. "Cinema juke box: just a novelty?" *Billboard*, July 10, 1965, pp. 45, 48.

29. Alan Penchansky. "Operators hail video jukebox future." *Billboard*, November 24, 1979, pp. 6, 46.

30. Jim McCullaugh. "Vid jukebox debuts." *Billboard*, May 15, 1982, pp. 48–49.

31. "Video jukebox uses promo clips, TV specials, old concert footage." *Variety*, July 7, 1982, p. 64.

32. "Video jukebox firm launches drive to license promo clips." *Variety*, March 30, 1983, p. 119.

33. "High tech clip jukebox bows." *Billboard*, July 10, 1983, p. 30.

34. Ken Terry. "Countdown begins for video jukeboxes." *Variety*, May 23, 1984, pp. 75, 78.

35. Kathleen Deveny. "Can high tech put Seeburg back in the groove?" *Business Week*, December 2, 1985, p. 89.

36. Peter H. Lewis. "Advances in jukeboxes." *New York Times*, November 19, 1986, p. D10.

37. Deborah Russell. "Juke biz finds new life via new technology, markets." *Billboard*, October 19, 1991, pp. 10, 83.

38. Neil Strauss. "Where the 45s keep spinning." *New York Times*, April 28, 1995, pp. C1, C25.

39. Ken Knauf. "1960 juke box & game exports jump 7.6% from 1959." *Billboard*, June 12, 1961, p. 44; Aaron Sternfield. "U.S. coin exports sets new mark." *Billboard*, July 11, 1964, pp. 42, 54.

40. "Jukebox exports up in 3–year totals." *Billboard*, July 6, 1968, p. 45.

41. Aaron Sternfield. "British juke box population at 20,000 — may hit 100,000." *Billboard*, May 30, 1960, pp. 85, 92.

42. Omer Anderson. "W. German musicians press for royalty payments on jukeboxes." *Billboard*, December 5, 1960, p. 68.

43. "Jazz juke box tunes no longer red taboo." *Billboard*, May 22, 1961, p. 46; "Red jukes in the black." *Billboard*, August 14, 1961, p. 63.

44. "Bulgarian Reds ban juke jazz; blast imperialistic cha cha disk." *Billboard*, August 14, 1961, pp. 6, 62.

45. "Jukeboxes banned in Bangkok." *New York Times*, June 25, 1962, p. 3.

46. "International report." *Billboard*, October 12, 1968, pp. MOA30+.

47. "Gordon spins happy tunes of soaring jukebox life in Europe." *Billboard*, May 10, 1969, p. 72.

48. "Int'l jukebox survey." *Billboard*, January 9, 1971, pp. 35–36, 38; "Int'l jukebox survey." *Billboard*, January 2, 1971, p. 36.

49. Kari Helopaltio. "See 6,000 more Finland spots via new juke boxes." *Billboard*, September 16, 1972, p. 30; Letty Kongalides. "Greek jukebox industry set for rapid expansion." *Billboard*, September 16, 1972, p. 30.

50. "The juke box: billion dollar threat." *International Musician* 60 (September, 1961): 14–15.

51. Sigmund Spaeth. "In and out of tune." *Music Journal* 20 (February, 1962): 80.

52. Stanley Green. "Jukebox piracy." *The Atlantic Monthly* 209 (April, 1962): 136.

53. "Joe Robbins letter takes Atlantic to task for phono royalty article." *Billboard*, April 14, p. 52.

54. E. R. Ratajack. "Jukebox piracy." *The Atlantic Monthly* 210 (August, 1962): 30–31.

55. Mildred Hall. "See juke bill getting to floor." *Billboard*, May 18, 1963, pp. 56–57.

56. "House copyright committee okays repeal of 1909 jukebox exemption." *Variety*, June 26, 1963, p. 51.

57. "Authors League of America says all creators must resent jukes' free ride." *Variety*, September 25, 1963, p. 56.

58. "Rewarding artistic achievement." *New York Times*, November 3, 1963, sec. 4, p. 8.

59. Larry Michie. "U.S. Senate warns ASCAP — jukes to make copyright deal — or else." *Variety*, March 22, 1967, pp. 1, 86.

60. Mildred Hall. "Copyright crossroads." *Billboard*, April 1, 1967, pp. 65, 68, 70.

61. "Jukebox industry's political power on copyright bill baffles music biz." *Variety*, April 26, 1967, p. 183.
62. Nicholas Allen. "Copyright still a key issue." *Billboard*, October 12, 1968, p. MOA23.
63. "Move to freeze $8 juke fee in copyright bill stirs ASCAP, BMI." *Variety*, August 17, 1974, p. 41; Mildred Hall. "McClellan bomb: $20 jukebox fee." *Billboard*, December 14, 1974, pp. 1, 14.
64. Mildred Hall. "Juke royalties." *Billboard*, November 15, 1977, p. 10.
65. Mildred Hall. "Campus and jukeboxes get break." *Billboard*, January 7, 1978, pp. 3, 102.
66. "Juke ops brush Copyright Act; ASCAP sues." *Variety*, August 2, 1978, pp. 1, 82.
67. Mildred Hall. "Jukebox operators slow in fee payoff." *Billboard*, August 12, 1978, p. 87.
68. "ASCAP-BMI to split jukebox royalties." *Variety*, December 12, 1979, p. 2; "ASCAP nears $100–mil take for new peak." *Billboard*, February 28, 1979, p. 97.
69. "Tribunal raises jukebox fee up to $25 in 1982, $50 in 1984." *Variety*, December 17, 1980, pp. 71, 78.
70. "Tribunal defends boost in copyright fees on jukeboxes." *Variety*, January 7, 1981, pp. 2, 68.
71. "Rights groups pact with jukebox ops; rebates promised." *Variety*, May 15, 1985, pp. 1, 94.
72. Bill Holland. "Crackdown on unlicenced jukes." *Billboard*, August 16, 1986, p. 6.
73. "C'right office eyes juke law followup." *Variety*, January 27, 1988, p. 91; "Tribunal finalizes juke royalty plan." *Variety*, November 27, 1985, p. 142.

74. Melinda Newman. "New license office to enforce jukebox performing rights pact." *Billboard*, April 7, 1990, p. 94.
75. Thomas Lea Davidson. "1961 music machine survey." *Billboard*, May 15, 1961, pp. 9+.
76. Aaron Sternfield. "1962 music machine survey." *Billboard*, May 12, 1962, pp. 52–53.
77. "Jukebox spins play trouble for operators." *Variety*, January 24, 1973, p. 49.
78. Alan Penchansky. "Rising simple prices hurt U.S. jukeboxes." *Billboard*, August 9, 1980, pp. 1, 39.
79. Alan Penchansky. "Jukeboxes 'endangered,' survey says." *Billboard*, November 15, 1980, pp. 3, 66.
80. Vance Muse. "Jukeboxes: reviving the joy." *Rolling Stone*, September 17, 1981, pp. 80, 82.
81. Ken Terry. "Jukebox biz is in a fatal decline." *Variety*, December 2, 1981, pp. 1, 110.
82. Peter McDermott. "Singled out for extinction." *Billboard*, December 15, 1981, p. 18.
83. "Arcade videogame profits nearly twice those of jukeboxes." *Variety*, January 25, 1984, p. 124.
84. Michael deCourcy Hinds. "The vintage jukebox still sounds sweet." *New York Times*, July 8, 1978, p. 12; Vance Muse. "Jukeboxes: reviving the joy." *Rolling Stone*, September 17, 1981, p. 82.
85. Charles R Cross. "Jukebox revival." *Esquire* 98 (December, 1982): 35–36; Robert Palmer. "A guide to the last great jukeboxes in town." *New York Times*, February 4, 1983, pp. C1, C20; James Barron. "Golden oldies: jukeboxes are big again." *New York Times*, February 23, 1989, pp. C1, C12.

Bibliography

Abrams, Samuel L. "Public relations success story." *Billboard*, May 18, 1946, pp. 128, 132.
Ackerman, Paul. "Juke box altering singles A&R." *Billboard*, July 17, 1961, pp. 1, 66.
"Ad campaign helps Denver ops to dime." *Billboard*, July 15, 1957, p. 124.
"Ads for the jukes." *Business Week*, October 27, 1945, pp. 82, 84.
Advertisement. *Billboard*, August 27, 1938, p. 109.
Advertisement. *Billboard*, February 25, 1939, p. 69.
Advertisement. *Billboard*, May 6, 1939, p. 78.
"Advertising paper quotes." *Billboard*, September 23, 1939, p. 69.
"Aireon facilities on block." *Billboard*, February 18, 1950, p. 93.
"Ala. turns down petition for jukes." *Billboard*, December 28, 1946, p. 93.
"Alabama governor appoints new ABC board." *Billboard*, February 7, 1948, pp. 106, 108.
"Albany liquor group on buyers' strike." *New York Times*, November 23, 1946, p. 26.
Allen, Herb J. "Records for operators' needs." *Billboard*, January 18, 1936, p. 72.
Allen, Nicholas. "Copyright: still a key issue." *Billboard*, October 12, 1968, p. MOA23.
Amann, Fred. "Location promotion pays off." *Billboard*, March 4, 1950, p. 20.
Amann, Fred. "Survey marginal locations." *Billboard*, August 23, 1947, pp. 115, 120.
"America's jookbox craze: coin phonographs reap harvest of hot tunes and nickels." *Newsweek* 15 (June 3, 1940): 48, 50.
"AMI sales policy, equipment revealed." *Billboard*, March 15, 1941, p. 62.
"AMI, Wurlitzer to all-dime output; Rock-Ola mulls move." *Billboard*, April 16, 1955, p. 71.
"Amusement biz puts music boxes to use in many ways." *Billboard*, August 24, 1940, p. 75.
"Analyze juke box trends." *Billboard*, January 10, 1948, pp. 87, 92.
Anderson, Omer. "British juke box boom in offing, as dollar bars ease." *Billboard*, June 22, 1959, p. 126.
Anderson, Omer. "Red Europe bows to juke box passion." *Billboard*, December 7, 1959, pp. 1, 81, 89.
Anderson, Omer. "W. German musicians press for royalty payments on juke boxes." *Billboard*, December 5, 1960, p. 68.
"Another dept. store installs juke box." *Billboard*, May 26, 1945, p. 73.
"Anti-delinquency." *Billboard*, July 23, 1949, p. 100.
"Anti 10–cent play." *Billboard*, May 29, 1948, p. 125.
"Anti-trust charges." *Billboard*, March 10, 1956, p. 84.
"APMA hits smutty disks." *Billboard*, January 20, 1940, p. 82.
"Arcade videogame profits nearly twice those of jukeboxes." *Variety*, January 25, 1984, p. 124.
"ASCAP-BMI to split jukebox royalties." *Variety*, December 12, 1979, p. 2.
"ASCAP endorses Kefauver plan on juke royalties." *Variety*, May 30, 1951, p. 41.
"ASCAP nears $100–mil take for new reach." *Billboard*, February 28, 1979, p. 97.
"ASCAP pulls a faux pas." *Billboard*, June 9, 1951, p. 10.
"ASCAP's two suits on copyright a test case on jukebox rendition." *Variety*, May 19, 1943, p. 39.
"Ask new law on juke box." *New York Times*, May 24, 1947, p. 10.
"Assn. members pledged to retain juke box control." *Billboard*, January 29, 1944, p. 62.

"Ass'n offsets bad press." *Billboard*, November 23, 1946, pp. 102, 106.

"Assn. pledges juke to each teen-age club." *Billboard*, January 29, 1944, p. 62.

Atlas, Ben. "Attempts to end copyright exemptions date back to '26." *Billboard*, December 4, 1954, pp. 21, 72.

"Atlas man says juke Mexico's top coin mach." *Billboard*, May 24, 1947, p. 108.

"Attention, phono ops." *Billboard*, September 4, 1937, p. 80.

"Australia takes to jukes." *Billboard*, December 1, 1945, pp. 110, 114.

"Austria swings to jukebox beat." *Variety*, January 9, 1957, pp. 4, 60.

"Authors League of America says all creators must resent jukes' free ride." *Variety*, September 25, 1963, p. 56.

"Auto. phono rental demand tops supply." *Billboard*, December 29, 1958, pp. 51, 60.

"Bacon finds European market still untapped." *Billboard*, July 12, 1952, p. 78.

"Badger over quota in sales drive." *Billboard*, May 6, 1939, p. 78.

Baker, Russell. "Pushing of disks bared at inquiry. *New York Times*, February 21, 1959, p. 10.

Barol, Bill. "The Wurlitzer 1015." *American Heritage* 40 (September/October, 1989): 28–29.

Barron, James. "Golden oldies: jukeboxes are big again." *New York Times*, February 23, 1989, pp. C1, C12.

"Begin the Beguine gets no. 1 spot on Denver phono 6 yrs." *Billboard*, April 21, 1945, p. 65.

"Better PR by ops seen aid to take hike." *Billboard*, July 9, 1949, pp. 149, 152.

"Big job ahead for disk makers." *Billboard*, August 12, 1944, p. 65.

"Big three main op source." *Billboard*, May 26, 1945, p. 73.

"Biggest record market is phonos, says A. P. writer." *Billboard*, January 20, 1940, p. 74.

Biro, Nick. "Dime conversion spurred: 53 cities." *Billboard*, July 22, 1957, pp. 104, 112.

Biro, Nick. "Miller Ratajack pinpoint MOA problems." *Billboard*, May 29, 1961, pp. 35, 61.

"Blank disk urged in jukes so one can buy silence." *New York Times*, January 1, 1953, p. 30.

"Bloomington passes machine license law." *Billboard*, June 21, 1947, p. 136.

"BMI's Kaye-bomb vs. jukeboxes." *Variety*, July 22, 1953, pp. 43, 45.

"Bogota curbs juke boxes." *New York Times*, May 2, 1956, p. 26.

Boldt, Ben. "Phonograph industry brings opportunities for musicians." *Billboard*, October 19, 1940, p. 65.

Bowers, Q. David. *Put Another Nickel In.* Vestal, New York: The Vestal Press, 1966.

Brack, Ray. "Cinema juke box: just a novelty?" *Billboard*, July 10, 1965, pp. 45, 48.

Brack, Ray. "Golden age of music merchandising." *Billboard*, October 12, 1968, pp. MOA3+.

"Bulgarian Reds ban juke jazz; blast imperialistic cha cha disk." *Billboard*, August 14, 1961, pp. 6, 62.

"Business assn set for largest show." *Billboard*, September 16, 1972, pp. 27–28.

"Canadian Ace, Century Music to test Sar juke-advertising unit." *Billboard*, February 19, 1949, p. 98.

Capehart, Homer E. "Americanism and music." *Billboard*, July 27, 1940, p. 78.

"Celebrates 66th year with good will drive." *Billboard*, June 26, 1954, p. 101.

"Celebration for 10,000th Aireon juke box in K.C." *Billboard*, December 7, 1946, p. 94.

"Census shows 99,000 jukes made in 1947." *Billboard*, June 11, 1949, p. 113.

"Centers meet war needs for both young and old." *Billboard*, June 12, 1943, p. 62.

"CFRB's Clair Wallace puts in plug on automatic phonographs." *Billboard*, November 23, 1940, p. 60.

Chandler, Robert. "Jukes want recognition." *Variety*, March 8, 1950, p. 43.

"Cheaters cheated." *Billboard*, August 8, 1936, p. 70.

"Chi commission fingers mobster control of jukes." *Variety*, April 27, 1955, pp. 1, 18.

"Chi op evolves own system for picking click disks." *Billboard*, July 29, 1944, p. 89.

"Chi ops push dime play; over 'hump.'" *Billboard*, June 9, 1951, pp. 76, 81.

"Chicago juke tax annulled." *Billboard*, December 8, 1945, pp. 79, 84.

"Chicago music ops try play price experiment." *Billboard*, November 1, 1947, p. 102.

"City tax on coin machine attacked." *Variety*, July 26, 1939, p. 41.

Clark, Edgar Rogie. "Juke box serenade." *Music Journal* 8 (October, 1950): 17, 38–39.

Cohen, Bernard. "Seeburg—creative energy and expansive bigness." *Billboard*, October 12, 1968, pp MOA20, MOA28.

Cohn, Nat. "Music for sale." *Billboard*, August 6, 1938, p. 66.

"Coin exports at $552,000." *Billboard*, March 30, 1946, p. 133.

"The coin machine industry." *Billboard*, February 27, 1943, p. 74.

"Coin machines hit $7,621,879 export." *Billboard*, April 4, 1953, pp. 1, 76.

"Coin machines' $175,000,000 U.S. gross." *Variety*, July 12, 1939, p. 39.

"Coin-operated phonograph not Sunday violation." *Variety*, February 8, 1939, p. 39.

"Composers sing the blues to reap juke box coins." *New York Times*, July 16, 1953, p. 19.

"Cong. Miller warns juke operators on drastic Fed amusement taxation." *Variety*, March 28, 1951, pp. 37, 40.

"Congresses add two copyright bills aimed at juke exemption." *Billboard*, June 22, 1955, p. 49.

"Consider ban on juke play." *Billboard*, April 17, 1943, p. 58.

"Consider the era—enter phonograph." *Billboard*, January 8, 1966, p. 50.

"Council Bluffs sets new juke, game licenses." *Billboard*, June 11, 1949, p. 113.

"Court hits high juke tax." *Billboard*, June 2, 1945, pp. 65–66.

"Court upholds city juke tax." *Billboard*, March 8, 1947, p. 103.

"C'right office eyes juke law followup." *Variety*, January 27, 1988, p. 91.

Crook, George. "How business profits from coin machines." *Billboard*, November 13, 1937, p. 76.

Cross, Charles R. "Jukebox revival." *Esquire* 98 (December, 1982): 35–36.

Dalziel, J.M. "The jook." *Billboard*, February 22, 1941, p. 73.

Davidson, Thomas Lea. "1961 music machine survey." *Billboard*, May 15, 1961, pp. 9+.

deCourcy Hinds, Michael. "The vintage jukebox still sounds sweet." *New York Times*, July 8, 1978, p. 12.

"Denver ops to ask locations for % changes." *Billboard*, April 1, 1950, p. 110.

Desrocher, Jack. "Database." *U.S. News & World Report* 112 (February 17, 1992): 10.

"Detroit music men ban competition one month." *Billboard*, November 5, 1938, p. 69.

"Detroiters hit naughty disks." *Billboard*, August 3, 1940, p. 70.

Deveny, Kathleen. "Can high tech put Seeburg back in the groove?" *Business Week*, December 2, 1985, p. 89.

Dietmeier, Bob. "Banner year ahead for juke industry." *Billboard*, July 30, 1955, pp. 1, 86.

Dietmeier, Bob. "How many jukes are there and is there room for more?" *Billboard*, May 20, 1957, p. 86.

Dietmeier, Bob. "How much do juke operators make?" *Billboard*, July 14, 1958, pp. 1, 72, 74.

Dietmeier, Bob. "Juke world boom still on upbeat." *Billboard*, July 22, 1957, pp. 1, 104, 107.

Dietmeier, Bob. "More jumbo jukes spell more disks." *Billboard*, February 2, 1957, pp. 1, 80.

Dietmeier, Bob. "New ideas, records pep up slow jukes." *Billboard*, April 6, 1957, pp. 1, 84, 98.

Dietmeier, Robert. "1953 export record: $6,000,000 in jukes." *Billboard*, March 6, 1954, p. 52.

"Dime juke play Missouri, Kan. operator trend." *Billboard*, November 2, 1946, p. 100.

"Dime juke play top topic." *Billboard*, January 4, 1947, p. 51.

"Dime jukes take Chicago beating." *Variety*, May 30, 1951, p. 41.

"Dime play poll results." *Billboard*, December 14, 1946, p. 100.

"Dime play question remains unanswered." *Billboard*, October 31, 1951, p. 68.

"Dime play tests still hit-or-miss." *Billboard*, November 11, 1950, pp. 78, 80.

"Disk makers see jukes platter sales hypo as hit tune popularizers." *Billboard*, May 18, 1946, p. 130.

"Diskeries vie for juke box biz with direct sales tack." *Billboard*, April 22, 1950, pp. 3, 24.

Dittman, James B. "Innovation: a trademark of Rowe." *Billboard*, October 12, 1968, p. MOA16.

"Do you recall the Panaram?" *Billboard*, July 10, 1965, p. 45.

"Doc Berenson gets action." *Billboard*, December 18, 1937, p. 72.

Dorsey, Tommy. "The importance of the music machine operator." *Billboard*, December 30, 1939, p. 146.

"Eastern juke ops dime shy; seek better commission deal." *Billboard*, January 6, 1951, pp. 47, 51.

"Editor gives phono figures." *Billboard*, October 5, 1940, p. 68.

"Ex-hillbillies find music they like at Baltimore spots." *Billboard*, August 28, 1943, p. 71.

"Export problems revealed by juke box manufacturer." *Billboard*, May 10, 1947, p. 116.

"FBI urges teen-age help." *Billboard*, December 22, 1945, pp. 76, 79.

"Few industries have so quickly given jobs to so many." *Billboard*, September 28, 1940, sup., p. 4.

Finkelstein, Herman. "These things are mine." *Variety*, January 5, 1955, p. 225.

"1st 45 juke is released by Seeburg." *Billboard*, October 28, 1950, pp. 3, 114.

"First Wurlitzer banquet sets high mark for tour." *Billboard*, July 16, 1938, p. 65.

"500,000 Wurlitzer phonographs." *Billboard*, August 4, 1962, p. 3.

Force, L. C. "Little Willie's growed up." *Billboard*, January 18, 1936, p. 74.

"Fortune magazine credits modern phonograph for reviving records." *Billboard*, September 23, 1939, p. 70.

"45s moving into greater prominence on jukes, threatening 78s' position." *Variety*, November 29, 1950, p. 42.

"40% of nation's music operators use written contracts." *Billboard*, May 28, 1955, pp. 91–92.

"France, once Debussy, now goes for jukes." *Billboard*, March 19, 1955, p. 85.

Freeman, William A. "A new 'juke box' finds popularity." *New York Times*, November 8, 1964, sec. 3, p. 5.

"Further analysis cues jukebox take nearer $150,000,000 a year." *Variety*, August 21, 1940, pp. 49, 60.

Gersh, Bill. "Music machine history." *Billboard*, July 10, 1937, pp. 79–80.

Gersh, Bill. "Slugs must go." *Billboard*, June 29, 1935, p. 107.

"Glenn Miller, heralded no. 1 swing king." *Billboard*, December 2, 1939, p. 134.

"Gordon spins happy tunes of soaring jukebox life in Europe." *Billboard*, May 10, 1969, p. 72.

"Grand jury cites juke box maker." *New York Times*, March 3, 1956, p. 29.

"The great jukebox shakedown." *Newsweek* 53 (February 9, 1959): 27–28.

Green, Abel. "Time for a change." *Variety*, November 4, 1953, p. 43.

Green, Stanley. "Jukebox piracy." *The Atlantic Monthly* 209 (April, 1962): 136.

Greenhouse, Steven. "Swan song." *New York Times*, March 10, 1974, sec. 3, p. 15.

"Griffin 'individually' (not for RIAA, it sez here) pro-jukebox ops." *Variety*, October 28, 1953, p. 39.

Hall, Mildred. "Campus and jukeboxes get break." *Billboard*, January 7, 1978, pp. 3, 102.

Hall, Mildred. "Cellar asks MOA-ASCAP arbitrate." *Billboard*, June 22, 1959, pp. 130–131.

Hall, Mildred. "Copyright crossroads." *Billboard*, April 1, 1967, pp. 65, 68, 70.

Hall, Mildred. "Juke royalties." *Billboard*, November 15, 1977, p. 10.

Hall, Mildred. "Jukebox operators slow in fee payoff." *Billboard*, August 12, 1978, p. 87.

Hall, Mildred. "McClellan bomb: $20 juke box fee." *Billboard*, December 14, 1974, pp. 1, 14.

Hall, Mildred. "See juke bill getting to floor." *Billboard*, May 18, 1963, pp. 56–57.

Hammergren, M. G. "An industry grows up." *Billboard*, January 20, 1940, p. 74.

Hartmann, A. C. "Coin-operated amusement machine industry gives depression a blow." *Billboard*, March 12, 1932, p. 28.

"H. C. Evans & Co. juke box division sold for $200,000." *Billboard*, April 16, 1955, p. 71.

Helopaltio, Kari. "See 6,000 more Finland spots via new jukeboxes." *Billboard*, September 16, 1972, p. 30.

"High tech clip jukebox bows." *Billboard*, July 30, 1983, p. 30.

"Hillbillies owe rise to jukes." *Billboard*, August 28, 1943, pp. 70, 75.

"Hit location-owned jukes." *Billboard*, September 13, 1947, pp. 104, 120.

"The hit parade." *Time* 73 (February 23, 1959): 20.

"Hit records boost play." *Billboard*, March 13, 1943, p. 59.

Holland, Bill. "Crackdown on unlicenced jukes." *Billboard*, August 16, 1986, p. 6.

Holland, Earl. "Selecting records and programs." *Billboard*, November 16, 1935, p. 64.

Horowitz, Is. "Juke box influence on record business." *Billboard*, May 23, 1953, p. 91.

Hoskins, Olin. "Rock-Ola: a dedication to dependability." *Billboard*, October 12, 1968, pp. MOA12, MOA28.

"House Copyright committee okays repeal of 1909 jukebox exemption." *Variety*, June 26, 1963, p. 51.

"House group mulls survey figures on juke operations." *Billboard*, June 22, 1959, p. 127.

"How exports grow." *Billboard*, April 4, 1953, p. 76.

"How juke boxes sustain disks, build them into hit category." *Billboard*, May 23, 1953, p. 81.

"How many jukes? 450,000 good bet." *Billboard*, April 6, 1959, pp. 32+.

Hughes, Arthur C. "Are risky records good business." *Billboard*, January 16, 1937, p. 93.

Humphrey, Harold. "Analyzing the hit records." *Billboard*, September 27, 1941, sup., pp. 30, 94.

Hurd, Walter. "The year 1940." *Billboard*, January 18, 1941, pp. 66–67, 70, 77.

Hurd, Walter. "America's new industry." *Billboard*, September 28, 1940, sup., pp. 3–5.

Hurd, Walter. "No junking of jukes." *Billboard*, September 25, 1943, sup., pp. 26–27, 166.

Hurd, Walter W. "A busy year." *Billboard*, September 27, 1941, sup., pp. 4, 84–85.

Hurd, Walter W. "Music." *Billboard*, September 4, 1937, p. 76.

Hurd, Walter W. "Music cheers." *Billboard*, June 1, 1940, p. 70.

Hurd, Walter W. "Permanent project." *Billboard*, November 6, 1943, p. 58.

Hurd, Walter W. "Social policy." *Billboard*, August 13, 1938, p. 68.

Hurd, Walter W. "The year 1937." *Billboard*, January 1, 1938, p. 126.

Hurd, Walter W. "Unemployment." *Billboard*, September 11, 1937, p. 74.

Hurd, Walter W. "Used phonograph prices." *Billboard*, April 16, 1938, p. 86.

"'I Wonder Who's Kissing Her Now' Cleveland's choice." *Billboard*, July 26, 1947, p. 112.

"Image-conscious operators shun double-entendre disks." *Billboard*, April 1, 1967, p. 69.

"In tune again?" *Forbes* 111 (March 1, 1973): 64.

"Industry mentions." *Billboard*, December 12, 1942, p. 60.

"Industry wins slug fight." *Billboard*, April 15, 1944, pp. 61, 68.
"Infant German juke box industry booming." *Billboard*, October 2, 1954, p. 85.
"Instant discotheque: just add dancers." *Business Week*, February 27, 1965, pp. 108–110.
"International phono association head addresses Los Angeles ops." *Billboard*, February 25, 1939, p. 69.
"International report." *Billboard*, October 12, 1968, pp. MOA30+.
"Int'l jukebox survey." *Billboard*, January 2, 1971, p. 36.
"Int'l jukebox survey." *Billboard*, January 9, 1971, pp. 35–36, 38.
"Int'l trade groups join Yanks in support of tax on jukeboxes." *Variety*, February 5, 1958, pp. 53, 58
"Iowa ops support 7½-cent coin; air legal problems." *Billboard*, March 19, 1949, pp. 113, 133.
"It's cheaper to fight." *Billboard*, August 12, 1957, p. 121.
"Jazz juke box tunes no longer Red taboo." *Billboard*, May 22, 1961, p. 46.
"Jimmy Dorsey praises music machines in Philly broadcast." *Billboard*, November 9, 1940, p. 68.
"Jivers featured by Mills Novelty." *Billboard*, February 17, 1940, p. 64.
"Joe Robbins letter takes Atlantic to task for phono royalty article." *Billboard*, April 14, 1962, p. 52.
"Johnson, E. C. "Don't give away your profits." *Billboard*, July 20, 1935, p. 65.
"Judge puts juke out of order to have quiet bite." *Billboard*, December 2, 1944, p. 91.
"Juke assn. execs adopt plan to mass-advertise via music boxes." *Billboard*, August 7, 1954, p. 14.
"Juke ban discouraged." *Billboard*, April 24, 1943, p. 66.
"Juke biz costly operation with small-profit returns." *Billboard*, February 9, 1952, pp. 78, 80.
"Juke box bill is unworkable." *Billboard*, February 16, 1952, pp. 17, 83.
"The juke box: billion dollar threat." *International Musician* 60 (September, 1961): 14–15.
"Juke box bonanza." *Business Week*, February 16, 1946, pp. 37–38.
"Juke box built in 1885 plays rolls, 3 musical instruments." *Billboard*, May 3, 1947, p. 118.
"Juke box disk purchases up to 50,000,000 a year." *Billboard*, January 19, 1952, pp. 1, 16, 73.
"'Juke box' going high hat." *New York Times*, December 21, 1946, p. 29.
"Juke box group to seek new coins." *New York Times*, March 8, 1950, p. 37.
"Juke box industry to mark 65th anniversary in May." *Billboard*, May 2, 1953, pp. 1, 92.
"Juke box men singing those red ink blues." *New York Times*, March 20, 1951, p. 30.
"The juke box network: part 2, the distributor's story." *Billboard*, January 22, 1949, sup., p. 18.
"The juke box network: the manufacturing story." *Billboard*, January 22, 1949, sup., p. 17.
"Juke box pix biz set for com'l use." *Variety*, December 12, 1945, p. 41.
"Juke box playing now a dime." *New York Times*, November 26, 1946, p. 35.
"The juke box's 60th birthday." *Billboard*, January 24, 1948, pp. 132+.
"Juke box suit settled." *New York Times*, April 16, 1958, p. 52.
"Juke box tops teen-age club fun; use games." *Billboard*, March 25, 1944, p. 90.
"Juke box trends." *Billboard*, March 24, 1956, p. 80.
"Juke boxes." *The Musician* 50 (January, 1945): 10.
"Juke boxes and youth." *Billboard*, January 30, 1943, p. 64.
"Juke boxes: big business booms around the world." *Billboard*, April 30, 1955, p. 87.
"Juke boxes bring fines." *New York Times*, August 28, 1945, p. 22.
"Juke boxes face uplift." *New York Times*, August 22, 1946, p. 29.
"Juke boxes limited by priority order." *New York Times*, December 11, 1941, p. 30.
"Juke boxes not all gold mines, Nebraskans report." *Billboard*, August 14, 1943, p. 62.
"Juke boxes prove worth." *Billboard*, November 27, 1943, p. 98.
"Juke boxes set stage for teen-age night clubs." *Billboard*, November 6, 1943, p. 62.
"Juke dispute causes tiff in taverns." *Billboard*, February 2, 1957, pp. 80, 89.
"Juke exports jump in value, may top $3 million for 1951." *Billboard*, March 22, 1952, pp. 80, 82.
"Juke leads Mexico entertainment." *Billboard*, July 28, 1945, pp. 73, 75.
"Juke legislative pot boiling." *Billboard*, March 8, 1947, pp. 103–104.
"Juke makers find good biz in exports." *Billboard*, April 19, 1952, pp. 84, 96.
"Juke medium spurs record sales." *Billboard*, February 17, 1945, p. 66.
"Juke operators see tele failing to nip their biz." *Variety*, February 22, 1950, p. 43.
"Juke op trend crimps potential." *Billboard*, May 2, 1953, p. 16.
"Juke ops brush Copyright Act; ASCAP sues." *Variety*, August 2, 1978, pp. 1, 82.
"Juke ops on tavern tele." *Billboard*, June 21, 1947, pp. 107, 136.
"Juke ops, performing rights societies in no mood to compromise in House hearings to revamp Copyright Act." *Variety*, June 17, 1959, pp. 39, 48.
"Juke ops' war chest to fight D.C. licensing." *Variety*, March 25, 1953, pp. 53, 58.
"Juke profits tops 24–hr. cafes & bars." *Billboard*, March 30, 1957, p. 110.

"Juke rentals—solution?" *Billboard*, May 3, 1947, pp. 114, 116.

"Juke romancers marry as Bing sings 'Gotta Be Free.'" *Billboard*, January 27, 1945, p. 63.

"Juke royalty battle heated as both sides meet head-on." *Billboard*, February 16, 1952, pp. 17, 80.

"Juke-royalty bill again to the fore." *Billboard*, February 17, 1951, pp. 10, 72.

"Juke 10c play hits op snag in twin cities." *Billboard*, March 10, 1956, p. 84.

"Jukebox Copyright Act amendment given good chance." *Variety*, October 31, 1951, p. 40.

"Juke-box exports up in 3–year totals." *Billboard*, July 6, 1968, p. 45.

"Jukebox industry bucks Kefauver in D.C. hearings on royalty bill." *Variety*, February 6, 1952, pp. 43, 50.

"Jukebox industry's political power on copyright bill baffles music biz." *Variety*, April 26, 1967, p. 183.

"Jukebox invasion." *Time* 56 (July 24, 1950): 32.

"The jukebox, it seems, is a hit of the past." *New York Times*, July 21, 1982, p. C12.

"Jukebox remains same even under different name." *Billboard*, January 9, 1971, pp. 35, 38.

"Jukebox spins play trouble for operators." *Variety*, January 24, 1973, p. 49.

"The jukebox story: 1880–1929." *Billboard*, December 27, 1969, p. 84.

"The jukebox story: 1930–1939." *Billboard*, December 27, 1969, p. 86.

"The jukebox story: 1940–1949." *Billboard*, December 27, 1969, p. 88.

"Juke-box tax drafted." *New York Times*, April 29, 1947, p. 22.

"The jukebox tune." *Time* 73 (March 2, 1959): 15.

"Jukeboxes banned in Bangkok." *New York Times*, June 25, 1962, p. 3.

"Jukeboxes back: forget old law." *Variety*, December 4, 1940, p. 44.

"Jukeboxes take big hold in Paris." *Variety*, July 10, 1957, p. 109.

"Jukeboxes try more elegant image in bid to expand number of locations." *Variety*, April 26, 1972, p. 57.

"Jukers vote diskery faves." *Billboard*, August 9, 1947, p. 112.

"Jukes battle tide rising against copyright exception." *Billboard*, June 2, 1941, pp. 3, 25.

"Jukes, cleffers get day in court on copyright bill." *Variety*, October 28, 1953, pp. 39, 42.

"Jukes helped disk firms recover from sales slump." *Billboard*, November 6, 1943, p. 63.

"Jukes score hit in Japan despite prices." *Billboard*, July 12, 1952, p. 78.

"Jukes set musical tastes." *Billboard*, February 10, 1945, p. 63.

"Jukes solid in South Africa." *Billboard*, May 31, 1947, pp. 108, 110.

"Jukes won't talk to ASCAP." *Variety*, December 19, 1956, pp. 51, 60.

Kandel, Myron. "Face-lifting set for jukeboxes." *New York Times*, September 17, 1962, p. 47.

Katz, Ben. "Music machines' influence on home record sales." *Billboard*, September 27, 1941, sup., p. 28.

Kaufman, Babe. "We doubled the take." *Billboard*, October 15, 1938, pp, 67–68.

"K.C. ops report disk price rise." *Billboard*, September 20, 1947, p. 120.

"KC paper notes 10c play move in story & column comments." *Billboard*, December 14, 1946, p. 100.

"Keeney busy on 5 games." *Billboard*, February 25, 1939, p. 79.

"Keeney wallbox in distrib's hands." *Billboard*, February 2, 1940, p. 71.

"Keys to profits: case in programming box." *Billboard*, May 23, 1953, p. 60.

Kline, K. C. "Operator can well spend hours watching patrons play machines." *Billboard*, November 14, 1942, p. 65.

Knauf, Ken. "Juke box bonanza: world market boom." *Billboard*, March 26, 1955, p. 52.

Knauf, Ken. "1960 juke box & game exports jump 7.6% from 1959." *Billboard*, June 12, 1961, p. 44.

Kongalides, Letty. "Greek jukebox industry set for rapid expansion." *Billboard*, September 16, 1972, p. 30.

Krivine, J. *Juke Box Saturday Night*. London: New English Library, 1977.

"Ky. Circuit court ruling hurts jukes." *Billboard*, December 23, 1944, p. 65.

"L.A.-Chicago op survey shows divided opinion on 6–for-quarter juke play." *Billboard*, March 13, 1948, pp. 100, 107.

"L.A. locations must pay new $7.50 license." *Billboard*, February 18, 1950, p. 93.

"Ladies, gents! Meet the juke box man." *Billboard*, October 15, 1955, pp. 1, 80.

"Lansing juke tax killed." *Billboard*, August 4, 1945, pp. 71–73.

"Lansky-Smith new Wurlitzer N.Y., N.J., Conn. distribs." *Billboard*, March 13, 1943, p. 59.

"Lease idea grows on juke ops." *Billboard*, June 29, 1946, pp. 118, 143.

Lennon, James L. "Coin machine biz grows up." *Variety*, October 1, 1952, p. 28.

Lewis, Peter H. "Advances in jukeboxes." *New York Times*, November 19, 1986, p. D10.

Littleford, W. D. "To the Reader's Digest." *Billboard*, October 29, 1955, pp. 1, 74.

"Local committees." *Billboard*, May 8, 1943, p. 58.
"Location ads boost play of juke boxes." *Billboard*, August 28, 1943, p. 70.
"Location letter warns of radio." *Billboard*, July 31, 1937, p. 89.
"Location owners, Chi juke ops lash out at smutty recordings." *Billboard*, May 24, 1947, p. 108.
"Location tele interest hits skids." *Billboard*, October 8, 1949, p. 116.
Loftus, Joseph A. "Juke box inquiry hears of gangster infiltration." *New York Times*, February 11, 1959, pp. 1, 34.
"Los Angeles juke box ops believe tavern video use only a temporary measure." *Billboard*, October 18, 1947, p. 103.
Lunzer Kritz, Francesca. "Video watch." *U.S. News & World Report* 110 (March 25, 1991): 72.
Lynch, Vincent. *Jukebox: The Golden Age*. New York: Putnam, 1981.
"Major pubs steam at Mitch Miller telling House diskers make the hits." *Variety*, February 13, 1952, p. 51.
"Makes grade!" *Billboard*, December 22, 1945, p. 76.
"Making an appointment to play a jukebox." *Variety*, July 23, 1958, p. 2.
"Man at bar turns into a music critic." *Billboard*, November 11, 1939, p. 69.
Mangan, James T. "Lecherous records." *Billboard*, December 4, 1937, p. 70.
"Manufacturer for 5c play." *Billboard*, December 7, 1946, pp. 94, 102.
"MAPOA sets delegates to state meet; revive hit tune parties." *Billboard*, June 25, 1949, p. 103.
"A march against juke boxes." *New York Times*, May 3, 1953, p. 27.
"Marian Anderson adds voice to great artists' praise of jukes." *Billboard*, February 10, 1945, p. 65.
"Market reports." *Billboard*, November, 13, 1943, pp. 60–61.
"Mass. House debates tax." *Billboard*, June 12, 1943, p. 62.
"Massachusetts ops plan test against Sunday juke fees." *Billboard*, August 29, 1942, p. 71.
McCormick, Moira. "Elvis tops list of jukebox hits." *Billboard*, August 20, 1988, pp. 6, 77.
McCullaugh, Jim. "Vid jukebox debuts." *Billboard*, May 15, 1982, pp. 48–49.
McDermott, Peter. "Singled out for extinction." *Billboard*, December 15, 1981, p. 18.
McDonough, Tom. "Export mart CM bonanza." *Billboard*, October 13, 1951, p. 67.
McDonough, Tom. "Exports heavy despite embargo." *Billboard*, April 2, 1949, pp. 103, 141.
McDonough, Tom. "Hit tune promotion." *Billboard*, January 24, 1948, p. 130.
"Memphis sings new tune." *Billboard*, January 15, 1944, pp. 63–65.
"Mex music union asks gov't aid vs. jukebox monster." *Variety*, August 5, 1959, p. 62.
"Mexican trade hit by curfew on juke boxes." *Billboard*, December 7, 1959, p. 81.
"Mexico enforces warning against phono loudness." *Billboard*, August 3, 1940, p. 70.
Michie, Larry. "U.S. Senate warns ASCAP — jukes to make copyright deal — or else." *Variety*, March 22, 1967, pp. 1, 86.
"Michigan phono assn. suggests steps for unifying industry's efforts in defense bond drive." *Billboard*, October 18, 1941, p. 62.
"Mills Do-Re-Mi has many novel features." *Billboard*, August 29, 1936, p. 112.
"Mills introduces new phono at convention." *Billboard*, January 18, 1936, p. 72.
Mills, Irving. "Phonograph records — the new talent medium." *Billboard*, August 27, 1938, p. 109.
Mills, Ralph J. "Consider the phonograph." *Billboard*, November 30, 1935, p. 117.
"Milwaukee firm boosts popular records in big promotion plan." *Billboard*, October 28, 1939, p. 74.
"Minneapolis has 1,000 juke boxes, survey reveals." *Billboard*, August 28, 1943, p. 71.
"Minneapolis passes juke box ordinance." *Billboard*, July 8, 1944, p. 64.
"MOA: hope, heritage of jukebox operators." *Billboard*, December 27, 1969, pp. 72, 74.
"MOA opens in Chi to 'beat ASCAP' theme on jukebox tap." *Variety*, May 9, 1956, pp. 41–46.
"MOA ops hear Pantages outline advertising plan." *Billboard*, April 16, 1955, p. 72.
"Mobile music operators vote for ten-cent play." *Billboard*, December 14, 1946, p. 100.
"Mobile taverns beat juke ban by renting equipment." *Billboard*, May 22, 1948, p. 115.
"Modern Vending record praised by Wurlitzer." *Billboard*, November 28, 1936, p. 125.
"Modern Vending sets a record." *Billboard*, June 13, 1936, p. 70.
"More folk disks say ops." *Billboard*, May 12, 1945, p. 65.
"More phonos in night clubs as fall season gets going." *Billboard*, October 5, 1940, p. 68.
"Most jukebox operators don't fear tele is threat to their industry." *Variety*, March 8, 1950, p. 43.
"Move to freeze $8 juke fee in copyright bill stirs ASCAP, BMI." *Variety*, August 17, 1974, p. 41.
"Movie juke boxes ... what about them?" *Billboard*, September 25, 1943, sup., p. 73.
"Mule train." *Billboard*, December 3, 1949, p. 99.
Murray, Tom. "Ops view advertising records." *Billboard*, February 25, 1939, p. 71.

Murray, Tom. "Year's trial proves Panther Novelty's weekly sponsored broadcast big biz booster." *Billboard*, September 5, 1942, p. 65.

Muse, Vance. "Jukeboxes: reviving the joy." *Rolling Stone*, September 17, 1981, pp. 80+.

"Music biz focuses on D.C. hearings over McCarran bill to license jukes." *Billboard*, October 14, 1953, pp. 73, 80.

"Music biz goes in town of 800." *Billboard*, May 29, 1937, p. 90.

"Music boxes lead field in collections, Baltimorean says." *Billboard*, August 28, 1943, p. 70.

"Music boxes win approval." *Billboard*, October 23, 1943, p. 62.

"Music goes 'round 25,000,000 times in juke boxes' day." *Billboard*, May 12, 1956, pp. 1, 43.

"Music guards teen-age morals." *Billboard*, December 18, 1943, p. 62.

"Music machines and the music industry." *Billboard*, September 27, 1941, sup., pp. 14–15, 90–91.

"Music machines booming in Detroit." *Billboard*, August 8, 1936, p. 70.

"Music men accept excise tax without objection." *Billboard*, October 31, 1942, p. 62.

"Music men meet phone demand with joint company." *Billboard*, February 28, 1942, p. 60.

"Music must make fair commission." *Billboard*, December 21, 1935, p. 61.

"Music operator survey." *Billboard*, October 7, 1950, pp. 78+.

"Music operators." *Billboard*, May 6, 1939, p. 78.

"Music operators again cautioned." *Billboard*, December 26, 1936, p. 124.

"Music operators shoulder record taxes in 21 states." *Billboard*, June 2, 1956, pp. 66, 81.

"Music operators talk problems." *Billboard*, March 20, 1937, p. 76.

"Music operators win injunction." *Billboard*, November 16, 1935, p. 64.

"Music publishers cast fierce frown at discs' slot machine methods." *Variety*, January 13, 1937, p. 47.

"Native jukeboxes threat to U.S. biz in West Germany." *Variety*, March 2, 1955, p. 55.

"N.E. ops wed jukes, cig mchs." *Billboard*, November 19, 1949, pp. 93, 95.

Neal, Ralph G. "Music operator analyzes his business." *Billboard*, April 10, 1937, p. 182.

Neal, Ralph G. "Profit tips for music operators." *Billboard*, December 5, 1936, pp. 78–79.

"Neat and very gaudy." *Newsweek* 30 (October 6, 1947): 62, 64.

"Newcomers in music choice." *Billboard*, March 13, 1943, p. 59.

Newman, Melinda. "New license office to enforce jukebox performing rights pact." *Billboard*, April 7, 1990, p. 94.

"Newspaper revives Jimmy Roosevelt's coin mach. career." *Billboard*, December 12, 1942, p. 62.

Nichols, Lewis. "The ubiquitous juke box." *New York Times Magazine*, October 3, 1941, p. 22.

"Nickel still tops with juke ops; no plans for upping tab to dime." *Variety*, December 16, 1953, p. 41.

"A nickel's worth of silence? An idea by Cleveland mayor." *Billboard*, January 1, 1944, p. 59.

"1958 juke box operator poll." *Billboard*, May 5, 1958, pp. 32–37.

"1953 juke exports up 50%; 14,089 units at $6,317,533." *Billboard*, April 24, 1953, p. 78.

"N.J. op crusades against smut disks." *Billboard*, October 30, 1937, p. 76.

"No chance for jukes to use classics, reporter discovers." *Billboard*, February 10, 1945, p. 63.

"No mid-season models pleases Rock-Ola ops." *Billboard*, June 11, 1938, p. 74.

"No summer price change." *Billboard*, June 26, 1937, p. 132.

Norman, R. G. "Music for long-pull profits." *Billboard*, November 30, 1935, p. 114.

"N.Y. Herald Tribune editorial cites automatic phono value in promoting patriotic songs." *Billboard*, February 28, 1942, p. 60.

"N.Y. juke ops up spins to 10c." *Variety*, March 2, 1955, p. 55.

"Objectionable records seen as a menace to the industry." *Billboard*, November 7, 1936, pp. 74–75.

"Obstacles to phono exports." *Billboard*, July 17, 1937, p. 80.

"Oklahoma sets up grab plan; doomed to failure." *Billboard*, April 10, 1943, p. 94.

"Open Alabama taverns to jukes." *Billboard*, November 29, 1947, pp. 156, 163.

"Open drive for dime juke play." *Billboard*, October 12, 1946, pp. 92, 100.

"The operator must decide." *Billboard*, December 14, 1946, p. 100.

"Operator poll, part 1." *Billboard*, May 20, 1957, pp. 50+.

"Operator survey panel airs nationwide 10c play." *Billboard*, March 19, 1955, pp. 74, 85.

"Operators, manufacturers set anniversary promotion drive." *Billboard*, May 23, 1953, p. 62.

"Ops air views on salaries." *Billboard*, June 25, 1949, pp. 94, 103, 106.

"Ops gear for dime play." *Variety*, February 14, 1950, p. 40.

"Ops go to dime on country-wide basis." *Billboard*, March 3, 1951, pp. 68, 75.

"Ops help set up teen clubs." *Billboard*, August 14, 1943, p. 62.

"Ops—industry's cornerstone." *Billboard*, September 13, 1947, p. 104.

"Ops pooh-pooh owned locations." *Billboard*, August 14, 1961, p. 62.

"Ops. see cocktail lounges as top p.-w. locations for juke boxes and photomatics." *Billboard*, January 13, 1945, p. 63.

"Ops. sked dime push in Boston on May 1." *Billboard*, March 19, 1955, pp. 74, 85.

"Ops to meet tele in 40 cities by '49." *Billboard*, May 29, 1948, p. 125.

"Ops win a lower tax." *Billboard*, July 22, 1939, p. 70.

"Ork leader boosts phonos on stage." *Billboard*, November 16, 1940, p. 70.

Orodenker, M. H. "Hot off the records." *Billboard*, December 18, 1937, pp. 3, 72.

"Over 30 years in music." *Billboard*, January 18, 1936, p. 74.

Paige, Earl. "The jukebox story." *Billboard*, July 4, 1976, pp. MR150, MR152.

Paige, Earl. "MOA's programs designed to assist members and instill new public image." *Billboard*, October 16, 1971, pp. MOA1, MOA7.

Palmer, Helene." "My two weeks visiting Europe." *Billboard*, June 29, 1935, p. 100.

Palmer, Robert. "A guide to the last great jukeboxes in town." *New York Times*, February 4, 1983, pp. C1, C20.

Parsons, Geoffrey Jr. and Robert Yoder. "A nickel a tune." *Reader's Digest* 38 (February, 1941): 113–115.

"Partners in business." *Billboard*, January 18, 1941, pp. 100–101.

Penchansky, Alan. "Jukeboxes 'endangered,' survey says." *Billboard*, November 15, 1980, pp. 3, 66.

Penchansky, Alan. "Operators hail video jukebox future." *Billboard*, November 24, 1979, pp. 6, 46.

Penchansky, Alan. "Rising single prices hurt U.S. jukeboxes." *Billboard*, August 9, 1980, pp. 1, 39.

"Penn ops set hit parties." *Billboard*, May 24, 1947, p. 108.

"Peoria ops try 10c play again; move is strong." *Billboard*, March 10, 1956, p. 84.

"Petrillo mixes plea for bite on juke take." *Billboard*, June 18, 1949, p. 110.

"Philly music men on record against smutty recordings." *Billboard*, February 28, 1942, pp. 60, 66.

"Phone music firm opens in Chi." *Billboard*, November 17, 1945, pp. 78, 80.

"Phono business may find way to capitalize on 'juke box' name." *Billboard*, October 5, 1940, p. 69.

"Phono exec speaks on music policy." *Billboard*, May 14, 1938, p. 84.

"Phono gets big play in Panama." *Billboard*, April 15, 1939, p. 74.

"Phono manufacturers in new move against smut." *Billboard*, December 28, 1940, p. 133.

"Phono-Mike tells success at show." *Billboard*, February 10, 1940, p. 66.

"Phono ops hit smutty records." *Billboard*, July 10, 1937, p. 80.

"Phonograph tax rulings." *Billboard*, October 18, 1941, p. 62.

"Phonographs fare better." *Billboard*, April 6, 1940, p. 67.

"Phonographs supplant radio as maker of song hits." *Billboard*, February 10, 1940, p. 66.

"Phonos avoid Arizona tax." *Billboard*, May 28, 1938, p. 91.

"Phonos being spotted in swank Philly night clubs." *Billboard*, April 13, 1940, p. 152.

"Phonos in France." *Billboard*, August 5, 1939, p. 66.

"'Phonos must be important,' declares Wisconsin paper." *Billboard*, October 26, 1940, p. 67.

"Picking records—an art or a science?" *Billboard*, January 3, 1942, p. 61.

"Picking the right records for the right spot." *Billboard*, September 28, 1940, pp. 6, 58–59.

"Picking the right records for the right spots." *Billboard*, September 27, 1942, sup., pp. 44+.

"Pinball games used frequently in movies, with results pro and con." *Billboard*, May 11, 1935, p. 63.

"Plan bigger program for teen-age clubs." *Billboard*, December 2, 1944, p. 91.

"Plan for youth clubs." *Billboard*, May 1, 1943, p. 62.

"Police curfew silences Irvington's juke boxes." *New York Times*, July 19, 1947, p. 15.

"Press plays up unfortunate news happening in Chi." *Billboard*, November 6, 1943, p. 62.

"Propose 20 per cent grab." *Billboard*, December 12, 1942, pp. 62, 67.

"Provisions of new Texas law." *Billboard*, May 25, 1935, p. 83.

"Public informed of phonograph benefits in radio announcement." *Billboard*, June 25, 1938, pp. 114–115.

"Public, location promotion top 10–cent play factors." *Billboard*, June 15, 1951, p. 72.

"Quizees say dime play won't work." *Billboard*, December 28, 1946, p. 93.

"Radio, BMI, films back ASCAP in bid for coin machine revenue." *Variety*, January 29, 1947, p. 42.

Rapoport, Roger. "Oldies but goodies." *Americana* 9 (November/December, 1981): 25–27+.

Ratajack, E. R. "Jukebox piracy." *The Atlantic Monthly* 210 (August, 1962): 30–31.

"RCA-Col battle of disk speeds spreads to jukebox industry." *Billboard*, July 5, 1950, p. 35.

"Radio promotion." *Billboard*, February 19, 1949, p. 98.

"Reader's Digest on 'racket' in the jukeboxes." *Variety*, October 15, 1955, pp. 61, 63.

"Record buying guide." *Billboard*, April 15, 1939, p. 74.

"Record buying guide." *Billboard*, August 26, 1939, p. 126.

"Record companies oppose juke's royalty payments." *Billboard*, November 3, 1951, pp. 1, 16.

"Record companies." *Billboard*, December 9, 1939, p. 64.

"Record guide chalks up 84 recording artists in 1939." *Billboard*, January 20, 1940, p. 74.

"Record plan is growing." *Billboard*, May 14, 1938, p. 84.

"Red jukes in the black." *Billboard*, August 14, 1961, p. 63.

"Reduced metal quotas cut juke boxes' manufacture." *New York Times*, November 9, 1951, p. 42.

"Reporter foresees oblivion for dime jukes—but quick!" *Billboard*, December 28, 1946, p. 94.

Reuter, Maynard L. "Music for millions." *Billboard*, September 27, 1941, sup., pp. 8–9, 85.

Reves, H. F. "Progress in the music field." *Billboard*, January 16, 1937, pp. 84–85.

Reves, H. F. "Vending machines in Detroit." *Billboard*, December 25, 1937, pp. 70–71.

Reves, Hal. "Tailor-made music offers new horizons to juke ops." *Billboard*, July 10, 1954, pp. 69, 72.

"Rewarding artistic achievement." *New York Times*, November 3, 1963, sec. 4, p. 8.

Richman, Dan. "Music machines prove foremost influence of retail record sales." *Billboard*, September 28, 1940, sup., p. 14.

Richman, Daniel. "Making records for the operator." *Billboard*, September 23, 1939, p. 3.

"Rights group pact with jukebox ops; rebates promised." *Variety*, May 15, 1985, pp. 1, 94.

"Riojas Co. history a trade parallel." *Billboard*, September 22, 1951, p. 94.

"Risque records." *Billboard*, April 1, 1967, p. 69.

Roberts, Henry T. "The percentage problem." *Billboard*, June 22, 1940, p. 78.

"Rock juke scores multi-selection record." *Billboard*, October 11, 1952, p. 88.

"Rockola calls jukes 'poor man's opera.'" *Billboard*, February 16, 1952, pp. 17, 80.

Rockola, David C. "Music enemy no. 1." *Billboard*, December 25, 1937, p. 68.

"Rock-Ola finds 20 records favored." *Billboard*, January 8, 1938, p. 68.

"Rock-Ola firm features 'idea exchange' for ops." *Billboard*, October 10, 1936, p. 76.

"Rock-Ola Imperial reaches new high." *Billboard*, July 31, 1937, p. 88.

"Rock-Ola machine abroad Queen Mary." *Billboard*, June 20, 1936, p. 70.

"Rock-Ola op tests new style location." *Billboard*, May 7, 1938, p. 84.

"Rock-Ola runs double shifts." *Billboard*, August 15, 1936, p. 70.

"Rock-Ola take biggest in 40 years as rival folds." *Billboard*, March 23, 1974, p. 38.

"Route study hypes nickel-dime fuss." *Billboard*, February 10, 1951, p. 76.

Russell, Deborah. "Juke biz finds new life via new technology markets." *Billboard*, October 19, 1991, pp. 10, 83.

"San Fran denies control of phonos to police dept." *Billboard*, March 18, 1944, p. 61.

Sanders, Arthur H. "Yesterday's juke-box." *Hobbies* 56 (August, 1951): 30–32.

Schickel, Steve. "Venezuela again top juke box importer." *Billboard*, April 4, 1953, pp. 79, 85.

Schoenfeld, Herm. "Jukebox: a windfall probe." *Variety*, February 18, 1959, p. 41.

Schreiber, Dick. "Machine output sets a record." *Billboard*, March 6, 1954, p. 48.

Schreiber, Dick. "1950: a solid market." *Billboard*, March 4, 1950, sup., p. 17.

Schrieber, Dick. "Only 17 per cent of music operators use contracts." *Billboard*, November 15, 1952, pp. 93–94.

Schreiber, Dick. "Operators talk commissions." *Billboard*, June 4, 1949, pp. 113–114.

Schreiber, Dick. "Ops discuss buying preferences." *Billboard*, June 11, 1949, pp. 113–114.

Schreiber, Dick. "Ops discuss incomes & expenses." *Billboard*, June 18, 1949, pp. 109–110.

Schulz, S. C. "Why jeopardize your biz? *Billboard*, December 11, 1937, p. 80.

"Scientist finds jitterbugs dying; ops, dancemen glad." *Billboard*, February 25, 1939, p. 77.

"Scooby-ooby Scopitone." *Time* 84 (August 21, 1964): 49.

Seals, Robert M. "Dime play ... or nickel?" *Billboard*, February 1, 1947, p. 144.

"See phonographs as prime exploitation outlet for pix." *Billboard*, March 28, 1942, p. 108.

"Seeburg announces features on new 1937 line of phonographs." *Billboard*, December 26, 1936, p. 124.

"Seeburg is fined $2,000." *New York Times*, January 16, 1957, p. 41.

"Seeburg phonos in restaurant chain." *Billboard*, November 27, 1937, p. 136.

"Seeburg settles antitrust action with consent decree." *Billboard*, February 9, 1957, p. 78.

"Sees bigger use of phonos in Mexico." *Billboard*, May 4, 1940, p. 76.

"Selectivity: the magic that built the juke box industry." *Billboard*, May 23, 1953, p. 81.

"Selling the U.S. jukebox abroad." *Business Week*, September 1, 1956, pp. 101–102.

"Senate currency group hears 7½ c suggestion as jukebox compromise." *Variety*, March 29, 1950, p. 58.

"Servicemen prefer jukes." *Billboard*, April 10, 1943, p. 94.

"Settle Chicago juke tax." *Billboard*, November 2, 1946, pp. 95, 100.

"75 wall box units on 10c play in K.C." *Billboard,* December 7, 1946, p. 98.

Shay, Grant. "Selling music." *Billboard,* February 8, 1936, p. 68.

"Silence is golden in Danish juke." *Billboard,* April 23, 1955, p. 30.

"$640,974 in music machines exported to 34 lands in '39." *Billboard,* March 2, 1940, p. 72.

"6th annual operator poll." *Billboard,* May 23, 1953, pp. 104+.

"Sked dime play move in Central Fla. in 2 weeks." *Billboard,* March 19, 1955, p. 74.

"Slugs a pinball menace." *Billboard,* June 29, 1935, p. 106.

"Smut records hurt phonos and games." *Billboard,* November 6, 1937, p. 80.

"Smutty discs plague ops." *Billboard,* February 11, 1939, p. 71.

"Soft phono volume soothes public gripes, Italians find." *Billboard,* October 10, 1960, p. 76.

"Soldier pushes button, music rolls out Bach as juke box quivers from frightful shock." *New York Times,* September 6, 1944, p. 21.

Solomon, Merl. "Wurlitzer — nearly 300 years in music." *Billboard,* October 12, 1968, pp. MOA10, MOA28.

"Solon calls for 'justice' to cleffers." *Variety,* March 16, 1955, pp. 1, 18.

Spaeth, Sigmund. "In and out of tune." *Music Journal* 20 (February, 1962): 80.

"Spike Jones's band starts tour: to court operators." *Billboard,* August 7, 1943, p. 62.

Sternfield, Aaron. "British juke box population at 20,000 — may hit 100,000." *Billboard,* May 30, 1960, pp. 85, 92.

Sternfield, Aaron. "Cinebox tests warm in Philly." *Billboard,* May 11, 1963, pp. 1, 53.

Sternfield, Aaron. "5c juke bastions crumbled by dime." *Billboard,* August 26, 1957, pp. 1, 34.

Sternfield, Aaron. "Juke box commercials may bring in extra operator loot." *Billboard,* April 17, 1961, pp. 1, 49.

Sternfield, Aaron. "Jukes build own niche in Mexico." *Billboard,* August 25, 1958, pp. 1, 4, 73.

Sternfield, Aaron. "1962 music machine survey." *Billboard,* May 12, 1962, pp. 52–53.

Sternfield, Aaron. "Operators look to movies, shows as greatest source of juke plays." *Billboard,* March 24, 1962, p. 12.

Sternfield, Aaron. "Union racketeer tells how he organized 100 operators." *Billboard,* August 12, 1957, pp. 121, 133.

Sternfield, Aaron. "U.S. coin exports set new mark." *Billboard,* July 11, 1964, pp. 42, 54.

Strauss, Neil. "Where the 45s keep spinning." *New York Times,* April 28, 1995, pp. C1, C25.

"Successful operator handles music exclusively in nation's capital." *Billboard,* May 11, 1935, pp. 61, 71.

"Suggest teenage centers." *Billboard,* August 7, 1943, p. 62.

"Survey juke volume problems." *Billboard,* July 26, 1947, pp. 112, 131.

"Syracuse juke box fee passes council." *Billboard,* January 11, 1947, p. 99.

"Tavern men nix juke ownership." *Billboard,* September 20, 1947, pp. 120, 126.

"Tavern tele in many Chicago spots music ops' biggest current location headache." *Billboard,* June 28, 1947, p. 113.

"Teen-age clubs grow." *Billboard,* May 29, 1943, pp. 92, 96.

"Teen-agers can afford a dime, juke exec says." *Billboard,* January 11, 1947, p. 99.

"Television in juke box." *New York Times,* June 28, 1949, p. 29.

"Tells locations to patronize op." *Billboard,* July 10, 1937, p. 81.

"10 best records for the week of Nov. 2." *Billboard,* November 16, 1935, p. 64.

"10 best sellers on coin-machines." *Variety,* December 4, 1940, p. 44.

"Ten-cent play still up in air." *Billboard,* June 8, 1946, pp. 110, 114.

Terry, Ken. "Countdown begins for video jukeboxes." *Variety,* May 23, 1984, pp. 75, 78.

Terry, Ken. "Jukebox biz is in a fatal decline." *Variety,* December 2, 1981, pp. 1, 110.

"Texas music ops select officers at conference." *Billboard,* October 5, 1935, p. 62.

"Texas taxes coin machines." *Billboard,* May 18, 1935, p. 73.

"Text of juke box week Detroit proclamation." *Billboard,* May 30, 1953, p. 82.

"Thousands of 5c music boxes are important market for discs." *Variety,* June 9, 1931, p. 59.

"3 house tunes build off-season grosses." *Billboard,* November 11, 1950, p. 78.

"Three shot in brawl over juke box tune." *New York Times,* March 2, 1948, p. 28.

"Trade on juke price hike." *Billboard,* October 19, 1946, pp. 96, 103.

"Trade watches 'music in color.'" *Billboard,* June 23, 1945, p. 65.

"Tribunal defends boost in copyright fees on jukeboxes." *Variety,* January 7, 1981, pp. 2, 68.

"Tribunal finalizes juke-royalty plan." *Variety,* November 27, 1985, p. 142.

"Tribunal raises jukebox fee up to $25 in 1982, $50 in 1984." *Variety,* December 17, 1980, pp. 71, 78.

"Tune announcement goes with new wall box music." *Billboard,* May 18, 1946, p. 128.

"Turnstile slugs circulate widely." *Billboard*, June 29, 1935, p. 106.

"20,000 U.S. venders shipped around the globe in 1954." *Billboard*, April 30, 1955, p. 89.

"Two Bridgeport ops voice opinion on 7½-cent coin." *Billboard*, March 25, 1950, p. 112.

"$232,000,000 in '46 from jukes." *Variety*, January 8, 1947, p. 218.

"Two of three cities in 800 have annual juke box tax." *Billboard*, May 5, 1958, pp. 52+.

"2,200 teen-age centers in U.S. with jukes, govt says." *Billboard*, November 17, 1945, p. 78.

Ulanov, Barry. "The jukes take over swing." *American Mercury* 51 (October, 1940): 172–177.

Ullendorff, Hans. "Coin machines in Europe." *Billboard*, March 5, 1938, pp. 80–81.

"U.S. record sales." *Billboard*, August 4, 1962, sup., p. 8.

"U.S. releases 1954 juke, game totals." *Billboard*, July 15, 1957, pp. 124, 136.

"Use of patriotic records in music boxes increasing." *Billboard*, July 27, 1940, p. 82.

Velie, Lester. "Racket in the juke box." *Reader's Digest* 67 (November, 1955): 65–71.

"Venezuela heads top 5 import list." *Billboard*, June 7, 1952, pp. 76, 83.

"Victor gives with hit disks in ops' Cleveland tie-up." *Billboard*, October 19, 1946, p. 103.

"Video jukebox firm launches drive to license promo clips." *Variety*, March 30, 1983, p. 119.

"Video jukebox uses promo clips, TV specials, old concert footage." *Variety*, July 7, 1982, p. 64.

"Video sports give ops headache." *Billboard*, February 5, 1949, pp. 101, 105.

"Videograph gets the jump with coin juke-TV combos." *Billboard*, October 18, 1947, p. 103.

"Wall boxes prove to be 'clinchers' for holding spots." *Billboard*, March 11, 1944, p. 69.

"Wall St. Journal recounts history of record industry." *Billboard*, November 29, 1941, pp. 90–91.

Warner, Eva M. "Buffalo survey shows interesting facts about phono record trends." *Billboard*, September 28, 1940, pp. 74, 76.

"Weekly MOA radio show gets under way Saturday." *Billboard*, October 15, 1955, p. 80.

"Weekly music notes." *Billboard*, October 12, 1935, p. 73.

"Weekly music notes." *Billboard*, November 6, 1937, p. 80.

"The week's best records." *Billboard*, December 18, 1937, p. 74.

Weinberger, Andrew D. "The law and the music machine." *Billboard*, September 28, 1940, sup., p. 41.

Weiser, Norman. "How can ops hike income?" *Billboard*, June 12, 1948, pp. 107–111.

Weiser, Norman. "Income vs. cost crisis." *Billboard*, March 17, 1951, p. 72.

Weiser, Norman. "Juke box Saturday night." *Billboard*, April 10, 1948, pp. 101, 109, 113.

Weiser, Norman. "Juke boxes jingle jangle." *Billboard*, February 19, 1949, pp. 98, 102.

Weiser, Norman. "Music ops find key to increased $." *Billboard*, October 8, 1949, p. 115.

Weiser, Norman. "New disks not to effect jukes." *Billboard*, April 2, 1949, pp. 133, 136.

Weiser, Norman. "New speed jukes." *Billboard*, May 27, 1950, p. 154.

Weiser, Norman. "Ops discuss 10–cent play." *Billboard*, May 22, 1948, pp. 112–113, 119.

Weiser, Norman. "Programming key to better take." *Billboard*, March 4, 1950, sup., p. 22.

Weiser, Norman. "10–cent play seen doomed." *Billboard*, May 29, 1948, pp. 115, 125, 128.

Wells, Margaret. "Coinmen and teen-age clubs." *Billboard*, March 4, 1944, pp. 66, 76.

"What is AFM?" *Billboard*, August 31, 1940, pp. 109–111.

"What is ASCAP?" *Billboard*, August 31, 1940, pp. 108, 110.

"What is BMI?" *Billboard*, August 31, 1940, pp. 109–111.

"What is MPAA?" *Billboard*, August 31, 1940, pp. 108, 110.

"What the records are doing for me." *Billboard*, October 22, 1938, p. 65.

"What's holding up dime music play?" *Billboard*, June 2, 1956, p. 67.

"Why are phonos called jook organs? Florida offers clue." *Billboard*, February 24, 1940, p. 71.

"Why the noise." *Billboard*, May 8, 1937, p. 80.

Wickman, Jim. "Color TV threatens tavern juke boxes." *Billboard*, May 29, 1954, pp. 1, 100.

Wickman, Jim. "U.S. finicky about juke boxes' music." *Billboard*, July 23, 1955, pp. 1, 126.

Winthrop, John B. "Boosting the phonograph take." *Billboard*, August 2, 1936, p. 76.

Wood, Frank W. "What's wrong with the coin machine industry?" *Billboard*, February 25, 1939, pp. 78–79.

"Worcester ops hike juke box price to dime." *Billboard*, January 4, 1947, p. 51.

"World game markets import $3 mil in U.S. units in '54." *Billboard*, April 30, 1955, p. 88.

"Writer reports one juke box for every 500 persons of U.S." *Billboard*, May 4, 1946, p. 136.

"Wurlitzer ad." *Billboard*, May 11, 1935, p. 63.

"Wurlitzer biz over 3 years." *Billboard*, May 29, 1937, p. 90.

"Wurlitzer in Chicago at end of second big week." *Billboard*, July 23, 1938, pp. 76, 86.

"Wurlitzer Co. develops record-counting device." *Billboard*, August 8, 1936, p. 70.

"Wurlitzer reveals Colonial model." *Billboard*, November 16, 1940, p. 70.

"Wurlitzer deal ends Capehart juke saga." *Billboard*, September 22, 1951, pp. 90, 94.

"Wurlitzer debuts new juke." *Billboard*, February 18, 1950, pp. 93, 99.
"Wurlitzer firm at full speed." *Billboard*, August 29, 1936, p. 112.
"Wurlitzer 1st coin firm to air radio show nation-wide." *Billboard*, February 10, 1945, p. 63.
"Wurlitzer plays for movie stars." *Billboard*, October 30, 1937, p. 76.
"Wurlitzer uses TV promotion to fight video competition." *Billboard*, June 24, 1950, p. 3.
"Yippee!" *New Yorker* 40 (July 11, 1964): 21–22.
Yohalem, Arthur E. "Traces ancestry of juke box." *Billboard*, July 20, 1946, pp. 116, 121.
"Youngstown phono tax trimmed." *Billboard*, July 6, 1946, pp. 112, 142.

Index